1994

ABOUT THE AUTHOR

Steven A. Meyerowitz graduated from Harvard Law School in 1979 and worked for more than four years as an attorney at a prominent Wall Street law firm. In 1984, he established Meyerowitz Communications Inc., a marketing communications consulting company now based in Northport, New York, which writes, prepares, produces, and places brochures, newsletters, bylined articles, and press releases for lawyers and other professionals to help them reach their marketing goals. As a contributing writer for *The Pennsylvania Lawyer* and a contributing editor of *Business Marketing*, his articles on marketing and management have appeared in many diverse publications, including *ABA Journal, Across the Bar, Barrister, Bench & Bar, New York Law Journal, The New York Times, The News Bulletin,* and *Of Counsel.* He is married and has two sons.

An Ounce of Prevention

MARKETING, SALES, & ADVERTISING LAW

for NON-LAWYERS

An Ounce of Prevention

MARKETING, SALES, & ADVERTISING LAW

for NON-LAWYERS

Steven A. Meyerowitz

Foreword by Bob Donath

 Gale Research Inc. • *DETROIT* • *WASHINGTON, D.C.* • *LONDON*

Gale Research Inc. Staff

Lawrence W. Baker, *Senior Developmental Editor*

Mary Beth Trimper, *Production Director*
Evi Seoud, *Assistant Production Manager*
Mary Kelley, *Production Assistant*

Cynthia Baldwin, *Art Director*
Barbara J. Yarrow, *Graphic Services Supervisor*
Kelly Schwartz, *Cover and Page Designer*

An Ounce of Prevention: Marketing, Sales, and Advertising Law for Non-Lawyers is designed to provide accurate and authoritative information in regard to the subject matter covered. It is sold with the understanding that neither the publisher nor the author is engaged in rendering legal or other professional services. If legal advice or other expert assistance is required, the services of a competent professional should be sought.

∞™ This book is printed on acid-free paper that meets the minimum requirements of American National Standard for Information Sciences–Permanence Paper for Printed Library Materials, ANSI Z39.48-1984.

To Eric and Glen
and
To Joanne

CONTENTS

▌ADVERTISING

▌SALES PEOPLE

▌LEGAL RESTRICTIONS ON MARKETING

▌ CUSTOMER RELATIONS

▌ ESPECIALLY FOR MARKETING EXECUTIVES

OUTLINE OF CONTENTS

▌LEGAL RESTRICTIONS ON MARKETING

▌CUSTOMER RELATIONS

FOREWORD

Marketing, among all the disciplines of business, seems to offer the widest selection of books to those practicing its craft. The titles range from solemn management disquisitions, through best-sellers flogging the latest business fads, to unabashedly cookbook-like how-to manuals promising enlightenments such as, "48 Ways to Save Your Job With Direct Mail!" Marketing folk are, after all, a communicative breed, loving to write as well as read.

The choices, however, begin to overlap each other substantially in content, as marketing, advertising, and sales managers building a professional bookshelf soon learn. Whether the subject is "one-minute managers" out "swimming with the sharks" or yet another step-by-step guide to getting publicity, much of what winds up cluttering our offices probably doesn't earn the space it takes up.

▌A Keeper for Your Bookshelf

A number of classics do earn their keep, of course, as does the occasional new release, particularly when it fills a critical gap in our marketing knowledge. Such books become prized possessions, not to lend casually to associates. I expect readers will feel that way about this book. Steve Meyerowitz, a leading writer about the legal vagaries of marketing, advertising, and sales, provides an estimable review of the law swirling around marketing today.

It's the right book for the times. The 1990s are proving to be the most turbulent of decades for business around the world, as greater social demands, novel corporate strategies, and new constraints rewrite the rules of commerce and society at large. For some businesses, the law has become a mine field, and none but the most myopic of managers can claim to not be affected by changes in the law.

Therefore, it is remarkable that a lay marketing manager's guide to legal issues had not been published and widely adopted before this book appeared. Some authors have written law books about marketing, but the arcane knowledge needed to fathom them renders them inaccessible to the typical executive reader who is not a lawyer, does not have the patience to wade through legalese and abstruse concepts, and who needs insights quickly. Hence the apt title, *An Ounce of Prevention: Marketing, Sales, and Advertising Law for Non-Lawyers.*

Neither this nor any other book substitutes for an ongoing business relationship with sound legal counsel, however. Do-it-yourself law is fine for prosecuting small claims court actions and defending your dog when he digs up the neighbors' azaleas. But not in the worlds of advertising, marketing, and sales where even seemingly minor blunders and unwitting oversights could cost you your business, your job, or even your personal estate.

Instead, think of *An Ounce of Prevention* as a manual for making more efficient and effective use of the law and professional counsel to protect your rights and, importantly, forthrightly seize business opportunities. Oddly enough, given the importance of the subject, marketing managers do not pay as much attention to legal issues as they should. In my experience working with and publishing for marketers, I've found their tendency to think narrowly about specific legal issues and not clamor for a bigger-picture view surprising. In companies big enough to have a bureaucracy promulgating formal policies, "Run it by legal" becomes something of an autonomic response for managers. They begin to see attorneys as obstacles. In small companies, managers don't have that luxury. Instead, they're tempted to forge ahead with programs, without benefit of legal vetting.

Neither type of manager has had the right guidebook to illuminate their blind spots. But now, *An Ounce of Prevention* speaks to them all, corporate employee to entrepreneur. Cynics will feel better prepared for what they anticipate will be encounters with lawyerly lackeys. Those of us with a more optimistic outlook will applaud the way Mr. Meyerowitz reports the outlines of legal restraint and permissibility, preparing us to work constructively with legal advisers.

▌Management in Mind

When a management-oriented book dwells on a highly specialized field—be it law, marketing research, industrial psychology, etc.—the author's appropriate mission is explaining the subject well enough to familiarize laymen with the key issues. When, for instance, is a particular specialist's technique likely to be most effective? What is the critical information the specialist needs to do the job? A working comprehension of the specialist's field will help the generalist manager find the right assistance, and protect him- or herself from dishonest advice.

In that spirit, Mr. Meyerowitz, a New York attorney, reviews 35 major legal issues affecting marketing, sales, and advertising. Each chapter discusses the legal conditions, the guiding logic, and several of the exemplary court cases that shape our business codes. Each chapter also includes a checklist of basic considerations that will suggest whether you need to consult an attorney about the issue at hand. Seemingly simple questions of fairness actually can be legal quagmires ready to trap the unwary; see Chapter 29 about how to cash full-payment checks, for instance.

The reasoning and probity that judges apply to the real-life dramas they face in court are among the most fascinating aspects of American society. So read this book as an issue-by-issue handbook if you like, but also read every chapter as an engrossing series of vignettes of how business really works when someone starts yelling about lawsuits. No doubt, you'll be surprised by at least some of the outcomes.

Was the radio station liable when its salesman beat up a customer after-hours in a bar, over a $15 invoice? Why can you be sued if a former employee repeats to a third party libelous statements *you* made about him or her? And in a case illustrating what can go awry in retail selling, did the pet store have to pay when the allegedly "docile dobe" nipped the neighbor?

▌Ignorance Is No Defense

Mr. Meyerowitz covers all the territory one would expect in a book about the issue at hand: advertising law, customer relations, the Uniform Commercial Code, the liabilities in marketing products and employing salespeople, patents, trademarks, copyrights, etc. Then he goes an extra distance for the reader, discussing a topic frequently ignored by those preoccupied with a company's legal exposure: the personal vulnerabilities of individual managers. Chapter 32, "The Risks of White Collar Crime," reminds managers about the responsibility to operate within the law. More surprising for some, however, will be the message in Chapter 33 about personal civil liability. It can be triggered innocently by ill-starred decisions and, regardless of the widely presumed shelter of incorporation, a misstep could cost a manager his or her personal fortune.

Ignorance of the law is no defense. Neither is the failure to be watchful. Perhaps this book's greatest contribution, therefore, is the heightened sensitivity, if not a justifiable paranoia, readers will develop for the ways they can get into trouble. Corporate "downsizing," for instance, forces greater workloads on company employees, and tends to push critical tasks and decision-making downward in the organization to less experienced staffers. How much damage can they cause? Chapter 2 points out, for instance, how a minor slip-up in choosing a product photo for a catalog can lead to trouble in a contract, and how costly liabilities can lurk in the paperwork's fine print. Similarly, Chapter 20 points out how the adequacy of product-use warnings is not necessarily obvious in liability cases, one of the most controversial areas of marketing law.

Mr. Meyerowitz has been writing about the law of marketing for more than a decade. As an editor of many of his columns and articles over the years, I have enjoyed working with him as he demystifies issues of critical importance to managers. Revealing the ambiguities and hidden pitfalls that await the unwary and then proposing practical solutions epitomizes the best of service journalism. In today's ever more litigious society, tough economic times and the opportunity to misuse new technologies create temptations for the unscrupulous and new worries for the just. This new book on marketing law is reaching the thoughtful manager's bookshelf just in time.

Bob Donath

Bob Donath is a well-known speaker and author on the subjects of business-to-business advertising and marketing. He now heads his own marketing and marketing communications consulting firm, Bob Donath & Co., in White Plains, New York, specializing in business-to-business marketing. In addition, he serves as managing editor for Marketing Management, *a new magazine for senior executives published by the American Marketing Association.*

INTRODUCTION

It certainly was easier to sell things in the old days. The right words and inflection by a carnival barker could persuade people to purchase elixirs guaranteed to cure baldness. Ads could say almost anything, and if they were pretty enough and slick enough they would sell enough. Telemarketing boiler rooms were hot!

Now, though, we have rules that protect customers, consumers, and copyrights. Laws demand fair competition, restrict a company's right to fire employees, and govern product reviews. Executives may face civil liability for actions that they may never have considered troublesome in the past, such as providing a reference for a former employee. Criminal liability for "doing one's job" almost seems possible, too.

Certainly, knowing the rules can help to keep people out of trouble.

But there is another benefit as well: Knowing the rules also may create opportunities. For instance, understanding the federal bankruptcy law can help a marketer determine how to safely sell to customers in Chapter 11. Understanding how arbitration and other forms of alternative dispute resolution work should help make it easier for executives who negotiate contracts to include simple arbitration provisions in them. And knowing whether a restrictive covenant is enforceable or not can play a large role in an employee's decision to leave—and compete against—an employer.

An Ounce of Prevention: Marketing, Sales, and Advertising Law for Non-Lawyers tries to show you the problems and the risks as well as the ways to push the limits, within the bounds of the law and morality. It tries to offer solutions, rather than roadblocks. It will not necessarily help you avoid all lawyers. But it should help you know when to contact a lawyer and what to ask.

An Ounce of Prevention is divided into five general sections: Advertising, Sales People, Legal Restrictions on Marketing, Customer Relations, and Especially for Marketing Executives. Thirty-five chapters make up the book and cover such topics as:

- Comparative Advertising in the 1990s
- How the Copyright Laws Affect Advertising

- Endorsements
- Product Reviews
- Liability for an Employee's Conduct
- Advertising Restrictions
- Telemarketing and "Junk" Faxes
- Product Liability
- FOB, FAS, and Other Such Terms
- When a Buyer Breaches
- Handling Checks Marked "Paid in Full"
- Selling to Customers in Bankruptcy
- The Risks of White Collar Crime
- Keeping Conflict Out of Court
- And 21 more chapters

Sprinkled throughout each chapter are examples of lawsuits, laws, and more that help illustrate each topic. Two sections end each chapter: one section presents in greater detail five court cases that deal with the subject at hand, the second is a checklist that sums up the key points of the chapter.

"For Further Reading" gives readers additional sources to go to if they desire more information on marketing, sales, advertising, and more. A subject index makes accessibility to *An Ounce of Prevention* quick and easy.

▌Acknowledgments

Special thanks go to Greg Michael and Larry Baker at Gale Research for their help in turning an idea into a book. Thanks, also, to Gina Misiroglu for her copyediting skills and Bernice Eisen for her indexing work. And, finally, thanks to my good friend Bob Donath for writing the foreword.

Steven A. Meyerowitz

ADVERTISING

COMPARATIVE ADVERTISING IN THE 1990s

■ What Is Comparative Advertising? ■ The Lanham Act
■ Truth as a Defense ■ Product Testing ■ Surveys ■ Damages
■ A Final Word

For many years U-Haul International, Inc. dominated the self-move consumer rental industry. Then, in mid-1979 Jartran, Inc. entered that market on a national basis. One of its principal tools: comparative advertising.

Jartran engaged in a $6 million nationwide newspaper advertising campaign comparing itself to U-Haul. The campaign lasted from the summer of 1979 to December 1980 and included more than 2,000 advertisements in 41 states and the District of Columbia. Perhaps as a direct result of these ads, Jartran's revenues increased from $7 million in 1979 to $80 million in 1980 and U-Haul's revenues declined for the first time in its history, from $395 million to $378 million. Jartran's executives boasted that newspaper advertising "has made us the fastest growing company in America." The tremendous success of Jartran's comparative advertising was demonstrated not only by the financial growth of Jartran but also by Jartran's receipt of the prestigious Gold Effie Award, which the American Marketing Association presents annually in recognition of effective advertising campaigns.

The only problem with Jartran's advertising campaign is that it apparently was not accurate. Jartran's ads advertised prices that were special promotional prices—but failed to identify them as such. Numerous times they compared Jartran's basic price with a U-Haul price that included a basic rate and a distribution fee, even though Jartran also charged a distribution fee. Indeed, in a large number of instances, rates Jartran charged customers exceeded the rates it advertised.

U-Haul filed suit against Jartran for false comparative advertising. The trial court found that Jartran's ads contained false, misleading, deceptive, and incomplete statements of fact and awarded U-Haul $40 million in damages and attorneys' fees as well as a permanent injunction against certain Jartran advertisements. The district court's calculation of damages was affirmed by the U.S. Court of Appeals for the Ninth Circuit, which ruled that it was appropriate to base the amount of the judgment on Jartran's advertising expenditures and the costs incurred by U-Haul in corrective advertising—and then to double that amount as permitted by a federal statute known as the Lanham Act, which is intended to ensure truthfulness in advertising.

▎What Is Comparative Advertising?

Comparative advertising is a relatively new trend. Up to the 1970s, ads rarely referred to a competitor's goods. And those that did would not mention the competition by name for fear that it both would give a competitor's product free publicity and risk a lawsuit. Instead, the competition became the ubiquitous "Brand X."

Businesses, advertising agencies, the Federal Trade Commission (FTC), and the television networks began to slowly recognize, though, that comparative advertising could serve a useful purpose. An ad that compared important characteristics of competing products provided useful information to consumers. If, for example, a General Motors car costs less to repair after an accident than a Toyota, potential automobile purchasers who were made aware of this difference in a comparative ad would have a tangible method of distinguishing GM and Toyota cars. And if a Toyota got better gas mileage than a similarly priced car made by GM, it would be useful for consumers to know that. When faced with these competing hypothetical ads, the marketplace would work as it theoretically was intended to, consumers could determine which characteristic—cheaper repairs or better gas mileage—was more important, and they could make informed, educated decisions about purchasing cars.

Comparative advertising is not without risk. When one manufacturer's ad mentions a competitor's product in a nonflattering way, the competitor is likely to become rather upset; indeed, the competitor is more likely to notice and respond to a comparative ad than to an ad that may just highlight (or even exaggerate) the benefits of the advertiser's product because the competitor's name, product, trademark, or package are in the ad. For instance, it did not take long after Jartran began its comparative advertising for U-Haul to file a lawsuit against Jartran.

As a result advertisers still may have a lingering fear about mentioning a competitor's product by name. It should be noted, too, that an ad need not necessarily mention the competition by name to fall within the scope of the laws relating to comparative advertising. For example, if there only are two major products in a field, an ad that refers to the "other leading product" or even "the competition" is a comparative ad that should follow the rules. Comparative advertisers that do follow these rules, which primarily are contained in section 43 of the Lanham Act, should be able to limit the problems their comparative advertisements may engender.

▌ The Lanham Act

Both state and federal laws technically govern comparative advertising. As a result, lawsuits challenging comparative ads usually tend to include claims under state unfair competition and false advertising laws and under state product disparagement rules. In addition, the FTC can regulate comparative and other forms of advertising under the Federal Trade Commission Act and on occasion has taken steps to challenge competitive ads, particularly where the ads made health-related or nutrition-related claims. But state laws tend not to provide sufficient recourse to aggrieved competitors and usually are not pursued once the lawsuit gets moving; similarly, the FTC now tends to stay out of most advertising disputes. This means that businesses generally must fight for their own rights under the federal Lanham Act.

Section 43 of the Lanham Act prohibits a company from making materially false representations about another company's goods, services, or commercial activities. It is intended to ensure truthfulness in advertising and to eliminate misrepresentations regarding the inherent quality or characteristics of another's product. Broad relief may be afforded to an injured party, including compensatory damages, punitive damages, permanent injunctions and possibly attorney's fees, corrective advertising, and recalls of the offending product.

Liability may be imposed under the Lanham Act on more than just advertisers—advertising agencies, research firms, and the like conceivably can be held liable, too. In one case, a research firm failed in its attempt to be dismissed from a lawsuit although it argued that it had not participated in the distribution of the advertised goods; the court ruled that that fact did not automatically exclude it from liability as a contributory infringer under the Lanham Act. In an even more recent case, a federal district court judge in New York City ruled that an advertising agency could be held liable to the Gillette Company for its part in preparing an ad that falsely claimed that razor blades manufactured by Wilkinson Sword, Inc. were better than Gillette's Atra Plus blades.

Perhaps surprisingly consumers generally are not authorized to bring lawsuits challenging these kinds of misrepresentations, even though one of the main benefits of comparative ads is generally recognized to be providing consumers with useful information. But a company that is harmed by a materially false representation about its product in a comparative ad may bring suit.

▌Truth as a Defense

Advertisers often use "puffery" in their ads, contending that their products are "the best" or represent "the most value for the money." These kinds of claims cannot be successfully challenged under the Lanham Act because, while they cannot necessarily be validated, they also cannot necessarily be deemed false. As one court has stated, "A statement which takes the form of an unfavorable comparison of products, or which 'puffs' or exaggerates the quality of one's own product, is not ordinarily actionable. . . . One is expected to believe in the superiority of his wares, and he may properly declare his belief to interested parties."

Generally speaking, though, the rule is that claims in comparative ads must be truthful and not misleading. That's what the manufacturer of Tropicana Orange Juice learned several years ago.

In mid-February 1982 Tropicana began airing a television commercial for its Premium Pack orange juice. The commercial showed the renowned American Olympics athlete Bruce Jenner squeezing an orange while saying, "It's pure, pasteurized juice as it comes from the orange." It then showed Jenner pouring the fresh-squeezed juice into a Tropicana carton while the audio stated, "It's the only leading brand not made with concentrate and water."

Soon after the advertisement began running, the Coca-Cola Company, the manufacturer of Minute Maid orange juice, brought suit against Tropicana for false advertising under the Lanham Act. Coke claimed that the commercial was false because it incorrectly represented that Tropicana Premium Pack contained unprocessed, fresh-squeezed juice when in fact the Tropicana juice was heated to about 200 degrees Fahrenheit when it was pasteurized and sometimes even was frozen prior to packaging.

The federal district court in which Coke had filed suit refused to block further broadcast of the ad. But the federal court of appeals in New York did so.

It ruled that the squeezing-pouring sequence was false on its face. It said that the ad made an explicit representation that Tropicana's Premium Pack was produced by squeezing oranges and pouring the freshly squeezed juice directly into the carton. But, the court noted, this was not a true representation of how the juice was prepared because it always was heated and sometimes was frozen prior to packaging. Additionally, the court found that the audio component of the ad that stated that the juice was "pasteurized juice as it comes from the orange" was blatantly false because pasteurized juice did not come from oranges. Even if the addition of the word "pasteurized" somehow made sense and effectively qualified the visual image, the appellate court said that Tropicana's commercial nevertheless was inaccurate because it represented that the juice was squeezed, heated, and packaged when it actually also may have been frozen. The bottom line for the court, and for Tropicana, was that its commercial was not literally true.

Being totally truthful and accurate in a comparative ad is not enough. Also comparative ads must not tend to confuse, deceive, or mislead; as one court has put it, "innuendo, indirect intimations, and ambiguous suggestions" are forbidden.

One interesting result of the truthful and non-misleading standard is that it may permit the use of another company's trademark in a comparative ad even without the trademark owner's permission so long as the trademark is used in a truthful and non-misleading manner. An advertiser also may use a picture of a competitive product in an ad. In one case, a court found that references to the laxative Metamucil on the packaging of the competing laxative Regacilium were truthful and could not be challenged on that ground. Indeed, one court even ruled that under the Lanham Act the manufacturer of the perfume Confess should not be prohibited from using a scent strip in advertising catalogs comparing its perfume to the Obsession perfume manufactured by the Calvin Klein Cosmetics Corporation!

∎ Product Testing

One of the best ways to support a claim of product superiority is to use the results of a test that support the claim in an ad. Because of the belief many people have in information categorized as "scientific proof," tests are carefully scrutinized by competitors that are negatively affected by claims made in ads based on these tests. And they also frequently form the basis for a lawsuit.

In one case, the manufacturer of Triumph cigarettes claimed that its cigarette was a "National Smoker Study Winner" based on a consumer test it had taken. In this test people first were asked to smoke two different cigarettes. Then they were told the tar content of the two cigarettes and asked, "Taking [the tar content] into consideration, which would you prefer to smoke?" The test was challenged by a competing cigarette manufacturer and the court ruled that it was deceptive and misleading because the participants in the test were low-tar cigarette smokers and asking them to take the tar content into account "dictated the test result." The court ruled that the advertiser's claim that Triumph was the "overall" preference of smokers therefore was misleading.

Where results of a test are truthfully reported, though, a competitor's ability to challenge a test is made more difficult. In another case, the Procter & Gamble Company began advertising its New Wondra hand and body lotion as superior to other leading lotions in the therapeutic treatment of dry skin. In particular, Procter & Gamble contended that New Wondra:

- Beat the leading lotions
- Was better than any top lotion
- Relieved dry skin better than any leading lotion
- Improved the condition of rough, dry skin better, as proved by dermatologists in clinical tests
- Worked better than any other leading lotion at turning rough, dry hands soft and smooth

In support of its advertising claims, Procter & Gamble relied on two large-scale clinical tests that it designated SC-207 and SC-215. Both were double-blind tests in which each of several groups of individuals used a version of New Wondra or one of the leading skin lotions over a period of several weeks, with a dermatologist periodically grading the efficacy of the product on the subjects' dry skin. The tests used an *ad libitum* procedure; that is, the subjects were told to apply the test lotions to their skin as they customarily used skin lotions, in whatever quantity and locations of the body they preferred. Procter & Gamble maintained that its tests led it to conclude that its New Wondra was superior to competitors' products in improving skin condition. SC-207 revealed an apparent difference in effectiveness that was statistically significant; SC-215 documented a statistically significant difference between lotions but only when the analysis was confined to data taken from a subgroup of those persons tested who initially had rough skin.

At about the same time that Procter & Gamble began running its ads, Chesebrough-Pond's, Inc., the manufacturer of what clearly was one of the "other leading lotions," began running its own comparative advertising. It asserted that its product, Vaseline Intensive Care Lotion, was equal in effectiveness to any other leading brand. According to the ads, "When it comes to relieving dry skin, no leading lotion beats Vaseline Intensive Care Lotion" and "You can't buy better lotions to heal winter dry skin."

When Chesebrough became aware of Procter & Gamble's superiority claims for New Wondra, it did not abort its parity claims but initiated its own tests to compare Vaseline Intensive Care Lotion with New Wondra. Its two small-scale tests, involving 28 and 11 subjects, and one large-scale clinical test, involving 73 subjects, revealed no significant difference between the two lotions.

Procter & Gamble then filed suit against Chesebrough, claiming that Chesebrough's ads violated the Lanham Act and seeking preliminary injunctive relief against the Chesebrough advertisements. On the next day, Chesebrough countered by suing for similar injunctive relief against Procter & Gamble's ads.

Each party to the lawsuits challenged the other party's tests in an attempt to show that the tests the other relied on were not sufficiently reliable to permit one to conclude with reasonable certainty that the tests established the proposition for which they were cited. That is not necessarily an easy thing to do, especially when the claims made are carefully tailored to reflect the test results obtained. But the reasons for which each of the tests were challenged should at least help advertisers recognize the kinds of things they should do—and should avoid doing—in their own tests.

Chesebrough first attacked Procter & Gamble's tests on the ground that, unlike Chesebrough's tests, they did not compare the currently advertised products at issue but compared in one case an earlier version of New Wondra with Vaseline Intensive Care Lotion and in the other instance the then-current version of New Wondra with Chesebrough formulas it claimed were significantly different. Procter & Gamble replied with evidence that the variations were not significant for purposes of the claims at issue.

Chesebrough also attacked Procter & Gamble's tests and results as unreliable and the product of highly questionable data manipulated to reach a predesigned conclusion. Procter & Gamble, on the other hand, challenged Chesebrough's tests as either too small to produce meaningful results or as "poorly designed, sloppily executed, and improperly analyzed," pointing to such alleged deficiencies as failure to use an articulated grading scale and employment of an erroneous and inappropriate statistical analysis.

There was a great deal of expert testimony at the trial regarding the reliability and acceptance of the *ad libitum* procedure; the use of a "one-tail" test that was used only to determine superiority rather than a "two-tail" test that was designed to discover whether one product was equal to or better than another; and reliance upon subjective rather than purely objective scientific judgments.

The district court judge found a number of weaknesses in Procter & Gamble's testing methods, including:

- Its failure to compare New Wondra directly with Vaseline Intensive Care Lotion

- Dependence on subjective visual observations by dermatologists or trained graders, which may have differed between graders

- Use of numerical designations that did not necessarily correspond to verbal descriptions on the numerical scale used

- Variations in the amount of each product applied by the subjects in *ad libitum* testing

- The selection of a subset of subjects with rough skin as indicated by a 1.5 figure on the scale rather than the 2.5 figure shown on the scale as the first indication of skin roughness

The court also found that Chesebrough's testing procedures had suffered from weaknesses, including:

- The inadequacy of the number of subjects used in the first two tests

- The risk that the unsupervised subjects in the third test might have become confused by the complicated instructions calling for them to apply New Wondra to one hand and Vaseline Intensive Care Lotion to the other, and might therefore accidentally have switched hands or contaminated the test application by using a hand treated with one lotion to apply the other lotion

- The fact that the subjects had such severe skin conditions that they were not representative users

- Defects in the grading scale and inconsistent grading by the tester

- The brevity of the tests

- The use of measured tests rather than the Procter & Gamble *ad libitum* tests with which they were compared

The lower court concluded that, although Procter & Gamble's tests were not worthless, they "were far from perfect and are subject to various infirmities." Chesebrough's tests, the court found, were "more questionable" than Procter & Gamble's but, the judge noted, had been used only to support a lesser claim of parity rather than a claim of superiority such as that asserted by Procter & Gamble for New Wondra. Despite these deficiencies the judge appeared to simply wash his hands of the matter. He stated that he could not determine whether either company's claims were true or false and refused to prohibit any of the comparative ads they had challenged. That decision was affirmed on appeal, but the value of the decision to other advertisers today is the lower court's analysis of the deficiencies of the Procter & Gamble and Chesebrough tests.

▌ Surveys

Scientific tests, which ascertain scientifically product specifications and quality, are different from consumer surveys, which measure popular opinion, and often serve different purposes. Both must be properly designed, though, and the conclusions drawn from each must be fair and truthful.

A company may use a consumer survey in response to a comparative ad that it wants to challenge. The survey could be used to support its claim that it would suffer "irreparable harm" if a court did not enjoin the offending ad. Generally speaking, a company need not prove that it would lose sales or that its goodwill would be damaged as a direct result of a false comparative advertisement. But it must submit some proof that provides a reasonable basis for its claim that it will be injured by the false ad.

In the case brought by Coke against Tropicana, for example, a consumer reaction survey and a test measuring commercial recall indicated that Tropicana's commercial was deceiving "a not insubstantial number of consumers." As the appellate court said, if consumers were misled by Tropicana's commercial, Coke probably would suffer irreparable injury because it was the leading national competitor for the chilled ready-to-serve orange juice market. That was sufficient for the appellate court to rule that Coke had demonstrated that it was likely to suffer irreparable injury and to rule that an injunction should be issued.

▌ Damages

How much of a risk does an advertiser face by running an improper comparative ad? The answer is that it faces a potentially very big risk. An opinion by Judge Clarence Thomas of the District of Columbia Court of Appeals, written shortly before he became a United States Supreme Court justice, illustrates the method courts may use to calculate damage awards.

That case arose several years ago after ALPO Petfoods, Inc. began claiming that veterinarians preferred the formula of ALPO Puppy Food over that of the leading puppy food, Puppy Chow, which was manufactured by the Ralston Purina Company. ALPO also asserted on its Puppy Food bags and in other media that the veterinarian preference was "2 to 1."

Over roughly the same period, Ralston claimed in print advertising directed to veterinarians, breeders, dog enthusiasts, and others interested in dog nutrition that its Puppy Chow products could lessen the severity of canine hip dysplasia, a crippling joint condition. The hypothesis behind Ralston's advertising was the "anion gap theory" of a Ralston nutritionist, Richard Kealy. Kealy proposed that the smaller the difference between the chlorine content and the combined sodium and potassium content of a dog's diet, the more snugly the dog's hip joints tended to fit. Beginning in 1980 Kealy conducted a series of studies exploring the effect of a low-anion-gap diet on dogs' hip joint fit. In 1984 results of Kealy's first four studies led him to prepare a monograph that reported a connection between low-anion-gap diet and reduced hip joint laxity. Kealy briefed Ralston's marketing executives about his findings and Ralston eventually made its canine hip dysplasia-related advertising claims.

Ralston and ALPO then sued each other alleging false advertising. After a 61-day trial, the district court decided that Ralston's canine hip dysplasia-related advertising lacked empirical support and was therefore false and deceptive. It also found no basis for ALPO's veterinarian preference advertising and found that it, too, violated the Lanham Act. The court awarded ALPO $10.4 million plus court costs and attorneys' fees. It awarded Ralston its costs and attorneys' fees but no damages because it saw Ralston as the greater wrongdoer. Ralston appealed.

After determining that the trial court was correct in ruling in favor of ALPO in its false advertising case against Ralston, Judge Thomas analyzed the lower court's decision to award ALPO damages. He noted that the Lanham Act authorized courts to award to an aggrieved plaintiff both plaintiff's damages and defendant's profits but said that a court's discretion to award these remedies "has limits." An award based on a defendant's profits required proof that the defendant acted willfully or in bad faith, he said. Ralston's decision to run canine hip dysplasia-related advertising that lacked solid empirical support did not, without more, reflect willfulness or bad faith in the view of Judge Thomas. The appellate court then overturned the $10.4 million judgment to ALPO and ordered the lower court to award ALPO its actual damages—and to award Ralston its actual damages, too. The court said that actual damages can include:

- Profits lost by the plaintiff on sales actually diverted to the false advertiser

- Profits lost by the plaintiff on sales made at prices reduced as a demonstrated result of the false advertising

- The costs of any completed advertising that actually and reasonably responds to the defendant's offending ads

- Quantifiable harm to the plaintiff's good will, to the extent that corrective advertising did not repair that harm

▌A Final Word

A number of organizations, including the American Association of Advertising Agencies (AAAA) and at least two of the television networks have, or in the past have had, guidelines for comparative advertising. Advertisers should check and follow all of these kinds of relevant guidelines before proceeding with their comparative advertisements.

Basically, though, once a business decides that it would be better off using a comparative ad than a more traditional kind of ad, and once it girds itself for the possible litigation battle that might follow, it should follow a very simple standard: be truthful, objective, and able to substantiate the claims made in the ad.

FIVE COMPARATIVE AD CASES

Companies of all sizes, in all geographical locations, and in all industries may use comparative ads or comparisons in their selling or promoting. Here is short list of some comparative ads that have resulted in lawsuits:

1. A full-page advertisement by Haynes Ambulance of Alabama, Inc. that contained a replica of an actual invoice from City Ambulance of Alabama, Inc. and a replica of Haynes's invoice for the same services disclosing that Haynes charged a lower price was true and accurate and not false and misleading. Therefore, it could not serve as the basis for a suit against Haynes charging unfair competition or disparagement, according to a decision of the Supreme Court of Alabama. (City Ambulance of Alabama, Inc. v. Haynes Ambulance of Alabama, Inc., 431 So.2d 537 (S.Ct. Ala. 1983).)

2. False statements about a brand of face powder that were made as part of a selling plan by sales clerks who were selling another brand that the competition contained mercury, white lead, or other ingredients injurious to the user's skin could be prohibited by the courts. (Bourjois, Inc. v. Park Drug Co., Inc., 82 F.2d 468 (8th Cir. 1936).)

3. After a judge found that two tablets constituted one of the authorized doses of Nuprin, an Ibuprofen-containing product, he ruled that the Lanham Act was not violated by a commercial pointing out the superiority of Nuprin over Extra Strength Tylenol, which is a non-aspirin analgesic, when Nuprin was taken in a dose of two tablets. The court rejected the argument by the manufacturer of Tylenol that the standard dose of Nuprin was one tablet and that one tablet of Nuprin was at best equipotent with the standard dose of Extra Strength Tylenol. (McNeilab, Inc. v. Bristol-Myers Co., 656 F.Supp. 88 (E.D. Pa. 1986).)

4. The Federal Trade Commission's challenge to advertisements that contended that Bayer Aspirin was pharmaceutically superior as to four specific attributes (purity, freshness, stability, and speed of disintegration) was upheld by a federal circuit court of appeals. The FTC had decided that an in-house study by the manufacturer of Bayer that showed Bayer's superiority did not support the manufacturer's claims as to those individual qualities. (Sterling Drug, Inc. v. Federal Trade Commission, 741 F.2d 1146 (9th Cir. 1984).)

5. A court refused to dismiss a Lanham Act claim by a manufacturer of portable electric tools for the home consumer market that alleged that statements in comparative ads by a competitor about the qualities and relative performance of the two company's products were false, misleading, deceptive, and incomplete. (Skil Corp. v. Rockwell International Corp., 375 F.Supp. 777 (N.D. Ill. 1974).)

Checklist for Comparative Advertising in the 1990s

✓ Weigh the benefits of comparative advertising against the drawbacks, and compare the net benefits to more traditional forms of advertising, such as ads highlighting a product's benefits or low cost, before proceeding with comparative advertisements.

✓ Include information of value to consumers and make comparisons about important product characteristics in comparative ads.

✓ Product testing should be objective, independent, and performed in accordance with generally accepted scientific and technical procedures.

✓ An effective consumer survey requires that a proper universe be examined and a representative sample chosen; the persons conducting the survey must be experts; the data must be properly gathered and accurately reported; the sample design, the questionnaires, and the manner of interviewing must meet standards of objective surveying and statistical techniques; the survey must be conducted by an independent entity; and the interviewers or sample designers should be trained and ideally should be unaware of the purpose of the survey.

✓ Make sure all claims made in comparative ads are made in good faith, are truthful, objective, and not misleading, and can be substantiated.

RECOGNIZING AND DEALING WITH EXPRESS WARRANTIES

▌What Can Constitute an Express Warranty
▌Disclaiming Express Warranties ▌Limiting Remedies for Breach
▌Unconscionable Contract Provisions
▌Express Warranties for Consumer Products ▌A Final Word

After a manufacturer of equipment for ice skating rinks sent a catalog of its products to the City of Utica, New York, the city ordered a resurfacing tank and five scrapers. The items were delivered to the city's skating rink, but the rink's manager realized that they were not what he expected them to be. The manager attempted to return them, but the manufacturer refused delivery. It then demanded payment from the city, and, when payment was not forthcoming, brought suit against Utica.

The resurfacing tank the city was interested in was a steel triangular tank placed on a carriage with rubber wheels. There was a pushing handle at one end and a water-release handle on top of the tank. As the tank was pushed over the ice, water was released from the tank onto a blade extending horizontally across the front of the tank at ice level so that a thin film of water was deposited upon the ice, creating a smooth surface. The description in the catalog gave the dimensions of the tank and stated that special sizes were made to order; there was no other description in words. However, there was an illustration in the catalog that showed a resurfacing tank with a water-release handle near the pushing bar and a blade in front of the tank that extended considerably beyond the width of the tank.

The resurfacing tank that the company delivered to Utica, however, apparently did not match the catalog illustration in several important respects. First, the water-release handle at the top of the tank, by which the operator of the machine could control the flow of water onto the ice, was located beyond the reach of the person pushing the tank. This meant that the tank had to be stopped for the release handle to be operated. Second, the blade near the surface of the ice only was as long as the width of the water tank instead of being wider than the tank. As a consequence, a witness for the city testified in court, the actual tank was too narrow and inconvenient for efficient use at the skating rink.

Third, the scrapers that the manufacturer had indicated in its catalog were made of "top quality aluminum" also apparently did not match the illustration contained in the catalog. The illustration showed a concave blade attached to a handle supported by two angle irons but the actual blade was flat instead of concave and the handle had no supporting angle irons. When one of the scrapers was used, it broke almost immediately.

The manufacturer contended in its lawsuit against the city that the items it delivered were the items that had been ordered and that the only reason they may have varied from the illustrations was that they were new and improved models. But the court rejected the company's claim.

In the court's view, the illustrations in the catalog created an express warranty from the company to the city that the products would conform to the illustrations. Because they did not, the court found that the company had breached this express warranty. The court concluded that the manufacturer therefore was not entitled to payment for the tank and scrapers it sold to Utica.

▌What Can Constitute an Express Warranty

Express warranties from sellers to buyers generally are governed by the Uniform Commercial Code (UCC). As its name would suggest, the UCC is a rather uniform law adopted by state legislatures across the country. It governs a variety of legal matters, including commercial relationships between buyers and sellers.

Under the UCC a warranty may be created by a seller even if the seller does not use formal words such as "warrant" or "guarantee" and even if the seller does not specifically intend to create a warranty. Thus, a seller does not have to say "I warrant that these rings are made of real gold" to create a warranty; it may be sufficient to tell a prospective customer that the rings "are made of real gold."

There are three ways that express warranties may be created by sellers, according to section 2-313 of the UCC:

- Any affirmation of fact or promise made by a seller to a buyer that relates to the goods creates an express warranty that the goods shall conform to the affirmation or promise.

- Any description of the goods creates an express warranty that the goods shall conform to the description.

- Any sample drawn from the bulk of goods that is the subject matter of the sale or any model that the seller offers to the buyer for inspection creates an express warranty that all of the goods shall conform to the sample or model.

Not every affirmation, description, sample, or model creates an express warranty. A seller that engages in "puffery" in promoting its product is not creating an express warranty even though it may say that its product is the "best." It is important to recognize, though, that words that one court might consider to be mere "puffing" may not be treated so lightly by a different court. And something that might otherwise constitute an express warranty but that is not in some manner "relied" on by the buyer or that does not form part of the conscious or subconscious reason the buyer is purchasing the product is not an express warranty either.

Express warranties may arise in many different situations. They may be created through words, technical specifications, blueprints, pictures, drawings, photographs, and, as the manufacturer of the ice skating rink equipment learned in the suit filed against it by Utica, product illustrations. Salespeople can give express warranties to customers orally in a sales talk and express warranties can be included in advertisements, instruction booklets, order and quotation forms, catalogs and brochures, and on labels and packaging. Past deliveries may set the description of quality by course of dealing. Also, trade custom on occasion may create warranties.

▌Disclaiming Express Warranties

The benefit that manufacturers, distributors, sellers, and others in the distribution chain receive when they create an express warranty is that it provides a buyer with a reason for purchasing their products. The risk they run, though, is that the products do not meet the standards established in the warranty. If the purchaser or an employee or family member of the purchaser is injured by the product or if the purchaser suffers financial or business losses attributable to the product, the warrantor may face a lawsuit.

One of the ways that companies try to limit the risks of giving purchasers express warranties is by disclaiming the warranties after they have been made. The difficulty with disclaimers, of course, is that the whole purpose of the law of warranty is to determine what it is that the seller in essence has agreed to sell. Take an extreme example: Should a computer seller that declares in a lengthy sales contract that it is selling a particular model of computer be permitted to disclaim "all warranties" in small printed type on the penultimate page of the sales contract so that it then can ship the purchaser a typewriter instead? Certainly not.

The law continues to struggle with the ability of warrantors to disclaim express warranties. In one case, a seller of heating and air conditioning units put a notice in bold print on the front page of its sales contract that said that it made "no warranties . . . which extend beyond the description of the appliance herein." Also on that page was, in bold print, "NOTICE TO THE BUYER: Do not sign this agreement before you read it or if it contains blanks." A court found the seller had sufficiently disclaimed all express warranties. The court in the ice skating equipment case said that the manufacturer could have relieved itself of the responsibility for delivering items in conformity with the illustrations in its catalog by merely indicating that the items were "not as illustrated." But the court was speaking of a hypothetical situation and it is not clear that it indeed would have upheld that kind of disclaimer had the company actually included that language in its catalog. At the least, it would have had to have been clear and explicit.

Many courts simply make it quite difficult to disclaim express warranties.

In the mid-1960s, a corporation named Community Television Services, Inc. was formed by two South Dakota-based broadcasting stations, KELO and KSOO, to construct near Rowena, South Dakota, a 2,000-foot tower to broadcast television signals for both stations. Dresser Industries, Inc. agreed to design, manufacture, and erect the tower for Community. A tower became operational in May 1969 at a cost to Community of $385,000.

A relatively thin metal structure, the tower was comprised of a mast and three interconnected legs held in balance by cables set to an appropriate tension. An antenna was placed on top of the tower for broadcasting television and FM radio signals. Community had the tower regularly inspected and properly maintained. The only significant maintenance operation Community took was to have an independent contractor it retained check and retension certain of the tower's cables.

On January 10 and 11, 1975, a severe winter blizzard occurred in the area where the tower was located. During the early morning hours of January 11, as the storm reached its height with wind speeds near the top of the tower of up to 80 miles per hour, the tower collapsed. Community contended that the collapse was not due to metallurgical or mechanical failure or abnormal wind loading but to a phenomenon known as mechanical resonance. It argued that because of the resonance, the tower members were inadequate to support the load that they sustained. Dresser argued, though, that a combination of ice, snow, and wind subjected the tower to a total force greater than the ultimate capacity of its structural elements. In its view, a substantial accumulation of rime ice (formed when water droplets, existing in clouds at temperatures below freezing, instantaneously crystallize and freeze as they collide with a structure) on the upper fourth of the tower enlarged the tower surface area exposed to the wind, thereby subjecting the tower members to a greater load than their designed wind loading capacity. In any event, Dresser urged that its warranty did not guarantee against mechanical resonance. Community filed suit and obtained a judgment against Dresser for more than $1 million, which it showed was the cost necessary for it to replace the tower and antenna, less depreciation, and adjacent buildings. Dresser appealed.

The focus of the appellate court's decision was an advertising catalog that Dresser had given to Community before it purchased the tower. In the catalog Dresser made the following affirmation: "Properly designed towers will safely withstand the maximum wind velocities and ice loads to which they are likely to be subjected. [Dresser] can make wind and ice load recommendations to you for your area based on U.S. Weather Bureau data."

The appellate court agreed with Dresser that a seller cannot be held to be the insurer of its product. But it noted that Dresser provided the catalog to Community to induce purchase of its product and that the affirmation contained in the catalog must be considered "part of the bargain." It said that the statements in the advertising catalog could reasonably have been found by the jury to be an affirmation of fact or a promise—in other words, an express warranty—concerning the actual durability or performance of the tower during the wind and ice storms to which it was likely to be subjected.

The court noted that while the blizzard was a severe one, Dresser did not provide evidence at trial that could lead to the conclusion that the wind alone, or the combination of wind and ice that Dresser claimed caused the collapse, was not within the range of storm conditions reasonably to be contemplated for the tower's location. The appellate court then determined that there was sufficient evidence for the jury to reasonably find that the tower was not as durable as it was warranted to be and that Dresser breached the express warranty contained in its catalog.

Next, the appellate court turned to Dresser's attempted disclaimer. On the back of each page of the two-page sale contract for the tower was a printed form entitled "Terms and Conditions of Sale" that included in item nine a warranty and limitation of liability clause. Dresser contended that the limitation of liability clause precluded it from incurring any liability for breach or, alternatively, limited its liability to the purchase price of the tower—$385,000 less depreciation.

The warranty issued by Dresser in item nine was that its product would be free of defects in material and workmanship and would meet applicable specifications. Item nine limited the warranty to those defects for which a buyer submitted a written claim immediately upon discovery and, in any event, within six months from final acceptance. It also limited the buyer's remedies for breach of warranty to repair, replace, or refund an equitable portion of the purchase price of any product that Dresser determined to be defective or found failed to meet applicable specifications and it gave Dresser the sole option of deciding which remedy it would provide.

The trial court refused to enforce the limitations of Dresser's liability set forth in item nine. It specifically ruled that the six-month period was a "manifestly unreasonable" time for discovery and notification of breach, in light of the tower's 25-year average useful life. While that ruling on its own could provide a great deal of concern to sellers, manufacturers, and other companies that issue express warranties, it may not have much lasting significance. The appellate court to which Dresser appealed relied on a different ground for its decision.

The appellate court said that the limitation clauses contained in item nine only applied to the purportedly exclusive warranty set forth in item nine— and not to the broader warranty created by the affirmation made in Dresser's advertising materials.

It said the six-month notification period provided for in item nine only related to the warranty that Dresser's products and construction "shall meet the applicable specifications incorporated in this contract, and be free from defects in material and workmanship." However, the appellate court said Dresser's affirmation in its advertising catalog went beyond the limited warranty contained in the written contract and created a promise concerning the tower's durability much broader than mere compliance with the contract's technical specifications. Dresser promised Community in its catalog that a nondefective, properly designed tower would "safely withstand the maximum wind velocities and ice loads to which [it is] likely to be subjected."

The appellate court then ruled that the general disclaimer of warranties in item nine did not restrict Community's right to recover. Language that limits or negates an express warranty is "inoperative when it cannot reasonably be construed consistently with language which creates the warranty" under the Uniform Commercial Code.

Therefore, because item nine contained in the sales contract did not limit the duration of the express warranty of durability or performance evident from the overall agreement of the parties as indicated by the catalog, nor limit remedies for its breach, the appellate court affirmed the judgment in favor of Community.

❙ Limiting Remedies for Breach

Another method for limiting the harm that an express warranty, if breached, can cause to a seller is to limit the kinds of remedies available to an aggrieved purchaser. Courts often uphold contractual provisions limiting a buyer's remedies to return of the goods and repayment of the price or to repair and replacement of nonconforming goods or parts.

In one case, Harold Brown, the president of Transamerica Oil Corp., saw an advertisement in a trade journal for "production injection packers" by the Baker International Corporation and its subsidiary, Lynes, Inc. A packer is a device inserted into an oil and gas well to seal off one zone from another, generally to stop water from entering the well bore and interfering with production. Frequently, packers are employed for temporary use in holes that have been cased and cemented. The Lynes ad, though, stated that its production injection packer was suitable for permanent use in open holes. Transamerica was in the business of drilling and completing oil and gas wells and Brown thought that that production injection packer might help it avoid the expensive casing and cementing process that Transamerica sometimes used. He telephoned Lynes and spoke with a sales representative. Lynes then sent Brown additional advertising and descriptive literature. This literature also stated that the production injunction packer was suitable for use as a permanent completion device in open well holes.

Transamerica purchased 10 production injection packers in six shipments from Lynes. Each invoice prepared and sent by Lynes contained language on its reverse side disclaiming any express warranties other than that the products were free from defects in materials and workmanship. Each invoice also purported to limit the purchaser's remedy to replacement of or credit for defective equipment or parts and to exclude any liability for consequential damages that might be suffered by a purchaser in the event of a breach of a warranty. Nonetheless, Transamerica later filed suit, claiming that the production injection packers failed to perform properly. A jury awarded Transamerica $196,577.62, much more than the purchase price of the packers.

On appeal, Baker and Lynes argued, among other things, that the invoices limited Transamerica's remedies and that the large damages award should be overturned on that basis. Transamerica countered that the limitation on remedies was not valid because it was unconscionable and because it was an attempt to alter a contract the parties had previously entered into.

■ Unconscionable Contract Provisions

The U.S. Court of Appeals for the Tenth Circuit noted that there are a number of factors that courts use to determine whether a provision in a contract is so unfair or one-sided as to be unconscionable and unenforceable. It said these factors are:

- The use of printed form or boilerplate contracts drawn by the party in the stronger economic position that establish take it or leave it provisions for the party in a weaker economic position

- A significant cost-price disparity or excessive price

- A denial of basic rights and remedies to a buyer of consumer goods

- The inclusion of penalty clauses

- An analysis of the circumstances surrounding the execution of the contract, including its commercial setting, its purpose, and actual effect

- The hiding of clauses that are disadvantageous to one party in a mass of fine print or in places that are inconspicuous to the party signing the contract

- Phrasing clauses in language that is incomprehensible to a layperson or that diverts the layperson's attention from the problems raised by technical language or the rights given up through them

- An overall imbalance in the obligations and rights imposed by the contract

- Exploitation of the underprivileged, unsophisticated, uneducated, and the illiterate

- Inequality of bargaining or economic power

Not all of these factors must necessarily be present for a court to determine that a particular contractual provision is unconscionable. But the appellate court said that, applying these standards, it could not rule that a clause excluding a seller's liability for consequential commercial damages always was unconscionable per se. It noted that Transamerica, Baker, and Lynes were business entities with much experience in the oil and gas business; Transamerica did not appear to be in a substantially weaker economic position than Baker or Lynes; the price for the packers apparently was not excessive; this was a commercial, rather than a consumer, setting; while the language limiting remedies was on the back of the invoice form there was language on the front, in red print, that referred to the terms and conditions of sale on the reverse side; and the limitation of remedies appeared in the first paragraph on the reverse of each invoice and was written in fairly large, legible print and in clear, concise language.

Nonetheless, the appellate court overturned the monetary award to Transamerica and ordered a new trial to determine what relief or damages Transamerica was entitled to and whether it should be held to the limited remedies provided by the invoice. It said that the trial court should have allowed Baker and Lynes to try to show that Brown had agreed to the limitation of remedies when he personally signed one of the invoices and to have a jury determine whether Brown was credible when he testified that he had not been aware of the limitation. Also, the appellate court ruled, Baker and Lynes should be permitted to introduce evidence at a retrial that the exclusive remedy of replacement or credit constituted a "usage of trade" in the oil and gas industry to which Transamerica should be held. If Baker and Lynes could prove either of these things, the appellate court suggested, Transamerica could be limited to the remedies set forth in the invoices for breach of the express warranty given as part of the transaction.

▌Express Warranties for Consumer Products

On January 4, 1975, President Gerald Ford signed into law a bill now known as the Magnuson-Moss Warranty Act, or the federal warranty act. In the words of Congress, this act was designed to "improve the adequacy of information available to consumers, prevent deception, and improve competition in the marketing of consumer products."

Significantly, the Magnuson-Moss Act does not require that sellers of consumer products give purchasers a warranty or warrant their goods for any length of time. It is a disclosure statute that requires that warranties that are provided for consumer products adequately disclose their terms and the nature of the warranty obligation.

Because the federal warranty act only applies to sales of consumer products, the definition of consumer products is important. The Magnuson-Moss Act defines consumer products as "any tangible personal property which is distributed in commerce and which is normally used for personal, family, or household purposes (including any such property intended to be attached to or installed in any real property without regard to whether it is so attached or installed.)"

The federal warranty act only applies when there is a written warranty. As defined in the federal warranty act, a written warranty means one of two things. First, it means any written affirmation of fact or written promise made in connection with the sale of a consumer product by a supplier to a buyer which relates to the nature of the material or workmanship and affirms or promises that such material or workmanship is defect-free or will meet a specified level of performance over a specified period of time. It also means any undertaking in writing in connection with the sale of a consumer product to refund, repair, replace, or take other remedial action with respect to the product in the event that the product fails to meet the specifications set forth in the warranty. It is necessary that these written affirmations, promises, or undertakings become "part of the basis of the bargain" between a seller and a buyer—in other words, that they are "relied" on by the buyer or that they form part of the conscious or subconscious reason the buyer is purchasing the product for them to constitute warranties.

Generally speaking, under the federal warranty act, any supplier or other company in the manufacturing and distribution chain that gives or offers to give a written warranty for consumer products costing the consumer more than $15 must state the following terms of the warranty in readily understandable language:

- The identity of the party or parties to whom the written warranty is extended, if the enforceability of the written warranty is limited to the original consumer purchaser or is otherwise limited to persons other than every consumer owner during the term of the warranty

- A clear description and identification of products, parts, or characteristics covered by and, where necessary for clarification, excluded from the warranty

- A statement of what the warrantor will do in the event of a defect, malfunction, or failure to conform with the written warranty, including the items or services the warrantor will pay for or provide, and, where necessary for clarification, those that the warrantor will not pay for or provide

- The point in time or event on which the warranty term commences, if different from the purchase date, and the time period or other measurement of warranty duration

- A step-by-step explanation of the procedure that the consumer should follow to obtain performance of any warranty obligation, including the persons or class of persons authorized to perform warranty obligations, the name of the warrantor, the warrantor's mailing address and/or the name or title and the address of any employee or department of the warrantor responsible for the performance of warranty obligations, and/or a telephone number that consumers may use to obtain information on warranty performance

- Information respecting the availability of any informal dispute settlement mechanism elected by the warrantor

- The statement "Some states do not allow the exclusion or limitation of incidental or consequential damages, so the above limitation or exclusion may not apply to you" accompanying any exclusions of or limitations on relief such as incidental or consequential damages

- The statement "This warranty gives you specific legal rights, and you may also have other rights which vary from state to state"

To further protect consumers from deception, the Magnuson Moss Warranty Act requires that any written warranty be labeled as either a full or a limited warranty. Only warranties that meet the standards of the federal warranty act may be labeled as full warranties. Generally speaking, for a warrantor warranting a consumer product by means of a written warranty to meet the federal minimum standards for warranty:

- The warrantor must at a minimum remedy the consumer product within a reasonable time and without charge, in the case of a defect, malfunction, or failure to conform with the written warranty.

- The warrantor may not exclude or limit consequential damages for breach of any written warranty on the product, unless the exclusion or limitation conspicuously appears on the face of the warranty.

- If the product (or a component part of the product) contains a defect or malfunction after a reasonable number of attempts by the warrantor to remedy defects or malfunctions in the product, the warrantor must permit the consumer to elect either a refund for, or replacement without charge of, the product or part. If the warrantor replaces a component part of a consumer product, the replacement must include installing the part in the product without charge.

▌A Final Word

Breach of warranty cases are different from product liability lawsuits that are based on a dangerous defect in a product. While many businesses focus on product liability law alone, express warranty law is something about which sellers, manufacturers, and distributors should take notice. As Dresser Industries learned with its radio tower, a breach of a warranty can be expensive.

FIVE LAWSUITS INVOLVING EXPRESS WARRANTIES

The provisions contained in sales contracts basically do not matter when everything goes well and the expectations of both buyer and seller are fulfilled. But when there is a problem, the words matter very much. Here are brief descriptions of five different cases where warranties reached the courthouse.

1. When a pebble from a passing car struck the windshield of the Model A Ford town sedan Sam Baxter was driving, small pieces of glass flew into Baxter's left eye. He filed suit against St. John Motors, the Ford dealer from which he had purchased the car, and against the Ford Motor Company. The basis for Baxter's suit: the catalogs and printed matter furnished by Ford to St. John Motors that were distributed to customers contained statements that said that the windshields of all Ford cars were made with a shatterproof glass that "will not fly or shatter under the hardest impact." The Supreme Court of Washington found in favor of Baxter, declaring that it would be "unjust" to permit manufacturers of goods to create a demand for their products by representing that they had qualities that they in fact did not have and then to deny the consumer the right to recover if damages result from the absence of those qualities, at least when the absence was not readily noticeable to the consumer. (Baxter v. Ford Motor Company, 12 P.2d 409 (Wash. 1932).)

2. In late 1972, the Singer Company became interested in an electro-deposition paint system for its Red Bud, Illinois, plant. Electrodeposition is a method of painting by which pretreated ware is conveyed through an electrically charged paint tank and the ware, serving as an anode, is coated with paint in an electroplating kind of process. After a period of nego-tiation between representatives from Singer and E. I. du Pont de Nemours and Company, du Pont contracted to provide Singer with paint for its approximately 22,000-gallon tank that would meet "all tests." From the beginning, Singer experienced problems with the electrodeposition system: ware frequently emerged from the paint tank with "blotches" and "streaks." Indeed, the plant needed to be repainted. Singer filed suit against du Pont. Du Pont argued, among other things, that the problem was with the pretreated ware while Singer argued that the paint was at fault. In a lengthy decision that covered numbers of different issues, the court ruled that the "all tests" provision of the contract, which specified such standards as colors and texture that the paint was to satisfy upon pretreated laboratory test panels, "was an express warranty pursuant to Section 2-313(1)(b) of the UCC." (Singer Co. v. E. I. du Pont de Nemours and Co., 579 F.2d 433 (8th Cir. 1978).)

3. After Guiseppe Ventura purchased a 1978 Mercury Marquis Brougham manufactured by the Ford Motor Corporation and sold by Marino Auto Sales, Inc., a Ford dealer, Ventura began having some prob-lems with the car. He filed suit against Ford and Marino and the court found that Ford had authorized Marino to perform repairs under the ex-press warranty on the car that Ford had issued; Ventura provided Marino with a reasonable opportunity to cure the car's defects by bringing it in for repairs five or more times with complaints of stalling and hesitation; despite Marino's attempts to effect repairs the stalling and hesitation con-tinued; Ventura's car was substantially impaired in value because of manu-facturing defects in workmanship or materials or both; Ford had breached its express warranty to Ventura; and Ventura was entitled under the Magnuson-Moss Warranty Act to return the car to Marino and receive his money back, with a credit for mileage driven. The court also found that

Ventura could recover from Ford the amount he paid his attorney in attorney's fees to litigate the suit. Taking into account the difficulty of the litigation and the quality of Ventura's attorney's work and his experience in similar litigation, the court determined that the lawyer's rates of $75 per hour for office time and $100 per hour for court time were reasonable and proper and that Ventura should recover from Ford the amount of $5,165 based upon the actual hours spent on the matter by Ventura's attorney. (Ventura v. Ford Motor Corp., 414 A.2d 611 (Sup. Ct. N.J. 1980).)

4. Robert and Frances Schneble claimed that they were told that the female Doberman pinscher that they purchased from the House of Hoyt was a "docile dobe," appropriate for one "who is in need of a dog for companionship and friendship, but wants very little aggressiveness" in a dog. More than two years after they purchased the Doberman, she was bred and gave birth to puppies. Several days later, a neighbor's child was looking at the puppies in the presence of the Schnebles when she was bitten by the puppies' mother. The girl filed suit against the Schnebles under the Illinois "dog-bite" statute and the Schnebles filed suit against the House of Hoyt seeking to be indemnified for any amounts they might be ordered to pay the girl. The Schnebles claimed, among other things, that the House of Hoyt was liable to them for breach of an express warranty about the Doberman's temperament. The court failed to find any express warranty. "Statements merely of the seller's opinion or sales talk do not constitute express warranties," it said. Even if there were an express warranty, the court said that it had not been breached: the express terms of the warranty did not provide that the dog would not bite and they only described the personality of the dog at the time it was sold. Concluding that it was "unfortunate of course that in this case the dog's bite was worse than her bark," the court ruled that the House of Hoyt should not be held liable to the Schnebles. (Whitmer v. Schneble, 331 N.E.2d 115 (App. Ct. Ill. 1975).)

5. On May 9, 1966, George W. Utter took his car to Three B's, an Aamco Transmissions, Inc. franchisee. At Utter's request, Three B's installed an "Aamco Custom Rebuilt Transmission with Lifetime Guarantee." Unfortunately, Utter's lifetime did not last long. On May 14, Utter told his wife he was going to do some work on the car. While the car was in the driveway, he started the engine, walked around to the front, and lifted the hood. As he was adjusting the carburetor, the car backed away from him down the driveway. A neighbor saw Utter walk along beside the car as it backed toward the street and saw him reach into the car in an apparent attempt to turn off the ignition. In trying to stop the car, Utter was knocked down and run over by the left front wheel. His wife, who had been inside their home, saw the accident and ran to help her husband. The driverless automobile continued to run in reverse, made a complete circle, and ran over both Mr. and Mrs. Utter. Finally, the neighbor was able to get inside the car and stop it by turning off the engine. Utter died of his injuries and his daughter filed suit against Three B's, which settled, and Aamco.

One of her principal claims: Three B's and Aamco had violated the express warranty as to the quality of the transmission repair. The court that issued a decision in this case noted that the franchise agreement between Aamco and Three B's required Three B's to use Aamco advertising materials and sales promotions and to contribute to national advertising by Aamco. Aamco sent Three B's camera-ready advertisements for newspapers and tapes for radio spots. Three B's used the materials to run advertisements in local newspapers and on local radio stations. The advertisements praised Aamco Transmissions with its "Coast-to-Coast Ironclad Guarantee." The court decided that the ads, together with the specific Aamco Transmission service guide given to Utter, provided substantial evidence to indicate that Aamco had expressly warranted the installation and performance of the transmission sold to Utter. As the court said, "Advertising may be the basis of or form a part of an express warranty." Aamco argued that there was no evidence that Three B's used any Aamco parts in its work for Utter, but the court concluded that Aamco expressly warranted the performance of the installed transmission whether or not it contained Aamco parts. (Scheuler v. Aamco Transmissions, Inc., 571 P.2d 48 (Ct. App. Kansas 1977).)

Express Warranty Checklist

✓ An express warranty is a promise about a product that, if breached, can result in a manufacturer, seller, distributor, or other entity in a product's distribution chain being held liable for damages.

✓ Express warranties can be created in virtually any advertising, marketing, or packaging materials and can be created without the use of the words "warranty" or "guarantee."

✓ Disclaiming express warranties is difficult to do because of the inherent conflict disclaimers create—the warrantor is hoping to create a sale by warranting a particular characteristic of the product but then it seeks to disclaim that warranty in the documentation, perhaps without the buyer even being fully aware of the disclaimer.

✓ Limiting a buyer's remedies can help limit a seller's risks; courts often uphold contractual provisions limiting a buyer's remedies to return of the goods and repayment of the purchase price or to repair and replacement of nonconforming goods or parts.

✓ The federal Magnuson-Moss Warranty Act does not require that warranties be provided to purchasers of consumer products but it does impose special obligations when warranties are offered.

HOW THE COPYRIGHT LAWS AFFECT ADVERTISING

■ Copyrights and Advertising ■ Fair Use ■ Works for Hire
■ A Final Word

In January 1987, the Allied Marketing Group, Inc., a mail-order retail company, began using a copyrighted postcard mailer to notify consumers that it had particular goods available for purchase. It registered its copyright in the postcard format with the U.S. Copyright Office in February 1987.

Several months later, Allied discovered that another mail-order retail company, the S & H Marketing Group, Inc., was using a similar postcard mailer. Allied filed suit against S & H, contending that S & H's mailer infringed on Allied's copyright in its mailer.

To establish the infringement of a copyright, a plaintiff must prove "ownership" of the copyrighted material and "copying" by the defendant. A plaintiff can prove ownership by proving that the material was original and copyrightable and that it complied with the requirements of the federal copyright law. It can establish copying by proving that the defendant had access to the copyrighted material and that there was a "substantial similarity" between the two works.

The district court found that Allied's certificate of copyright registration was sufficient to show that it owned the copyright in its postcard. The court noted that S & H stipulated that it had received at least one version of Allied's postcard as early as August 1986 and found S & H had access to and had been specifically aware of Allied's postcard promotions prior to the alleged conception of the S & H postcard. Concluding that the two post-cards were "substantially—indeed, strikingly—similar," the court then issued a preliminary injunction precluding S & H from using postcards that were similar to Allied's copyrighted card.

However, the U.S. Court of Appeals for the Fifth Circuit reversed the district court's decision to issue a preliminary injunction. It ruled that the court should have considered S & H's defenses to Allied's copyright claim, which included that Allied lost any protection it may have had in the post-card mailer because it failed to place a copyright notice on more than one million postcards that it mailed, as required by the Copyright Act.

▐ Copyrights and Advertising

While the law at one time did not even permit an advertiser to have a copyright in an ad, today the federal copyright laws play an important role in many advertising and marketing decisions. The basic rules are rather straightforward, but they become much more complicated when considering questions of how much of one business's copyrighted material another business may use and when analyzing the ownership of free-lanced works.

Article I, Section 8, of the Constitution provides: "The Congress shall have Power . . . To promote the Progress of Science and useful Arts, by securing for limited Times to Authors and Inventors the exclusive Right to their respective Writings and Discoveries." Under the Copyright Act as enacted by Congress, copyright protection exists in original works of authorship fixed in any tangible medium of expression. Most original works may be copyrighted. Significantly, ideas may not be copyrighted—although the words used to express the ideas may be. Furthermore, facts may not be copyrighted—although a compiler of facts may be able to copyright the compilation.

No registration is required for copyright, although registration is required before an infringement suit may be filed. And, as Allied discovered, copyright notice is essential. The owner of a copyright that omits the notice on the copyrighted materials will lose the copyright unless it can meet one of three conditions:

1. The notice was omitted from no more than a relatively small number of copies distributed to the public.

2. The owner registered the work within five years after the publication without notice and made a reasonable effort to add notice to all copies distributed to the public in the United States after discovering the omission.

3. The notice was omitted in violation of an express written requirement.

Thus, if a copyright owner omits copyright notice from a copyrightable work, copyright protection may still be accorded the work if it falls within one of the three exceptions. (Innocent infringers who are misled by the absence of copyright notice may not be held liable for damages for infringing a copyright.)

The copyright law grants the copyright holder "exclusive" rights to use and to authorize use of its works in five qualified ways:

1. To reproduce the copyrighted work in copies or phonorecords

2. To prepare derivative works based upon the copyrighted work

3. To distribute copies or phonorecords of the copyrighted work to the public by sale or other transfer of ownership, or by rental, lease, or lending

4. In the case of literary, musical, dramatic, and choreographic works, pantomimes, and motion pictures and other audiovisual works, to perform the copyrighted work publicly

5. In the case of literary, musical, dramatic, and choreographic works, pantomimes, and pictorial, graphic, or sculptural works, including the individual images of a motion picture or other audiovisual work, to display the copyrighted work publicly

Anyone who violates any of the exclusive rights of the copyright owner is an infringer of the copyright. The law provides the owner with a potent arsenal of remedies against an infringer, including the right to obtain an injunction to restrain the infringer from violating its rights, the right to impound and destroy all reproductions of its work made in violation of its rights, and the right to recover its actual damages and any additional profits realized by the infringer or statutory damages and attorney's fees.

▍Fair Use

All reproductions of a copyrighted work, however, are not within the exclusive domain of the copyright owners; some are in the public domain. Any individual may reproduce a copyrighted work for a "fair use."

The doctrine of fair use has been called the most troublesome in the whole law of copyright. Simply put, no one really knows what constitutes fair use. May someone take just a "little" from a copyrighted work and claim that it is fair use? What if the little bit is the essence of the work? For instance, the U.S. Supreme Court decided several years ago that *The Nation* violated the copyright held by Harper & Row Publishers, Inc. and the Reader's Digest Association, Inc. in former President Gerald Ford's memoirs although it only published several hundred words from the book. The Court found that those words were "the heart of the book" because they dealt with former President Richard Nixon's resignation and pardon.

What if someone makes only one or a few copies of a complete copyrighted work, such as a newsletter? Does it matter if the copier is a for-profit business? In recent years, courts have not been very understanding when businesses have attempted to argue fair use if they could have avoided the problem by purchasing additional subscriptions to a newsletter, book, or other copyrighted work and thus avoided the copying.

Although courts have constructed lists of factors to be considered in determining whether a particular use is fair, no fixed criteria have emerged by which that determination can be made. Nor did Congress provide definitive rules when it codified the fair use doctrine in the 1976 act; it simply incorporated a list of factors to be considered:

- The purpose and character of the use

- The nature of the copyrighted work

- The amount and substantiality of the portion used

- The effect of the use upon the potential market for or value of the copyrighted work

Whether or not something may be deemed fair use in a particular case is often rather difficult to know in advance. However, in recent years, courts have suggested that copying for a commercial purpose can almost never be a fair use. Even taking a few sentences from a longer work may be not be a fair use if the purpose is commercial. As Judge Learned Hand once stated, "No plagiarist can excuse the wrong by showing how much of his work he did not pirate."

▌ Works for Hire

The copyright law provides that copyright ownership vests initially in the author or authors of the work. As a general rule, the author is the party who actually creates the work, that is, the person who translates an idea into a fixed, tangible expression entitled to copyright protection. The law carves out an important exception, however, for "works made for hire." If the work is for hire, the employer or other person for whom the work is prepared is considered the author and owns the copyright unless there is a written agreement to the contrary. Classifying a work as made for hire determines not only the initial ownership of its copyright, but also the copyright's duration, and the owner's renewal rights, termination rights, and right to import certain goods bearing the copyright. The contours of the work for hire doctrine therefore carry profound significance for free-lance creators—including artists, writers, photographers, designers, composers, and computer programmers— and for the industries that commission their works.

Suppose that a company's in-house advertising department employee, an ad agency, or independent contractor prepares a marketing campaign and associated marketing materials for the company. Who owns the copyright? The U.S. Supreme Court addressed the difficult issue of the copyright in works for hire in a 1989 decision.

That case arose after the Community for Creative Non-Violence, a nonprofit unincorporated association, dedicated to eliminating homelessness in America, decided in the fall of 1985 to sponsor a display in Washington D.C. to dramatize the plight of the homeless. Mitch Snyder, a member and trustee of the organization, and other members of the group conceived the idea for the display: a sculpture of a modern Nativity scene in which, in lieu of the traditional Holy Family, the two adult figures and the infant would appear as contemporary homeless people huddled on a streetside steam grate. The family was to be black (most of the homeless in Washington being black); the figures were to be life-size; and the steam grate was to be positioned atop a platform "pedestal" or base, within which special effects equipment would be enclosed to emit simulated steam through the grid to swirl about the figures. They also settled upon a title for the work—Third World America—and a legend for the pedestal: "and still there is no room at the inn."

Snyder spoke to James Earl Reid, a Baltimore, Maryland, sculptor, about the sculpture. In the course of two telephone calls, Reid agreed to sculpt the three human figures. The association agreed to make the steam grate and pedestal for the statue. Reid proposed that the work be cast in bronze, at a total cost of approximately $100,000, taking six to eight months to complete. Snyder rejected that proposal because the association did not have sufficient funds and because he wanted the statue completed by December 12. Reid then suggested, and Snyder agreed, that the sculpture be made of a material known as Design Cast 62, a synthetic substance that could meet the group's monetary and time constraints, be tinted to resemble bronze, and withstand the elements. The parties agreed that the project would cost no more than $15,000, not including Reid's services, which he offered to donate. The parties did not sign a written agreement and neither side mentioned copyright.

After Reid received an advance of $3,000, he made several sketches of figures in various poses. At Snyder's request, Reid sent the association a sketch of a proposed sculpture showing the family in a crèchelike setting: the mother seated, cradling a baby in her lap; the father standing behind her, bending over her shoulder to touch the baby's foot. Upon Snyder's suggestion, Reid visited a family living at the association's Washington shelter but decided that only the family's newborn child was a suitable model. While Reid was in Washington, Snyder took him to see homeless people living on the streets. Snyder pointed out that they tended to recline on steam grates, rather than sit or stand, to warm their bodies. From that time on, Reid's sketches contained only reclining figures.

On December 24, 1985, 12 days after the agreed-upon date, Reid delivered the completed statue to Washington. There it was joined to the steam grate and pedestal prepared by the association and placed on display. Snyder paid Reid the final installment of the $15,000. The statue remained on display for a month. In late January 1986, the association returned it to Reid's Baltimore studio for minor repairs. Several weeks later, Snyder began making plans to take the statue on a tour of several cities to raise money for the homeless. Reid objected, contending that the Design Cast 62 material was not strong enough to withstand the ambitious itinerary. He urged the association to cast the statue in bronze at a cost of $35,000 or to create a master mold at a cost of $5,000. Snyder declined to spend more of the association's money on the project.

In March 1986 Snyder asked Reid to return the sculpture. Reid refused and filed a certificate of copyright registration for "Third World America" in his name and announced plans to take the sculpture on a more modest tour than the one the association had planned. Snyder, acting in his capacity as the association's trustee, immediately filed a competing certificate of copyright registration.

Snyder and the Community for Creative Non-Violence then filed suit against Reid, seeking return of the sculpture and a determination of copyright ownership. The case reached the Supreme Court.

The Court noted that Section 101 of the copyright law provides that a work is for hire under two sets of circumstances. Section 101(1) provides that a work is a work for hire if it is prepared by an employee within the scope of his or her employment. Section 101(2) provides that a work is a work for hire if the work is specially ordered or commissioned for use as a contribution to a collective work, as a part of a motion picture or other audiovisual work, as a translation, as a supplementary work, as a compilation, as an instructional text, as a test, as answer material for a test, or as an atlas, if the parties expressly agree in a written instrument signed by them that the work should be considered a work made for hire.

Neither Reid nor Snyder argued that the sculpture fit within any of the nine categories of specially ordered or commissioned works; in any event, they had no written agreement establishing Third World America as a work for hire.

The Court then examined whether Third World America was a work prepared by an employee within the scope of his or her employment. It noted that the copyright law did not define these terms. But relying on the common understanding of the terms, it ruled that Reid was not the association's employee but rather an independent contractor. It then concluded that because he was an independent contractor, and because the association could not meet the requirements of Section 101(2), Third World America was not a work for hire and the association was not entitled to the sole copyright. (It did say, though, that because of the extent of the association's involvement in the sculpture, it could be a joint author and, if that were so, it and Reid would be co-owners of the copyright.)

▌A Final Word

The federal copyright law protects advertisements and similar creative marketing materials from being used by third parties. The holder of a copyright is entitled to the exclusive right to use the copyright, subject to a third party's "fair use." When used properly, the copyright laws can be just as important as the patent and trademark laws in establishing creative rights, and a marketing and advertising advantage.

FIVE COPYRIGHT CASES

1. In November 1946 a former professional fashion model incorporated the Vogue School of Fashion Modeling to conduct courses in fashion and photographic modeling and "self improvement." The school was licensed as a trade school by the New York State Department of Education—but it was not affiliated with *Vogue*, published at that time by

Conde Nast Publications, Inc. To promote and advertise itself, the school printed a booklet that described the school, its work, and its personnel. On the back of the school's 1948 catalog were photographic reproductions of several magazine covers, including one from the April 15, 1948 issue of *Vogue* and one from the May 1948 issue of *Glamour*, which also was published by Conde Nast. The school printed a subsequent catalog with the same text, but the back cover displayed three reproductions of *Vogue* covers and two of *Glamour* from 1948 and 1949. Conde Nast filed suit against the school, arguing among other things that the school's use of seven of its covers had infringed its copyright.

The court that issued a decision in this case noted that Conde Nast had copyrighted the contents of *Vogue* and *Glamour* and that the school had reproduced the covers without permission for a commercial purpose. After finding that the covers were copyrightable and had in fact been copyrighted, it analyzed whether the school's copying had been within the permissible limits of fair use. It acknowledged that the school had not attempted to claim that the covers were the product of its own genius and effort or to offer them for sale. But, it ruled, the copying had not been the reasonable use permitted by fair use. It noted that the extent of the copying had been substantial; although the school did not reproduce the entire cover, "its very essence—the picture of the model—was, as was also the title." At the time the school reproduced the covers, the court said that, in addition to their artistic value, "they had the element of time-liness, for the copying took place shortly after these issues had appeared."

Even though the defendants may have lacked the intention to deliberately infringe, the court said that the purpose of the school's copying was to promote its business with the aid of an attractive catalog and the prestige of Conde Nast's magazines. It said this was exactly the prohibition that limited the privilege granted by the fair use theory, that "no one is entitled to save time, trouble, and expense by availing himself of another's copyrighted work for the sake of making an unearned profit." It then granted Conde Nast an injunction restraining the school from copying, distributing, or using in any manner Conde Nast's seven copyrighted covers. (Conde Nast Publications, Inc. v. Vogue School of Fashion Modeling, Inc., 105 F. Supp. 325 (S.D.N.Y. 1952).)

2. On March 2, 1983 the *Enterprise*, a weekly newspaper in Tangipahoa Parish, Louisiana, published an advertisement for Community Motors, Inc. at the request of one of Community Motors' salesmen, Frank Kraemer. The ad announced that Kraemer had joined the Community Motors' staff, displayed a photograph of Kraemer, listed Community Motors' address, and indicated that a variety of automobiles were available. Kraemer provided the *Enterprise* with the information for the ad, chose the size of the ad, and posed for a photograph taken by the *Enterprise*. In addition to photographing Kraemer, the *Enterprise* designed, composed, and printed the ad. The *Enterprise* did not inform Kraemer that it claimed any copyright interest in the advertisement. Subsequently, Kraemer contacted another weekly newspaper in Tangipahoa Parish, the *Ponchatoula Times*, and asked it to run a similar ad. Kraemer gave the *Times* a copy of the ad that had run in the *Enterprise* and told the *Times* to use that format, including the same photograph. The *Times* made only insignificant changes and published an almost identical ad on March 3, 1983.

On May 31, 1983, the *Enterprise* acquired a Certificate of Copyright Registration from the Register of Copyrights for the entire March 2, 1983, edition of the *Enterprise*. The *Enterprise* had printed a notice of copyright for the entire newspaper under the masthead on the front page, but it affixed no separate copyright notice to the Community Motors ad itself. The copyright it obtained specifically covered all original photographs; the *Enterprise* claimed that covered the photograph it had taken of Kraemer. It then filed suit against the *Times*, contending that the *Times* had violated its copyright in the Commercial Motors ad. The federal district court ruled that absent a written agreement to the contrary, the advertiser, Frank Kraemer or Community Motors, owned the copyright on the ad as a "work made for hire." Alternatively, the district court held that if the

Enterprise did own the copyright, specific notice was required on the ad to protect it from copyright infringement. Accordingly, the district court dismissed the suit and granted summary judgment for the *Times*.

The *Enterprise* appealed to the U.S. Court of Appeals for the Fifth Circuit. The appellate court stated that it did not have to decide whether the *Enterprise* or the advertiser owned the copyright on the ad because it found that even if the *Enterprise* owned the copyright, it failed to provide sufficient notice of the copyright to protect its rights. Under the Copyright Act, a newspaper is a "collective work." The law states that the individual contributions comprising a collective work may be protected under a single notice of copyright applicable to the collective work as a whole. However, advertisements are different. Advertisements inserted in a collective work on behalf of persons other than the collective work copyright owner are not protected by a copyright notice applicable to the work as a whole, the Fifth Circuit said. Rather, separate notice is required for any advertisement inserted on behalf of someone other than the collective work copyright owner regardless of whether the publisher or advertiser owns the copyright. "Consequently, when an advertiser gives a publisher an advertisement which has been published previously in another publication and has no copyright notice affixed, it would be logical for the publisher to presume both that no copyright was claimed by the prior publisher and that reprinting of the advertisement verbatim would not infringe any right of the prior publisher." The circuit court then upheld the district court's decision dismissing the case against the *Times*. (Canfield v. Ponchatoula Times, 759 F.2d 493 (5th Cir. 1985).)

3. In the late 1970s, "Saturday Night Live" ran a skit poking fun at New York City's public relations campaign and its "I Love New York" theme song. The satire ended with the singing of "I Love Sodom" to the tune of "I Love New York." Elsmere Music, Inc., the copyright owner of the "I Love New York" song, brought suit against the National Broadcasting Company for copyright infringement. A New York Federal District Court judge rejected Elsmere's claim, concluding that the "Saturday

Night Live'' parody was protected by "fair use." The U.S. Court of Appeals for the Second Circuit agreed, ruling that ''in today's world of often unrelieved solemnity, copyright law should be hospitable to the humor of parody.'' (Elsmere Music, Inc. v. National Broadcasting Co., 623 F.2d 252 (2d Cir. 1980).)

4. In May 1985, the United Telephone Company of Missouri published its Jefferson City telephone directory. The following June, the Johnson Publishing Co., Inc. published two editions of a Jefferson City directory. One, a softcover edition, was the residential edition and, the other, a hardcover directory, was Johnson's business edition. One of the steps Johnson took to prepare its 1986 directory was to update the listing information contained in the white pages of its 1985 directory by comparing in alphabetical sequence the white pages of United's 1985 Jefferson City directory with Johnson's 1985 white pages to identify any listings in the United directory that did not appear in the white pages of Johnson's 1985 directory. It marked any such listings with either an *R*, indicating a residential listing, or a *B*, indicating a business listing. A keyboard operator entered the names, addresses, and telephone numbers for such listings into Johnson's listing information data base. Johnson then prepared, in telephone sequence, computer printout sheets containing the updated listing information. In addition, Johnson conducted a telephone canvass of listings contained in the printout sheets. It instructed surveyors to call each of the listings to verify the accuracy of the information appearing on the sheets for each listing and to acquire new or corrected information. It instructed the surveyors to make three attempts at different times (morning, afternoon, and evening) to contact the persons listed on the sheets. If a surveyor was unable to contact the person listed after making three attempts, the surveyor was instructed to refer to United's 1985 Jefferson City telephone directory to verify the name, address, and telephone number shown on the printout sheet for the person listed. Johnson also conducted a post-canvas audit of the surveyors' results.

Of the white page listings that Johnson entered into its listing information data base as a result of the comparison that Johnson did with United's 1985 Jefferson City phone directory, all but 214 were contacted either by the surveyors during the telephone canvass or by Johnson during the post-canvas audit. Johnson's directory contained a total of 23,629 white page listings. Of those total listings, 4,188 were not found in United's 1985 Jefferson City directory. Furthermore, about 2,819 of the white page listings in United's 1985 directory were not included in Johnson's 1986 directory. United had inserted three fictitious listings in its 1985 directory for the purpose of showing copying of its telephone directory, but none of these listings were included in Johnson's directory.

Contending that Johnson had infringed its copyright in the 1985 directory, United filed suit. Noting that telephone directories were clearly copyrightable, the court said that the issue came down to whether Johnson had copied United's directory. The element of copying may be shown by either an admission of copying by the defendant, or by the indirect route of proving access to the directory and substantial similarity between plaintiff's and defendant's works. One of the most significant evidences of copying, the court said, is the copying of errors. The court found that while Johnson's 1986 Jefferson City directory did not contain any of the fictitious listings contained in United's 1985 directory, the evidence "clearly established that Johnson copied from United's 1985 Jefferson City telephone directory." It then ruled that Johnson had not made fair use of United's copyrighted directory. It said that a compiler of a directory or the like may make fair use of an existing compilation serving the same purpose if it first makes an honest, independent canvass; it merely compares and checks its own compilation with that of the copyrighted original; and it publishes the result after verifying the additional items derived from the copyrighted publication. Because Johnson did not first conduct an independent canvass, the court concluded that it did not meet the fair use exception. (United Telephone Co. of Mo. v. Johnson Publishing Co., 671 F. Supp. 1514 (W.D. Missouri 1987).)

5. In 1976, Universal City Studios, Inc. and Walt Disney Productions, which owned the copyrights to some of the television programs broadcast on the public airwaves, filed a copyright infringement action against the Sony Corporation and the Sony Corporation of America, which manufactured and sold home videocassette recorders, and several retailers that sold the machines. Universal and Disney argued that some individuals had used Sony's Betamax machines to record some of their copyrighted works and that Sony should be held liable for the copyright infringement allegedly committed by Betamax consumers because it sold and marketed the recorders. The district court denied Universal and Disney any relief, but the U.S. Court of Appeals for the Ninth Circuit reversed, finding that Sony should be held liable for contributory copyright infringement. At Sony's request, the United States Supreme Court agreed to review the case. The Court found that most people used their VCRs for "time-shifting," the practice of recording a program to view it once at a later time, and thereafter erasing it, without any commercial or for-profit motive. Over the dissent of four justices, and with an invitation to Congress to change the result, the majority then ruled that home time-shifting is fair use and that the copyright act did not prohibit that conduct. (Sony Corp. v. Universal City Studios, Inc., 464 U.S. 417 (1984).)

Copyright Checklist

✓ Advertisements, labels, brochures, catalogs, and other similar marketing communications materials may all be copyrighted.

✓ The holder of a copyright is entitled to the exclusive right to use the copyrighted work, subject to a third party's right to make fair use of it.

✓ When an employee creates a work within the scope of the employee's employment, the employer is entitled to the copyright.

✓ In many cases, when an independent contractor creates a work and agrees in writing to transfer the ownership of the copyright to the company that retained the contractor, the company is entitled to the copyright. Thus, businesses that hire independent contractors should ask their contractors to sign written agreements granting them the copyright.

✓ The copyright law, together with the law on trademarks and patents, is an important part of a marketer's and advertiser's arsenal and its requirements should be kept clearly in mind.

4

ENDORSEMENTS

▌Reflect Endorser's Honest Views ▌Consumer Endorsements
▌Expert Endorsements ▌Endorsements by Organizations
▌Disclosure of Material Connections ▌A Final Word

Several years ago, the Federal Trade Commission (FTC) discovered that Pat Boone had not investigated the claims he made in print and television advertisements in support of Acne-Stain, an acne medication. The FTC also learned that despite his claim that his daughters liked the product, not all of them used it and, in any event, none of them had anything more than mild acne. Following these disclosures, Pat Boone reached an agreement with the FTC that provided that he would not misrepresent the effectiveness of Acne-Stain and would make reasonable inquiries before agreeing to endorse any other products.

But the FTC did not stop with the crooner. It brought a complaint against Acne-Stain's manufacturer for improperly using Pat Boone's endorsement. Nearly a year later, the manufacturer agreed to resolve the FTC's complaint by offering refunds to customers—and it deposited $175,000 in a fund from which those refunds could be paid.

Endorsements (which sometimes are referred to as testimonials) are advertising tools that reflect the opinions, beliefs, findings, or experiences of an entity other than the sponsoring advertiser. They can be effective when an endorser is a celebrity if the celebrity's views carry weight with consumers—that's why, for example, basketball players endorse sneakers and breakfast cereals. Even a non-celebrity endorsement can be effective if the endorser appears to be honest and acting in good faith. As a result, en-

dorsements frequently are used by advertisers: a film critic's review of a movie may be excerpted in a print advertisement purchased by the movie's producer; a well-known professional automobile racing driver may speak of the smooth ride, strength, and long life of a certain manufacturer's tires in a television commercial; a prominent golfer may be shown in an ad hitting golf balls.

Not every ad that uses a person to promote a product should be considered an endorsement subject to the rules and laws that courts and the FTC have developed over the years. For example, suppose a television commercial depicts two women in a supermarket buying a laundry detergent with one of the women telling the other how well her brand of detergent cleans her family's clothes. Or suppose that a generally nonrecognizable male voice on a radio commercial praises a particular product in a way that makes it clear he is speaking on behalf of the manufacturer rather than on the basis of his own opinions. Neither the fictional dramatization of the supermarket scene nor the voice-over commercial should be considered endorsements by the courts or the FTC.

▌ Reflect Endorser's Honest Views

Actual endorsements do have to comply with a variety of rules, though. The first rule is that endorsements should be used with consent and always must reflect the honest opinions, findings, beliefs, or experiences of the endorser. They may not contain any representations that are deceptive or misleading or that could not be substantiated if made directly by the advertiser.

Certainly, the endorsement message need not be phrased in the exact words of the endorser—unless the advertisement claims that it is. But the endorsement may not be presented out of context or reworded to distort in any way the endorser's opinion or experience with the product. (For example, an ad should not claim that a restaurant review called a particular restaurant "a great choice" with "exciting menu options" if the reviewer actually said the restaurant was "a great choice if the only alternative is starvation" and that it had "exciting menu options for people who have never seen food before.")

Furthermore, where an advertisement represents that the endorser used the endorsed product, the endorser must be an actual user of the product at the time the endorsement is given. Additionally, an advertiser may continue to use an endorsement only if it has good reason to believe that the endorser remains an actual user of the product.

The effect of this rule can be seen in the following hypothetical story: Suppose a building contractor states in an advertisement that he recommends a particular exterior house paint because of its remarkable quick-drying properties and durability. The contractor only can say this if he actually does recommend the paint and if it actually does have quick-drying properties and is durable.

Then suppose that the paint manufacturer reformulates the paint to allow it to cover exterior surfaces with only one coat. Before continuing to use the contractor's endorsement, the advertiser must contact the contractor to determine whether the contractor would continue to recommend the paint.

▌Consumer Endorsements

The FTC has a number of specific guidelines for consumer endorsements. First, the FTC says that an advertisement using an endorsement by an individual or a group of consumers on a central or key attribute of a product must reflect what consumers generally will achieve with the advertised product in actual use. Therefore, an advertiser should have adequate substantiation for this kind of representation or should disclose the limited applicability of the endorser's experience as to what consumers generally may expect to achieve.

Imagine that an ad presents the endorsement of the owners of a television set, including their statement that they have only needed to have their TV repaired once at a cost of under $10. If the television manufacturer does not have evidence that this reflects what a significant proportion of consumers would be likely to experience, it should include a disclosure that either states clearly and conspicuously what the generally expected performance would be or clearly and conspicuously informs consumers that the performance experienced by the endorser is not what they should expect to experience. According to the FTC, the mere disclosure that "not all consumers will get this result" is insufficient because that may imply that while all consumers cannot expect the advertised results, a substantial number can.

A second FTC rule for consumer endorsements requires that endorsements by what are or appear to be "actual consumers" utilize actual consumers, in both the audio and video, or clearly and conspicuously disclose that the persons in the ad are not actual consumers of the advertised product.

This kind of situation may occur, for instance, in an ad using a "hidden camera" in a crowded cafeteria at breakfast time where a spokesperson for the advertiser asks a series of cafeteria patrons for their spontaneous, honest opinions of the advertiser's coffee. Even if not one of the actual patrons is specifically identified in the ad, the net impression may well be that these are actual consumers and not actors. If the ad in fact uses actors, that should be disclosed.

▍Expert Endorsements

When an ad represents that an endorser is an expert regarding the endorsement message, the FTC requires that the endorser's qualifications in fact give the endorser the expertise the endorser is represented as possessing. For example, if a person described as an "engineer" endorses an automobile, the endorser's professional training and experience should be related to the design and performance of automobiles; if the endorser's field is chemical engineering, the endorsement might be deceptive. And if a product is endorsed by something called the "American Institute of Science," the institute must be an actual independent organization.

Of course, an expert endorser may take into account factors not within his or her expertise, such as matters of taste and price. But an expert's endorsement must be supported by the expert's evaluation of product features or characteristics with respect to which the endorser is an expert and that are relevant to an ordinary consumer's use of or experience with the product.

Where an ad implies that an endorsement is based upon a comparison of competing products, the expert indeed must have conducted the comparison and the expert must have reached the conclusion that the endorsed product is at least equal overall to the competition's products (if that is what the ad explicitly or implicitly contends) or that the advertised product is superior to other products with respect to those significant features for which the endorser is an expert (if that is the contention of the ad).

Suppose an association of professional athletes states in an ad that it has "selected" a particular brand of beverage as its "official breakfast drink." The association may be regarded as an expert in the field of nutrition because consumers would expect it to rely upon the selection of nutritious foods as part of its business needs. Consequently, the FTC would require that the association's endorsement be based upon an expert evaluation of the nutritional value of the endorsed beverage. Furthermore, the use of the words "selected" and "official" in the endorsement imply that it was given only after direct comparisons had been performed among competing brands. As a result, the advertisement could be deceptive if the association had not in fact performed these comparisons between the endorsed brand and its leading competitors in terms of nutritional criteria, or if the results of the comparisons do not conform to the net impression created by the ad.

Furthermore, an advertiser may use an endorsement of an expert only so long as it has good reason to believe that the endorser continues to subscribe to the views presented in the ad. An advertiser may satisfy this obligation by securing the endorser's views at reasonable intervals where reasonableness is determined by such factors as new information on the performance or effectiveness of the product, a material alteration in the product, changes in the performance of competitor's products, and the advertiser's contract commitments.

▋ Endorsements by Organizations

The FTC views endorsements by organizations, especially expert ones, as representing the judgment of a group whose collective experience exceeds that of any individual member and whose judgments generally are free of the kind of subjective factors that vary from individual to individual. Therefore, an organization's endorsement must be reached by a process sufficient to ensure that the endorsement fairly reflects the collective judgment of the organization. Moreover, if an organization is represented as being expert, then, in conjunction with the proper exercise of its expertise in evaluating the product, it must use an expert or experts recognized as such by the organization or standards previously adopted by the organization and suitable for judging the relevant merits of the products.

As an example, imagine that a mattress manufacturer advertises that its product is endorsed by a chiropractic association. Because the association would be regarded as expert with respect to judging mattresses, its endorsement must be supported by an evaluation by an expert or experts recognized as such by the organization or by compliance with standards previously adopted by the organization and aimed at measuring the performance of mattresses in general, and not designed with the particular attributes of the advertised mattress in mind.

▋ Disclosure of Material Connections

When there exists a connection between the endorser and the seller of the advertised product that might materially affect the weight or credibility of the endorsement because the connection might not be reasonably expected by the ad's audience, the connection must be fully disclosed. (Ordinarily, payment or promise of payment to an endorser who is an expert or well-known personality need not be disclosed because it is expected by viewers, as long as the advertiser does not represent that the endorsement was given without compensation.) Therefore, if a restaurant informs in advance all of its patrons who enter the restaurant that they may be interviewed by an advertiser as part of its promotion for a new soy protein "steak," and the advertiser prepares an ad asking these actual patrons for their "spontaneous" opinions, it should make the circumstances under which the endorsements were obtained clear in the ad.

▌ A Final Word

Endorsements are an important part of advertising. Some companies seem to believe that there is almost nothing better than having well-recognized personalities highlight the benefits of their products. Whether that makes sense from a marketing point of view is something that marketing executives can discuss and debate; from a legal viewpoint, though, the rules are clear and advertisers should make sure they comply with them.

FIVE ENDORSEMENTS THAT RAISED LEGAL CONCERNS

1. Joseph G. Branch operated a correspondence school known as the Joseph G. Branch Institute of Engineering and Science out of his home office in Chicago. For a number of years, he sold and distributed correspondence courses by mail in Latin American countries. The courses were extensively advertised in newspapers published in various Central and South American countries. Branch also circulated letters, leaflets, circulars, catalogs, and other advertising material among his prospective students in which he represented that he maintained an institute of engineering and science in Chicago that was founded in 1910; that "[t]he diplomas and degrees awarded by this worthy Institute are signed and sealed by the

Officials of our Institute, acknowledged before a Notary Public, certified by the County Court Clerk and authenticated by the Secretary of the State of Illinois, U.S.A."; and that it was "the only officially recognized University in accordance with the laws of United States for extension courses [by correspondence.]" Branch's school, however, was neither a university nor an institute. It had no entrance requirements, no resident students, no library, no laboratory, and no faculty. The staff primarily consisted of a messenger, eight translators, Branch's daughter, a person who apparently had a bachelor of science degree from the University of Mexico, and Branch.

Branch was not authorized by law or by any educational association to issue diplomas or give degrees and the provisional approval he received from the superintendent of Public Instruction of Illinois was disapproved of and withdrawn after his school was inspected. Branch nonetheless ignored that fact and continued to represent that his courses of instruction were approved by the Illinois Department of Education. His diplomas and degrees had signatures attested to by public officials in such a manner as to make it appear that they had official sanction. After investigating, the Federal Trade Commission issued an order requiring Branch to cease and desist from using the words "Institute" or "University" in connection with the conduct of his business and from representing that his business was either an institute or university. The order also prohibited him from using the words "officially recognized" or words of similar import in connection with his school, or otherwise representing directly or by implication that the school was recognized or approved as an institution of learning by the United States government or by any state government or governmental agencies. Finding that the record before the FTC contained an abundance of evidence to support the FTC's findings that the representations made by Branch in the conduct of his "diploma mill" were false and fraudulent, the U.S. Court of Appeals for the Seventh Circuit upheld the FTC's order. (Branch v. Federal Trade Commission, 141 F.2d 31 (7th Cir. 1944).)

2. One of the products sold by Niresk Industries, Inc. was an electric cooker-fryer that was manufactured by Merit Enterprises, Inc. In conjunction with its sales campaign for that cooker-fryer, Niresk employed advertisements that appeared in a large number of periodicals of national circulation. The Merit fryer was equipped with a Westinghouse thermostat and, as part of its sales campaign, Niresk prominently displayed the Westinghouse name in its ads. The FTC issued a complaint against Niresk, contending that its ads were false or deceptive because the name Westinghouse was being used in a fashion that tended to induce the belief that the appliance was manufactured by Westinghouse when that was not so. The FTC issued a cease and desist order, to which Niresk objected in court. But the court upheld the FTC, finding that "the use of labels or trade names in a manner having a capacity or tendency to mislead the purchaser" was prohibited by the Federal Trade Commission Act. (Niresk Industries, Inc. v. Federal Trade Commission, 278 F.2d 337 (7th Cir. 1960).)

3. According to a complaint filed by the FTC against American International Industries, Inc., American was in the business of selling records and record vending racks through distributors. It advertised for people to become distributors in a number of newspapers and through brochures and other promotional literature that it mailed to prospective purchasers. In its materials it posed a question that a potential distributor might ask: "Q: How do I know that your company is reliable?" The answer contained in the materials: "A: We are listed by Dun & Bradstreet." The FTC objected to the reference to the credit rating company Dun & Bradstreet, finding that American's listing "signified nothing more than that it had a certain credit rating and a certain estimated financial worth." It then issued a cease and desist order requiring that American stop directly or indirectly representing that its integrity was vouched for by Dun & Bradstreet. (In re American International Industries, Inc., 57 F.T.C. 119 (1969).)

4. More than 40 years ago, the FTC charged that certain testimonials used by the R. J. Reynolds Tobacco Company were false, misleading, and deceptive. The FTC contended that they represented to the public "that the smoking of Camel cigarettes, during, after, or between meals, irrespective of what, where, or when one eats, is good for, advantageous to, and aids digestion, in that it renews and encourages the flow of digestive fluids and increases the alkalinity of the digestive tract; that the smoking of such cigarettes relieves fatigue and creates, restores, renews, and releases a new flow of body energy giving needed bodily strength and vigor, and that this is 'a basic discovery of a famous research laboratory and throws new light on the subject of cigarette smoking'; that the 'wind' and physical condition of athletes will not be affected or impaired in any way by the smoking of as many Camel cigarettes as they desire; that Camel cigarettes, unlike other brands of cigarettes, are always gentle to and never harm or irritate even a sensitive throat, nor leave an aftertaste; that the smoking of such cigarettes is soothing, restful, and comforting to the nerves, and protects one against becoming 'jittery' or 'unsure' when subjected to intense nerve strain; that one with healthy nerves may smoke as many Camel cigarettes as he or she likes without the risk of keyed-up or jangled or frazzled nerves, and that Camels are in these respects different from all other brands of cigarettes; and that the smoke of Camel cigarettes contains less nicotine than does the smoke of any of the four other largest selling brands of cigarettes." The FTC found these representations to be false and issued an order barring Reynolds from "using in any advertising media testimonials of users or purported users of said cigarettes which contain any of the representations prohibited." (R. J. Reynolds Tobacco Co. v. Federal Trade Commission, 192 F.2d 535 (7th Cir. 1951).)

5. C. I. Energy Development, Inc. paid former astronaut Gordon Cooper to endorse its automobile retrofit device, a tool that a car owner could add to an engine to, C. I. claimed, improve fuel economy. The ads contended, among other things, that competent scientific tests for fuel economy proved the claims, and that Cooper had the education, training, and knowledge necessary to qualify him as an expert in the field of automotive engineering. The FTC determined, though, that the device would not improve fuel economy; there were no scientific tests to prove those claims; and Cooper was not an automotive engineering expert. The government issued an order to which the company consented that, among other things, prohibited it from claiming that any of its endorsers was an expert in a particular field unless the endorser had the education, training, and knowledge necessary to be qualified as an expert in that field; prohibited it from using, publishing, or referring to any testimonial or endorsement from any person or organization unless, within 12 months immediately preceding any such use, publication, or reference, it had obtained from that person or organization an express written and dated authorization for such use, publication, or reference; and prohibited it from misrepresenting in any manner the purpose, content, or conclusion of any test or survey pertaining to its products. (In re C. I. Energy Development, Inc., 94 F.T.C. 1337 (1979)

Tips for Advertisers Considering Endorsements

Businesses considering using third party endorsements in their advertisements should make sure that:

✓ The claims in the ad reflect the endorser's honest views.

✓ An endorsement that reflects the experience of an individual or a group of consumers on a central or key attribute of the product is representative of what consumers generally will achieve with the advertised product in actual use.

✓ Endorsements by what are or appear to be "actual consumers" utilize actual consumers or disclose that they are made by actors.

✓ Where an ad implies that an endorsement is based upon a comparison of competing products, the expert actually conducted the comparison.

✓ An organization's endorsement is reached by a process sufficient to ensure that the endorsement fairly reflects the collective judgment of the organization.

5

HOW TO DEFEND YOUR TRADEMARKS

■ The Value of Trademarks ■ Registering a Trademark
■ Protecting Trademarks ■ Infringement ■ A Final Word

Successful commercial marketing has many rewards. Most important to the marketer are the financial rewards to be reaped. However, when a manufacturer develops a novel marketing approach—a commercial concept meeting with a receptive consumer—the concept is often imitated. To hear Häagen-Dazs, Inc. tell it, that's allegedly what happened several years ago in the premium ice cream market.

In 1980 Häagen-Dazs filed suit against the producers and distributors of Frusen Glädje ice cream. Häagen-Dazs contended that the defendants packaged their product in such a way as to "cash in on the commercial magnetism of the exclusive marketing technique developed . . . by the family which owns and operates Häagen-Dazs." In particular, Häagen-Dazs focused upon five features of Frusen Glädje's ice cream container that it charged Frusen Glädje took directly from its ice cream container in an effort to appeal to Häagen-Dazs customers and confuse them into believing that Frusen Glädje was related to the Häagen-Dazs line. These features were:

- *The phraseology Frusen Glädje used in reciting its product's ingredients*

- *The recitation of the artificial ingredients not contained in the product*

- *The manner in which the product was to be eaten to enhance its flavor*

- *A two word Germanic-sounding name having an umlaut over the letter a*

- *A map of Scandinavia*

Häagen-Dazs contended that Frusen Glädje intentionally packaged its product in a manner calculated to trade upon "plaintiff's unique Scandinavian marketing theme." It sought a preliminary injunction to prevent Frusen Glädje from continued use of the allegedly infringing container.

The court said that there was a serious question as to the merits of Häagen-Dazs's claim. Häagen-Dazs's only trademark was for the name "Häagen-Dazs." It held no trademark, nor could it, upon the so-called "unique Scandinavian marketing theme" it employed. "This is simply a vehicle by which plaintiff has chosen to market its product."

The names Häagen-Dazs and Frusen Glädje were "clearly distinguishable," the court said. While it was true that both names contained two words to identify an ice cream product, the court noted that that was not unusual—"so do the names 'Louis Sherry' and 'Dolly Madison.'" The court also noted that the Häagen-Dazs and Frusen Glädje names seemed to be of Swedish origin, and, as appropriate in that language, an umlaut appeared over the letter a. But, it said, that was a matter of grammar and not a basis upon which Häagen-Dazs could bring a trademark infringement suit.

The court found it equally apparent that the containers were clearly distinguishable "and would appear so to all but the most obtuse consumer." The coloring and designs of the containers, as well as the shape of the containers themselves, were so different "that only the most unobservant and careless consumer would mistake one product for the other."

Finding that Häagen-Dazs had failed to demonstrate even the remotest possibility of confusion at the consumer level as to the source of Frusen Glädje's products, the court then rejected Häagen-Dazs's request for an order prohibiting Frusen Glädje from using its container.

▌ The Value of Trademarks

A trademark may be any word, name, symbol, device, or design or any combination thereof adopted and used by a manufacturer or merchant to identify its goods and distinguish them from those manufactured or sold by others. (A service mark is any mark used in the sale of advertising of services so as to distinguish the services from the services of others.)

Trademarks are important because they help consumers identify the source of goods—and that is why Häagen-Dazs was concerned about the Frusen Glädje container that it thought would confuse consumers. Trademarks distinguish one company's products from products manufactured by another company. A company that has a registered trademark may prohibit others from using the mark anywhere in the United States. Because they can facilitate sales, trademarks may be among a business's most important assets—and they should be treated as such.

A company that fails to take proper care of its trademark risks losing it. At one time, shredded wheat, aspirin, cellophane, dry ice, and escalator all were valid and enforceable trademarks that entitled only the owners of the trademarks to make shredded wheat, sell aspirin, advertise cellophane, promote dry ice, and manufacture escalators. However, because the trademarks became associated in the public's mind with the actual goods—rather than their manufacturer or source—the owners lost the trademarks and now anyone may use them. These trademarks simply became the generic terms for the goods.

▌ Registering a Trademark

In the past federal trademark law required that a company must actually use a trademark before it was permitted to register the mark. That changed in 1989 when the statute was amended to permit companies to obtain trademark registration by showing an "intent to use" the trademark. That can be shown through marketing, advertising, and distribution plans. After obtaining a trademark registration, which is valid for 10 years and renewable for additional 10-year periods, a company has six months to begin using the trademark in commerce. It should be noted that a trademark need not be registered for it to be valid.

▌ Protecting Trademarks

There are a number of ways trademarks can be lost. For instance, a company can lose a trademark after the ten-year registration period by failing to renew the mark. In practice, that really should not happen. More troublesome is when a company loses a mark because of its failure to properly protect it. One of the worst ways that can happen is when a trademark becomes a generic term referring to the product rather than to the source of the product. To try to prevent that, businesses should make sure to take the following steps:

- *Select a Good One:* Mere descriptive words are difficult to register and protect as trademarks. Thus, Prime Beef is less likely to be a valid trademark than Kodak, which was a word coined by the company. (TV Guide, a rather descriptive trademark, has managed to remain protected through the years, in part due to the trademark owner vigorously taking many of the actions described below.) Choosing a good trademark—and even using it on more than one product—is the first step in protecting a trademark.

- *Use It Right:* A trademark is an adjective and should be used as an adjective. Say, "Pass me a tissue" or "Pass me a Kleenex tissue"—not "Pass me a Kleenex." Say, "I need to use the IBM computer"—not "I need to use the IBM." Say, "Please make a copy," "Please make a photocopy," or "Please make a Xerox copy"—not "Please make a Xerox." Businesses should ensure that they use their trademarks properly internally—some companies even have usage guides for employees. They also should use their trademarks properly in all promotional materials. Trademarks should be in distinctive typefaces. In addition, a trademark owner should reflect the fact that its trademark is a trademark by using the designation ™ for trademark or ℠ for service mark (if the mark is not registered with the U.S. Patent and Trademark Office) or ® or "Reg. U.S. Pat & Tm. Off." (if it is registered) following the trademark. In the court decision many years ago that found that aspirin was a generic term, the judge focused on the Bayer aspirin label, which read "Bayer—Tablets of Aspirin." He stated that Bayer "itself recognized the meaning which the word had acquired, because the phrase most properly means that these tablets were Bayer's make of the drug known as 'aspirin.'"

- *Prevent Third Party Misuse:* Third parties that misuse a company's trademark should be informed of their error and asked—or warned—to cease doing so. Policing competitor's advertising, newspapers stories, and even crossword puzzles (a five letter word for "copy" is not "xerox") can reveal misuse. Indeed, informational advertising that alerts the world to the company's trademark and sets up a policy against misuse may be critical to the trademark owner's attempts to protect its trademark. Here are excerpts from some informational ads that trademark owners published in an attempt to protect their trademarks:

The Word Frigidaire Always Ends with a Capital ® (for the registered trademark designation).

What's in a name? A Lot . . . When The Name Is Kelly®. Kelly is a brand name for temporary help services provided exclusively by Kelly Services, Inc. The following are registered trademarks of Kelly Services, Inc.: Kelly®; Kelly Girl®; Kelly Services®. Nobody Puts Temporaries to the Test Like Kelly®.

Don't confuse a weedeater with Weed Eater®. Sometimes people say they want a 'weedeater' when they really want a Weed Eater® brand trimmer. And, while a weedeater might be anything from a voracious goat to a little green creature from a gardener's nightmare, there is only one Weed Eater® brand trimmer. It's America's number one brand of trimmer—the one people ask for time after time.

FORMICA® IS A SPECIAL BRAND. "Formica" is the name of a very particular product. It's both a registered trademark and a special brand name. As such, we ask that you use the name Formica® only when referring to our particular brand of products. This protects you as well as us. Because by properly using our name, whenever you ask for Formica brand, you'll be sure of getting the real Formica brand.

To all the writers and typists and proofreaders and editors who help us protect our trademark Kleenex® by always starting it with a capital K followed by l-e-e-n-e-x and following it with a proper generic: be it tissue, towels, or diapers; Kimberly Clark says "Bless you!"

Dear *New York Times:* 8 Down has us puzzled. Let's see, 6 Across is W-A-X-Y. That leaves us with a five letter word for "duplicate" beginning with the letter *X*. Obviously, it couldn't be X-E-R-O-X. That's because "Xerox" isn't a verb. It's our trademark. As a trademark, it should only be used as a proper adjective followed by the descriptive term, like a Xerox copier, a Xerox printer, a Xerox typewriter, or a Xerox duplicator. But you probably know this already. You of all newspapers are a stickler for this sort of thing. Which still leaves us with the original problem . . . a five-letter word for "duplicate" beginning with *X*. (XEROX® is a trademark of XEROX CORPORATION.)

▌Infringement

Trademark owners have the right to stop infringing trademarks. In other words, a trademark is a form of a monopoly. Among the factors courts consider when deciding whether confusion exists between trademarks are:

- The degree of similarity between the owner's mark and the alleged infringing mark

- The strength of the owner's mark

- The price of the goods and other factors indicative of the care and attention expected of consumers when making a purchase

- The length of time the defendant has used the mark without evidence of actual confusion

- The intent of the defendant in adopting the mark

- The evidence of actual confusion

- Whether the goods, if noncompeting, are marketed thorough the same channels and advertised through the same media

- The extent to which the targets of the parties' sales effects are the same

- The relationship of the goods in the minds of the public because of the similarity of function

- Other facts suggesting that the consuming public might expect the prior owner to manufacture a product in the defendant's market

The ability of a trademark owner to prohibit competing businesses from using identical or confusingly similar trademarks can be seen in a recent lawsuit filed by Kenner Parker Toys, Inc., the owner of the Play-Doh trademark, against Rose Art Industries, Inc., which sought registration in 1986 for the mark Fundough for its own modeling compound and related accessories.

The court noted that a trademark owner may oppose the registration of any competing mark that is likely, when used on or in connection with the goods of the applicant for a trademark, "to cause confusion or to cause mistake or to deceive." The court said that the test for likelihood of confusion does not focus on similarity of competing marks in the abstract. Rather, it said, the test evaluates objective evidence that the competing marks, when used in the marketplace, are likely to confuse the purchasing public about the source of the products. The court then proceeded to compare the two marks.

The court said that the prefixes *play* and *fun*, in the overall context of these competing marks, conveyed a very similar impression. "Both are single syllable words associated closely in meaning. Particularly in the context of a child's toy, the concepts of fun and play tend to merge." It added that in context, the prefixes *play* and *fun* seemed at least as similar as *tree* and *valley* or *island* and *valley,* which, it noted had been held to be components of the confusingly similar marks *spice tree* and *spice valley,* in one case, and *spice island* and *spice valley,* in another.

In addition, the court stated, the single-syllable suffixes *doh* and *dough* sounded the same. "In light of a modern trend to simplify the spelling of 'gh' words, consumers may even perceive one as an interchangeable abbreviation for the other."

The court also noted that the following factors supported its view that Fundough was an infringing mark:

- The marks Play-Doh and Fundough were used for practically identical products, namely modeling compounds and related modeling accessories

- Both Kenner and Rose Art marketed their products in practically identical channels of trade, namely toy outlets

- Both marks appeared on inexpensive products purchased by diverse buyers without exercising much care

Finally, the court noted that the multitude of similarities in the trade dress of Play-Doh and Fundough products "cries out for recognition." The color (dominated by yellow), size, and shape of the packaging for both products were the same. Comparable fictitious characters in a hat adorned the packaging of both products. Both products featured promotions—discounts, rebates, and the like—in a circle with serrated edges. The marks themselves appeared in coinciding locations on both products' packages. The instructions and color charts on both packages were nearly identical. Both products displayed a rainbow motif. The court noted that "[t]hese trade dress features and more—original to Play-Doh—have appeared on products bearing the Fundough mark." It then ruled in favor of Play-Doh.

▌ A Final Word

Trademarks can be important business assets and advertising and marketing executives are at the forefront of trademark protection—they must ensure that the right trademark is chosen, that it is used properly, and that competitors and the general public do not misuse it. When properly protected, trademarks can lead to increased sales and market share. Losing them, however, can lead to much embarrassment.

FIVE TRADEMARK CASES

1. On July 28, 1960, the Minneapolis-Honeywell Regulator Company filed an application to register the trademark AccuData for data handling apparatus including amplifiers, power supplies, relay rack fixtures, test equipment, and accessories, alleging that it had first used the mark in September 1958. The Industrial Nucleonics Corporation filed a notice of opposition, alleging ownership of the trademark AccuRay for industrial beta gauges used in measuring the weight, thickness, and area of sheet materials, radiation gauges used in measuring the physical properties of materials, and control equipment that included such gauges for regulating industrial processes. Industrial alleged that its use of the trademark AccuRay in interstate commerce had been continuous since approximately 1951. The trademark trial and appeal board ruled that the marks AccuRay and AccuData "do not look at all alike; their connotations are not the same; and, while they are similar to the extent that both embody the term 'Accu,' the similarity between them in this respect is considered not to be such as would lead to confusion or mistake or deception, since this term to purchasers would be more than likely to suggest the high degree of accuracy of the goods to which the marks are applied." It then found that the use of AccuRay and AccuData as contemplated by the two companies would not be likely to lead to confusion or mistake or deception of the purchasing trade, and it dismissed Industrial's opposition. A federal appellate court affirmed that decision. (Industrial Nucleonics Corp. v. Minneapolis-Honeywell Regulator Co., 328 F.2d 942 (U.S. Ct. Customs and Patent Appeals 1964).)

2. After a New York Committee on Professional Standards discovered that attorney Jan L. Shephard was advertising the availability of his legal services under the name "The People's Law Firm of Jan L. Shephard, Attorney, P.C.," it filed two charges against him. The first charge contended that his use of the phrase "The People's Law Firm" was deceptive and misleading because it suggested or implied that the firm was controlled by the public, received public funds for its existence, provided free legal services, or was a nonprofit legal service. The second charge alleged that the name "The People's Law Firm of Jan L. Shephard, Attorney, P.C." constituted a trade name in violation of the prohibition against lawyers conducting their practice under trade names. A New York appellate court sustained both charges, noting that advertising that is misleading or deceptive is not protected by the First Amendment to the United States Constitution and that the prohibition against the use of a trade name by a lawyer in private practice was valid and enforceable. It then ruled that Shephard should be censured. (In re Shephard, 459 N.Y.S.2d 632 (3d Dep't 1983).)

3. In 1967 Sizzler Restaurants International, Inc. filed suit against another operator and franchisor of budget steak restaurants then known as Sizzler's for trademark and service mark infringement. The suit resulted in a 1968 judgment prohibiting Sizzler's from using the Sizzler mark or any confusingly similar mark but allowing it to use the name Western Sizzlin Steak House, Inc. The two companies apparently coexisted peacefully for the next few years. In 1980, however, Sizzler once again sued Western. Sizzler was troubled by the fact that Western had obtained federal trademark and service mark registration of the word "Sizzlin" standing alone. Western and its franchisees were using "Sizzlin" by itself as a service mark for their restaurants on some signs, and as a trademark to describe one of their steak offerings. In addition, even when "Sizzlin" appeared in tandem with "Western," the former word often was much more prominent. Sizzler contended that "Sizzlin" was confusingly similar to "Sizzler," and hence that Western should be barred from using the mark.

In 1984, after a full trial, the district court called the two companies together for what it termed a "final settlement conference." The court fashioned a judgment from which neither party took an appeal. It required that Western cancel its service mark registration for "Sizzlin" though it permitted it to keep the trademark registration. Western and its franchisees also were required to modify exterior wall and pole signs at their restaurants so that any use of "Sizzlin" on such signs was accompanied by the word "Western" displayed in an equally prominent fashion. The court imposed a timetable for the conversion of signs to meet requirements and retained jurisdiction for enforcement purposes.

Skeptical of Western's ability or commitment to ensure compliance with the judgment—it seems that Western ran a rather loose franchise operation—Sizzler went to considerable expense to determine whether Western's restaurants were complying with the court's requirements. It found that many were not. Close to half had not complied with the court's order that "Sizzlin" wall signs at certain restaurants be permanently disconnected from electricity by October 1, 1984. In addition, some restaurants were violating the 1984 judgment by using pole signs on which "Sizzlin" was unduly prominent, and two were found to be violating the 1968 judgment by using the term Sizzler. Consequently, Sizzler filed a motion for contempt.

In January 1985, the district court granted the motion. It thereafter imposed a $25,000 contempt sanction on Western, prohibited Western from outside use of the Sizzlin trademark, and entered an order establishing a schedule of prospective sanctions for future violations. Sizzler appealed, claiming that the $25,000 award was too small; Western also appealed. The court rejected Sizzler's appeal as not timely filed. It also held that Western's admitted violations of the district court order restricting its use of the service mark warranted the district court's finding of contempt and the imposition of sanctions for the purpose of compensating Sizzler even though Western's franchisees moved to correct the violations after Sizzler had filed its contempt motion. In addition, the appellate court said that the district court's decision to extend the prohibition on the use of the term Sizzlin was within its authority. Finally, the circuit court stated that Western's past indifference toward adequate enforcement of the 1984 judgment among its franchisees warranted the imposition of prospective sanctions. (Sizzler Family Steak Houses v. Western Sizzlin Steak House, Inc., 793 F.2d 1529 (11th Cir. 1986).)

4. For many years, Official Airline Guides, Inc. has continuously used its federally registered trademark "OAG Travel Planner." When registering that trademark, it was required to disclaim as descriptive the words "Travel Planner." However, OAG claimed a non-statutory trademark over the term "Travel Planner." It published under its trademark travel directories, including the *OAG Travel Planner North American Edition,* containing information on transportation and hotel and motel accommodations in the United States and abroad. To obtain information for its guides, OAG sent listing forms to hotels, airlines, car rental agencies, and other travel-related concerns. These forms also solicited paid advertisements.

In the early 1980s, Ashbyweb Ltd., an English corporation, began the promotion, sale, distribution, and solicitation of advertisements for *The Travel Planner USA,* a directory similar to OAG's travel guide. Ashbyweb's principals knew of OAG's *Travel Planner* for about 20 years. Ashbyweb's guide was not sold in the United States, while OAG's guide was rarely sold outside the United States. However, Ashbyweb annually sent more than 20,000 listing forms to travel related entities in the United States, requesting corrections and soliciting optional advertisements. The logo on Ashbyweb's listing forms read "The Travel Planner," while fine print elsewhere on the form referred to "The USA Travel Planner." Ashbyweb's letterhead, used on individual letters soliciting advertisements, referred only to "The Travel Planner." OAG brought suit against Ashbyweb, alleging among other things trademark infringement. The complaint sought a temporary restraining order and preliminary and permanent injunctive relief prohibiting Ashbyweb from selling, distributing, or soliciting advertisements for any publication using the mark "Travel Planner."

The district court denied a preliminary injunction, finding that the term "Travel Planner" was generic and could not be trademarked. OAG appealed. The appellate court recognized that OAG could not take advantage of the special protection afforded to registered trademarks because its registration of the mark expressly disclaimed the words "Travel Planner." However, the appellate court said OAG's disclaimer of the phrase "Travel Planner" in its registration did not deprive it of any nonstatutory rights it may have had. The appellate court said that the arrangement of the letters "OAG" coupled with the more descriptive term "Travel Planner" constituted a mark that qualified for trademark protection. While refusing to grant OAG a preliminary injunction, it said the district court should seriously consider whether Ashbyweb's use of the term "Travel Planner" infringed OAG's common law mark over the term "OAG Travel Planner." The appellate court said that if OAG held a protectable mark over the term "Travel Planner" or the term "OAG Travel Planner," the lower court should decide whether Ashbyweb had infringed OAG's mark or marks—that is, whether there was a likelihood of confusion between OAG's mark and the term used by Ashbyweb. In that analysis, the district court had to keep in mind the "the effect of Ashbyweb's use of the term 'Travel Planner' to solicit advertisements." (Official Airline Guides, Inc. v. Goss, 856 F.2d 85 (9th Cir. 1988).)

5. On September 2, 1969, the United States Patent and Trademark Office issued registration no. 876,139 to Usen Products Company for Fancy Fixin's cat food. On December 22, 1969, the registered trademark owner became Lipton Pet Foods, Inc. On June 24, 1977, the Ralston Purina Company filed a petition with the United States Patent and Trademark Office to cancel the Fancy Fixin' trademark on the ground of abandonment due to nonuse. Ralston had made one shipment of Fancy Fixins cat food in an attempt to show use, obtain a trademark on the name, and support its application challenging Lipton's mark. On July 6, 1977, Lipton assigned the registration to Lipton Industries, Inc., which defended the Ralston petition. The Patent and Trademark Office Trial and Appeal Board granted the petition, invoking the presumption of abandonment arising from two years' nonuse of a mark with no explanation that justified the nonuse. Lipton appealed, but the court upheld the board's finding, noting that Lipton had admitted nonuse. (Lipton Industries, Inc. v. Ralston Purina Co., 670 F.2d 1024 (U.S. Ct. Customs and Patent Appeals, 1982)

Trademark Checklist

✓ A trademark may be any word, name, symbol, device, or design, or any combination thereof, adopted and used by a manufacturer or merchant to identify its goods and distinguish them from those manufactured or sold by others.

✓ Trademarks are important because they help consumers identify the source of goods. Thus, trademarks may be among a business's most important assets.

✓ A company that fails to take proper care of its trademarks risks losing them. Trademarks that have been deemed "generic" terms available to all include shredded wheat, aspirin, cellophane, dry ice, and escalator.

✓ There are three steps that trademark owners should take to protect their trademarks: choose good trademarks; use them properly; and prevent third party misuse.

✓ Trademark owners may file infringement suits to prevent others from using identical or confusingly similar trademarks. A trademark owner will succeed in such a case upon showing that the competitor's trademark is likely to confuse the purchasing public about the source of the products.

6

CHOOSING AND PROTECTING SLOGANS

▋ Choosing A Slogan ▋ Secondary Meaning ▋ A Final Word

In the mid-1970s, Wileswood, Inc. filed an application with the U.S. Patent and Trademark Office to register the slogans America's Best Popcorn! and America's Favorite Popcorn! for its unpopped popcorn. Wileswood's position was that a slogan or other form of trademark, to be refused registration, must be "only" or "solely" descriptive of the goods but that its slogans were more than that. It said that they should be considered as a whole and that they were "attention-getting, tongue-in-cheek, self-laudatory, or boastful designations or characterizations of its popcorn" and therefore registrable.

The examiner agreed that the registrability of each mark must be determined on the basis of the expression as a whole. But, the examiner found, the slogans America's Best Popcorn! and America's Favorite Popcorn! were merely laudatorily descriptive phrases not subject to registration. The U.S. Patent and Trademark Office Trial and Appeal Board upheld that decision.

▋ Choosing a Slogan

Slogans are a kind of trademark that serve important marketing and advertising purposes. They are intended to convey a particularly valuable thought about a manufacturer's product. The best slogan is one that can be distinguished from the balance of a company's advertising and can stand on its own.

Businesses use many different kinds of slogans. A term that a company chooses as a slogan or other kind of trademark generally fits somewhere in the spectrum of classifications ranging from generic or common descriptive, merely descriptive, or suggestive to arbitrary or fanciful.

A generic or common descriptive term is one that is commonly used as the name or description of a kind of goods. It cannot become a trademark under any circumstances (for example, light beer and decaffeinated coffee).

A merely descriptive term specifically describes a characteristic or ingredient of an article (for example, bubbly champagne, and auto page). Descriptive terms can become a valid trademark by acquiring a secondary meaning. Secondary meaning exists when the trademark is interpreted by the consuming public to be not only an identification of the product, but also a representation of the product's origin. Secondary meaning is generally established through extensive advertising that creates in the mind of consumers an association between different products bearing the same mark. This association suggests that the products originate from a single source. Once a trademark that could not otherwise have exclusive appropriation achieves secondary meaning, competitors can be prevented from using a similar mark.

A suggestive term suggests rather than describes an ingredient or characteristic of the goods and requires the observer or listener to use imagination and perception to determine the nature of the goods. Such a term can be protected without proof of a secondary meaning (for example, Tide and Coppertone).

Finally, an arbitrary or fanciful term enjoys the same full protection as a suggestive term but is far enough removed from the merely descriptive not to be vulnerable to possible attack as being merely descriptive rather than suggestive. These are known as strong marks (for example, Kodak and Black & White scotch).

The trademark spectrum reflects levels of judicial skepticism concerning whether a term actually serves the source denoting function that a mark is supposed to perform. Terms that are arbitrary, fanciful, or suggestive as applied to a given product or service are naturally understood by the consuming public as designations of origin. Indeed, it is unlikely that they would be understood as anything else. Descriptive terms, on the other hand, are ill-suited to serve as designations of origin, because they are naturally understood by the consuming public in their ordinary descriptive sense.

The rationale for prohibiting the appropriation of a descriptive term as a trademark rests upon the equal right of another company producing and marketing a similar product to describe its product with similar accuracy. Were this right not protected by the law, elements of the language could be monopolized in such a way as to impoverish others' ability to communicate. Thus, courts have rejected the following phrases as slogans, holding that they are merely descriptive:

72

- I love you
- Auto shampoo
- Car shampoo
- Smackin' good
- Another delicious marine protein product
- More gun for the money
- America's freshest ice cream
- Best and biggest cigar
- Easy clean
- Sudsy (for household ammonia)
- Tender fresh (for fresh cut chicken)
- The professional health care people

On the other hand, distinctive slogans are upheld and are able to be registered. These include:

- Dedicated to Achieving the Highest Level of Professionalism
- Quality through Craftsmanship
- Your Financial Security Is Our Business

Acronyms and initials also have been held to be proper slogans:

- CAX (for community automatic exchange)
- PAX (for private automatic exchange)
- PTS (for programmed tax system)

▌ Secondary Meaning

Secondary meaning can be important to protect weaker slogans. One of the best cases to discuss secondary meaning involves the slogan of Clairol, Inc., Hair Color So Natural Only Her Hairdresser Knows For Sure, for Clairol's hair tinting, dyeing, and coloring preparation.

Since 1950 Clairol has marketed products for tinting and dyeing hair under the trademark Miss Clairol. In 1956 Clairol embarked on an extensive advertising campaign to promote the sale of its Miss Clairol hair color preparations, which included advertisements in national magazines, on outdoor billboards, and on car cards for bus and subway transit systems; mailing pieces; radio and television ads; and point-of-sale display material designed to be used by beauty salons and retailers as window or counter displays in association with the Miss Clairol product.

The format for the advertising Clairol used remains quite familiar even today: a large, color photograph of an attractive woman, often accompanied by a young child; the question Does she . . . or doesn't she? prominently imprinted on or above the photograph; the slogan Hair Color So Natural Only Her Hairdresser Knows For Sure also conspicuously imprinted on or below the photograph and set apart from the other portions of the ad; the mark Miss Clairol in large type; a representation of the packaged Miss Clairol hair coloring product; and, perhaps, advertising text extolling the virtues and advantages of the product.

Between 1956 and 1966 Clairol sold more than $50 million worth of its Miss Clairol hair coloring product and spent approximately $22 million for advertising material containing the slogan. During that period, there were more than 100 million "impressions" of advertisements prominently displaying Clairol's slogan.

In the early 1960s Clairol filed an application to register the slogan. The application was opposed by Roux Laboratories, Inc., which also manufactured and sold hair tinting, dyeing, and coloring preparations. Roux contended that the slogan was descriptive. Clairol relied chiefly on the fact that it had used the slogan in nearly all of its extensive advertising of Miss Clairol products in various media since 1956 to establish that the slogan had become well-known to the purchasing public and served to point to Clairol as the source of the products.

The court of customs and patent appeals assumed that the slogan was descriptive. It then analyzed whether it served an origin-indicating function in addition to describing attributes of the Clairol product. As the court put it, "Is it . . . or isn't it?"

The court said that mere advertising or other evidence of supposed secondary meaning cannot convert something unregistrable by reason of its being the common descriptive name or generic name for the goods—the antithesis of a trademark—into a registrable mark. But, it concluded, considering all of the factors—Clairol's exclusive, prominent, and repeated use of the slogan for at least 10 years in association with its products, expenditures of more than $22 million for point-of-sale displays and other advertising material resulting in a multitude of separate audio and visual impressions of the slogan, and substantial sales of the product with which the slogan had been associated—it was clear that it had acquired a secondary meaning.

❚ A Final Word

Slogans can be important marketing and advertising tools. Descriptive slogans are the most difficult to get registered and to protect. Suggestive or fanciful slogans are the most likely to be effective—that is, to remind consumers of the source of the product—and to be protectable. Certainly, a creative albeit descriptive slogan, with a great advertising budget behind it, may be able to acquire a secondary meaning and thus become valuable. But it may not.

FIVE SUITS OVER SLOGANS

1. Superba Cravats, Inc. filed an application with the U.S. Patent and Trademark Office to register the slogan "Soil It—Wash It—Never Needs Pressing" for its neckties. After the trademarks examiner refused to register the mark, finding that it was a mere statement of fact and therefore incapable of functioning as a trademark to identify Superba's goods and distinguish them from similar goods of others, Superba appealed to the trial and appeal board. Superba contended that the expression was a slogan that possessed some degree of origination or ingenuity and that its exact meaning required some analysis and thought. It argued that its slogan also had a certain ring or catchiness to it. However, the trial and appeal board also rejected Superba's contentions. It said that it could not agree that Superba had coined a slogan that possessed any originality or ingenuity or that it was either catchy or had a ring to it. "[W]e see no more ingenuity in this statement than if [Superba] had stated 'Soil—Wash—But Don't Press,' which is an obvious statement of fact." The trial and appeal board concluded that the phrase "Soil It—Wash It—Never Needs Pressing" was a completely informative expression as applied to Superba's neckties and that it was therefore incapable of being registered as a trademarked slogan for the company. (In re Superba Cravats, Inc., 149 U.S.P.Q. 852 (Trial and Appeal Board, 1966).)

2. The Standard Oil Company sought to register "Guaranteed Starting" as a service mark for "inspecting, conditioning, and otherwise servicing motor vehicles to facilitate their operation in cold weather, and starting or arranging for the payment of starting expense of motor vehicles which fail to start after being so serviced." After the assistant commissioner of patents refused to register the words "Guaranteed Starting" as a service mark, the oil company asked the court of customs and patent appeals to review the decision. It noted that what Standard Oil would do included testing the battery, adding certain antifreeze ingredients to the fuel, installing special lubricants, and the like. After completing the work, Standard Oil's service station operator would give the customer a certificate containing an agreement to the effect that if, at any time during the winter, a mechanic was required to start the car, Standard Oil would get it started or would reimburse the customer for the cost of starting. The court noted that Standard Oil had extensively used "Guaranteed Starting" in connection with its "winterizing" motor service. It recognized that Standard Oil may have hoped that in using the words "guaranteed starting" to bring its services to the attention of the public, the words would have distinguished it from similar services offered by others. "However, having chosen words which, taken in their normal meaning, do no more than inform the public with reasonable accuracy what is being offered, it did not succeed." The court stated that the words were well understood, English words in common use. Taken together, they amounted to no more than a sort of condensed announcement that Standard Oil would guarantee the work done to insure the starting of the customer's car. "It must be assumed that the ordinary customer reading the advertisements displayed by an automobile service station would take the words at their ordinary meaning rather than read into them some special meaning distinguishing the services advertised from similar service of other station operators." It concluded that whatever may have been Standard Oil's intention in using the words, its "use has not accomplished what [it] wished to do. Hence, they are not a service mark." (In re The Standard Oil Company, 125 U.S.P.Q. 227 (Ct. Customs and Patent Appeals, 1960).)

3. On March 5, 1975, the McDonald's Corporation sought to register the following as a slogan: "Twoallbeefpattiesspecialsaucelettucecheese-ppicklesonionsonasesameseedbun." The trademarks examiner rejected McDonald's application, ruling that it was highly descriptive; indeed, the examiner said, the slogan consisted solely of a complete list of ingredients for a sandwich that McDonald's sold in its restaurants. McDonald's countered that its slogan was an arbitrary, but definite, arrangement of words that was used, visually and audibly, in a unique and arbitrary manner in connection with the advertising and sale of its restaurant services to identify and distinguish its services from those of others. It argued that the evidence clearly showed that, as a result of its extensive use of its slogan, the public had come to associate it with McDonald's and its restaurant services.

McDonald's said while the slogan was formed of words arranged in a particular, selected order, others could use the words to describe their own goods or services except in an order or arrangement, or visual or verbal presentation, confusingly similar to McDonald's slogan. In addition, the McDonald's director of advertising and promotion asserted in an affidavit that McDonald's had continuously used the slogan in connection with the sale and advertising of its restaurant services throughout the United States from at least December 1974 to December 16, 1975 (the date he executed the affidavit); that McDonald's had spent in excess of $2 million advertising and promoting its services under the slogan; that advertising and promotion of its services under the slogan had included the preparation and production of at least three nationally run television commercials featuring the slogan prominently, each of which was shown on an average of 10 times per month during the period between December 1974 and March 5, 1975 (the date McDonald's filed the application); that each such commercial reached an average of 18 million adults per showing; that in addition at least six national radio commercials of 30- and 60-second lengths had been repeatedly played over that medium; and that special local store promotions had occurred throughout the United States involving extensive advertising using the slogan in local television, radio, and print media, in point-of-purchase advertising in individual restaurants, and in connection with T shirt premiums and contests. McDonald's submitted samples of newspaper advertisements, copies of television storyboards, counter toppers, a sample scratch-off word game that contained the slogan and was used in McDonald's restaurants to promote its restaurant services; and a sample of a button that contained the slogan and was worn by McDonald's employees.

The U.S. Patent and Trademark Office Trial and Appeal Board said the McDonald's slogan was "obviously not the common descriptive name" of McDonald's restaurant services, and was not even the common descriptive name of a hamburger sandwich or specialty sandwich made of the listed ingredients. It found that McDonald's slogan was "something more than just a list of ingredients for a sandwich sold in [McDonald's] restaurants; that is, it is a unique and somewhat catchy arrangement and combination which in its entirety creates a commercial impression quite different from that of the individual words as they are ordinarily used." The trial and appeal board then ruled that the slogan had become distinctive of McDonald's restaurant services and that it was therefore entitled to the registration McDonald's sought. (In re McDonald's Corporation, 199 U.S.P.Q. 490 (Trial and Appeal Board, 1978).)

4. On June 8, 1976, the European American Bank & Trust Company filed an application with the U.S. Patent and Trademark Office to register the slogan Think About It as a service mark for banking and financial services. The trademarks examiner refused registration on the ground that the slogan Think About It did not function as a service mark to identify and distinguish the bank's services from those of others but rather was informational or instructional in nature. The bank appealed to the trial and appeal board. It contended that it prominently displayed the slogan in bold block letters in its ads; that the words were the only important words for potential customers to remember; that it adopted the words in their particular pattern to create a fanciful phonetic rhythm; and that the slogan was distinct and unique because the personal impression it conveyed was somewhat incongruous with the cold, detached, and unemotional image of a bank. The court stated that there could be no doubt that slogans are registrable as trademarks when they are used to identify the goods and services of the applicant and distinguish them from the like goods or services of others. Moreover, it said, a slogan or expression did not necessarily have to be unique, catchy, or rhyming for it to perform the function of a trademark. It stated that at the same time, though, not all words, devices, symbols and the like could necessarily function as trademarks notwithstanding that they may have been adopted with the intent of doing so. The trial and appeal board ruled that the phrase Think About It was a familiar expression "and we believe that the ordinary customer or prospective customer reading [the bank's] advertisement would take the phrase at its ordinary meaning rather than attributing thereto the special meaning of a service mark used to distinguish [the bank's] services from the banking services of others." It then affirmed the examiner's refusal to register. (In re European American Bank & Trust Co., 201 U.S.P.Q. 768 (Trial and Appeal Board, 1979).)

5. Finding that the slogan Proudly Made in USA was an unimaginative embellishment of a common informational phrase, the trademarks examiner refused the application of Remington Products, Inc. to register the slogan for Remington's electric shavers and parts. Remington appealed to the trial and appeal board, contending that the word "proudly" added a new dimension to what it admitted was a commonly used expression on numerous products. It also noted that it had used the letters ™ in connection with the slogan and that in the three years before the date of its application, it had sold $120 million worth of shavers and had expended $450,000 in advertising its products. The trial and appeal board upheld the examiner's decision. It said that the slogan provided only information to the public and did not indicate the source of the shavers. It also noted that the use of the letters ™ on a product did not make unregistrable matter into a trademark. (In re Remington Products, Inc., 3 U.S.P.Q. 2d 1714 (Trial and Appeal Board, 1987).)

Slogan Checklist

✓ Slogans, a special kind of trademark, are intended to convey a particularly important thought about a manufacturer's product.

✓ There are four general categories of slogans: generic or common descriptive, merely descriptive, suggestive, and arbitrary or fanciful.

✓ Generic or descriptive slogans are not registrable as trademarks.

✓ A slogan that is not much more than a description of a good's characteristics and that acquires a secondary meaning (which means that the public understands the source) may be registered as a trademark.

✓ Arbitrary or fanciful slogans are strong trademarks that can serve as the building blocks for successful advertising and marketing campaigns.

7

PATENT POWER

▌ The Power of Patents ▌ Novel and Useful Requirements
▌ Nonobvious Requirement ▌ Federal Circuit Court ▌ A Final Word

On July 23, 1867, J. B. Blair, an artist, alleging that he was the original and first inventor of "a new and useful rubber head for lead-pencils," received a patent for his invention. The specification and claim he filed in support of his patent application were, in part, as follows:

Be it known that I, J. B. Blair, of the city of Philadelphia . . .
have invented a new and useful cap or rubber head to be applied
to lead-pencils . . . for the purpose of rubbing out pencil-marks;
and I do hereby declare the same to be fully described in the
following specifications . . . :

The nature of my invention is to be found in a new and useful
or improved rubber or erasive head for lead-pencils . . . and con-
sists in making the said head of any convenient external form,
and forming a socket longitudinally in the same to receive one
end of a lead-pencil or a tenon extending from it. . . .

The said head may have a flat top surface, or its top may be of a
semicircular or conical shape, or any other that may be desirable.
Within one end of the said head I form a cylindrical or other
proper-shaped cavity. This socket I usually make about two-
thirds through the head, and axially thereof; but, if desirable, the
socket or bore may extend entirely through the said head. The
diameter of the socket should be a very little smaller than that of
the pencil to be inserted in it. The elastic erasive head so made is
to fit upon a lead-pencil at or near one end thereof, and to be so
made as to surround the part on which it is to be placed, and be
held thereon by the inherent elasticity of the material of which
the head may be composed. The said head is to be composed of

india-rubber, or india-rubber and some other material which will increase the erasive properties of the head. . . .

[I]t is evident that the contour of the said head may be varied to suit the fancy or the taste of an artist or other person; and I do not limit my invention . . . so long as [the head] is made to encompass the pencil and present an erasive surface about the sides of the same.

A head made in my improved manner and applied to a pencil as above set forth is of great practical utility and advantage to bookkeepers, accountants, and various other persons. The pointed form of the head . . . will be found very useful for draughtsmen in erasing lines from their drawings when it may be desirable not to erase other lines in close proximity to that which it is desirable to erase. The elastic or rubber pencil head, made as above set forth, may be applied not only to lead pencils, but to ink-erasers and other articles of like character.

I claim as a new article of manufacture an elastic erasive pencil-head, made substantially in manner as described.

J. B. Blair

After the Rubber-Tip Pencil Company acquired the patent from Blair, it filed suit against someone it claimed was manufacturing rubber-tipped pencils similar to those covered by the patent. The case reached the United States Supreme Court, which analyzed whether Blair's "invention" had been patentable.

The Court noted that an idea in and of itself is not patentable. It noted that a patent only could be obtained for a new or useful art, machine, manufacture, or composition of matter, or any new and useful improvement thereof. Blair's eraser, it found, was not patentable. "Everybody knew, when the patent was applied for, that if a solid substance was inserted into a cavity in a piece of rubber smaller than itself, the rubber would cling to it." The Court noted that the small opening in the piece of rubber was not patentable, and that neither was the elasticity of the rubber. It said, "What, therefore, is left for this patentee but the idea that if a pencil is inserted into a cavity in a piece of rubber smaller than itself the rubber will attach itself to the pencil, and when so attached become convenient for use as an eraser?" It then ruled that Blair's eraser had not been patentable.

▌ The Power of Patents

Lesser things than pencil erasers have been found to be patentable, and have provided manufacturers with a monopoly on their production and substantial income. Indeed, patents can be powerful marketing tools. The statement in 1899 by the commissioner of patents that "[e]verything that can be invented has been invented" seems quite ridiculous.

Article I, Section 8, clause 8 of the Constitution gives Congress the power "[t]o promote the Progress of Science and useful Arts by securing for limited Times to Authors and Inventors the exclusive Right to their respective Writings and Discoveries." The patent clause reflects a balance between the need to encourage innovation and the avoidance of monopolies that stifle competition without any concomitant advance in science.

From their inception, the federal patent laws have embodied a careful balance between the need to promote innovation and the recognition that imitation and refinement through imitation are both necessary to invention itself and the very lifeblood of a competitive economy. Soon after the adoption of the Constitution, the First Congress enacted the Patent Act of 1790, which allowed the grant of a limited monopoly of 14 years to any applicant that "hath . . . invented or discovered any useful art, manufacture, . . . or device, or any improvement therein not before known or used." In addition to novelty, the 1790 law required that the invention be "sufficiently useful and important" to merit the 14-year right of exclusion. That act also required that the patentee deposit with the secretary of state a specification and if possible a model of the new invention, "which specification shall be so particular, and said models so exact, as not only to distinguish the invention or discovery from other things before known and used, but also to enable a workman or other person skilled in the art or manufacture . . . to make, construct, or use the same, to the end that the public may have the full benefit therefore, after the expiration of the patent term."

The first patent law established an agency known by self designation as the "Commissioners for the promotion of Useful Arts," composed of the secretary of state, the secretary of the Department of War, and the attorney general, any two of whom could grant a patent. Thomas Jefferson was the first secretary of state, and the driving force behind early federal patent policy. He also played a large role in the drafting of the country's second patent act, which became law in 1793, and known as the Patent Act of 1793. That law carried over the requirement that the subject of a patent application be "not known or used before the application." It also created a defense to an infringement action where "the thing, thus secured by patent, was not originally discovered by the patentee, but had been in use, or had been described in some public work, anterior to the supposed discovery of the patentee." From the outset, in Jefferson's words, federal patent law has been about the difficult business "of drawing a line between the things which are worth to the public the embarrassment of an exclusive patent, and those which are not."

▎Novel and Useful Requirements

The current patent law is remarkably similar to the early laws. Protection is afforded to "[w]homever invents or discovers any new and useful process, machine, manufacture, or composition of matter, or any new and useful improvement thereof." Congress also has made protection available for "any new, original and ornamental design for an article of manufacture." To qualify for protection, a design must present an esthetically pleasing appearance that is not dictated by function alone, and must satisfy the other criteria of patentability. The novelty requirement of patentability is expressed in Section 102(a) and 102(b) of the federal patent law, which provides that:

A person shall be entitled to a patent unless—

(a) the invention was known or used by others in this country, or patented or described in a printed publication in this or a foreign country, before the invention thereof by the applicant for patent, or

(b) the invention was patented or described in a printed publication in this or a foreign country or in public use or on sale in this country more than one year prior to the date of application for patent in the United States.

Sections 102(a) and 102 (b) operate in tandem to exclude from consideration for patent protection knowledge that is already available to the public. They express a congressional determination that the creation of a monopoly in such information would not only serve no socially useful purpose but would in fact injure the public by removing existing knowledge from public use. Thus, once an inventor has decided to lift the veil of secrecy from the invention, the inventor must choose the protection of a federal patent or dedicate the idea to the public at large.

▮ Nonobvious Requirement

In addition to the requirements of novelty and utility, the federal patent law long has required that an innovation not be anticipated by the prior art in the field. Even if a particular combination of elements is "novel" in the literal sense of the term, it will not qualify for federal patent protection if its contours are so traced by the existing technology in the field that the improvement can be said to be "the work of the skillful mechanic, not that of an inventor." The nonobviousness requirement extends the field of unpatentable material beyond that which is known to the public under Section 102 to include that which could readily be deduced from publicly available material by a person of ordinary skill in the pertinent field of endeavor.

Taken together, the novelty and nonobviousness requirements express a congressional determination that the purposes behind the Constitution's patent clause are best served by free competition and exploitation of either that which is already available to the public or that which may be readily discerned from publicly available material.

The applicant whose invention satisfies the requirements of novelty, nonobviousness, and utility, and who is willing to reveal to the public the substance of his or her discovery and the best mode of carrying out the invention, is granted "the right to exclude others from making, using, or selling the invention throughout the United States" for a period of 17 years. The federal patent system thus embodies a carefully crafted bargain for encouraging the creation and disclosure of new, useful, and nonobvious advances in technology and design in return for the exclusive right to practice the invention for a period of years. Upon expiration of that period, the knowledge of the invention inures to the members of the public, who are thus enabled without restriction to practice it and profit by its use.

▮ Federal Circuit Court

For a good part of this century, courts seemed quite willing to strike down patents that were challenged. Indeed, in 1949, U.S. Supreme Court Justice Robert H. Jackson exaggerated just a bit when he complained in a dissenting opinion that "the only patent that is valid is one which this Court has not been able to get its hands on." About 10 years ago, though, that started changing.

In the early 1980s, perhaps with the intent to clarify patent law and expand patent protection, Congress created the U.S. Court of Appeals for the Federal Circuit and granted that court jurisdiction over every appeal in a patent lawsuit.

The federal circuit has established standards more favorable to patent holders and has been more likely than other courts in the past to uphold patents. It has seemed more likely to approve or grant preliminary injunctions challenging alleged patent infringements. In short, it has become more pro-patent and therefore made patents more valuable.

▌ A Final Word

Should a company seek a patent for its new, useful, innovative, and nonobvious product? Perhaps, and perhaps not. Such a product can be protected under trade secret law as well as under patent law, and there are benefits to each. For instance, a trade secret can be kept secret forever; a patent is only protectable for 17 years. And a trade secret need not be disclosed; a patent must be disclosed.

On the other hand, a company does not have to be concerned with competitors' attempts at obtaining their patented product because it is already contained in federal government files; thus, a patent holder does not have to worry about commercial espionage, dishonest employees, or unfair competition. Furthermore, patent law is a uniform federal law with a uniform federal interpretation; trade secret law may vary from state to state and could provide companies with less protection than the patent laws. The question of whether to proceed through patent or trade secret protection is a good one to have to deal with, of course, because it means that a company has something important and valuable to protect. And, one therefore hopes, to sell.

FIVE PATENT CASES

1. In September 1976, Bonito Boats, Inc. developed a hull design for a fiberglass recreational boat that it marketed under the trade name Bonito Boat Model 5VBR. Designing the boat hull required substantial effort on Bonito's part: it prepared a set of engineering drawings, created a hardwood model from the drawings, and then sprayed the model with fiberglass to create a mold, which then served to produce the finished fiberglass boats for sale. Bonito placed the 5VBR on the market in September

1976. It apparently did not file a patent application to protect the utilitarian or design aspects of the hull or the process by which it manufactured the hull. The boating public favorably received the 5VBR in Florida and many other states. In May 1983, the Florida legislature enacted a statute that made it unlawful for anyone to use the direct molding process to duplicate for the purpose of sale any manufactured vessel hull or component part of a vessel made by another without the written permission of that other person. The statute also made it unlawful for a person to knowingly sell a vessel hull or component part of a vessel duplicated in violation of that law.

On December 21, 1984, Bonito filed an action alleging that Thunder Craft Boats, Inc. had violated the Florida statute by using the direct molding process to duplicate the Bonito 5VBR fiberglass hull and had knowingly sold such duplicates in violation of the Florida statute. Bonito sought a temporary and permanent injunction prohibiting Thunder Craft from continuing "to unlawfully duplicate and sell Bonito Boat hulls or components" as well as an accounting of profits, treble damages, punitive damages, and attorney's fees. Thunder Craft argued that the Florida statute was invalid because it conflicted with federal patent law. The Florida Supreme Court ruled that the law was impermissible because it interfered wit the scheme established by the federal patent laws, and the case reached the United States Supreme Court. The U.S. Supreme Court said "We believe that the Florida statute at issue in this case so substantially impedes the public use of the otherwise unprotected design and utilitarian ideas embodied in unpatented boat hulls as to run afoul" of the federal patent laws. By offering patent-like protection for ideas deemed unprotected under the federal scheme, the Supreme Court said that the Florida statute conflicted with the strong federal policy favoring free competition in ideas that did not merit patent protection. It then agreed with the Florida Supreme Court that the Florida statute was preempted by federal law and could not be relied on by Bonito in its suit against Thunder Craft. (Bonito Boars, Inc. v. Thunder Craft Boats, Inc., 489 U.S. 141 (1989).)

2. The owner of the Mead patent no. 1,736,544, for improvements in automobile lighters, filed an infringement action against another manufacturer. Before the Mead lighter, there were lighters of the "reel type." In those lighters, the igniter unit was connected with a source of current by a cable that was wound on a spring drum so that the igniter unit and cable could be withdrawn from the socket and used for lighting a cigar or cigarette. As the removable plug was returned to the socket, the wires were reeled back into it. The circuit was closed either by manual operation of a button or by withdrawal of the igniter from its socket. Then, in 1921, the Morris patent was issued for a so called "wireless" or "cordless" lighter. This lighter eliminated the cables and the mechanism for winding and unwinding them, provided for heating the ignited unit without removing it from its socket, and eliminated all electrical and mechanical connections of the igniter unit with the socket once it was removed therefrom to use. In the Morris lighter, the circuit was open when the plug rested in the socket and closed when the plug was pushed farther into the socket against the resistance of a spring. Another patent was issued for a lighter that required the operator to press and hold down a push-button to close the circuit. In yet another case, the operator was obliged to hold the plug, or the circuit-closing part, in place until the heating coil became hot enough to use. These lighters required rather continual attention on the part of the person using them so that there would be no over heating or burning out of the heating coil. Mead claimed that his lighter eliminated this inconvenience and hazard by incorporating automatic features. The Mead lighter added to the so-called "wireless" or "cordless" lighter a thermostatic control responsive to the temperature of the heating coil. In operating, it automatically returned the plug to its "off" position after the heating coil had reached the proper temperature. To operate Mead's device, one had to turn the knob on the igniter plug to a point where an electrical connection was established from the battery through the heating coil. There the plug remained temporarily latched. When the heating coil was sufficiently hot for use, the bimetallic elements in the thermostat, responsive to the temperature conditions of the heating coil, caused the igniter plug to be released and to be moved by operation of a spring to open-circuit position. The plug might then be manually removed for use in the manner of a match. When replaced in the socket after use, it was held in open-circuit position until next needed. The Supreme Court noted that thermostatic controls of a heating unit, operating to cut off an electric current energizing the unit when its temperature had reached the desired point, were well known to the art when Mead made his device. It said that to incorporate such a thermostatic control in a so-called "wireless" or "cordless" lighter was not to make an "invention" or "discovery" within the meaning of the patent laws. Mead merely incorporated the well-known thermostat into the old "wireless" lighter to produce a more efficient, useful, and convenient article. But, the Court said, a new application of an old device may not be patented "if the result claimed as new is the same in character as the original result" even though the new result had not before been contemplated. It said that the use of a thermostat to break a circuit in a "wireless" cigar lighter was analogous to, or the same in character as, the use of such a device in electric heaters, toasters, or irons, whatever may be the difference in detail of design. "Ingenuity was required to effect the adaptation, but no more than that to be expected of a mechanic skilled in the art." The Court concluded that the Mead device was not patentable because it was not the result of invention but a "mere exercise of the skill of the calling," an advance "plainly indicated by the prior art." (Cuno Engineering Corp. v. Automatic Devices Corp., 314 U.S. 84 (1941).

3. Several years ago Power Lift, Inc. filed suit against Lang Tools, Inc. and Wendell Lang, Lang Tools' president, founder, majority owner, and director, for infringement on Power Lift's patent for a Blow-Out Preventer Lift System and Method. The patent related to a device used to lift equipment, such as a blow-out preventer, during oil and gas well drilling operations. The device was placed on the drilling rig platform and attached to the equipment to be raised through a central aperture in the platform's rotary table. During drilling operations, equipment located at the mouth of the well sometimes needs to be raised toward the underside of the drilling platform. For example, a blow-out preventer, which weighs many tons, may need to be raised a short distance to service the well bore casing to which the blow-out preventer is connected. Power Lift contended that Lang based his lift system on inspection of the Power Lift blow-out preventer system that was already in field use. His son, Darrell Lang, had been seen measuring the width of the Power Lift winches and drums. Lang's system, while not identical to Power Lift's system, was based on it. Immediately after receiving its patent, Power Lift contacted Lang by phone and offered him a license, alleging that Lang Tools was infringing its patent. Lang apparently refused the offer, stating "before he would pay [Power Lift] a nickel, he'd see [Power Lift] in the courthouse" and decided not to stop production of Lang's lift system. In response, Power Lift filed suit against Lang and his company for patent infringement. Power Lift did not sue Lang directly but rather on the theory that he had induced Lang Tools to infringe the Power Lift patent. A jury found Lang liable, and he appealed. He contended that his actions were the actions of Lang Tools, Inc. and that he therefore could not be said to have actively induced infringement of the patent. The U.S. Court of Appeals for the Federal Circuit, finding that the law permits liability to be imposed on corporate officials who actively aid and abet their corporation's infringements, upheld the decision (including the award of attorney's fees, a quite exceptional situation) against Lang personally and against his company. (Power Lift, Inc. v. Lang Tools, Inc., 774 F.2d 478 (Fed. Cit. 1985).)

4. Beginning in 1953 the University of Maryland conducted an extensive study of the wind resistance of tractor-trailer vehicles to seek methods of reducing drag. Under the direction of a professor of aerodynamics, the University's Wind Tunnel Operations Department tested more than 7,000 configurations in wind tunnel tests on trailer models. The study concluded that one of the best drag reduction methods was to use a continuous "fairing." That is a deflector attached to the back of the tractor cab roof that extends in a curved or modified *S* configuration to the top leading edge of the trailer where it also is attached. While the Maryland fairing proved in wind tunnel tests to be very effective at reducing the drag from wind resistance, it was recognized to be impractical, if not useless, because the tractor-trailer could not be turned when such a fairing was employed. In 1958 the Stamm patent was issued. The Stamm device consisted of two principal parts, one being curved pieces mounted on the top and sides of the tractor cab and the other being conduits mounted on the top and sides of the trailer. The curved pieces were designed to direct air flow smoothly from the cab through the conduits on the trailer. In 1966 Walter Selden Saunders obtained a patent for an air-deflecting device for reducing wind resistance encountered by tractor-trailer combination vehicles. The device was a panel-like deflector mounted on top of the cab of the tractor to produce "a relatively wide diffusion of the air . . . and cause the same to readhere to the body of the truck rearwardly of the front portion thereof in a relatively smooth and even manner."

Saunders granted an exclusive license of the patent to the Rudkin-Wiley Corp. in 1966. Rudkin-Wiley's commercial embodiment of the Saunders invention was roughly rectangular and had a smaller cross sectional area than the cross-sectional area of the front face of the trailer that extended above the tractor cab. When the vehicle was in motion, significant fuel savings could be achieved because of the reduced resistance or drag. Uniroyal, Inc. manufactured a device similar to Rudkin-Wiley's embodiment of Saunders' invention, although it was more rounded on the corners and edges. In 1975 Uniroyal filed suit seeking to have Saunders' patent declared invalid for obviousness, and the district court ruled that it was. The case reached the U.S. Court of Appeals for the Federal Circuit. The court stated that the obviousness standard was sometimes difficult to apply because it required the court to return to the time when the invention was made. "The invention must be viewed not with the blueprint drawn by the inventor, but in the state of the art that existed at the time . . . That which may be made clear and thus 'obvious' to a court, with the invention fully diagramed . . . may have been a breakthrough of substantial dimension when first unveiled." The appellate court then determined that the district court had impermissibly used hindsight to reconstruct the claimed invention from prior art with the invention before it and aided by Uniroyal's expert, "rather than viewing the invention from the position of a person of ordinary skill at the time it was made." It then reversed the district court's decision that the Saunders patent was invalid. (Uniroyal, Inc. v. Rudkin-Wiley Corp., 837 F.2d 1044 (Fed. Cir. 1988).)

5. The clotting or pro-coagulant factor, Factor VIII:C, is found in all mammals. When a patent entitled Ultrapurification of Factor VIII Using Monoclonal Antibodies was issued to inventors Theodore S. Zimmerman and Carol A. Fulcher, it was known that human Factor VIII:C was a complex protein produced by the Factor VIII:C gene and secreted into the blood stream. It occurred in normal blood plasma at a concentration of about 200 nanograms per milliliter. Most of the problems faced by researchers attempting to isolate Factor VIII:C were due to the amount and nature of the other proteins in the plasma. Before Zimmerman and Fulcher's invention, scientists had succeeded in concentrating Factor VIII:C in plasma; that concentrate had been used to replace transfusions of whole blood in the treatment of hemophilia. The process was expensive and, because of the large volume of whole blood needed as starting material, the possibility of contamination and disease from impurities in the source blood, the large amount of extraneous plasma proteins in the concentrate, and the large volume of concentrate that still had to be administered to the patient, scientists continued searching for an improvement. Zimmerman and Fulcher succeeded in isolating and, for the first time, characterizing Factor VIII:C, by a process of chromatographic absorption of the Factor VIII:C complex using monoclonal antibodies specific to Factor VIII:RP, followed by separation of the Factor VIII:C.

Contending that Genentech, Inc. had infringed that patent, the Scripps Clinic & Research Foundation (which held the patent on the invention by Zimmerman and Fulcher) filed suit. Among other things, Genentech asserted that the inventors had deliberately withheld an analysis from the patent examiners and had misrepresented that impurities were "trace" when in fact they were not. The district court ruled in favor of

Genentech, finding that the inventors had not provided sufficient information about the claimed invention to the patent examiners. The U.S. Court of Appeals for the Federal Circuit reversed that decision. It ruled that Genentech had not proved that the inventors had intended to deceive or mislead the examiners. "Conduct that requires forfeiture of all patent rights must be deliberate," the appellate court concluded. (Scripps Clinic & Research Foundation v. Genentech, Inc., 927 F.2d 1565 (Fed. Cir. 1991).)

Patent Checklist

✓ The federal patent law can offer important protection to marketers and advertisers—it creates the ultimate in marketing opportunity, a monopoly.

✓ For a product to be patentable, it must be novel, useful, and nonobvious.

✓ In recent years, the U.S. Court of Appeals for the federal circuit, which Congress created in the early 1980s and which has sole jurisdiction over appeals of all patent lawsuits, has taken a much more pro-patent and pro-patentee viewpoint than courts did before.

✓ Among other things, the Federal Circuit has created standards favorable to patentholders, has shown itself likely to uphold patents that have been issued, and has seemed rather willing to allow patent holders to protect themselves with preliminary injunctions.

✓ Businesses with novel inventions must consider whether to seek protection under a patent or trade secret route. Both have their benefits and drawbacks, but having to choose between them is the "good news"—it means that a manufacturer has something valuable to protect that could, or should, lead to increased sales.

8
PRODUCT REVIEWS

▌ Bad Reviews ▌ Using a Review in an Ad ▌ A Final Word

The United States Supreme Court issues scores of decisions every year. For the most part, though, Supreme Court rulings do not tend to directly determine legal issues of importance to marketers. But one decision issued about a decade ago clearly sets forth the rules for a company that wants to challenge a review of one of its products.

▌ Bad Reviews

That case began when *Consumer Reports* published a seven-page article evaluating the quality of numerous brands of medium-priced loudspeakers in its May 1970 issue. In a boxed-off section occupying most of two pages, the magazine commented on "some loudspeakers of special interest," one of which was the Bose 901, which had been placed on the market by the Bose Corporation. Bose had been founded in 1964 by Dr. Amar Bose, whom Consumers Union of United States, Inc. (CU), the publisher of *Consumer Reports,* conceded was an expert in the field of loudspeaker design. The Bose 901 loudspeakers that Dr. Bose designed were unique and unconventional. Each of the two loudspeaker cabinets in the system had the five-sided shape of a baseball home plate when viewed from above; one side in the front faced the listener and two sides in the rear faced away from the listener. The front face of each cabinet contained one driver and each of the two rear faces had four drivers. As a result, the listener received one-ninth of the sound directly from the loudspeakers and eight-ninths of the sound by reflection off the wall behind the speakers.

After describing the system and some of its virtues, and after noting that a listener "could pinpoint the location of various instruments much more easily with a standard speaker than with the Bose system," the *Consumer Reports* article made the following statements: "Worse, individual instruments heard through the Bose system seemed to grow to gigantic proportions and tended to wander about the room. For instance, a violin appeared to be 10 feet wide and a piano stretched from wall to wall. With orchestral music, such effects seemed inconsequential. But we think they might become annoying when listening to soloists."

After stating opinions concerning the overall sound quality, the article concluded: "We think the Bose system is so unusual that a prospective buyer must listen to it and judge it for himself. We would suggest delaying so big an investment until you were sure the system would please you after the novelty value had worn off."

Bose took exception to numerous statements made in the article and, when Consumers Union refused to publish a retraction, Bose filed a product disparagement suit in federal district court in Massachusetts.

The district court conducted a 19-day trial and ruled in favor of Consumers Union on most issues. Among other things, the court ruled that Bose was a "public figure" and, therefore, the First Amendment precluded recovery for Bose in this case unless it proved by clear and convincing evidence that Consumes Union had made a false disparaging statement about a Bose product with "actual malice."

On three critical points, however, the district court agreed with Bose. First, it found that one sentence in the article contained a "false" statement of "fact" concerning the tendency of the instruments to wander. Based primarily on testimony by the author of the article, the district court found that instruments heard through the speakers tended to wander "along the wall" rather than "about the room" as the article had indicated. Second, it found that the statement was disparaging to Bose. Third, it concluded that Consumers Union had published that false statement of material fact with knowledge that it was false or with reckless disregard of its truth or falsity—in essence, that Consumers Union had been guilty of actual malice. It entered judgment for Bose on its product disparagement claim. In a separate trial, Bose was awarded approximately $100,000 in damages.

The Supreme Court disagreed with the district court's ruling. It said that the error in the review was the kind of inaccuracy that was inevitable in "free debate" and that it must be protected if the freedom of expression guaranteed by the First Amendment was to have the "breathing space" that the Court believed it needed to survive. As the Court said, under the district court's analysis, "any individual using a malapropism might be liable, simply because an intelligent speaker would have to know that the term was inaccurate in context, even though he did not realize his folly at the time."

The Court noted that there may be some doubt as to whether the "actual malice" standard should be applied to a claim of product disparagement based on a critical review of a loudspeaker system but it did not specifically deal with that issue. It simply stated that the error in the article "fits easily within the breathing space that gives life to the First Amendment."

Conceivably, there may be situations where a manufacturer that is challenging an unfavorable product review does not have to meet the "actual malice" standard. If it is not a so-called "public figure" (which requires a degree of prominence in a community or, perhaps, in a particular industry), it may be able to challenge unfavorable reviews that contain careless errors rather than errors under the more-difficult-to-prove reckless or intentional standard. But it could be difficult as a practical matter to show that a manufacturer is not a public figure for purposes of a review—if a trade publication reviews a product produced by a company in that trade, the company may be deemed a public figure for purposes of that magazine's review in the industry. In any event, it is awfully difficult to challenge a reviewer's opinion even if the opinion is that the manufacturer's product is no good because opinions can be neither true or false and generally are protected by the First Amendment.

Of course, in many instances a product review is favorable to a manufacturer's product. Can portions of the review be used in an ad? A decision of the U.S. Court of Appeals for the First Circuit identifies the parameters.

▌ Using a Review in an Ad

The issue of *Consumer Reports* that evaluated lightweight vacuum cleaners a number of years ago contained the following notice: "Consumers Union accepts no advertising or product samples and is not beholden in any way to any commercial interest. Its Ratings and product reports are solely for the use of readers of *Consumer Reports*. Neither the Ratings nor the reports may be used in advertising or for any commercial purpose. CU will take all steps open to it to prevent such uses of its material, its name, or the name of *Consumer Reports*."

In the vacuum cleaner evaluation, the Regina Power Team was "check-rated" and effusively praised. Models were check-rated when Consumers Union judged the product tested to be of high overall quality, low price, and appreciable superiority to the non-check-rated models examined. *Consumer Reports'* comments regarding this product included:

- "Regina Power Team—far ahead of the pack in cleaning ability."

- "[O]nly one model, the check-rated Regina Power Team, was an adequate substitute for a full-sized vacuum."

- "Only the Regina Power Team vacuumed the floor thoroughly."

- "The Regina Power Team also stood out in our carpet-cleaning test. It alone left the carpet presentable after only one sweep, pristine after two sweeps."

The Regina Power Team lightweight vacuum cleaner was marketed by the Regina Company, a division of General Signal Corporation's wholly owned subsidiary, the General Signal Appliance Corporation. As part of its marketing strategy, Regina and its outside advertising agency, Gray-North, Inc., a division of Grey Advertising, Inc., prepared three half-minute commercial messages for broadcast on television. The first did not mention *Consumer Reports,* but the other two did.

The second ad, entitled "Squid," emphasized the lightweight convenience of the Regina Power Team compared to full-size vacuums. During one of the many different visual portions of the message, the voice-over announcer stated that the Regina Power Team was "the only lightweight that *Consumer Reports* says, quote, was an adequate substitute for a full-sized vacuum." The statement "*Consumer Reports* is not affiliated with Regina and does not endorse products" was superimposed on the screen the entire time the *Consumer Reports* quotation was mentioned.

The third ad, entitled *"Consumer Reports,"* included several quotations from *Consumer Reports* visually displayed on the screen as they were read by an announcer. As with "Squid," each time material from *Consumer Reports* was mentioned, there appeared the statement that it was not affiliated with Regina and did not endorse products. This disclaimer appeared on the screen for a total of 14 seconds out of the 29.5-second duration of the commercial. The print size used for the disclaimer was comparable with normal television advertising practice for required disclosures and remained on the screen for a longer period of time than was normal for such disclosures.

Regina notified Consumers Union that it planned to broadcast these commercials. It offered to provide copies to Consumers Union and to meet to discuss the matter. But Consumers Union instead sent Regina a telegram demanding that Regina cease and desist from airing its commercials; Consumers Union then filed suit.

Consumers Union alleged that specific defects in the commercials had a misleading effect. The court granted Consumers Union a temporary restraining order blocking the ads over Regina's objections.

Upon receiving Consumers Union's court papers, Regina changed the commercials' disclaimer to state *"Consumer Reports* is not affiliated with Regina and does not endorse Regina products or any other products." This was intended to allay concerns of Consumers Union that the initial wording of the disclaimer might convey the impression that, while Consumers Union generally did not endorse products, it had made an exception in Regina's case. Responding to Consumers Union's complaint, Regina also revised the voice-over of the "Squid" commercial to insert the word "unquote" at the end of the quotation attributed to *Consumer Reports* and changed the last visual of that message to eliminate pictures of Regina models other than the Power Team.

After a hearing, the district court prohibited Regina from using those commercials and Regina appealed.

Among its arguments on appeal, Consumers Union contended that Regina's ads were false and misleading in three respects. First, it claimed that the ads conveyed the false impression that the *Consumer Reports* review of the Power Team was exclusively favorable. Although *Consumer Reports* did check-rate the Power Team, it also noted that its dust-holding capacity was not good and found other minor defects. But the appellate court noted that as a factual matter, Regina's ads did not convey the impression that the *Consumer Reports* review was wholly favorable. Rather, they merely conveyed what the appellate court said was the accurate impression, that *Consumer Reports* concluded that the Power Team lightweight vacuum was superior to others tested. Consumers Union, the court said, virtually admitted that the negative factors were of little consequence: another issue of the magazine listed the Power Team as a "Best Buy Gift" with no negative qualifications.

Second, Consumers Union asserted that Regina's original ads conveyed the false impression that Consumers Union's favorable review applied to the entire Regina line, when in fact models other than the Power Team were not rated so highly. The appellate court questioned the accuracy of that assertion. It said that the Power Team was the only machine shown and named during the commercial. The group picture that flashed rapidly past the viewers' eyes at the very end had been changed; that made the point moot.

Third, Consumers Union objected to the failure of the commercial announcer to close the quotation from *Consumer Reports*. Instead of saying "unquote" following the excerpt, the announcer continued with the rest of the commercial's text. But the court noted that Regina changed the commercial to include the word unquote and found this issue to be moot, too.

The court noted that ads that are not technically false but that lead to a mistaken public belief that a trademark's owner sponsored or otherwise approved of the use of its trademark can be enjoined. The theory is that advertisements should not be allowed to create a likelihood of confusion by consumers regarding the origin or sponsorship of the product.

But, the court said, Regina's ads were not shown to have given rise to that kind of confusion. "We are satisfied that the disclaimer is adequate to distance CU and Regina," it added. (It noted with respect to the value of disclaimers that "[p]resumably the disclaimer printed in each issue of CU's magazine dissuades the readers of *Consumer Reports* from concluding that CU is affiliated with the companies whose products it reviews. In view of its faith in the efficacy of its own disclaimer, CU's position that no disclaimer by Regina would be sufficient to prevent consumer confusion does not ring true.")

Consumers Union also relied on a section of New York law that prohibited the use of the name of a nonprofit corporation for advertising purposes without first obtaining written consent. But the appellate court found that that law was not intended to apply to a situation where the nonprofit corporation's business was that of evaluating products and where it widely disseminated the results. The purpose of the law was to protect the right to privacy, the court said. "By going public with its views, CU places itself in a position where its privacy is not infringed when these views are repeated."

The appellate court then reversed the order of the district court enjoining Regina from running the commercials.

▌A Final Word

Reviews from independent sources provide valuable information to consumers precisely because they are independent. That's why they are protected to a great extent by the First Amendment. And because the information they contain is so important, they generally may be republished in ads so long as the ads meet the standard that so many other kinds of ads must meet: they must be truthful, fair, and not misleading.

FIVE CASES CHALLENGING REVIEWS OR THEIR USE IN ADS

1. Medical Directors, Inc. and Weight Reduction Medical Centers, Inc. operated weight-loss clinics throughout Texas and other states. As a part of its advertising program the companies used testimonials from satisfied clients. A typical ad featured the photograph and personal endorsement of an individual who had completed the companies' program. One particular ad sparked a legal controversy: it stated that the satisfied clients giving their endorsements of the program, Bill and Beverly Hickman, were actually "investigators" or "spies" working "on behalf of the Better Business Bureau." The Hickmans' contact with the companies began when Beverly gave Bill as a Father's Day gift a program of treatment at the companies' facility near their home in Beaumont, Texas. Bill Hickman, a self-described skeptical consumer, checked the reputation of the program with the Beaumont office of the Better Business Bureau of Southeast Texas before beginning treatment. When he found that the Bureau had little information about the program in its files, he offered to furnish it with periodic reports on his experiences in the weight-loss program. The Bureau regularly accepted information from the consuming public as raw data on the practices of local businesses and readily agreed to take what information Hickman cared to volunteer.

Hickman's reports were favorable. Over the three weeks during which he participated in the weight-loss program, he lost 33 pounds. Beverly Hickman, who also joined the program, lost 15 pounds over the same period. After he completed the program, Hickman mentioned to a member of the companies' staff that he had been keeping the Better Business Bureau apprised of his progress. Very shortly thereafter, the companies asked the Hickmans to appear in testimonial advertisements for their program. The Hickmans agreed to give their endorsements. The text of the ads prepared by the companies claimed that the Hickmans engaged in a "personal investigation for the Better Business Bureau" and discovered that the program "really works." The newspaper ad was headed with the attention-grabbing phrase "BBB Spy" printed in large type above a photograph of Bill Hickman; the television spots, featuring both Bill and Beverly Hickman, were overlaid with the words "BBB investigators."

After the television commercials were taped, but before any of the ads were published, the companies' advertising director initiated and taped a telephone conversation with the executive vice-president of the Bureau's southeast office regarding the Bureau's involvement with the Hickmans' investigation. Under questioning, the bureau official repeatedly stated that

Hickman had not been acting under the aegis of the Bureau when he undertook his investigation, that the Bureau received only the information Hickman volunteered to it, and that the Bureau did not approve or endorse the companies' weight-loss program. Only when pressed for a characterization of Hickman's relationship with the Bureau did the Bureau official state that the companies' advertising director's description of it as a "personal investigation on the Better Business Bureau's behalf" was "more or less" correct.

The ads were thereupon run in Texas, Louisiana, and Arizona. The Bureau disclaimed them and took steps to secure their withdrawal immediately upon becoming aware of their publication. A federal appellate court agreed with the decision of a district judge that the ads were misleading because they implied that the Better Business Bureau had reviewed the companies' weight reduction program and vouched for its safety and effectiveness when that was not the case. It then ruled that the companies could be enjoined from using the designations "Better Business Bureau" or "BBB" in their advertising unless they included a disclaimer that the "Better Business Bureau does not approve or endorse the Weight Reduction Medical Centers or their weight reduction program." (Better Business Bureau v. Medical Directors, Inc., 681 F.2d 397 (5th Cir. 1982).)

2. An article in an issue of *Consumer Reports* published in November 1968 reported on the generally favorable research results obtained by Consumers Union of United States, Inc. concerning the safety of a microwave oven produced by Amana Refrigeration Inc. In April 1973, however, *Consumer Reports* published an unfavorable article on Amana's microwave oven. Amana then printed more than 200,000 copies of a brochure in an attempt to offset the effects of the unfavorable article. The brochure was entitled "Let's Talk About the Safety of the Radarange Oven." It included various expert opinions on the safety of microwave ovens and then directly quoted a full paragraph from the 1968 article, although it did not mention the unfavorable 1973 article.

Consumers Union wrote to Amana requesting that it stop circulating the brochure because it infringed the copyright held by Consumers Union and because it misled consumers. Amana filed suit against Consumers Union, which filed counterclaims against Amana. Amana claimed that it had not violated the copyright held by Consumers Union in the 1968 story because its use of the one paragraph was a "fair use." But the court disagreed. It said that if Amana had referred to both articles in an attempt to show that Consumers Union had an inconsistent position on microwave ovens, fair use "might be involved." But, it said, the only possible conclusion to be reached from a reading of the brochure was that Amana was attempting to convey the impression that Consumers Union approved of Amana's microwave oven as of 1973 when the exact opposite was true. That was misleading and, the court said, impermissible. The court then issued an injunction prohibiting Amana from continuing to print or distribute the brochure. (Amana Refrigeration, Inc. v. Consumers Union of United States, Inc., 431 F.Supp. 324 (N.D. Iowa, 1977).)

3. After Abraham J. Briloff reviewed a preliminary prospectus from the Reliance Insurance Company that Reliance circulated to the investment community with the intention of offering at public sale two million shares of its Series A Cumulative Preferred Stock, Briloff wrote an article for Barron's analyzing Reliance's proposed public offering. He also analyzed the relationship between Reliance and the Reliance Group, Inc., the company that owned all of the common stock of Reliance. Briloff concluded that the purpose of the public offering was to serve the interests and needs of Reliance Group rather than Reliance Insurance. The article charged that the proceeds of the sale were to flow upstream to Reliance Group to the detriment of Reliance Insurance and its policyholders and minority shareholders. The article also implied that Reliance Group was employing certain "creative accounting" concepts and engaging in improprieties, bad business judgment, and breach of fiduciary duties, all of which led to its decision to market the proposed stock.

After publication of the article, Reliance Insurance revised its preliminary prospectus, filed a final prospectus with the Securities and Exchange Commission, and sold two million shares of preferred stock to the public at an interest rate that it claimed was approximately one percentage point higher than it would have been had Briloff's article not been published—a cost over the 25-year life of the preferred issue of approximately $7.5 million. Reliance Insurance also filed suit against *Barron's* and Briloff. The court that issued a decision in this case noted that the article was clearly defamatory of Reliance Insurance, a public figure, and probably also of Reliance Group. But, it said, the article was written by a reputable member of the accounting community who held strong and genuine views about Reliance Insurance and about what he regarded as some of the failings of accountants. In addition, it said, the article was primarily no more than a critique or a personally held opinion concerning matters of public record. Strong public policies exist in favor of the right to publish such critiques as those contained in Briloff's article, the court said. It added that if "the financial press, or the press at large, had to fear libel suits when expressing dislike of certain persons or firms, or of business or other practices, the self censorship that would inevitably occur would have a stifling if not smothering effect on the functioning of a free press." It then dismissed the libel claim brought by Reliance Insurance. (Reliance Insurance Co. v. Barron's, 442 F.Supp. 1341 (S.D.N.Y. 1977).)

4. The August 1969 issue of *Consumer Reports* published an article entitled "Beers." While acknowledging that the number of brands of beer ran well into the hundreds, the article stated that Consumers Union chose for testing 35 brands of beers—24 domestic and 11 imported brands. The 35 brands of beer tested, all of which were rated "Acceptable," were divided into three groups according to the taste panel's judgment of body: light bodied, medium-bodied, and heavy-bodied. Each of the three groups was further subdivided into classes in order of overall quality as judged by the panel: the light-bodied group had two classes, I and II; the medium-bodied group, four classes, I, II, III, and IV; and the heavy-bodied group, two classes, II and III (no heavy-bodied beer received Class I stature). The introductory paragraph of the ratings also stated that "[e]xcept as noted, closely ranked products differed little in overall quality; judgments of overall quality are comparable from body group to body group." Under Class I of the light-bodied group were listed two brands of beer in the following order: Hamm's and Coors. Under Class II of the medium-bodied beer were listed six brands of beer with the Hamm's Waldech brand mentioned first. Hamm's Beer and Hamm's Waldech were brewed and sold by the Theodore Hamm Brewing Co., Inc.

Obviously pleased with the positions attained by its products on the ratings sheet, the brewing company instituted a large advertising campaign designed to call the public's attention to the *Consumer Reports* rating. This advertising took the following forms:

- Distribution of the *Consumer Reports* article on beers

- Tagline announcements over radio and television indicating that Hamm's Beer had been rated the top beer in the country in the August issue of *Consumer Reports*

- Newspaper and poster advertisements that depicted a large bottle of Hamm's Beer in front of smaller bottles of 15 other brands of beer

- Memoranda to Hamm's employees stating that "Hamm's was rated among the two best light-bodied beers in America," and that "Hamm's Waldech was selected best in Class II of the medium bodied beers ahead of many other well known premium beers"

- "Counter-cards" asserting, among other things, that Hamm's was "Rated FIRST Among Beers Americans Like Best by *Consumer Reports* Magazine."

Consumers Union claimed that Hamm's conduct constituted copyright infringement, unfair competition, and unjust enrichment and sought a preliminary injunction to prohibit the ads. The court divided its decision into various categories. With respect to the fact that Hamm's had distributed copies of the *Consumer Reports* article on beers, the court said that that was in violation of the Consumers Union copyright and enjoined Hamm's from continuing to do so. With respect to Hamm's references in its ads to the *Consumer Reports* article on beers, the court said that there was a practice in manufacturers' advertisements to quote correctly from leading periodicals a favorable mention of their products. It then denied Consumers Union's request for an injunction on this aspect of its claim. Finally, the court enjoined Hamm's from using any false and misleading tagline that indicated that its beer was rated "the top beer in the country" or the "No. 1 beer in the country" by *Consumer Reports* because that was not technically true. (Consumers Union of United States, Inc. v. Theodore Hamm Brewing Co., 314 F.Supp. 697 (D.Conn. 1970).)

5. For many years, John Yiamouyiannis was an active opponent of the fluoridation of public water supplies. He was a paid employee of the National Health Federation, an organization that was actively opposed to fluoridation, the author of numerous articles on fluoride, and a coeditor of a quarterly journal published by the International Society for Fluoride Research. Several years ago Yiamouyiannis claimed that he was defamed by two articles published in *Consumer Reports* entitled "Fluoridation: The Cancer Scare" and "The Attack on Fluoridation—Six Ways To Mislead the Public." The first article explained how Yiamouyiannis's colleague, Dean Burk, an American biochemist, helped to kill a proposal before the Dutch Parliament to fluoridate water supplies by virtue of a television interview in Holland in which he told the audience that "fluoridation is a form of public mass murder." The article said that opposition to fluoridation in this country was led by the National Health Federation, whose roots "run deep into the soil of medical quackery." The article went on to say that in 1974 the National Health Federation decided to "break the back" of fluoridation efforts and hired Yiamouyiannis "to do the job." It said that he was successful in influencing a debate in Los Angeles and that a study with Burk "failed [according to the National Cancer Institute] to take into account widely recognized risk factors known to affect the death rate." It added that a later study was even more "amateurish," according to a National Cancer Institute official, and ignored "the most fundamental factors involved in cancer mortality rates—age, sex and race." The article reported that Burk and Yiamouyiannis were successful in Holland but unsuccessful in England and said that "independent investigations by seven of the leading medical and scientific organizations in the English-speaking world have unanimously refuted the National Health Federation's cancer claims."

The second article referred to other claims that fluoridation caused harm yet nowhere mentioned Yiamouyiannis, Burk, or the National Health Federation in refuting theories that fluoride was a poison, caused birth defects, was mutagenic, caused allergic reactions, caused cancer in animals, and contributed to heart disease. However, the article did state that "every type of misrepresentation known to Disraeli" had "been used to attack fluoridation," referring to the "misleading information" that appeared regularly in a paper called the *National Fluoridation News.* The article concluded that the "simple truth is that there is no 'scientific controversy' over the safety of fluoridation" and that the "survival of this fake controversy represents, in CU's opinion, one of the major triumphs of quackery over science in our generation." Yiamouyiannis's complaint complained of defamation mainly by innuendo. In essence, he read the articles as saying that his work was "grossly and irresponsibly misleading" the American people; that he sold his scientific integrity and objectivity to contrive a deliberately false case against fluoridation; that his work was incompetent "claptrap" and overlooked the fundamental risks factors that elementary principles required; and that he was a man of no credibility or honor.

The author of the *Consumer Reports* articles informed the court that he had investigated the background and qualifications of Yiamouyiannis before the article was published. He also said that he had consulted with the Consumers Union library staff to determine the reliability of supporting references; the technical department; an in-house medical consultant; an outside medical advisor; a dental consultant; a Ph.D. with experience in epidemiology and the safety of water supplies; a psychiatrist who had investigated and written about the National Health Federation; the head of the Environmental Studies Section of the Environmental Epidemiology

Branch of the National Cancer Institute; and a professor of biochemistry of the University of Minnesota.

The court found that Yiamouyiannis was a public figure and that, as a result, he had to prove with convincing clarity that Consumers Union had published the article with actual malice. But, the court said, it was clear that Consumers Union had made a thorough investigation of the facts: scientific writings and authorities had been consulted; and authoritative scientific bodies speaking for substantial segments of the medical and scientific community had been investigated. Indeed, the court stated, the unquestioned methodology of the preparation of the article exemplified the very highest order of responsible journalism: the entire article was checked and rechecked across a spectrum of knowledge and, where necessary, changes had been made in the best interests of accuracy. The court then ruled that neither the article's writer nor the editors at *Consumer Reports* had acted with actual malice and that other portions of the allegedly defamatory matter were protected as statements of opinion; it then concluded that the claim by Yiamouyiannis should be dismissed. (Yiamouyiannis v. Consumers Union of the United States, Inc., 619 F.2d 932 (2d Cir. 1980).)

Product Review Checklist

✓ Product reviews by experts are difficult for manufacturers to challenge because of protections afforded by the First Amendment. This is especially true where the review is prepared by an expert in the area and where the expert proceeds carefully.

✓ The First Amendment requires that a public figure, a term broad enough to include a well-known national company and a well known company in a particular industry (at least with respect to the other participants in the industry), prove that any errors in a review were the result of actual malice. In practice, that is a difficult, if not impossible, standard to meet.

✓ Non-public figures can recover for errors in reviews where they can show that the reviewer was negligent or careless or intended to harm the manufacturer.

✓ Companies may use reviews in their ads, but the ads have to be truthful, fair, and not misleading.

✓ Ads that contain reviews from independent sources should make it clear that the reviewer is not associated with the advertiser.

9

ADVERTISING AND PRIVACY RIGHTS

▌Privacy Rights ▌Look-alikes and the Right of Privacy
▌Sound-alikes and the Right of Publicity
▌Death and the Right of Publicity ▌A Final Word

In a complaint filed almost 100 years ago in a New York courthouse, Abigail M. Roberson alleged that without her permission the Franklin Mills Company and the Rochester Folding Box Company of Rochester, New York, made 25,000 advertising posters using her picture below the slogan Flour of the Family, clearly indicating that the posters were advertising for Franklin Mills's flour. She contended that the posters were displayed in "stores, warehouses, saloons, and other public places" and that her friends and other people recognized her picture. She said that she was greatly humiliated by the scoffs and jeers of people who recognized her face and that her "good name" had been attacked. She became ill and was confined to bed and suffered losses in the amount of $15,000. Roberson asked the court to prohibit Franklin Mills and Rochester Folding Box from continuing to circulate her picture in any form whatsoever and to require that they pay her damages.

The case reached the New York Court of Appeals. The court noted that Roberson had not contended that the portrait was libelous; indeed, the court said, it was "said to be a very good one, and one that her friends and acquaintances were able to recognize." The court understood that Roberson was claiming that her right of privacy had been invaded, but it refused to find that any such right of privacy existed under the law. For one thing, it feared that a "vast field of litigation" would be created if it were to determine that privacy existed as a legal right enforceable in court.

How times have changed. The year after that decision, the New York legislature enacted a statute specifically recognizing a right of privacy. Today, courts across the country also recognize a right of privacy and a somewhat related right—a right of publicity. The development of these rights means, for one thing, that Franklin Mills would lose the suit filed by Roberson if it were decided now; it also means that advertisers and manufacturers must be careful in their ads, product packaging, and related marketing materials to make sure that they do not invade anyone's right of privacy or harm anyone's right of publicity. The best insurance is for advertisers to make sure they have the proper consents and releases or otherwise conform to the general requirements set forth by the courts and in various state statutes.

▌ Privacy Rights

Generally speaking, there now are four kinds of privacy rights accepted by the courts:

- Intrusion upon one's seclusion or solitude
- Public disclosure of embarrassing private facts
- Publicity that places one in a false light
- Appropriation of one's name or likeness for another's advantage.

The first three kinds of the right of privacy generally protect the right to be let alone. These privacy rights stem from the publication of an article in 1890 in the *Harvard Law Review* by Samuel D. Warren and Louis D. Brandeis, who later became a justice of the United States Supreme Court. They urged the legal system to recognize the right of privacy and, to a very large extent, it has done so.

The fourth kind of privacy right, which has come to be known as the right of publicity, protects the interest of celebrities in the commercial exploitation of their identities. It covers the names, likenesses, achievements, and identifying characteristics of celebrities. The theory of the right of publicity is that a celebrity's identity can be valuable in the promotion of products, and the celebrity has an interest that should be protected from the unauthorized commercial exploitation of that identity. As one court has stated, "The famous have an exclusive legal right during life to control and profit from the commercial use of their name and personality."

On occasion in certain states, the right of privacy and the right of publicity is seen as the same thing. For instance, the Civil Rights Law that was adopted in New York after the 1902 Roberson decision provides in section 50 that, "A person, firm or corporation that uses for advertising purposes, or for purposes of trade, the name, portrait or picture of any living person without having first obtained the written consent of such person, is guilty of a misdemeanor." Section 51 of that law now states that, "Any person whose name, portrait or picture is used within the state for advertising purposes or for purposes of trade without the written consent first obtained as above provided may maintain an equitable action in the supreme court of this state against the person, firm or corporation so using his name, portrait or picture, to prevent and restrain the use thereof; and may also sue and recover damages for any injuries sustained by reason of such use and if defendant shall have knowingly used such person's name, portrait or picture in such a manner as is forbidden or declared to be unlawful by the last section, the jury, in its discretion, may award [punitive] damages."

The New York Court of Appeals ruled a decade or so ago that there was no right of publicity in New York but that all such claims stemmed from these two sections of the Civil Rights Law. It stated that any so-called right of publicity was merely a misnomer for the privacy interest protected by the Civil Rights Law as applied to public figures. "By its terms, the statute applies to any use of a person's picture or portrait for advertising or trade purposes whenever the defendant has not obtained the person's written consent to do so." Even given this decision, it is clear that to a large extent the right of publicity of well-known figures or personalities is as protected in New York and across the country as the right of privacy belonging to the unfamous.

There is a tension in the law, though, between the right of publicity and other "rights," such as the First Amendment's protection of free speech. The right of publicity conflicts with the economic and expressive interests of others. It creates a monopoly in an individual (and perhaps in the individual's heirs, as discussed later). Strong policies support the free use of words and ideas that are in general circulation and not protected by a valid copyright, patent, or trademark. As a result, businesses that work within the legal guidelines may be able to engage in advertising or marketing activities at the boundaries of the law that do not invade any person's privacy rights while at the same time maximizing their advertising and marketing efforts.

▌Look-alikes and the Right of Privacy

In the 1980s Christian Dior-New York, Inc. was the corporate entity that controlled advertising and publicity for 35 United States licensees that sold varied lines of merchandise under the coveted Dior label. J. Walter Thompson's Lansdowne Division, in conjunction with noted photographer Richard Avedon, developed a campaign for Dior that involved a series of ads featuring a trio known as the Diors (one female and two males). They were characterized by an article in *Newsweek* as idle rich, suggestively decadent, and aggressively chic. It was suggested that this trio, putatively inspired by Noel Coward, Alfred Lunt and Lynn Fontanne in Coward's 1933 play *Design for Living*, would become the most notorious personalities in advertising since Brooke Shields refused to let anything come between her and her Calvins. To emphasize the impression of the unconventional, the copy for one ad read, "When the Diors got away from it all, they brought with them nothing except 'The Decline of the West' and one toothbrush." Evidently, to stir comment, the relationship portrayed in the ad campaign was meant to be ambiguous. The 16 sequential ads were intended to depict this steadfast trio in varying situations leading to the marriage of two (but not the exclusion of the third), birth of a baby, and their ascent to heaven (subject to resurrection on demand).

Thus, the Diors, and by association their products, would be perceived as chic, sophisticated, elite, unconventional, quirky, audacious, elegant, and unorthodox.

The wedding advertisement was titled "Christian Dior: Sportswear for Women and Clothing for Men." Portrayed in the ad were the happy Dior trio attended by their ostensible intimates, all ecstatically beaming: television personality Gene Shalit; model Shari Belafonte; actress Ruth Gordon; and Barbara Reynolds, a secretary who bore a remarkable resemblance to Jacqueline Kennedy Onassis. The copy, in keeping with the desired attitude of good taste and unconventionality, read: "The wedding of the Diors was everything a wedding should be: no tears, no rice, no in-laws, no smarmy toasts, for once no Mendelssohn. Just a legendary private affair." One of the things that stamped it as "legendary" was the presence of the eclectic group, the most legendary of whom was clearly Onassis, shown discreetly behind Gordon and Shalit, obviously delighted to be in attendance at this event.

That the person behind Gordon and Shalit bore a striking resemblance to Onassis was no mere happenstance. The ad agency and the advertiser knew there was little or no likelihood that Onassis would ever consent to being depicted in this kind of ad campaign for Dior. Indeed, she had never permitted her name or picture to be used in connection with the promotion of commercial products. Her name has been used sparingly only in connection with certain public services, and civic, art, and educational projects that she had supported. Accordingly, Lansdowne and Avedon, once the content of the picture and the make-up of the wedding party had been determined, contacted Ron Smith Celebrity Look-Alikes to provide someone who could pass for Onassis. That agency, which specialized in locating and providing persons who bore a close resemblance to well-known personalities on request (and for a fee), came up with Barbara Reynolds who, with appropriate coiffure and appointments, looked remarkably like Onassis.

The ad was run in September and October 1983, in several upscale publications, including *Esquire, Harper's Bazaar, The New Yorker,* and the *New York Times Magazine.* It received widespread circulation and was the subject of considerable comment, as was the entire ad series. Dior reportedly committed $2.5 million to the campaign and boasted that as a result its sales went through the roof. But Onassis filed suit against Dior, Lansdowne, Avedon, Reynolds, and Ron Smith, seeking an injunction to restrain further use or distribution of the ad on the ground that it violated Sections 50 and 51 of the New York Civil Rights Law. Although the court decision focuses on that law, its analysis is significant because of its broad interpretation of the right of privacy.

The defendants, urging a strict and literal compliance with the law, stated that there was no violation. The court recognized that Onassis's name did not appear in the ad. It then analyzed whether the ad violated the law notwithstanding that it also did not use her actual portrait or picture.

It noted a number of cases in which the statutory term "portrait or picture" had been analyzed. In one case, Pola Negri, the well-known movie actress of the 1920s, objected to the publication of an ad in 1969 showing a scene from one of her early movies with words issuing from her mouth in the balloon caption suggesting the use of the antihistamine drug Pola-ramine. The defendant argued that the picture did not really show Negri as she was then, but the court ruled that so long as the ad portrayed a recognizable likeness it was objectionable. "If a picture so used is a clear and identifiable likeness of a living person, he or she is entitled to recover damages suffered by reason of such use."

In another case, the portrait or picture complained of was not an actual photo but a composite photo-drawing depicting a naked black man in a boxing ring with the recognizable facial features of Muhammad Ali, the former world heavyweight boxing champion. The court ruled that the phrase "portrait or picture" as used in the New York Civil Rights Law was not restricted to actual photographs but comprised any representation that was recognizable as a likeness of the complaining individual.

The principle the court in the Onassis case distilled from the New York Civil Rights Law and the various cases construing its provisions was that "all persons, of whatever station in life, from the relatively unknown to the world famous, are to be secured against rapacious commercial exploitation." The statute, the court said, was intended to protect "the essence of the person, his or her identity or persona from being unwillingly or unknowingly misappropriated for the profit of another." It said that Shakespeare may not have been aware of advertising techniques, media hard-sell, or personal endorsements for product promotion, but that the words he put in Iago's mouth in *Othello* were right on target:

Good name in man or woman, dear my lord,

Is the immediate jewel of their souls;

Who steals my purse steals trash; 'tis something, nothing;

'Twas mine, 'tis his, and has been slave to thousands;

But he that filches from me my good name

Robs me of that which not enriches him,

And makes me poor indeed.

It then ruled that the essence of what was prohibited by the law was the exploitation of one's identity. To permit an "illusionist" to act in this manner, in the court's view, would be sanctioning an obvious loophole to the statute. "If we truly value the right of privacy in a world of exploitation, where every mark of distinctiveness becomes grist for the mills of publicity, then we must give it more than lip service and grudging recognition." It said that Barbara Reynolds could capitalize on her striking resemblance to Onassis at parties, in television appearances, and in dramatic works but not in commercial advertisements. Similarly, Ron Smith could market its clients for fun and profit in various areas but could not capitalize on natural resemblance to a well-known person for trade or advertisement. It concluded "Let the word go forth—there is no free ride. The commercial hitchhiker seeking to travel on the fame of another will have to learn to pay the fare or stand on his own two feet."

∎ Sound-alikes and the Right of Publicity

A different issue arose from a 1985 ad campaign entitled The Yuppie Campaign that was prepared by the advertising agency of Young & Rubicam, Inc. for the Ford Motor Company. The aim was to make an emotional connection with yuppies, bringing back memories of when they were in college. Different popular songs of the 1970s were sung on each commercial. The agency tried to get the singers who had popularized the songs to sing them. But failing in that endeavor in 10 cases, the agency had the songs sung by "sound-alikes." One of the sound-alikes was for actress/singer Bette Midler, who filed suit.

Midler won a Grammy in 1973 as the Best New Artist of that year. Records she made since that time have gone Platinum and Gold. She was nominated in 1979 for an Academy Award for Best Female Actress in the movie *The Rose,* in which she portrayed a pop singer. She has been described as an "outrageously original singer/comedian," a "legend," and "the most dynamic and poignant singer-actress of her time."

When Young & Rubicam was preparing the Yuppie Campaign it presented the commercial to Ford by playing an edited version of Midler singing "Do You Want to Dance," taken from the 1973 Midler album, *The Divine Miss M.* After Ford accepted the idea and the form of the commercial, the agency contacted Midler's manager. The conversation apparently went as follows:

> *"Hello, I am Craig Hazen from Young & Rubicam. I am calling you to find out if Bette Midler would be interested in doing . . . ."*
>
> *"Is it a commercial?"*
>
> *"Yes."*
>
> *"We are not interested."*

Undeterred, Young & Rubicam sought out Ula Hedwig, whom it knew to have been a backup singer for Midler for 10 years. Hedwig was told by Young & Rubicam that it wanted someone who could sound like Bette Midler. She was asked to make a "demo" tape of the song if she was interested. She made an a capella demo, got the job, and sang the song for the commercial, imitating Midler to the best of her ability.

After the commercial was aired, Midler claimed that she was told by "a number of people" that it "sounded exactly" like her record of "Do You Want to Dance." Hedwig was told by "many personal friends" that they thought it was Midler singing the commercial. But neither Midler's name nor picture was used in the commercial and Young & Rubicam had a license from the copyright holder to use the song. The issue in Midler's lawsuit came down to whether the law prohibited imitation of Midler's voice.

The First Amendment protects much of what the media do in the reproduction of likenesses or sounds, the U.S. Court of Appeals for the Ninth Circuit recognized. But, the court said, the purpose of the media's use of a person's identity is central. If the purpose is "informative or cultural," the use is permitted; "if it serves no such function but merely exploits the individual portrayed, immunity will not be granted." Moreover, the court stated, federal copyright law preempts much of the area.

The court noted that Nancy Sinatra had once sued the Goodyear Tire and Rubber Company on the basis of an advertising campaign by Young & Rubicam featuring "These Boots Are Made for Walkin'," a song closely identified with her; the female singers of the commercial were alleged to have imitated her voice and style and to have dressed and looked like her. The basis of Sinatra's complaint was unfair competition; she claimed that the song and the arrangement had acquired "a secondary meaning" that, under California law, was protectable. The court that decided the case noted that Goodyear and Young & Rubicam had paid a "very substantial sum to the copyright proprietor to obtain the license for the use of the song and all of its arrangements." To give Sinatra damages for their use of the song would clash with federal copyright law and her case was dismissed.

The court in Midler's case said that if she were claiming a secondary meaning to "Do You Want to Dance" or seeking to prevent the defendants from using that song she would fail like Sinatra. But she was arguing something else. The ad used an imitation to convey the impression that Midler was singing, much like the Onassis court found that the look-alike was an imitation intended to convey the impression that Jacqueline Onassis was at the wedding of the Diors.

Why did the defendants ask Midler to sing if her voice was not of value to them? Why did they studiously acquire the services of a sound-alike and instruct her to imitate Midler if Midler's voice was not of value to them? What they sought, the court said, was an attribute of Midler's identity. Its value was what the market would have paid for Midler to have sung the commercial in person. To impersonate a singer's voice was "to pirate her identity."

The court did not decide that every imitation of a voice to advertise merchandise could be prohibited. It said only that when a distinctive voice of a professional singer was widely known and was deliberately imitated to sell a product, the sellers appropriated what was not theirs.

▌Death and the Right of Publicity

Just how long does the right of publicity continue? As one judge has said, if it continues after death, may the descendants of George Washington sue the secretary of the treasury for placing his likeness on the dollar bill? May the descendants of Abraham Lincoln obtain damages for the commercial exploitation of his name and likeness by the Lincoln National Life Insurance Company or the Lincoln Division of the Ford Motor Company? May the descendants of James and Dolly Madison recover for the commercialization of Dolly Madison confections? For this and other reasons, many of the courts that have decided the issue have ruled that the right of publicity dies with the celebrity.

For instance, a fight that professional boxer Jimmy Reeves had against Jake Lamotta in the old Cleveland Arena on September 24, 1941 was recreated and included immediately after the opening scenes of the motion picture *Raging Bull,* a biographical account of the life of boxer Jake Lamotta, who was portrayed by Robert DeNiro. The dramatized fight scene comprised approximately two minutes of the movie, which was produced by United Artists Corporation.

Louise Reeves, the widow of Jimmy Reeves, filed suit in Ohio against United Artists and several others for appropriating the name, identity, likeness, character, ability, achievement, and performance of Reeves. The trial court found that Ohio recognized the right of publicity but that it is not descendible after the person's death because it is a personal right.

The California Supreme Court issued a similar ruling in a case brought by the widow and surviving son of the movie actor Bela Lugosi, who played the title role in the 1930 film *Dracula,* seeking to recover profits made by Universal Pictures from its licensing of the use of the Count Dracula character. The court decided that the right to exploit a name and likeness was personal to an artist and must be exercised, if at all, by the artist during the artist's lifetime.

That California decision led the California legislature to pass a law on this subject in 1984. It prohibits any person from using a deceased personality's name, voice, signature, photograph, or likeness, in any manner, on or in products, merchandise, or goods, or for purposes of advertising or selling, or soliciting purchases of products, merchandise, goods, or services, without prior consent from someone designated by the personality. Deceased personality is defined to mean any person whose name, voice, signature, photograph, or likeness had commercial value at the time of his or her death, whether or not during the lifetime of that person the person used his or her name, voice, signature, photograph, or likeness on or in products, merchandise, or goods, or for purposes of advertising or selling, or the like. The statute states that it does not apply to the use of a deceased personality's name, voice, signature, photograph, or likeness in a play, book, magazine, newspaper, or similar product; for political or newsworthy purposes; in single and original works of art; or in ads for any of these other excepted purposes. Texas and other states have similar laws.

▌A Final Word

Today it is commonplace for individuals to promote or advertise commercial services and products or to have their identities infused in the products. Individuals prominent in athletics, business, entertainment, and the arts are frequently involved in such enterprises. Courts recognize that an unauthorized commercial appropriation of a person's identity converts the potential economic value in that identity to another's advantage. Advertisers must be careful either to obtain permission or to make sure that they comply with the applicable legal rules—and for a national campaign, those rules may involve the laws from New York and California and all of the states in between.

PRIVATE LIVES IN FIVE PUBLIC CASES

The irony when people file lawsuits alleging interference with their right of privacy is that there may be nothing in the United States more public than litigation—court records, hearings, and proceedings traditionally are open to the public and to the media; some jurisdictions now even allow television cameras. There may be more logic to suits involving claims of interference with a right of publicity—if that kind of suit has a result favorable to the celebrity, the celebrity's value may increase. Here is a brief discussion of five actual cases that may help to throw light on right of privacy and right of publicity issues and the question of what advertisers are and are not permitted to do in this regard.

1. From the time Johnny Carson began hosting "The Tonight Show" in 1962, he was introduced on the show each evening with the phrase "Here's Johnny." Indeed, a substantial segment of the television viewing public associated Carson with that phrase. (It is not at all clear that his retirement from "The Tonight Show" will change that fact.) In 1967 Carson first authorized use of this phrase by an outside business venture, permitting it to be used by a chain of restaurants called Here's Johnny Restaurants. Several years ago, though, a Michigan company engaged in the business of renting and selling portable toilets called itself Here's Johnny Portable Toilets, Inc., called its product "Here's Johnny" portable toilets, and used the motto The World's Foremost Commodian to promote its product. Carson filed suit alleging, among other things, invasion of his privacy and publicity rights.

The U.S. Court of Appeals for the Sixth Circuit decided that Carson's right of privacy was not violated. Apparently, the gist of his claim was that Carson was embarrassed by and considered it odious to be associated with the portable toilet. Clearly, the court said, the association did not appeal to Carson's sense of humor. But the court did not issue its decision on this basis, preferring to analyze the right of publicity issue. It found that Carson's identity was exploited and his right of publicity invaded, even though neither his name nor his picture were used. (Indeed, it said that there would have been no violation of Carson's right of publicity if the manufacturer had called its product the "John William Carson Portable Toilet" because even though literally using Carson's name it would not have appropriated Carson's identity as a celebrity.) Over the objection of one dissenting judge who argued that the right of publicity should not extend to phrases or other things that are "merely associated" with a celebrity, the court ruled that the company had appropriated Carson's identity in connection with its corporate name and its product without Carson's permission. (Carson v. Here's Johnny Portable Toilets, Inc., 698 F.2d 831 (6th Cir. 1983).)

2. Several years ago, National Video, Inc. placed an ad to promote its nationally franchised video rental chain that contained a photograph of Phil Boroff, who looked remarkably like actor and filmmaker Woody Allen. The photograph portrayed a customer in a National Video store with physical features and a pose characteristic of Allen. The staging of the photograph also evoked associations with Allen. Sitting on the counter were videotape cassettes of *Annie Hall* and *Bananas,* two of Allen's best known films, as well as *Casablanca* and *The Maltese Falcon.* The latter two Humphrey Bogart films were associated with Allen and his film *Play*

It Again, Sam, in which the spirit of Bogart appeared to the character played by Allen and offered him romantic advice. The individual in the ad held a National Video V.I.P. card, which apparently entitled the bearer to favorable terms on movie rentals. The woman behind the counter was smiling at the customer and appeared to be gasping in exaggerated excitement at the presence of a celebrity. The headline on the ad was "Become a V.I.P. at National Video. We'll Make You Feel Like a Star."

The court that issued a decision in this case sidestepped the issue of whether Allen's privacy rights had been violated, finding it was not necessary to determine whether a photograph of a look-alike was a "portrait or picture" of Allen for purposes of the New York Civil Rights Law, under which Allen had filed suit. The court decided, though, that the ad created the likelihood of consumer confusion over whether Allen endorsed or was otherwise involved with National Video's goods and services and that it therefore violated the federal Lanham Act. Any disclaimer that National Video might use, the court said, would have to boldly make it clear that Allen did not endorse National, its products, or its services. National also could make those facts clear in the staging of the photograph or in the accompanying advertising copy, the court concluded. (Allen v. National Video, Inc., 610 F.Supp. 612 (S.D.N.Y. 1985).)

3. On the July 4th weekend in 1977, while visiting friends in Woodstock, New York, Susan Cohen and her four-year-old daughter Samantha went bathing in a stream located on their friends' private property. Without their consent, James Krieger took photographs of Cohen and her daughter and subsequently sold them to Herbal Concepts, Inc., a seller and advertiser of consumer products. Herbal Concepts used one of the photographs in an advertisement for Au Naturel, a product designed to help women eliminate body cellulite, those "fatty lumps and bumps that won't go away." The advertisement appeared in two editions of *House and Garden* and in single editions of *House Beautiful* and *Cosmopolitan.* Ira Cohen subsequently recognized his wife and daughter in the advertisements while reading one of the magazines; the Cohens then filed suit.

The case reached New York's highest court which noted that for the Cohens to win their suit they had to show that the people in the photograph were capable of being identified from the ad alone. The court said that the picture depicted two nude persons, a woman and a child, standing in water a few inches deep. It said the picture quality was good and that there were no obstructions to block the view of the subjects. The woman was carrying a small unidentified object in her left hand and was leading the child with her right hand. Neither person's face was visible but the backs and right sides of both mother and child were clearly presented and the mother's right breast could be seen. The identifying features of the subjects included their hair, bone structure, body contours, and posture. Considering these factors, the court concluded, someone familiar with the people in the photograph could identify them by looking at the ad. It permitted the Cohens' lawsuit to proceed to trial. (Cohen v. Herbal Concepts, Inc., 63 N.Y.2d 379 (1984).)

4. After Chemical Bank took photographs and motion pictures of employees in the bank's electronic customer services department, the bank began to use them for advertising purposes. One of the employees filed suit on behalf of himself and the other employees alleging that the bank used the photographs and motion pictures in advertising without the employees' written consent as required by the New York Civil Rights Law. The bank countered that it had the employees oral and implied consent but New York State's highest court ruled that written consent was required by the statute; it said that partial judgment as to liability was properly granted to the employees. (Caesar v. Chemical Bank, 66 N.Y.2d 698 (1985).)

5. When Agnes Bayer asked a friend, Jay Benton, to care for the registered Appaloosa horse she owned, she allowed him to take her horse to a nearby ranch. While visiting the ranch, Ed Smyth, an employee of the Ralston Purina Company, took a photograph of the horse and of Benton while the horse was being unsaddled. Smyth obtained a release from Benton, who told Smyth that he was the trainer and part owner of the horse. Smyth did not attempt to discover the other owner. No release was obtained from Bayer. The photograph was used in Ralston Purina's advertising and Bayer filed suit. A jury awarded Bayer $5,000 for the use of the photograph in the ad without her permission and the case reached the Supreme Court of Missouri. That court ruled that a person's privacy is not violated when a picture of something that the person owns is published if nothing indicates who the owner is. It then ruled that the case should be dismissed. (Bayer v. Ralston Purina Co., 484 S.W.2d 473 (Sup. Ct. Missouri 1972).)

Privacy Checklist

✓ The right of privacy and the right of publicity are now generally recognized in the United States.

✓ Properly drafted consents can go a long way toward avoiding invasion of privacy lawsuits.

✓ The right of publicity affords celebrities and well-known personalities the ability to exploit their own commercial value.

✓ Sound-alikes and look-alikes often present courts with difficult legal questions; but if it appears that an advertiser is getting a free ride, courts are likely to prohibit them.

✓ Dead celebrities cannot easily file a lawsuit—but their representatives can. If a state statute prohibits use of the personality of a dead celebrity, an advertiser should be careful about breaching that rule.

AN ADVERTISER'S LIABILITY FOR ADVERTISING COSTS

■ Agency Rules ■ Television and Radio Ads ■ Print Ads
■ A Final Word

In the first few months of 1982 Creative Media Services, Inc., an ad agency working on behalf of Citytrust Bank, which primarily operated in the Bridgeport, Connecticut area, placed several ads in small daily and weekly newspapers published by the Housatonic Valley Publishing Company. Citytrust created its own ads and used Creative Media to buy space and place them. Housatonic billed Creative Media, and Creative Media in turn billed the bank. Citytrust paid Creative Media $1,500 per month for its services, plus the costs of placing ads.

Housatonic carried the account under the name of Citytrust c/o Creative Media and used Creative Media's address. Housatonic performed no credit check on Citytrust or Creative Media.

When the account became delinquent, the publisher called the bank. The publisher spoke to Nancy Horton, who had previously worked for Creative Media but who then had an office on the bank's property and was doing the same job for the bank that Creative Media had done previously. Citytrust and Horton had arrived at their relationship after Horton had been laid off by Creative Media in March 1982 when it seemed that Creative Media might be having financial difficulties. Failing to receive payment, and after Creative Media went bankrupt, Housatonic filed suit against the bank even though the bank had already paid Creative Media for the cost of the newspaper advertisements.

The trial court ruled in favor of the publisher, finding that because an agency relationship existed between Creative Media and the bank, the bank was liable to the publisher for the cost of the ads—even though the bank had already paid the ad agency for the ads. An appellate court reversed that decision, though, on rather narrow (and rather questionable) grounds (finding that Creative Media was not the bank's agent). Nonetheless, the appellate court decision freed the bank from its obligation to pay twice for something it had received once.

▌Agency Rules

Advertising agencies developed before radio and television. In those days they bought space in newspapers and magazines as principals. They resold the space to advertisers, but if they failed to resell the space the advertising agencies were still liable for it. To make sale of the space easier, the early agencies employed writers to produce advertising copy that could be shown to the space prospects; that was the beginning of the present-day advertising agency.

In those beginning days, the publishers of newspapers and magazines looked to the credit of the advertising agencies and not to that of the advertisers; the publishers did not deal with the advertisers but only with the agencies.

The advent of radio did not change this. Agencies bought time on radio as principals and on their own credit.

When television came, the situation again did not change at first. The television networks accepted the concept that the agencies were solely liable for advertising time purchased, the same concept early adopted and promoted by the agencies themselves.

Since as far back as 1930, the trade association for advertising agencies, known as the American Association of Advertising Agencies (AAAA) and often called the four A's, had a form of contract for advertising between agency and the media that provided that the agency would be solely liable for advertising purchased, and that the advertiser would not be liable. The AAAA and the larger agencies believed in this position, believed it was correct also as a matter of law, and promoted it actively in booklets, speeches, and the like.

The agencies' position that the advertiser was not liable to the media was in part based on selfish reasons. The agencies wanted no direct dealings between advertisers and the media, fearing that could lead to elimination of the agencies. Thus, the custom and usage developed whereby the media sent their invoices only to the agencies, the agencies paid the media, and the agencies (rather than the media) collected from the advertisers. This increased the cash flow through the agencies and, they believed, helped them to improve their standing with their lenders. Thus, the agencies did not want the system changed to one where the advertisers paid directly to the media. Moreover, as they explained their position to advertisers they made it easier to collect from advertisers—the advertisers were often assured that there was no possibility of paying twice, once to the agency and later to the media.

Ad agencies traditionally have been compensated by commissions, usually of 15 percent, paid by the media. Thus, if a newspaper ad cost $1,000, an advertiser would pay the agency $1,000 and the agency would forward $850 to the newspaper. (In certain cases, agencies are paid other fees or compensated in different ways.)

For more than 60 years, the standard agreement prepared by the AAAA has provided that agencies are "solely liable" for the cost of advertising. Recognizing this, media traditionally have investigated the creditworthiness of ad agencies—not the advertisers themselves.

But in the early 1970s, a number of ad agencies failed and entered bankruptcy. In addition, as the volume of television advertising increased, and the money involved as well, the networks became concerned that the advertisers be liable ultimately for the advertising time bought for them. In the case of big advertisers, their financial responsibility was much greater than that of the agencies. The placement contracts prepared by the media were then revised to provide that ad agencies and/or their advertisers could be liable for payment. Indeed, the AAAA form dropped the sole liability provision. Sometimes, though, agencies failed to sign these contracts because they did not want to compromise their position that their advertiser clients were not liable to the media.

Generally speaking, the media did not alert advertisers to their changed view—primarily because they had no dealings with the advertisers and knew that the larger agencies, at least, asserted that they were solely liable and had informed advertisers that they would not be liable to the media. The reason for the media's actions (or non-actions) were rather clear—they wanted to be able in an emergency to assert their legal position that the advertiser was liable on the contract, but at the same time they wanted to retain the goodwill of advertising agencies, which placed the majority of the advertising, and did not want to antagonize them by informing their clients of their new legal views.

Today there are two issues that courts analyze to determine who may be held liable for unpaid advertising costs. First, they look to the terms of the particular contract to determine whether it allocates liability. If not, they analyze the question under general principles of agency law.

An agent is someone who acts on behalf of another party and is subject to that party's control. Most courts that have analyzed the subject have found that an ad agency is an advertiser's agent, and not the media's agent or the agent for both the advertiser and the media. Generally speaking, if the media in that case know that an ad agency is acting for a particular advertiser, the ad agency is said to be acting for a fully disclosed principal and the ad agency may not be deemed solely liable for advertising costs. If the media know only that the agency is acting for a principal but does not know the full identity of the principal (a rather uncommon advertising situation) the ad agency and the principal both may be held liable for advertising costs.

What happens if an ad agency fails to pay the media? Can the media hold the advertiser liable? If the advertiser already paid the ad agency but the agency did not forward payment, perhaps because it entered bankruptcy, can the advertiser be required to pay twice for the same ad—once to the ad agency and once to the media? What if an advertiser wants to negotiate a different fee arrangement with its ad agency? In other words, who is liable for advertising costs?

▍Television and Radio Ads

The leading court decisions in this area were issued by the federal district court for the Southern District of New York and the U.S. Court of Appeals for the Second Circuit in a case stemming from the failure of the Lennen & Newell, Inc. advertising agency in the early 1970s. The CBS television network filed suit against Stokely-Van Camp, Inc., seeking payment for advertising placed by Lennen for which Stokely had paid Lennen but for which Lennen had not paid CBS. The question was whether Stokely or CBS should shoulder the loss.

For more than 17 years, Lennen, a full-service advertising agency, had handled Stokely's account on the basis of an unwritten arrangement. On behalf of Stokely, Lennen would produce television commercials, with Stokely's approval, pursuant to an advertising budget approved by Stokely. Lennen gave Stokely advertising advice and made the arrangements for the advertising. Stokely did not know what contracts, if any, Lennen made with the media but did know that Lennen was being paid by means of a 15 percent commission based on the gross amount of the invoices. Stokely never asked for or received copies of the agency-media contracts and simply paid Lennen on its invoices.

CBS sold time for Stokely commercials both on its network under so-called network agreements and on five specific CBS stations under a series of 13 specific contracts. Lennen prepared and sent Stokely schedules containing the station, date, program, and time for each Stokely commercial to be shown during a three-month period on network television, and also advised Stokely of the station, date, and time for each Stokely commercial to be shown locally by the CBS television stations. Under both the network agreements and station contracts CBS billed Lennen for the cost of the advertising time less 15 percent. CBS never billed Stokely directly. The bills to Stokely from Lennen were for 100 percent of the cost of the advertising, so that upon Stokely's payment Lennen would receive its 15 percent commission.

The first network television agreement that CBS sent to Lennen but that Lennen never signed and returned specifically referred to Lennen as "acting as agent for Stokely-van Camp, Inc." Among other things, it stated that "Agency and Advertiser will indemnify and hold harmless CBS and any stations" from and against various claims arising out of the broadcast of the "Agency Package." The second network contract also was not signed, although the court found that Lennen's actions in forwarding commercials to CBS constituted its acceptance of the terms.

The station contracts signed by CBS and Lennen were on a standardized form styled "CBS Television Stations National Sales Schedule Agreement." Each referred to Lennen as agent for Stokely and each was signed by Lennen "As Agent for Stokely-Van Camp, Inc." They contained the following provision:

> CBS shall bill Advertiser via Agency monthly or weekly whenever CBS shall so elect, for the charges due hereunder for such period. Advertiser shall pay CBS, in accordance with such billing, within ten calendar days after receipt thereof. Any failure whatsoever by Advertiser to make timely payment charges under this Agreement or any other breach whatsoever by Advertiser or Agency of this Agreement shall give CBS the right in addition to its other rights, to cease performance of this Agreement.

From sometime in August or September 1970, CBS knew that Lennen was in financial difficulty, was being paid by Stokely for its television advertising but was not using the payments to discharge its obligations to CBS, and was behind in settling invoices of CBS. Apparently because CBS wanted Lennen to survive and to retain its goodwill, CBS did not notify the advertisers who might otherwise have withdrawn their accounts from Lennen. In addition, when CBS and other creditors agreed that payments due from Lennen on or before October 31, 1971, could be deferred on condition that payments due after that date would be "on a current basis," CBS did not advise Stokely.

The court ruled in favor of Stokely. It found no evidence that advertising agencies generally executed contracts binding their clients. Indeed, it said, the evidence was to the contrary. The court noted that after CBS had revised its contracts to attempt to impose liability on advertisers by language in a contract form that it sent only to agencies, the agencies generally declined to sign the contracts because they were inconsistent with the position that the agencies were solely liable to CBS and to the other networks. "The evidence establishes that CBS did not believe, and could not reasonably have believed, that Lennen was authorized to bind Stokely," the court concluded. Although Lennen was an advertising "agency," the court found that it had no actual or apparent authority from Stokely to bind Stokely to the media and, therefore, no agency relationship existed for that purpose under the law.

▍ Print Ads

A bankruptcy court reached a different conclusion in a print media case.

In 1972, Astra Pharmaceutical Products, Inc. engaged the advertising agency of Dean L. Burdick Associates, Inc., pursuant to an oral agreement, as its ad agency to promote Astra's pharmaceutical products. In 1975 they signed a written agreement similar to that of their oral agreement.

Burdick worked on a noncommission basis and received, instead, payment from Astra on a time billing basis. During March and April 1975, Burdick billed Astra $35,156.67 in time charges that Astra did not pay.

In May 1975, Burdick entered bankruptcy. Astra ceased doing business with Burdick and began removing all of its material from Burdick's offices. Around that same time, various media representatives contacted Astra directly and claimed that Burdick had not paid them for work done on the Astra account. After apparently denying liability, Astra paid the media $19,988.67.

In addition, Astra received invoices from Burdick for print production costs that Burdick had allegedly incurred in March 1975. Astra paid $12,559.48 directly to the suppliers on account because the bills had not been paid by Burdick and Astra believed it was primarily liable to the suppliers. The Burdick trustee contended, however, that Astra was not contractually liable to pay the costs to the suppliers and that the costs should have been submitted by the creditors as creditor claims against Burdick's estate; therefore, the trustee concluded, Astra still owed that amount to Burdick.

Astra filed a claim against Burdick, and the Burdick trustee counterclaimed, seeking payment of the March and April 1975 bills. Astra alleged that the total amount it had paid to the media it also had paid to Burdick for the express purpose of meeting those obligations, and because Burdick never used that money to pay those debts Astra contended that it was entitled to offset that amount from the amount it owed to Burdick.

Astra and the Burdick trustee agreed that Astra was entitled to a $10,000 setoff. Astra concluded that it was obligated to pay Burdick only an additional $5,168. It calculated that it was obligated for the $35,156.67 in time charges for March and April less $10,000 for the agreed setoff, less $19,988.67 for the media costs that Astra paid twice, and that it had no further obligation for the production costs of $12,559.48 that Astra paid directly to the suppliers.

The trustee concluded that Astra owed $37,756.15, amounting to $35,156.67 for time charges plus $12,559.48 for production costs, less $10,000 for the agreed setoff, plus interest.

The trustee argued that the Stokely case was the guiding case but the court disagreed. It noted that the Stokely case dealt solely with television and radio advertising but that the Astra case dealt with print media. It said the law in New York was that a print publication was entitled to assume that an advertising agency was seeking space on behalf of its principal and could look to the advertiser for outstanding obligations incurred by the advertising agency.

The court noted that Astra and Burdick had not been engaged in a typical advertiser/advertising agency relationship. Typically, it said, an advertising agency was paid on a commission basis but Burdick did not receive commissions; rather, it billed time charges to Astra. The court also said that in the Stokely case, the advertising agency was a full-service advertising agency and Stokely had no knowledge of the contracts made by the agency. Conversely, it found that Burdick was a small specialized agency and not only did Astra know with whom Burdick had contracted, but the written agreement between Burdick and Astra specified that the work done by Burdick had to be authorized by Astra.

Finding that a principal-agent relationship did exist between Astra and Burdick, the court ruled that Astra had been obligated to pay the debts incurred on its behalf by Burdick. It therefore ruled in favor of Astra's calculation and rejected the trustee's claims.

▌ A Final Word

The cases, as few as they are, are in disarray. What's an advertiser to do?

The first thing is to make sure or attempt to make sure to work with financially stable ad agencies.

Second, to the greatest extent possible, advertisers should try to document that their ad agencies are solely liable for advertising costs.

If the issue is not resolved in advance and, because of an ad agency's bankruptcy or fraud, becomes something that has to be resolved, advertisers could litigate it. Even if they win, though, they will have incurred litigation costs. And the possibility remains that they may lose.

FIVE AD AGENCY SUITS

1. After the advertising agency used by Goozh Gifts, Inc. to purchase time on radio station WOL went bankrupt, the station demanded payment from Goozh; when Goozh failed to pay, the station filed suit. Testimony at trial indicated that the agency brought the Goozh account to WOL; that all the station's dealings were with the agency and none were with Goozh directly; and that there was no formal contract between them but simply an understanding under which the station sent all bills to the agency. The president of WOL testified that he had relied on Goozh's credit, but admitted that he had never investigated Goozh directly. He also admitted that the agency had been an accredited agency at the time the account was placed and that one of the factors of such accreditation was the agency's financial responsibility. The head of the agency testified that under his arrangement the agency was to be solely responsible for the cost of advertising it placed and that the advertising media knew very little about the accounts the agency placed with them because "they are doing business with us." He also said that Goozh did not pay anything for the agency's services but that its compensation came from WOL by way of a commission or discount of 15 percent of the gross advertising charge. The court that issued a decision on the station's suit stated that "the surest criterion of liability is to be found in the intention of the parties. Granting that [the agency] was authorized to place advertising for Goozh, there was no evidence whatever of any intention that Goozh was to be liable to WOL." Indeed, the court said, "It seems to have been established that WOL never intended to hold Goozh [liable], but relied on [the agency] as its direct contracting party." The court concluded that Goozh was entitled to prevail in the suit. (Washington Broadcasting Co. v. Goozh Gifts, Inc., 118 A.2d 392 (Mun. Ct. App. D.C. 1955).)

2. In the spring of 1978, the Climate Control Corporation, a distributor for a national air conditioning firm, decided to run commercials on local Chicago television stations. Because it understood that media representatives would not deal directly with advertisers, so that it could not purchase air time itself, Climate Control secured the services of an advertising agency, Sander Rodkin/Hechtman/Glantz Advertising, Ltd. Sander Rodkin recommended both the ABC and CBS stations and June and July 1978 dates for running the commercials. Sander Rodkin never discussed the terms of the billings with Climate Control except to say that Sander Rodkin would bill Climate Control, pay the media, and receive a commission from the media. Sander Rodkin told Climate Control that that was standard procedure in the advertising industry.

Unfortunately, Sander Rodkin was in financial distress. Although it received full payment from Climate Control promptly after each billing, it was slow in honoring its billings from ABC television affiliate WLS-TV. Moreover, it did not designate the checks it did remit to WLS-TV to reflect that they should be applied to the invoices covering Climate Control commercials—some checks designated other accounts, while others bore no designation at all. When Sander Rodkin failed on April 13, 1979, WLS-TV's accounts showed $13,175 still unpaid for television air time used for Climate Control commercials. From Climate Control's point of view, however, it had paid for the time in full—it made a final payment of $15,000, designated as payment for WLS-TV air time, to Sander Rodkin on August 28, 1978. Climate Control did not learn from WLS-TV until December 1979 that it considered it liable for the unpaid balance; on its refusal to pay, WLS-TV filed suit. The court stated that the key issue was whether Sander Rodkin was an agent for Climate Control with the power to bind it to a contract to pay for the purchase of advertising time. Finding many issues of fact that needed to be resolved, the court ordered a trial on that question. (American Broadcasting Companies, Inc. v. Climate Control Corp., 524 F. Supp. 1014 (N.D. Illinois 1981).)

3. For some time, the Tire Supply Corporation of Long Island had placed advertisements in the *Pennysaver* newspaper. Beginning in May 1967, ads for Tire Supply were placed by the Palmer, Wilson and Worden advertising agency. These ads were placed with the *Pennysaver* by insert orders on Palmer Wilson's letterhead. A description of the ad was on the front of the orders and certain terms and conditions appeared on the back. They provided that Palmer Wilson was to be solely responsible for payment and all invoices were to be sent to Palmer Wilson. The *Pennysaver* ran the ads and sent invoices to Palmer Wilson. Tire Supply paid Palmer Wilson for advertisements but, when Palmer Wilson did not pay the *Pennysaver*, the publisher filed suit. Emphasizing that the insertion orders sent by Palmer Wilson to the *Pennysaver* provided that all invoices were to be sent to the agency, which would be solely responsible for payment, the court ruled that the *Pennysaver* could not hold Tire Supply liable. (Huntington Pennysaver, Inc. v. Tire Supply Corp., 298 N.Y.S.2d 824 (D.Ct. Suffolk Co. 1969).)

4. After the ad agency Glynn-Palmer Associates, Inc. failed to pay a bill from the *New York Times* for an ad it prepared for its client, Worldwide S.O.S., the newspaper sued the agency. The agency contended that the *Times* knew that it was acting for Worldwide and therefore Worldwide, not the agency, should be liable for the cost of the advertisement. The *Times*, to the contrary, contended that it only dealt with the agency and that it had no knowledge of its client's creditworthiness, and, according to the custom and usage in the industry, the agent should be liable. The court said that the *Times* was aware that the Worldwide ad was not for Glynn-Palmer because Worldwide's name appeared on the insertion order and on the *Times* bill. It found that the paper had not introduced sufficient proof about any industry custom "by which advertising agents implicitly agree to be liable for the cost of advertisements placed for their clients." The court then ruled that the *Times* had failed to prove that the agency should be held liable for the cost of the ad, and it dismissed the lawsuit. (The New York Times Co. v. Glynn-Palmer Associates, Inc., 525 N.Y.S.2d 565 (Civ. Ct. N.Y. Co. 1988).)

5. In late 1979 and early 1980, Scott, Lancaster, Mills & Atha, Inc., an advertising agency, ordered air time from several television stations on behalf of its client advertiser, National Service Corporation. After the TV spots had run, Scott Lancaster denied that it was liable for payment on behalf of National Service, which had declared bankruptcy. The TV stations filed suit against the ad agency to collect on the delinquent accounts. The ad agency contended that it was not liable to the stations because the stations knew that the ads were for National Service. The court found that independent television stations customarily looked to advertising agencies for payment of air time, absent other prior arrangements. Determining that the agency new of that custom, it concluded that the TV stations could hold the agency liable for unpaid advertising costs. (Midwest Television, Inc. v. Scott, Lancaster, Mills & Atha, Inc., 252 Cal.Rptr 573 (Cal.App. 1988).)

Payment Checklist

✓ Although ad agencies may have been "solely liable" for advertising costs in the past, that may no longer be the case.

✓ Today, the media is quite likely to want to hold ad agencies—and advertisers—liable for unpaid advertising costs.

✓ Courts will examine contracts to determine the parties' intent and, if those agreements are not clear, they will look to industry customs.

✓ To limit their financial exposure, advertisers should examine the financial stability of their ad agencies and make sure to work only with ad agencies that are in good financial condition.

✓ In addition, advertisers should try to include provisions in their contracts with their ad agencies (and perhaps with the media) that state that the ad agencies are solely liable for advertising costs.

SALESPEOPLE AND OTHER EMPLOYEES

11

THE LEGAL SIDE OF HIRING

▌Oral Versus Written Agreements ▌Statute of Frauds
▌What to Cover in a Contract
▌Independent Contractor or Employee?
▌Negligent Hiring and Retention ▌A Final Word

Many years ago, when the Allied Insulation Company, Inc., decided that it needed to hire additional salespeople, it placed an ad in a daily newspaper in Baton Rouge, Louisiana, that stated:

OPPORTUNITY KNOCKS

WE WANT enthusiastic, ambitious men to represent us locally. Professional training program w/$450.00 monthly guarantee if qualified. Enthusiasm and ambition quickly rewarded with advancement. Be in the four figure bracket. For appointment call Mr. Johnson, 357-9756 before 1 P.M. daily.

In response to the ad, Bobby Willis went to Allied's office, completed an employment application, and was hired as a salesperson beginning February 24, 1964. He asked a young man in the office when he applied for the position whether he would receive the minimum guaranteed wage of $450.00 per month and was told, "I guess so." Willis then began to work and received commissions for the first month in the amount of $171.84. After he worked for about two weeks during the month of April, he was asked to sign a formal employment contract. He refused to do so, but continued working for Allied.

When he finished his second month of work, he received commissions totaling $417.61. He resigned and brought suit for $300.00, which was ap-

proximately the balance to which he claimed he was entitled under his contract for $450.00 per month less the commissions he had received.

Allied argued that the advertisement was not an irrevocable offer to hire salespeople at $450.00 per month but merely an invitation to proposed employees to enter into a contract of employment. It also contended that the guarantee was only for "qualified" salespeople and that Willis was not "qualified."

The court rejected Allied's defenses. It said that the newspaper ad constituted an offer of employment that Willis had accepted, resulting in a contract that bound Allied. Indeed, the court said, Willis must have been qualified because "he was put to work and worked for two months and only resigned when [Allied] did not continue his guaranteed salary of $450.00 per month." The court added that if he had not been qualified, Allied could have discharged him or terminated his employment—which it had not done even though Willis had refused to sign Allied's proposed employment contract.

The rule announced by the court in the Allied case—that an employment ad constitutes an offer by an employer to hire an employee on the terms described in the ad—generally is not accepted by most courts across the country. However, the court's decision is important for a number of reasons. For one thing, it shows that employers can face liability for words or actions taken at the very inception of the employment relationship. The case also should make it clear that written employment contracts are so very important. Even if the court in the Allied case had followed the general rule that ads do not constitute employment offers and had granted judgment to Allied, Allied nonetheless would have been faced with litigation costs (including attorney's fees) and lost executive time to defend itself in the lawsuit. If Willis had signed a contract before beginning work, his compensation would have been made perfectly clear and there would have been less of a likelihood of a lawsuit.

▌Oral Versus Written Agreements

Of course, a contract does not have to be written to be enforceable. A contract can be implied—that is, a court can find an enforceable agreement between two parties based on their acts or conduct. And a contract can be oral. In one case, Gordon Stephen Buttorff sought unpaid commissions to which he claimed he was entitled under an oral agreement he had with the president of United Electronic Laboratories, Inc.

According to Buttorff, the agreement provided that he would sell and market a camera manufactured by United Electronic that it called the Cam-eye and that was used primarily for security purposes by banks and other money-handling institutions as a protective device.

Buttorff contended that he was to develop a market for the sale of the Cam-eye and to establish distributorships in major population areas; that he was to have an exclusive agency to sell or distribute the product unlimited as to territory; and that he would be compensated by purchasing the camera at a net price of $440 and reselling the product to his customers for $985, plus installation cost. He said that the orders for the product were always forwarded directly to United Electronic, which then shipped the product to the customer and billed the customer directly. Upon collection from the customer, United Electronic sent him his commission. Buttorff also stated that this arrangement was to continue until United Electronic and he could agree on the terms of a written agreement.

United Electronic claimed that a contract had never been formed; among other things, it said that it never agreed to grant Buttorff an exclusive distributorship or agency, principally because it and Buttorff had never agreed on the terms of a sales quota that he would have to meet.

Courts generally will find that if two parties clearly intend not to be bound except by a written agreement, they will not be bound until the agreement is signed. However, parties may have a valid and binding contract before a contract has been completed and signed even though they may intend to put their agreement in writing.

The court in the *United Electronic* case ruled that a written agreement was not necessary so far as the sale of cameras and the payment of commissions to Buttorff were concerned. It noted that the parties continued in the relationship for more than a year and that cameras were sold and commissions paid during the time. It concluded that "a contract [had been] formed."

▌Statute of Frauds

Not all oral agreements are enforceable. The most common reason relied on by courts that refuse to enforce oral agreements is the Statute of Frauds. The Statute of Frauds is a law enacted by states to prevent fraud and to protect against perjured testimony by limiting the enforceability of certain oral agreements. Among other things, it states that a contract that cannot be performed within one year is unenforceable unless the party seeking to enforce the contract produces a writing signed by the opposing party that contains the major terms of the alleged agreement.

Suppose a saleswoman contends that her employer orally promised that she would have her job for three years but that she was fired after 15 months. Because the contract could not have been completed in one year, it is within the Statute of Frauds and unenforceable unless evidenced by a written document containing the major terms of the agreement signed by the employer. On the other hand, suppose an employee is hired for a certain salary under an oral employment contract that also states that it is terminable for any just and sufficient cause whenever dismissal is deemed necessary for the welfare of the company. Because the company could terminate the employee within a year, the Statute of Frauds does not apply and the contract is enforceable—even if the employee works for the company for a decade and then files suit for some alleged breach of the agreement.

On occasion, the effect of the Statute of Frauds seems particularly unfair to courts; perhaps as a result, they have developed a number of exceptions. Significantly, though, from an employer's point of view, it may seem that the exceptions favor employees or former employees—this further supports the value of having written employment agreements. That's what the American Insurance Company discovered several years ago.

Royden C. Tomlins had been employed for approximately four years in San Francisco by the Crum & Forster Group, Inc. when a vice president of American Insurance named Maas asked Tomlins whether he was interested in working for American Insurance. After negotiations with Maas, Tomlins went to American Insurance's home office in New Jersey, at the company's expense, for an interview with officers there.

When Tomlins left, he was told that American Insurance would transmit its decision through Maas in San Francisco. A few days later, Tomlins and Maas met and agreed that Tomlins would begin working for American Insurance at a certain salary. Tomlins stated that Maas said, "There's no way of getting a contract," but that the company would provide a "letter of intent." Tomlins also stated that he was assured that he could expect to work for American Insurance for three years and that it would be confirmed in writing.

Tomlins left his position at Crum & Forster and went to work for American Insurance. He was fired a week later and brought suit against American Insurance for breach of an employment contract.

The court noted that the agreement Tomlins claimed he had with American Insurance was obviously one that could not be performed within one year. Because Tomlins had no written contract, memorandum, or letter of intent, American Insurance therefore contended that the alleged oral agreement was unenforceable under the Statute of Frauds. Tomlins argued, though, that to permit American Insurance to rely on the Statute of Frauds would result in "unjust and unconscientious injury" to him.

The court upheld Tomlins's legal argument. It said that if he could prove that he suffered an unjust injury and that he had been promised that American Insurance would sign a document indicating the term of his employment, he could recover in his breach of contract suit notwithstanding the Statute of Frauds.

▌ What to Cover in a Contract

The safer course may be for an employer to insist on written contracts for all employees. However, because many lawsuits seem to involve claims by or against salespeople, a middle ground is to have contracts only for them.

After a business has established a policy of using written contracts (or understands the risks of having only oral agreements) for salespeople, the next issue to consider is what to include in the written documents.

To limit litigation risk, a contract for a salesperson should at a minimum deal with the following 10 items:

1. Term of employment

2. Reasons for which employment may be ended

3. The salesperson's duties

4. Salary or commission rate

5. A definition of the sales that are subject to commission, perhaps specifically including a definition of "net sales"

6. Territory in which sales must occur

7. When payments are payable

8. Whether a salesperson must still be employed to receive commissions or bonuses

9. Whether advances in excess of commissions must be returned

10. A system that explains, upon request of a salesperson, how bonuses or commissions are calculated and that permits the salesperson to request that the calculation be reviewed

▮ Independent Contractor or Employee?

One of the other things that an employer must decide is whether the contract should include provisions to make a worker an employee or an independent contractor.

The law imposes many obligations on businesses that have employees that are not imposed on businesses that retain independent contractors. For instance, employers generally are obligated to withhold federal, state, and social security taxes and to contribute to state workers' compensation and unemployment insurance funds for their employees. Employees—but not independent contractors—may participate in group, life, and health insurance plans and in a company's profit sharing program. Furthermore, an employer is more likely to be held liable for the negligent acts of an employee than for the negligence of an independent contractor.

The benefits of hiring independent contractors are clear, but there is one major drawback—an employer does not have the same right to control the actions of an independent contractor as it does to control the actions of an employee. Put another way, a worker that is subject to the control of a business (whether or not the business actually exercises control) usually will be found to be an employee; an independent contractor is one who is hired to perform a certain task but is allowed the latitude to determine where, how, and when to do so. The title used—employee or independent contractor—will not influence a court's decision as to whether a person is one or the other; the substance of the worker's actions and the significance of the employer's right to control will govern.

▮ Negligent Hiring and Retention

Businesses must take care when hiring employees *and* independent contractors. In recent years, courts have imposed liability on employers who were negligent in hiring a worker when that worker subsequently injured or damaged another person's business or property. There appears to be no general requirement that employers must check to see if the people they are intent on retaining have a criminal record, but they must at least perform a minimal investigation into an applicant's background.

Furthermore, when a business has prior knowledge of a worker's propensity to commit certain harmful acts (perhaps including drunk driving or getting involved in fights) the employer may best be advised to discharge the worker or risk having liability imposed under the doctrine of negligent retention. A broader discussion of an employer's potential liability for a worker's acts is contained in chapter 12.

▌A Final Word

The terms of an employment contract can affect many things, including the ability of an employer to fire an employee, an employer's liability for certain acts of the employee, and post-employment issues such as liability for bonuses and commissions. All of these issues can lead to litigation; all are discussed in later chapters.

FIVE CONTRACT CASES

Employment contract cases constitute one of the most common forms of litigation. Often, a properly drafted and clear contract agreed to by both employer and employee could have avoided a lawsuit being filed in the first place. Here are five cases to keep in mind.

1. In 1965 the Rio Grande Pickle Company, a Colorado corporation engaged in the business of raising and selling cucumbers for the pickling industry, hired George Fujimoto as the supervisor of its planting and growing operations and Jose Bravo as labor recruiter. In response to their request for additional compensation, Rio Grande orally agreed to pay them a bonus of 10 percent of the company's annual profits; Bravo told the president of Rio Grande that he wanted the agreement in writing and the president replied, "I will prepare one and send you a contract in writing."

Rio Grande sent Fujimoto and Bravo signed contracts calling for each of them to receive a bonus amounting to 10 percent of the company's net profits for each fiscal year. Fujimoto and Bravo signed the agreements but did not return them to their employer. They remained employed until November 1966; shortly thereafter, Rio Grande ceased doing business in Texas. Fujimoto and Bravo then filed suit, seeking 10 percent of Rio Grande's net profits for the fiscal year ending September 30, 1966, and 10 percent of the profits of the following two months. Rio Grande argued that Fujimoto and Bravo had not accepted the offered bonus contracts and that as a result they were not entitled to their bonuses, but the court disagreed. It found that because the contracts did not specify the means by which they could be accepted, Fujimoto and Bravo did not have to return them to the company after signing them.

"One usually thinks of acceptance in terms of oral or written incantations," the court stated, "but in many situations acts or symbols may be equally effective communicative media." In this case, the court noted that Fujimoto and Bravo, who had threatened to quit unless their remuneration was substantially increased, continued to work for the company for 14 months after receiving the written contracts and did not again express dissatisfaction with their compensation. In the court's view, that meant that they had accepted the bonus contracts and they were valid and binding on the company. (Fujimoto v. Rio Grande Pickle Company, 414 F.2d 648 (5th Cir. 1969).)

2. George B. Dickinson was a certified public accountant with a practice in El Paso, Texas, for many years. In 1971 Martha McLeod engaged Dickinson to organize records and to prepare a tax return for her Florida business. At that time, McLeod's business was a sole proprietorship; with Dickinson's help, Auto Center Manufacturing Co. was incorporated in Florida in March 1972. Martha McLeod owned all of the company's stock and her husband John was its president. The McLeods began encouraging Dickinson to move to Cocoa Beach, Florida, to become a full-time employee of the company. They discussed the conditions of his possible employment on several occasions, but the negotiations were inconclusive.

According to Dickinson, in May 1972 John McLeod telephoned Dickinson at his home in El Paso and agreed to employ Dickinson on Dickinson's terms—those terms included paying him a salary of $60,000 per year and, after the end of his first year of employment, a $25,000 bonus with which he could purchase 25 percent of the company's stock. Dickinson claimed that during that telephone conversation he also told John McLeod that he considered the transfer a permanent one and that he intended to work for Auto Center until his retirement and that John McLeod answered, "Fine, come on down." However, the parties did not sign a written employment contract; Dickinson never received the stock; and his employment with the company was terminated four days before he would have completed his first year with the company.

Dickinson then sued the corporation and John McLeod, arguing that they breached their employment contract with him. The trial court found that the alleged oral contract could not be performed within one year from the date it was made and therefore was unenforceable under the Statute of Frauds. The trial court also found that Dickinson had failed to show that his case was such an "egregious situation" to permit an exception to the Statute of Frauds and that his claim should be dismissed; the dismissal was upheld on appeal. (Dickinson v. Auto Center Manufacturing Co., 594 F.2d 523 (5th Cir. 1979).)

3. In 1966 Thomas M. Conard received $12,000 during the year from his employer, Mitchell Industries, Inc., and $12,000 at year-end. At his request, he was paid $15,000 during the year and $9,000 at year-end for 1967 and 1968. The year-end checks had the word "Xmas" written on them. However, during 1969, he was paid $15,0000 during the year and nothing at year-end. Conard sued Mitchell Industries for $9,000. Conard testified that he did not know how the year-end bonus was figured but that in December 1966 the president and vice-president of the company told Conard concerning his compensation "that I had no worry." They denied ever saying this and testified that they unilaterally determined the amount of the year-end bonus, depending on the company's profits and individual performance. They also testified that there was no discussion or negotiation of the amount with any employee and that no precedent had been set. The evidence during trial also showed that Mitchell Industries' income declined from $206,579.82 in 1967 to $25,130.01 in 1968 and that the company suffered a loss of $90,242.60 in 1969. As the court said, "It appears that Conard made more money in 1969 than Mitchell Industries." The court found that there had been no agreement between Conard and his employer as to the amount of compensation he was to be paid and that there was no formula or ascertainable method for determining the amount of any year-end payment to Conard. It then dismissed his suit. (Conard v. Mitchell Industries, Inc., 291 N.E.2d 577 (Ct. App. Indiana 1973).)

4. Several years ago Harold H. and Randy Klein, partners in a real estate development company and shareholders in a salvage company specializing in scrap iron, hired Vince Kobida, an independent contractor, to demolish a dilapidated factory on their land. The Kleins did not supervise the demolition or exercise any control over the activities. The one-page contract stated simply that Kobida would abide by all government regulations, would hold the Kleins harmless for injuries and damages arising from the project, and would provide the necessary insurance, including worker's compensation. Although Kobida had started in the wrecking business in 1936, he had not demolished a building in more than 25 years.

When the Kleins hired Kobida, Kobida had no equipment or employees with which to perform the demolition. He did, however, acquire equipment and hire personnel after undertaking the job. Among the workers hired by Kobida was Robert J. Wagner, a 20-year-old with no demolition experience. During the demolition, Wagner and a co-worker were working on the roof of the factory at least 40 feet above the ground. The roof was riddled with holes. As Wagner and his co-worker rolled a heavy steel tripod off the roof, Wagner caught his glove on the tripod. Wagner was thrown into the air and fell through the roof to the ground, sustaining permanent injury to his left foot. He received worker's compensation benefits from Kobida, his employer, and then filed a suit against the Kleins, seeking additional recovery from them. One of his theories: the Kleins had negligently hired Kobida.

The court noted that Randy Klein had not investigated Kobida's qualifications; had not inquired whether Kobida was a member of the National Association of Demolition Contractors, an organization of people involved in demolition that compiles a safety manual for demolition and provides safety information to those in the field; had not inquired as to whether Kobida had the proper equipment; and had not called any references. At trial, Wagner's expert witness testified that without safety precautions the conditions on the roof were inherently dangerous. The expert stated that a competent contractor would have used a crane to remove the roof. He testified that a person who hired an independent contractor to perform demolition work should check the contractor's background to make sure the contractor had the proper equipment. The jury concluded among other things that the Kleins had negligently hired Kobida and found the Kleins liable for 95 percent of the $481,750.58 in damages it awarded to Wagner.

However, on appeal, the appellate court ruled that negligent hiring did not by itself constitute an affirmative act of negligence upon which the liability of a principal employer to an independent contractor's employee could be based. "Stated another way, a principal employer or general contractor owes no duty to an independent contractor's employee to carefully select the independent contractor." It then reversed the judgment against the Kleins. Wagner v. Continental Casualty Co., 421 N.W.2d 835 (Sup. Ct. Wisc. 1988).)

5. When Clarence Hansen went to a parking lot in Portland, Oregon, to pick up the car he had left there earlier in the day, he paid the attendant, Millard Waters, the parking fee. Hansen then invited Waters to play dice with him—the wager being the parking fee. Waters agreed to do so but, after they were finished, a dispute arose and Waters assaulted Hansen. Hansen sued the owners of the lot to recover damages resulting from the assault. He presented evidence that made it clear that the lot's owners knew that Waters was a person of "vicious propensities and was prone to the use of physical force and violence" and argued that they had negligently retained Waters in their employ and should be accountable for the damages he caused. The court ruled that even if the owners of the parking lot had been negligent in retaining Waters, Hansen was not entitled to any recovery—he had been using the parking lot for an unlawful purpose and, being an unlawful guest at the time of the fight, the owners did not owe him any duty to avoid negligence in retaining their employees. (Hansen v. Cohen, 276 P.2d 391 (Sup. Ct. Oregon, 1954).)

Hiring Checklist

✓ Oral "agreements" can lead to litigation because parties may not agree on the provisions of the contract when push comes to shove. Written employment contracts that carefully define essential terms can help to avoid expensive and lengthy litigation.

✓ While many oral agreements are enforceable, a large number are not, principally because of the Statute of Frauds. It sometimes appears that courts adopt exceptions to the Statute of Frauds that penalize employers to the benefit of employees. The message for businesses: Get it in writing.

✓ Fewer legal risks and obligations are associated with independent contractors than with employees. The benefits to each should be considered when hiring a salesforce.

✓ Hire carefully! Negligent hiring (which simply may involve a failure to check references and conduct at least a minimal investigation into an applicant's background) can lead to liability.

✓ Fire when necessary! An employer's retention of careless, negligent, or perhaps dangerous employees also may lead to liability for personal injury caused by, or property damaged by, those employees.

12

LIABILITY FOR AN EMPLOYEE'S CONDUCT

■ Scope of Employment ■ Smoking ■ Drunk Driving ■ A Final Word

In his role as a salesperson for the National Biscuit Company, Ronnell Lynch visited numerous grocery stores to sell National Biscuit's products. On May 1, 1969, Lynch came to the store managed by Jerome Lange to place previously delivered merchandise on the shelves.

An argument developed between Lange and Lynch regarding Lynch's servicing of Lange's store. Lynch became very angry and started swearing. Lange told Lynch either to stop swearing or to leave the store, because children were present. Lynch then became uncontrollably angry, saying, "I ought to break your neck." He went behind the counter and dared Lange to fight him. Lange refused, whereupon Lynch proceeded to viciously assault him. After he finished beating up Lange, he threw merchandise around the store and left.

Lange filed suit against National Biscuit, arguing that because Lynch worked for National Biscuit, it should be held liable for damages resulting from his conduct.

Generally speaking, courts will hold an employer liable for an employee's conduct under the legal doctrine known as "vicarious liability" or "respondeat superior" (which means the master is liable for the actions of the servant) where the employee is acting within the scope of his employment. Courts impose responsibility on an employer for an employee's actions even where the employer is not directly at fault as a means of spread-

ing losses and the costs for an employee's actions across a wide range of people and companies. Courts believe that an employer that knows that it may be held liable for the actions of its employees will consider that liability as a cost of business and will attempt to avoid the cost by insuring against these kinds of contingencies or by adjusting its prices so that its customers bear part, if not all, of the burden. In addition, courts believe that an employer, knowing that it may be held liable, will be alert to prevent actions by an employee that might result in liability.

There is a wide disparity in the law in the application of the "scope of employment" test to factual situations involving intentional acts by employees that cause injury. The court in the Lange case decided that an employer should be held liable for an assault by its employee when the source of the attack was related to the duties of the employee and the assault occurred within work-related limits of time and place.

The court noted that Lynch's assault "obviously occurred within work-related limits of time and place, since it took place on authorized premises during working hours." It added that the precipitating cause of the initial argument concerned the way Lynch performed his work. Accordingly, it ruled that National Biscuit should be held responsible for Lynch's aggression and that Lange should be granted judgment on his suit.

▌ Scope of Employment

The key issue in virtually all cases that seek to impose liability on an employer for an employee's actions—whether the employee's actions consisted of intentional acts of assault, as in Lange's case, or negligence or carelessness—is whether the employee was acting within the "scope of employment" when the damages occurred. There are a number of factors that courts examine to determine whether an employee's actions occurred within the employee's scope of employment:

- Was the employee's conduct, to some degree, in furtherance of the interests of the employer?

- Did the employee intend to act on behalf of the employer?

- Was the employee authorized to perform the actions in question?

- Did the employee's actions occur substantially within authorized time and space restrictions?

One of the best cases to show the breadth of the scope of employment test was brought against Ray Korte Chevrolet by Caroline F. Simmons after she had been severely injured when her car was struck head-on by an automobile driven by James L. Stone, a salesperson who worked for Ray Korte.

According to the testimony at trial, on the day of the accident Stone ended his regular shift and went to a neighborhood bar with another salesperson, where he drank approximately three beers. He then returned to his office and made several business phone calls—including one to Charles Urban, a customer to whom he had sold a number of vehicles and with whom he had been dealing on the sale of a truck. Stone then left to pick up Urban to take him to the Ray Korte showroom. On his way to Urban, he was in the auto accident with Simmons.

A jury found in favor of Simmons and awarded her $671,520.00 in damages. The appellate court upheld the judgment, noting that there was considerable evidence from which the jury could have found that Stone was acting within the scope of his employment at the time of the accident.

First, the court noted, Stone was a regular employee of Ray Korte Chevrolet. He had been known to pick up customers on off shift hours to try to sell them cars. (Apparently, it was customary practice for car salespeople to work during off-hours because their on-duty hours often failed to coincide with their customers' available time for viewing or test-driving cars.) Stone had done business with Urban on previous occasions; was seen making business calls in the office just prior to the accident; and had arranged to pick Urban up and bring him to the showroom. In addition, the court noted that the route taken by Stone from the Ray Korte lot was the precise one that he would have taken to meet Urban. This evidence, the appellate court determined, was "more than sufficient" to uphold the jury's decision.

▌Smoking

Scope of employment issues come in a wide range of lawsuits. One of the more interesting questions is whether an employer can be held liable for injuries resulting from an employee's smoking. In other words, when employees smoke for their own pleasure, are they acting outside the scope of their employment? In a case filed by Edgewater Motels, Inc., against the Walgreen Company, the Supreme Court of Minnesota ruled that an employer can be held vicariously liable for an employee's negligent smoking of a cigarette if the employee is otherwise acting in the scope of his or her employment at the time of the negligent act.

In July 1973, A. J. Gatzke, a 31-year Walgreen employee and then district manager, spent approximately three weeks in Duluth, Minnesota, supervising the opening of a new Walgreen's restaurant. During that time, he stayed at the Edgewater Motel at Walgreen's expense. On or about August 17, 1973, Gatzke returned to Duluth to supervise the opening of another Walgreen owned restaurant. Again, he lived at the Edgewater at the company's expense. While in Duluth, Gatzke normally would arise at 6:00 A.M. and work at the restaurant from about 7:00 A.M. to 12:00 or 1:00 A.M. the next morning. In addition to working at the restaurant, Gatzke remained on call 24 hours per day to handle problems arising in other Walgreen restaurants located in his district. Gatzke thought of himself as a "24-hour-a-day man." He was allowed to call home at company expense. He was reimbursed for his laundry, living expenses, and entertainment. There were no constraints as to where he would perform his duties or at what time of day they would be performed.

On August 23, 1977, Gatzke worked at the restaurant for about 17 hours—the seventh consecutive day that he put in these kind of long hours. He worked that day with Curtis Hubbard, a district manager from another territory. Gatzke's supervisor, B. J. Treet, a regional director, also was present.

Between 12:00 and 12:30 A.M., Gatzke, Hubbard, Treet, and a chef left the restaurant in a company-provided car. The chef was dropped off at his hotel and the other three proceeded to the Edgewater, where they each had a room. Treet went to his room but Gatzke and Hubbard decided to walk across the street to the Bellows restaurant to have a drink.

In about an hour's time, Gatzke consumed four brandy Manhattans, three of which were doubles. While at the Bellows, Gatzke and Hubbard spent part of the time discussing the operation of the newly opened Walgreen restaurant. Additionally, Gatzke and the Bellows' bartender talked a little about the mixing and pricing of drinks; Gatzke apparently was interested in learning about the bar business because the new Walgreen restaurant served liquor.

Between 1:15 and 1:30 A.M., Gatzke and Hubbard left the Bellows and walked back to the Edgewater. Witnesses testified that Gatzke acted normal and appeared sober. He went directly to his motel room and then "probably" sat down at a desk to fill out his expense account because "that was [my] habit from traveling so much." During the five minutes or so that it took Gatzke to complete the expense account he admitted that he "probably" smoked a cigarette. After filling out the expense account, he went to bed; a fire broke out soon thereafter. Gatzke escaped from the burning room but the fire spread rapidly and caused more than $300,000 in damage to the motel.

A fire reconstruction expert testified that the fire started in, or next to, the wastebasket located to the side of the desk in Gatzke's room; he also stated that the fire was caused by a burning cigarette or match based on his x-ray examination of the remains of the basket, which disclosed the presence of cigarette filters and paper matches.

The court that issued a decision in the case noted that other courts that have faced the question of whether an employee's smoking of a cigarette can constitute conduct within the scope of the employee's employment have not agreed on the resolution of the question. A number of courts that have dealt with the issue have ruled that the act of smoking, even when done simultaneously with work-related activity, was not within the employee's scope of employment because it was a matter personal to the employee that was not done in furtherance of the employer's interests.

Other courts that have considered the question have reasoned that the smoking of a cigarette, if done while engaged in the business of the employer, was within an employer's scope of employment because it was a minor deviation from the employee's work-related activities, and thus merely an act done incidental to general employment.

The court in the Edgewater Motel case said that it was persuaded by the reasoning of the courts that ruled that smoking can be an act within an employee's scope of employment. "It seems only logical to conclude that an employee does not abandon his employment as a matter of law while temporarily acting for his personal comfort when such activities involve only slight deviations from work that are reasonable under the circumstances, such as eating, drinking, or smoking." In order to release an employer from liability, the court said, the employee's deviation must be so material or substantial as to amount to an entire departure.

The court then found that there was sufficient evidence from which a jury could find that Gatzke was involved in serving Walgreen's interests while he was at the bar. For instance, Gatzke testified that, while at the Bellows, he discussed the operation of the newly opened Walgreen's restaurant with Hubbard. Also, the bartender stated that on that night "[a] few times we would talk about his business and my business, how to make drinks, prices."

But the court said that even assuming that Gatzke was outside the scope of his employment while he was at the bar, there was evidence from which a jury could have reasonably found that Gatzke resumed his employment activities after he returned to his motel room because at that time he filled out his expense account. The expense account was, of course, completed so that Gatzke could be reimbursed by Walgreen's for his work-related expenses and, in this sense, Gatzke was performing an act for his own personal benefit.

However, the completion of the expense account also furthered Walgreen's business in that it provided detailed documentation of business expenses so that they were properly deductible for tax purposes. In light of all that, the court said that it was reasonable for the jury to find that Gatzke was acting within the scope of his employment when he completed his expense account. Therefore, the court ruled, he was working within the scope of his employment at the time he was negligent with the burning cigarette and the motel could recover from Walgreen's.

▌ Drunk Driving

Unfortunately, drunk driving—and an employer's liability for an employee's drunk driving—remains an important and frequently litigated subject despite public service advertising campaigns, politicians' pronouncements, and the efforts of antidrunk driving organizations. A recent case illustrates the legal problems associated with drunk driving as well as the costs—in terms of lives and dollars and cents.

Stephen VanDekken was a liquor salesman for the Eber Brothers Wine & Liquor Corporation. On June 25, 1984, VanDekken visited several of his customers' taverns, where he consumed alcohol. That evening, at approximately 8:30 P.M., the car he was driving collided with a motorcycle operated by Martin James. James was killed instantly and VanDekken was seriously injured. A state police officer arrived at the accident and smelled alcohol on VanDekken's breath. VanDekken was taken to the hospital and arrested for criminally negligent homicide, driving while intoxicated, and related traffic offenses.

VanDekken pleaded guilty to the criminal charges and violations and returned to work for Eber three months after the accident; his employment was conditioned on his retaining his State Liquor Authority solicitor's permit and arranging for someone to drive him on his sales route.

The parents of Michael James filed suit against Eber and were awarded $250,000 in compensatory damages and $2.5 million in punitive damages. (Punitive damages are awarded as a means of punishing a defendant.) The Jameses based their entitlement to punitive damages on the theory that Eber knew of VanDekken's habit of drinking on the job yet did nothing to change his behavior. They also suggested that Eber's offer of continued employment to VanDekken after he had recovered from the accident was in exchange for VanDekken's promise to testify favorably for Eber at trial.

On appeal, Eber challenged both the compensatory damages award and the punitive damages award.

The court quickly upheld the compensatory damages award, finding that the amount awarded by the jury was not excessive and clearly indicating that VanDekken had been operating in the scope of his employment at the time of the accident.

However, it said that the punitive damage award was not supported by the evidence because there was no proof of any complicity by Eber in or ratification of VanDekken's actions. The appellate court ruled that punitive damages can be imposed on an employer for the intentional wrongdoing of its employees only where management has authorized, participated in, consented to, or ratified the conduct giving rise to a plaintiff's injuries, or deliberately retained the unfit employee, or where the wrong was committed in connection with a recognized business system of the employer.

The court found insufficient evidence that Eber had condoned or ratified VanDekken's conduct. It recognized that Eber had not strictly prohibited its salespeople from having an occasional drink with a customer to foster business relationships, but said that Eber had not permitted or condoned drinking on a regular basis and, on the contrary, warned employees about doing that. Moreover, the court said, there was no evidence to support the Jameses' claim that VanDekken had a drinking "problem" or, even if he had, that Eber was aware of it. VanDekken had no history of driving while intoxicated or other alcohol-related incidents. The court said that the fact that VanDekken listed on his employment application an alcohol-related arrest in 1972—more than 12 years before the accident—was not proof that he had a drinking problem at the time of the accident. "In order for an award for punitive damages to stand against an employer, there must be more than a showing that the employee was acting in the scope of his employment," the court concluded.

While state law and the facts of each case will determine whether an employer can be held responsible for damages for an employee's drunk driving, there are a number of steps that employers should take to attempt to limit their potential liability. For instance, employers should:

- Make salespeople aware that company policy does not condone drunken driving

- Limit a salesperson's access to an automobile if that person has a known drinking problem, perhaps by providing alternative means of transportation

- Never engage in a cover-up of any accident involving alcohol, or risk imposition of punitive damages

▌A Final Word

In 1834 a British judge limited an employer's liability for actions of an employee who went "on a frolic of his own." An employer still may be able to avoid liability by showing that the employee's negligence occurred during a frolic—a substantial departure from the employer's business—or a detour—a slight departure. The general rule, though, is that an employer may be held responsible even if it specifically forbade an employee's actions; courts still attempt to use employer liability as a means of spreading costs across a wide range of companies and industries.

Employers that use independent contractors can see their potential liability reduced. However, there are a growing number of exceptions to the "rule" that an employer is not liable for the negligence of its independent contractor that courts justify on the grounds that employers select independent contractors just as they hire employees and employers can best determine how to spread the costs (such as by insurance).

The bottom line, then, is that, given the public policies behind court decisions on the issue of employer liability for worker negligence, there is little chance to escape litigation and only a somewhat larger chance of avoiding liability. Prevention and employee education are the best steps employers can take to attempt to limit their risks.

FIVE LIABILITY LAWSUITS

The cases in which employers are sued for employees' actions are legion. Here are five that present interesting fact patterns, as well as important lessons.

1. According to a complaint filed by James E. Henderson against radio station KATZ a number of years ago, Del Cook was a salesman engaged in soliciting advertising for KATZ. Henderson, a photographer, purchased advertising time on the radio station from Cook. After his ads were broadcast, he received a bill from the radio station. He claimed that he called the station about the bill and was told by the woman with whom he spoke that he either could pay by mail or give it to the collector. Henderson told her that Cook was the person with whom he did business and she told him that Cook would collect it and, if he did not, that Henderson could mail it in. At 4:00 A.M. the following morning, and with no expectation of seeing Cook, Henderson was at an all-night cafe in East St. Louis where he was waiting to take some commercial photographs of a group of people who were then inside a tavern next door to the cafe.

Henderson was putting a coin in the jukebox when he heard Cook call to him and ask him for the money. Henderson said he told Cook that he had called the radio station and had been told that he could pay the bill the following week. Henderson said Cook demanded the money because "he was my collector." When Henderson, who was about five foot nine and weighed about 150 pounds, did not give him the money, Cook, who was about six feet tall and weighed more than 200 pounds, "ran into me with his body and all, knocking me to the floor, and said he wanted the money." According to Henderson, he was on the floor with Cook on top striking him until someone pulled Cook off. Three or four of the customers put Cook outside. Henderson, thinking Cook had gone, went outside after three or four minutes, but Cook was there and allegedly ran into Henderson again, knocking him down. At the same time, Henderson dropped his camera and case and when he started to pick them up, Cook kicked him in the face, using the toe of his shoe, kicking him below the left eye with sufficient force to break a bone in his face, trap one of the eye muscles in the dislocated bone, produce bleeding, and permanently impair the eyesight in Henderson's left eye.

Henderson got to his feet, said he did not know what to do, and paid Cook the amount of the bill—$15. He then went to a hospital where he was treated for his injuries. Thereafter, he filed suit against the radio station. The court said that giving the benefit of all disputed facts to Henderson, the evidence indicated that the radio station's salesperson was guilty of an "outrageous and unforeseeable act. Over the collection of a

$15 account, he made an unprovoked and powerful attack" on Henderson. But because the attack was so "outrageous," the court held it to be unforeseeable and, therefore, not within the scope of Cook's employment. It ruled that the suit against the radio station should be dismissed. (Henderson v. Laclede Radio, Inc., 506 S.W.2d 434 (Sup. Ct. Missouri 1974).)

2. In the early 1970s, the management of the Estate Life Insurance Company of America gave George W. Blood the title Director-Special Marketing and asked him to supervise the sale of a so-called GP-800 policy from its home office in Roanoke, Virginia. In December 1972, Blood met Richard W. Walters, a Roanoke tire salesperson. After Walters said that he would like to get into the insurance business, Blood told him that he had to purchase a GP-800 policy and attend a "school" for insurance salespeople at a cost of $75.00. Upon completion of the training, he would be a marketing representative of Estate Life entitled to a commission of 35 percent of the first year premiums on policies sold by him. Blood told Walters that a representative could advance to the position of marketing director, entitled to a 55 percent commission, by selling 10 GP-800 policies and by recruiting five other GP-800 salespeople. Blood also told Walters that he could be promoted immediately to marketing director (and be entitled to a percentage of the premiums on GP 800 policies) by paying him $10,000 in cash. Walters purchased the policy, paid the additional $75, and attended a three-hour "school" conducted, in part, by Blood at a local motel. Walters subsequently received a six-month temporary license to sell insurance for Estate Life. He later introduced Blood to Philip Thomas Dudley, who gave Blood a check for $10,000 payable to Blood's insurance agency to become a marketing director. When Walters heard that Dudley had paid Blood $10,000, he decided to become a marketing director and gave Blood a note for $8,000 and a check for $2,000 payable to Blood's agency.

Several weeks later, Dudley and Walters realized they had "been took." Blood disappeared and Dudley and Walters filed suit against Estate Life. Estate Life argued that Blood's fraud was outside the scope of his authority, that it did not know he was making fraudulent misrepresentations for his own personal gain, and that it therefore could not be held liable to Dudley and Walters. The court disagreed. It cited a general rule of agency law that states that a principal who puts an agent in a position that enables the agent, while apparently acting within his authority, to commit a fraud upon third persons is subject to liability to those third persons even if the principal is entirely innocent. The rationale: The person relying upon the appearance of agency knows that the apparent agent is not authorized to act except for the benefit of the principal, but that is something that the person normally cannot ascertain and therefore a risk that the principal, rather than the third party, ought to bear. While the court recognized that not all employers can always be held liable for fraud committed by all employees or agents, it ruled that a jury should determine whether the evidence presented by Dudley and Walters was sufficient to prove that Blood's conduct should be deemed attributable to Estate Life. (Dudley v. Estate Life Insurance Company of America, 257 S.E.2d 871 (Sup. Ct. Virginia 1979).)

3. The window display prepared by the general manager of the J. C. Penney store in Healdsburg, California, was intended to directly take on Rosenberg & Bush, which operated a competing retail store across the street. The display consisted of placards that compared the garments offered for sale by Penney with similar garments offered by Rosenberg & Bush. In reference to a Rosenberg & Bush garment, one of the signs said, "Decide for yourself. This garment is either a poorly made second or prison-made merchandise. Seams crooked. Slovenly made. Long loose stitches. . . . Note the shoddy appearance, the wrinkled waist and hems of this garment." Rosenberg & Bush filed suit against Penney, seeking to hold it responsible for the actions of its general manager.

The court found that the general manager had charge of the window displays, the goods to be displayed, and their manner of arrangement. While Penney had a policy book admonishing managers to maintain a spirit of friendliness and courtesy toward competitors, the court ruled that a "master is liable if he employs an employee to speak for him, and it is immaterial if, acting in the scope of his authority, he makes a mistake as to the truth." Then the court, finding the placards libelous, upheld a $10,000 award to Rosenberg & Bush. (Rosenberg v. J. C. Penney Co., 86 P.2d 696 (Dist. Ct. App. Calif. 1939).)

4. After Joanne E. Meany was injured in an automobile accident on December 23, 1981, she filed suit against the Cardinal IG Company, which was the employer of Preston Cortright, the person driving the other car involved in the accident. She contended that Cardinal should be held liable for her injuries because it served Cortright, a night quality assurance manager, intoxicating beverages at a Christmas party during normal working hours and because it allowed Cortright to drive home in an intoxicated state. Meany argued that the state's Dram Shop Act, which imposed liability on commercial liquor vendors for accidents caused by patrons that have had too much to drink in certain instances, should be applied to Cardinal, but the Supreme Court of Minnesota rejected her contentions. It stated that extending liability under the Dram Shop Act to an employer would "open a virtual Pandora's box." It then ruled that, at least under Minnesota law, an injured third party has no claim against an employer-social host that negligently served alcohol to an employee. (Meany v. Newell, 367 N.W.2d 472 (Sup. Ct. Minn. 1985).)

5. Rose Marie Drexel contended in a lawsuit that her husband had been given a prescription for the drug Aldactone that was properly filled on March 3, 1975, by a retail drugstore located in Reading, Pennsylvania. She also alleged that her husband returned to the same drugstore to have the prescription refilled on April 14, 1975, but that he did not receive Aldactone, a diuretic, but Coumadin, a blood thinner. As a result of taking Coumadin, Drexel's husband sustained massive traumatic injuries from which he died on May 12, 1975. Drexel's suit was against Union Prescription Centers, Inc., the corporation that had franchised the Reading drugstore to Joseph J. Todisco, Jr. She contended that Union Prescription had control of the Reading drugstore and should be held responsible for the "negligence and carelessness and malpractice" that occurred when her husband's prescription was improperly refilled.

The court recognized that some degree of control by a franchisor over a franchisee would appear to be inherent in the franchise relationship. However, it said, the mere existence of a franchise relationship neither automatically triggered an employer-employee relationship nor insulated the parties from such a relationship. "Whether the control retained by the franchisor is also sufficient to establish a master-servant relationship depends in each case upon the nature and extent of such control as defined in the franchise agreement or by the actual practice of the parties." Union Prescription pointed to the following provisions in the franchise contract as evidence that it had no right to control the Reading store. For one thing, the contract provided that Todisco was merely the recipient of a license granted by Union Prescription to operate a Union Prescription Center under that name in return for which Todisco agreed to pay the company a 4.5 percent monthly royalty from the store's gross receipts. In addition, it provided that Todisco was obligated to pay all business expenses and taxes, assumed the risk of litigation arising out of the store's operation, had some say in choosing the inventory, and was required to identify himself as the owner of the store on all signs and printed matter bearing the Union Prescription mark. Drexel contended, conversely, that the franchise agreement as a whole provided sufficient control to Union Prescription to raise a question about the nature of the relationship between the company and Todisco that should be resolved by a jury. She pointed to a number of provisions, including several that stated that Todisco was required to avail himself of Union Prescription's marketing and management advice; Todisco only could operate under the Union Prescription name and logo; Union Prescription had the right to approve the location of the store and the right to inspect the premises during normal business hours; and Todisco had to keep the store open for a minimum number of hours per week, use Union Prescription's standard forms and accounting system, and maintain the exterior and interior of the store premises in a "clean, orderly, and attractive condition" using Union Prescription's standard colors, lighting, design, equipment, and fixtures.

The case reached the U.S. Court of Appeals for the Third Circuit, which stated that the agreement indicated that Union Prescription had reserved the right to control numerous specific facets of the franchisee's business operation. It then determined that whether the Reading store was sufficiently subject to the control of Union Prescription was an issue that should be decided by a jury. (Drexel v. Union Prescription Centers, Inc., 582 F.2d 781 (3d Cir. 1978).)

Liability Checklist

✓ Employers can be held responsible for personal or property damage resulting from intentional or careless acts of employees—and, on occasion, independent contractors.

✓ The general test for imposing liability is whether an employer has a "right to control" the worker, even if the right is not fully exercised.

✓ Careful selection, training, and oversight of employees is crucial to limiting an employer's potential liability.

✓ If litigation occurs, it is important to determine whether the employee's actions took place in the scope of the employee's employment. This requires an examination of where, when, why, and how they occurred.

✓ Because courts impose liability on employers as a means of spreading costs beyond injured parties alone, businesses must ensure that they take steps to spread potential liability expenses, through liability insurance, increased prices, or a combination of both.

13

THE LEGAL SIDE OF FIRING

■ Written Contracts ■ Public Policy Limitations ■ Promises to Keep
■ A Final Word

Joseph Murphy was first employed by the American Home Products Corporation in 1957. Over the course of the succeeding two decades, he held a variety of accounting positions at the company, but American Home never gave him a formal written employment contract.

On April 18, 1980, when he was 59 years old, Murphy was fired. He filed suit against American Home and argued that his discharge, which he said occurred in part because he had disclosed alleged accounting improprieties on the part of corporate personnel, had been improper.

The top court in New York, the New York Court of Appeals, ruled that an employee hired on an "at-will" basis—which means that the employee does not have a formal employment contract containing a specified employment term and can leave or be discharged for virtually any reason, or even no reason at all—may not bring suit in New York for wrongful discharge.

The at-will employment doctrine that formed the basis of the decision by the New York Court of Appeals in the American Home Products case and that has been the general rule throughout the country is slipping. Nearly 40 years ago, a California court ruled that an employee of a union could not be fired for failing to commit perjury before a legislative committee. During the past 10 or 20 years, numerous other courts across the country also have found exceptions to the at-will employment doctrine.

While the majority rule continues to be that an at-will employee can be fired when an employer so desires, there now are many instances when an employer may not fire an employee. They can be divided into three basic categories:

- *When an employee has a contract that provides for employment for a certain period of time and discharge for specified reasons—in this case, the employee is no longer an at-will employee*

- *When an employer's discharge violates public policy as announced by the courts—such as firing an employee for serving on a jury or for filing a workmen's compensation claim*

- *When an employer's words, written materials, or actions can be interpreted as having modified the at-will employment agreement—such as when an employment manual states that employees can be discharged only "for cause"*

Furthermore, state and federal legislatures have enacted laws that limit an employer's right to fire an at-will employee. For instance, employers may not discharge employees because of their race, religion, gender, or place of national origin and certain "whistle-blower" laws prohibit retaliatory actions against employees who report their employer's illegal actions to the government.

▌Written Contracts

The starting point to determine whether and when a business can fire an employee is the employment agreement. A properly drafted agreement, as indicated in chapter 11, will explain an employee's rights and the term of employment. If the agreement says that an employee must be employed for a number of years but may be terminated for cause, the agreement even may define cause. On the other hand, if an employment agreement says that the employment is "at-will," then, subject to the public policy limitations imposed by the courts and legislature, the employee generally may be discharged at any time.

Where an employee does not have a written employment agreement, any oral agreement or agreement implied by the actions of the employer and employee must be reviewed. To the extent that an unwritten agreement is unenforceable because of the Statute of Frauds, as discussed in chapter 11, the employer may be able to discharge the employee at will.

▌ Public Policy Limitations

Public policy. The words are enough to scare some people half to death. That's because it is sometimes not really clear exactly what "public policy" is until it is relied on by a court for a decision in a particular case. In essence, public policy is anything that the courts use as a rationale to reach a decision they want to reach. They can use public policy to expand the protections contained in the Constitution's Bill of Rights to reflect modern day matters that could not have been contemplated 200 years ago. On the other hand, they can cite public policy as the reason for limiting individual rights.

Many so-called public policy limitations have been imposed by courts to prohibit employers from discharging employees; a number of them are included at the end of this chapter in the section Five Firings. But public policy does not limit every firing for any reason. Here is a brief description of a number of suits that failed:

- A company advised an employee/shareholder who was suing the company that he would be fired if he did not dismiss his complaint; he refused to do so, and the company fired him. The court ruled that conditioning continued employment on termination of the lawsuit is not against public policy.

- An employee who claimed that he was fired just as he was "about to uncover criminal activities" by another employee was not entitled to protection as a whistle-blower

- A suit by a research scientist who objected to continued work on a particular project involving what she claimed was a controversial—but lawful—drug and then resigned was not permitted to sue the pharmaceutical company that had employed her for wrongful discharge, because use of the drug was not clearly against public policy.

- An employee who was discharged after notifying his employer that he was going to attend law school at night could not bring a wrongful discharge suit despite his contentions that public policy favored education; the court found that his "attendance at night school was a private matter rather than a public concern."

As a review of the cases indicates, courts take a hard look at alleged public policy arguments and, other than in the clearest cases, seem to need very good reasons to expand the exceptions to the general at-will rule.

▌Promises to Keep

If the law of contracts can be said to relate to one thing, that thing is a promise. After all, a contract is really nothing more than promises between sides to take or refrain from taking certain action. The essence of the promise is the essence of the parties' agreement. Courts become involved in contract disputes because contracts often are not written as clearly as they should be, or because circumstances may arise that the parties never considered, requiring that their contract be interpreted in light of the new developments. When forced to analyze a contract, a court will try to determine what the parties intended when they wrote it.

When it comes to the employer/employee relationship, though, courts may find a contract when an employer never considered one existed; it then may interpret it against the employer's interests. Look at what happened in a recent case decided by the Minnesota Supreme Court.

When the Equitable Life Assurance Society of the United States interviewed Carol Lewis, Mary Smith, Michelle Rafferty, and Suzanne Loizeaux in the spring of 1980, a manager or supervisor assured them that if hired, their employment would continue so long as their production remained at a satisfactory level. They all were hired to work in Equitable's office in St. Paul, Minnesota. While they did not receive written contracts of employment, they each received a copy of the company's employee handbook. Among other topics, the handbook discussed company policies regarding job security, dismissals, and severance pay.

With respect to dismissals, the handbook stated:

> Dismissals usually come about because of an individual's indifference to work quality or attendance standards. Except for misconduct serious enough to warrant immediate dismissal, no employee will be discharged without previous warning and a period in which to bring performance up to a satisfactory level. When a dismissal is necessary and the employee has been with [the company] for six months or longer, severance pay may be granted, depending on the reason for the dismissal.

Several months after they began working for Equitable, the company's Pittsburgh office requested assistance from its St. Paul office. The four St. Paul workers were among two groups sent to assist the Pittsburgh office for two-week periods.

When they returned to St. Paul, each received a personal letter from Equitable management commending them on their job performance while in Pittsburgh. However, they were asked to change the expense reports they filed at least two times to comply with company guidelines. They did so, but then refused to make further changes, maintaining that the expenses shown on their original reports had been honestly and reasonably incurred and were submitted based upon the instructions they had received prior to leaving for Pittsburgh.

In January 1981, though, the four workers each received a letter from the office manager requesting again that they revise their expense reports. The letter set out still another, different set of guidelines to be followed. Additionally, three of the workers met individually with a manager from Equitable's Chicago office. At the meetings, they were once again asked to change their expense reports to conform to company policies. They refused and were told that they were being put on probation. They were also warned, for the first time, that termination might be considered.

A week later, the office manager received orders from Chicago to obtain from two of the workers monies they had agreed to refund to Equitable and then to fire all four. The office manager called the two to his office and had them refund the money, saying nothing of the fact that they were to be terminated later that day. Late in the afternoon, he called each of the four to his office individually and again asked them to change their reports. When they stated that they were standing by their reports, he terminated them for "gross insubordination." Because they were fired for gross insubordination they received no severance pay. Had they been fired for other reasons, they would have been entitled to as much as one month's severance pay. The four workers, primarily relying on the employee handbook, filed suit against the company and contended, among other things, that the company had breached their employment agreement. A jury found in their favor and Equitable appealed.

The case reached the Supreme Court of Minnesota, which noted that it was undisputed that the four workers had been hired for indefinite terms, had no written employment contracts, and could have left their employment with the company at any time. Generally speaking, it added, those kinds of employment relationships may be terminated by an employer at any time without cause. However, it noted that it had ruled that, under certain circumstances, employee handbook provisions may create contractual obligations enforceable against an employer.

In one case, the court ruled that the following four-step discipline and dismissal provisions in a company's employment manual contractually bound an employer:

> *"If an employee has violated a company policy, the following procedure will apply:*

1. An oral reprimand by the immediate supervisor for the first offense, with a written notice sent to the Executive Vice President.

2. A written reprimand for the second offense.

3. A written reprimand and a meeting with the Executive Vice President and possible suspension from work without pay for five days.

4. Discharge from employment for an employee whose conduct does not improve as a result of the previous action.

In no instance will a person be discharged from employment without a review of the facts by the Executive Officer."

The court in the Equitable case found that the statements in Equitable's policy manual, while not as explicit as the four-step procedures listed above, plainly stated that in certain circumstances all employees were entitled to a warning and to a probationary period prior to dismissal and were sufficient to limit Equitable's right to freely dismiss its employees.

The court ruled that because the four workers had received handbooks at the time they began employment the handbook's dismissal provisions were part of the four workers' employment contracts. It then upheld the jury's decision that Equitable had breached the employment contracts and its award of compensatory damages to the four former employees.

▌A Final Word

Personnel handbooks, company manuals, oral statements made by interviewers, and even pre-employment recruitment and interview documents all may contain implied promises that restrict an employer's ability to discharge employees. In certain cases, courts have ruled that employees need not even have seen the documents to be able to argue that they limit an employer's termination rights. Even those courts that are unwilling to expand the public policy exceptions to the at-will termination rule may be willing to allow an employer's own words or written materials to limit its rights. That makes it crucial that all businesses review their written employment materials, change provisions that are unacceptable, and educate recruiters to the kinds of promises that they are—and are not—willing to make and keep.

FIVE FIRINGS

1. Patricia Jirak was employed by Federal Express Corporation from November 5, 1987, until August 1, 1988, as a part-time courier. Her job duties included unloading cargo and delivery and pick-up routes on a fill-in basis for other couriers who had not reported to work. During the first five months of her employment, she was absent from work three times and was late on numerous occasions, and consequently was issued two warnings stating that if this conduct continued, further disciplinary action might be necessary. On April 28, 1988, she was issued a "decision day" letter on account of another day that she was absent. Under Federal Express's decision day policy, she was given a day off with pay and was required to present a written personal performance agreement acceptable to her manager, detailing specific actions she would take to correct her attendance problem and stating a personal commitment to abide by that agreement. Although Jirak promised to improve, she was late a few more times in the next two months and was issued a second decision day letter on June 17, 1988. Despite all of these warnings, she called in sick on August 1, 1988, with back pain and menstrual cramps and did not report for work. Her employment was terminated.

Jirak filed suit against Federal Express, alleging that her termination was due to discrimination on the basis of sex in violation of Title VII of the Civil Rights Act of 1964 and the Pregnancy Discrimination Act of 1978. She claimed that menstruation, like pregnancy, was a uniquely female attribute for which an employer may not lawfully discharge an employee. Federal Express contended that there was a legitimate non-discriminatory business reason for discharging Jirak—her poor attendance record and ultimately her violation of the second decision day agreement. The court agreed with the company. It found first that while the Pregnancy Discrimination Act prohibited discrimination in employment "because of or on the basis of pregnancy, childbirth, or related medical conditions," menstrual cramps were not a medical condition related to pregnancy or childbirth and therefore were not covered by that law. The court also ruled that the decision of an employer to treat a high number of absences regardless of the reason for those absences as an attendance problem justifying disciplinary action did not violate Title VII so long as the policy was applied equally to all employees. Because Jirak failed to provide any evidence that Federal Express's policy of termination for violation of a second decision day letter was not applied equally to male and female employees, the court dismissed her suit. (Jirak v. Federal Express Corp., 805 F.Supp. 193 (S.D.N.Y. 1992).)

2. After Dorothy Frampton was fired by the Central Indiana Gas Company, she filed a suit against Central Indiana seeking damages for a retaliatory discharge. Frampton contended that she injured her arm while working and that Central Indiana and its insurer paid her hospital and medical expenses, as well as her full salary, during the four months she was unable to work. She alleged, though, that Central Indiana did not tell her of any further benefits to which she might have been entitled. When she returned to work, she performed her job capably. Approximately 19 months after the injury, she notified Central Indiana of a 30 percent loss in the use of her arm; she said she was hesitant to file a claim for fear of losing her job, but she did so and received a settlement for her injury. She claimed that she was discharged from her position the next month without any reason being given. The Indiana Supreme Court ruled that an employee who can prove that he or she was discharged in retaliation for filing a claim under the state's workmen's compensation act would be entitled to a judgment against a former employer. While acknowledging the general rule that, under ordinary circumstances, an at-will employee may be discharged without cause, the court concluded that when an employee is discharged for exercising a statutorily conferred right, an exception to the general rule must be recognized. (Frampton v. Central Indiana Gas Co., 297 N.E.2d 425 (Sup. Ct. Indiana 1973).)

3. Olga Monge contended in a lawsuit she filed against the Beebe Rubber Company that she had been fired by Beebe because she had refused to date her boss. A jury found in her favor and the case reached the Supreme Court of New Hampshire. That court, joining a large number of other courts across the country, limited the ability of an employer to discharge an at-will employee. It recognized an employer's interest in running its business as it sees fit (although it said the employment at-will defense was "based on an ancient feudal system"). However, it said that interest must be balanced against the interest of employees in maintaining their employment and the public's interest in maintaining a "proper balance" between the two. It ruled that a termination by an employer of an at-will employment contract that "is motivated by bad faith or malice or based on retaliation is not in the best interest of the economic system or the public good and constitutes a breach of the employment contract." It then upheld the jury's decision that she had been improperly discharged. (Monge v. Beebe Rubber Co., 316 A.2d 549 (Sup. Ct. N.H. 1974).)

4. When Vickie Nees was first called for jury duty, she requested and was granted a 12-month postponement because of her honeymoon. The next year, she was again subpoenaed to serve on a jury. She told her employer, Hocks Laboratories, which gave her a letter stating that they could spare her only "for awhile." The letter asked that she be excused. She presented the letter to the court clerk and told the clerk that she had been called before and had to be excused but that she would like to serve on a jury. The clerk told Nees that she would not be excused and Nees returned to her office and told her employer that she would have to serve a minimum of two weeks. She did not tell that she had told the court clerk she really wanted to serve. Several days after Nees began her jury duty, she received a letter from Hocks telling her that she had been terminated. The letter stated, in part: "Although we asked you to request an excusal from Jury Duty and wrote a letter confirming [our] position, it has been brought to our attention you, in fact, requested to be placed on Jury Duty." Stating that the jury system and jury duty are high on the scale of American institutions and citizen obligations, the court limited the at-will defense and ruled that employers may not discharge an employee for fulfilling the employee's obligation of jury duty. (Nees v. Hocks, 536 P.2d 512 (Sup. Ct. Oregon, 1975).)

5. From December 1966 until November 18, 1981, John Novosel was employed by the Nationwide Insurance Company. In late October 1981, a memorandum was circulated through Nationwide's offices soliciting the participation of all employees in an effort to lobby the Pennsylvania House of Representatives in support of the No-Fault Reform Act, then before the state legislature. Novosel contended that he was discharged solely because he refused to participate in the lobbying effort and his privately stated opposition to Nationwide's political stand. This case reached the U.S. Court of Appeals for the Third Circuit, which determined that a former employee may bring suit against a former employer for an employment termination that abridged a significant and recognized public policy. It ruled that the protection of an employee's freedom of political expression "would appear to involve no less compelling a societal interest than the fulfillment of jury service or the filing of a worker's compensation claim." (Novosel v. Nationwide Insurance Company, 71 F.2d 894 (3d Cir. 1983).)

Termination Checklist

✓ Firing employees is not as simple as it used to be. In recent years, many courts and legislatures have imposed a number of restrictions on the right to discharge at-will workers.

✓ Where a termination is against public policy or contravenes the implied or explicit words of an employment agreement (perhaps as modified by employee handbooks or other written company materials), courts may limit an employer's right to fire.

✓ Clearly written employment contracts setting forth employment terms and the reasons an employee may be discharged are most helpful.

✓ Employers should avoid creating the impression that employees are entitled to their jobs, unless they mean it. Thus, for example, while a probationary period for employees might seem to be a good idea, there should be no suggestion that once an employee passes the probationary period the employee has a "permanent" job—unless the employer wants that to be the case.

✓ Employers can be aided by disclaimers in handbooks and manuals and statements signed by new employees that state that they understand they are at-will employees subject to being discharged at any time for any or no reason.

14

POSTEMPLOYMENT ISSUES

■ Recovering Excess Commissions ■ Paying Bonuses
■ A Note on Attorney's Fees ■ Defaming Former Salespeople
■ Self-Publication ■ A Final Word

A number of years ago, Orville E. Fortune, a salesperson, entered into a written employment contract with the National Cash Register Company. The contract stated that it was terminable at will, without cause, by either party on written notice. It also provided that Fortune, operating in Massachusetts, would receive a weekly salary in a fixed amount plus a bonus for sales made within the territory assigned to him for "coverage or supervision," whether the sale was made by him or someone else. The amount of the bonus was determined on the basis of bonus credits, which were computed as a percentage of the price of products sold. The contract said that Fortune would be paid a percentage of the applicable bonus credit as follows:

1. Seventy-five percent if the territory was assigned to him at the date of the order

2. Twenty-five percent if the territory was assigned to him at the date of delivery and installation

3. One hundred percent if the territory was assigned to him at both times

The contract further provided that the bonus interest would terminate if shipment of the order was not made within 18 months from the date of the order unless the territory was assigned to him for coverage at the date of delivery and installation or special engineering was required to fulfill the contract. In addition, National Cash Register reserved the right to sell products in Fortune's territory without paying a bonus.

In 1968 Fortune's territory included First National Stores, Inc. This account had been part of his territory for the preceding six years; he had been successful in obtaining several orders from First National, including a million-dollar order in 1963.

Sometime in late 1967 or early 1968, National Cash Register introduced a new model cash register, the Class 5. Fortune corresponded with First National in an effort to sell the machine. He also helped to arrange for a demonstration of the Class 5 to executives of First National on October 4, 1968. National Cash Register had a team also working on this sale.

On November 27, 1968, National Cash Register's manager of chain and department stores and the Boston branch manager, both part of National Cash Register's team, wrote to First National regarding the Class 5. The letter covered a number of subjects, including price protection, trade-ins, and trade-in protection against obsolescence. While the company normally offered price protection for only an 18-month term, apparently the size of the proposed order from First National caused National Cash Register to extend its price protection terms for either a two-year or four-year period.

On November 29, 1968, First National signed an order for 2,008 Class 5 machines to be delivered over a four-year period at a purchase price of approximately $5 million. Although Fortune did not participate in the negotiation of the terms of the order, his name appeared on the order form in the space entitled "salesman credited." The amount of the bonus credit as shown on the order was $92,079.99.

On January 6, 1969, the first working day of the new year, Fortune found an envelope on his desk at work. It contained a termination notice addressed to his home, dated December 2, 1968. Shortly after receiving the notice, Fortune spoke to the Boston branch manager, with whom he was friendly. The manager told him, "You are through," but, after considering some of the details necessary for the smooth operation of the First National order, told him to "stay on" and to "[k]eep on doing what you are doing right now." Fortune remained with the company in a position entitled "sales support." In this capacity, he coordinated and expedited delivery of the machines to First National under the November 29 order and serviced other accounts.

Beginning in May or June, Fortune began to receive some bonus commissions on the First National order. Having received only 75 percent of the applicable bonus due on the machines that had been delivered and installed, Fortune spoke with his manager about receiving the full amount of the commission. Fortune was told "to forget about it." Sixty-one years old at that time, and with a son in college, Fortune concluded that it "was a good idea to forget it for the time being."

Approximately 18 months after receiving the termination notice, Fortune, who had worked for National Cash Register for almost 25 years, was asked to retire. When he refused, he was fired. He did not receive any bonus payments on machines that were delivered to First National after that date. Fortune then filed suit against National Cash Register.

The court noted that his employment contract was a "classic terminable at-will employment contract." It said that under the express terms of the contract, Fortune had received all the bonus commissions to which he was entitled. The court found that, under a literal reading of the contract, National Cash Register correctly concluded that it had not breached the contract and had no further liability to Fortune.

However, the court said, when commissions are to be paid for work performed by an employee, an employer's decision to terminate its at-will employee "should be made in good faith." It said that an employer could be held liable for damages if it sought to deprive an employee of compen-

sation by terminating the employee's contract when the employee was on the brink of successfully completing a sale; the result should be the same, it said, where an employer attempts to deprive an employee of any portion of a commission due the employee.

National Cash Register argued that there was no evidence of bad faith in connection with its decision to terminate Fortune, but the court disagreed. It said the evidence and the reasonable inferences to be drawn from the evidence supported the jury's decision that the termination of Fortune's 25 years of employment as a salesperson with National Cash Register the next business day after the company obtained a $5 million order from First National was motivated by a desire to pay Fortune as little of the bonus credit as it could. The fact that Fortune was willing to work under those circumstances did not constitute a waiver of his claim, the court said; it only showed that the company had him "at their mercy."

The Fortune case brings together many of the subjects discussed in the preceding three chapters of this book: it shows the importance of the terms of written employment agreements and the role public policy plays when an employer seeks to terminate an employee. This chapter discusses two important postemployment issues; both ultimately involve money.

Whether an employee is entitled to commissions or bonuses when no longer employed by a company is a question that arises frequently, and not just when an employer terminates an employee to avoid paying commissions. It also occurs when an employer seeks to recover the excess of advances over commissions from salespeople, as happened in a case brought by National Memorial Park, Inc., against Harry Geller, its former sales director.

▌ Recovering Excess Commissions

Geller's written five-year employment contract, dated January 1, 1964, with National Memorial and its affiliates, the National Mausoleum Corporation and National Memorial Park Cemetery, Inc., stated that, as compensation, he would receive commissions on sales made under his supervision of ground burial spaces, bronze memorials, cremation niches, underground crypts, and the like. The agreement further provided that National Memorial would advance Geller $650 per week against his commission account.

Geller resigned on November 6, 1966. At that time, advances to him exceeded his earned commissions by $12,780.07; National Memorial filed suit seeking to recover that amount. The court that issued a decision in this lawsuit first turned its attention to the written contract.

It noted that the paragraph of the contract dealing with advances stated as follows:

ADVANCES

The companies agree to advance the Sales Director $650 per week against his commission account. No decrease will be considered until June 1, 1964, if this sum is not earned by volume. These advances shall be offset against his earnings. The Sales Director may draw in excess of that figure if due him, in light of commission on net sales.

The court noted that Geller's contract did not either expressly or impliedly obligate him to repay National Memorial for any excess of advances over commissions earned. Advances were to be "offset against" his commissions and not charged to him personally as a loan or other indebtedness, the court said. "Had there been an intention to require [Geller] to repay the excess of advances over commissions, certainly a short statement would have been included in the document dealing not only with the obligation of repayment but also with the date for such repayment." However, the court found, nothing in the contract indicates whether any repayment was required when each quarterly accounting was given to Geller or upon termination of the contract. It ruled that the parties to the contract had no intention to obligate Geller to make repayment.

The court noted that, generally speaking, most judges rule that when a contract of employment provides for advances to an employee to be charged to and deducted from commissions, the employer cannot recover from the employee the excess of advances over the commissions earned in the absence of an express or implied agreement to repay any such excess. It then ruled that the complaint against Geller should be dismissed.

▌ Paying Bonuses

An employer that cannot recover money already out the door to a departed employee has one set of problems. But it even may be worse if an employer has to pay a bonus of *new* money to a former employee. The terms of the employment agreement are crucial here, too, as the American Optical Corporation was pleased to learn.

American Optical said the sales incentive plan that it put in place for its salesforce was "an opportunity to earn additional income by improving [its] sales performance in 1970." Under the terms of the plan, salespeople who exceeded their "incentive quota" would be paid a bonus in addition to their base salary. The amount of each salesperson's bonus was to be computed in terms of a percentage of the base salary, depending upon the percentage of the total sales of the salesperson for 1970 in relation to the salesperson's incentive quota.

The plan also provided as follows:

> *Payments will be made semi-annually and [are] expected to be during October, 1970 (based on the first six months performance) and April, 1971. 40% of any incentives computed for the interim payment will be withheld until the final settlement. . . .*

> *ADDITIONAL RULES*

> *1. To receive payment of earned incentive including amounts withheld during the incentive period, a salesman must be on the payroll at the time of distribution.*

During 1970, Walker exceeded 140 percent of his sales quota. Under the terms of the plan, he was paid a bonus of $948 in October 1970. If he had continued working through April 1971, at which time further bonus payments were distributed by American Optical to its salespeople, Walker would have been entitled to an additional $2,452.00 as the balance of his bonus for 1970.

However, on December 31, 1970, Walker voluntarily quit his job. When American Optical refused to pay him the balance of the bonus to which he claimed he was entitled, he filed suit.

The case reached the Oregon Supreme Court, which ruled against Walker. It said that when a bonus plan specifically provided that a bonus did not become payable until a certain date—and only to employees who continued in employment until that time—an employer had no duty to pay the bonus to employees who voluntarily quit their jobs before that date.

∎ A Note on Attorney's Fees

Employers should recognize that state law often provides that a worker who successfully sues a former employer for unpaid wages, salary, or commissions also may be entitled to payment of attorney's fees incurred in connection with the suit and to reimbursement for expenses of litigation. (Some statutes also provide for penalty charges against the employer.) These costs could in certain cases more than double the amount due the worker, and should be kept in mind when such a dispute arises.

▌Defaming Former Salespeople

The other major postemployment issue that can cost an employer a lot of money involves statements made by an employer or its representatives about former employees. The statements can be to customers, a former employee's co-workers, or other businesses seeking information about a former worker, or to any combination of these three groups. The basic legal requirement: Be careful, or risk suffering the same kind of losses suffered by the Larson Distributing Company.

A few years ago, Larson's carpet division manager, Robert Fitzsimmons, hired Ned Pittman to work as a carpet salesperson. Fitzsimmons agreed to give Pittman all accounts in a specified area of the Denver territory and to pay him 17 percent of gross profits on sales.

Pittman sold large volumes of merchandise and earned substantial commissions in the first 10 months of his employment. At the beginning of the following fiscal year, the company reduced Pittman's commissions to 15 percent. There was evidence that the reason for the reduction was that Pittman earned more money than the owner of the company. Pittman protested the reduction, but continued to work. Indeed, his earnings continued to increase.

Beginning in the third year, over Pittman's protest, his commission was again reduced, this time to a sliding rate, depending upon sales volume. Also, several of Pittman's accounts, including some that he had developed himself, were given to other salespeople. These salespeople were paid 17 percent even though Pittman had been earning a lower commission on them.

After the second reduction in commission, Pittman consulted an attorney. The attorney wrote a letter to the company, demanding back payment of commissions and restoration of territory. The letter concluded by requesting a response within five days, and stated that Pittman had authorized a lawsuit if it should become necessary.

Larson's response: It terminated Pittman. Pittman then began looking for a new job in the same industry.

In response to inquiries from a factory representative of a supplier to the company, Fitzsimmons stated that the reason Pittman had been terminated was because he "spent too much time in the office and on the telephone" rather than calling on customers. In response to inquiries from a customer,

Fitzsimmons stated that Pittman had been terminated because he "wasn't doing as good a job."

Pittman, contending that he had been slandered, filed suit against Larson.

The court noted that a statement is slanderous or defamatory if it tends to harm the reputation of another so as to lower him or her in the estimation of the community or to deter third persons from associating or dealing with him or her. More specifically, a person who ascribes to another person conduct, characteristics, or a condition that adversely affects his fitness for the proper conduct of that person's lawful business, trade, or profession can be held liable for slander.

The court said that the statements Fitzsimmons made to the customer and factory representative were "clearly defamatory." The court rejected Larson's contention that the statements constituted only Fitzsimmons's opinion—it said that neither statement was cautiously phrased but were unqualified statements of fact. "No other reasons were given or hinted at for Pittman's firing." Furthermore, the court noted, as Pittman's supervisor, "Fitzsimmons's was in a position to know the real reasons for Pittman's firing."

Many courts do recognize a "qualified privilege" for statements that former employers make to employees or in response to an inquiry from a prospective employer, so long as the statements are made in good faith and without malice. The court in the Pittman case rejected Larson's claim that Fitzsimmons' statements should be entitled to that defense. Among other things, it found evidence that Fitzsimmons had "abused the privilege" because there was evidence that the statements were false—Pittman apparently was fired not because of poor job performance or failure to call on customers but because he demanded satisfaction of his claims for compensation. While falsity alone would not support a decision finding an abuse of privilege, the court noted that Fitzsimmons was in a position to know the reasons he gave for firing Pittman were false and was required to answer truthfully.

▌ Self-Publication

For a statement to be considered defamatory, it must be communicated (or "published") to someone other than the person the statement is about. Therefore, it would appear that an employer could not be held liable for defamation of a former employee if the employer did not speak to anyone other than the employee. Yet some courts have found what they refer to as compelled self-publication to be sufficient to meet the publication test.

In one case, employees who were improperly fired for "gross insubordination" claimed that they had communicated this information to prospective employers themselves when asked why they had left their previous employment. They admitted that their former employer never made any such statements to their prospective employers.

The court said that if a defamed person was in some way compelled to communicate the defamatory statements to a third person and if it was foreseeable to the employer that the defamed person would be so compelled, then the employer could be held liable for the defamation. It stated that the concept of compelled self-publication "does no more than hold the originator of the defamatory statement liable for damages caused by the statement where the originator knows, or should know, of circumstances whereby the defamed person has no reasonable means of avoiding publication of the statement or avoiding the resulting damages." The court said that it was foreseeable to the employer that its former employees would be asked by prospective employers to identify the reason that they were discharged. Their only choices would be to repeat the defamatory statement—"gross insubordination"—or to lie. "Fabrication, however, is an unacceptable alternative," the court concluded.

▌ A Final Word

Two major post-employment issues can cost an employer money. First, bonuses and commissions may be payable to or, at the least, not recoverable from former salespeople. Businesses can try to limit these expenses by placing appropriate language in employment contracts.

Employers also face potential liability when speaking about former employees to current employees or customers or to former employees' prospective employers. A qualified privilege can protect them, so long as statements are made in good faith and without malice.

FIVE POSTEMPLOYMENT LAWSUITS

1. While Chester W. Markham was employed as a commission salesperson by the Nu-Tone Products Company, advances from the company to him exceeded the commissions he earned. The written contract Markham had signed provided that any excess of advances over commissions earned "shall remain a debt of [Markham] until paid in full" and that if "collection is required at any time, [Markham] shall pay the reasonable cost thereof including attorney's fees." After Markham left Nu-Tone, the company filed suit to collect the excess advances. In its decision in this case, the Supreme Court of Colorado noted the general rule that an express or implied agreement is required to impose a personal obligation on a commission salesperson to repay advances in excess of earned commissions and that without such an agreement, an employer cannot recover the excess of advances over commissions earned. It then found that the contract signed by Markham contained "clear and unambiguous" contractual language to the effect that the excess of advances over commissions earned was Markham's debt until paid in full to Nu-Tone. (Nu-Tone Products Company v. Markham, 481 P.2d 719 (Sup. Ct. Oregon, 1971).)

2. John L. Huber, who was doing business as Huber Claim Service, hired Corbertt R. Landry on September 1, 1959, to manage one of his offices. Landry's written employment agreement provided that his compensation was to be based on one-half of the net profits of the office. It also provided that he could draw $450 per month, to be deducted from the share of the net profits he was to receive as compensation. On December 23, 1959, after giving appropriate notice to Landry under the agreement, Huber terminated him because the office had made no profits. Landry had taken his monthly draw up to November 15, but Huber refused to pay Landry any compensation for the period between November 15 and December 23, contending that the draw was only an advance against Landry's share of the net profits and that, because there were no net profits, he did not owe anything to Landry. Landry filed suit.

The court noted that most similar cases involved employers seeking to recover from employees the excess of advances or draws paid over the commissions or profits actually earned and that Landry's case involved the converse. It said, though, that the same general rule should apply and concluded that in the absence of contrary agreement, a contract to pay an employee a specified sum periodically, which is to be charged against future commission or profits, entitles the employee to recover the promised amount regardless of the commissions or profits earned. (Landry v. Huber, 138 So.2d 449 (Ct. App. Louisiana, 1962).)

3. After Michael LaForte recovered unpaid wages in a lawsuit against his former employer, Rubenstein Brothers, he contended that he was entitled to an award of attorney's fees under a state statute permitting attorney's fees to be awarded to a victorious employee in a suit for "any unpaid wages whatsoever." A trial judge found that LaForte's attorney performed "considerable work" in connection with the case and ordered Rubenstein to pay LaForte's reasonable attorney's fees. Employers should recognize that this kind of statute increases the likelihood that disgruntled employees will bring suit for amounts they claim due because it can remove the burden of legal fees from their shoulders. (Rubenstein Brothers v. LaForte, 320 So.2d 303 (Ct. App. Louisiana, 1975).)

4. A business that sold and distributed candy and related items to schools, churches, and other groups for use in their fund raising activities operated primarily through sales representatives, all of whom were employed under written agreements that assigned a particular exclusive geographic territory to each. The agreements also expressly prohibited any sales representative from selling competitors' products during the term of employment and for one year thereafter. In May 1986, the company's regional sales manager received information from a customer that one of the company's sales reps, Alfred Payne, was violating his employment agreement by selling outside his assigned territory. The sales manager discussed the situation with the sales rep whose territorial exclusivity allegedly was being violated and whose sales and commissions would suffer if the allegations were true. He also discussed the customer report with two officials at the company's headquarters.

Payne filed suit against the company, charging it with, among other things, defamation. The company argued that the statements complained of by Payne were subject to a qualified privilege, and the court agreed. It said the sales manager had "a clear interest and duty regarding whether one of his employees was violating key terms of his employment contract." Moreover, the court said, the sales manager's statements were directed toward individuals with a similarly strong interest and duty, including the sales rep whose efforts to sell the company's products in the relevant area was allegedly being compromised. Because Payne failed to show that the statements he complained about were motivated by actual malice, ill will, or personal spite, the court ruled that Payne's defamation claim should be dismissed. (Payne v. Kathryn Beich & Nestle, 697 F.Supp. 612 (E.D.N.Y. 1988).)

5. "I have enough against you for an indictment," Frank Dovidio, an investigator in the Asset Protection Department of the Lincoln First Bank, N.A., allegedly told Kenneth H. Loughry, a collection manager in the bank's Consumer Credit Services Department who was responsible for both debt collections and property repossession and disposition. Dovidio allegedly then threw an envelope containing tinfoil packets on the table and demanded, "Come on Ken, you know what these are. Have you ever used cocaine?" At the meeting, Robert Lee, a bank vice-president, manager of its Real Estate Division, and director of security, then allegedly accused Loughry of larceny when he stated, "We know that you gave a truck to Charles Johnson for bringing back a car from out of state. We've verified that this truck is registered in the name of Chuck Johnson." Although Loughry denied ever having used cocaine and denied having improperly transferred a truck to Johnson, he was discharged the next day. Loughry filed suit, contending that the bank officers' "slanderous statements" had resulted in his discharge and had damaged his reputation in the banking community. A jury found in Loughry's favor and awarded him $55,000 in damages to compensate him for his losses and $133,000 in punitive damages—$22,000 as to Lee, $6,000 as to Dovidio, and $105,000 as to the bank.

The bank appealed the compensatory and punitive damages award to the New York Court of Appeals. The court acknowledged that statements among employees in furtherance of the common interest of the employer, made at a confidential meeting, "may well fall within the ambit of a qualified or conditional privilege." However, it said, the privilege is conditioned on its proper exercise and cannot shelter statements published with malice or with knowledge of their falsity or reckless disregard as to their truth or falsity. The court upheld the compensatory damages award, noting that the jury had determined that the two statements by Lee and Dovidio were false, that Lee and Dovidio "solely from malice intend[ed] to injure [Loughry] when [they] made the statements," that the statements were made "solely as a result of [the individuals'] malice toward [Loughry]," and that they injured Loughry. The court said that consonant with risk allocation theories, liability for compensatory damages is properly placed on an innocent employer for slander by its agents committed in the course of their employment. However, it said, punitive damages "are a different matter entirely." Unlike damages that compensate an individual for injury or loss, punitive damages—damages over and above full compensation—serve the societal purpose of punishing and deterring the wrongdoer, as well as others, from similar conduct in the future.

Because of a dual recognition that blameless shareholders or owners likely suffer the ultimate burden of punitive damages vicariously imposed on an employer, and yet vicarious punitive damages can advance the goal of deterrence by motivating the employer to take corrective action, the issue of vicarious liability for punitive damages has for decades fueled heated controversy among courts and commentators. In New York, the court stated, the issue has long been settled: an employer may not be punished for malicious acts in which it was not implicated. Punitive damages only can be imposed on an employer for the intentional wrongdoing of its employees only where management has authorized, participated in, consented to, or ratified the conduct giving rise to such damages, or deliberately retained an unfit employee, or the wrongdoing was in pursuit of a recognized business system of the employer. Loughry did not contend that Lincoln had authorized or ratified the Lee and Dovidio statements, or had deliberately retained unfit employees, or had promulgated such statements as part of its regular business policy. Finding that neither Lee nor Dovidio were "superior officers" so as to equate their conduct with participation by their employer, the court reversed the punitive damages award against the bank. (Loughry v. Lincoln First Bank, N.A., 502 N.Y.S.2d 965 (Ct. App. N.Y. 1986).)

Postemployment Checklist

✓ Even when an employer properly terminates a salesperson without fear of a "wrongful discharge" suit, the employer has two issues to be concerned about—payment of post-employment bonuses or commissions, and possible defamation lawsuits.

✓ Generally speaking, an employee paid commissions will be entitled to keep any excess advances over earned commissions unless the employee's contract specifically provides otherwise.

✓ Similarly, a former employee may be entitled to a promised draw for the period while the employee was working even if the employee does not seek that payment until the postemployment period—unless a written agreement provides otherwise.

✓ Statements about former employees to customers, other employees, and the former employees' prospective employers can subject an employer to liability for defamation.

✓ In many instances, however, those kinds of statements can be subject to a qualified privilege, at least to the extent they were not made as a result of malice, ill will, or in bad faith.

LEGAL
RESTRICTIONS
ON MARKETING

15

ADVERTISING RESTRICTIONS

■ Content Regulations in Federal Law ■ State Content Regulations
■ The American Flag Cases ■ A Final Word

Over the course of a number of years, Time, Inc., the publisher of several popular magazines, had been advised by United States Secret Service agents that particular photographic reproductions of currency appearing in its magazines violated provisions of federal law that imposed criminal liability on anyone who "prints, photographs, or in any other manner makes or executes any engraving, photograph, print, or impression in the likeness of any . . . obligation or other security [of the United States]" except in certain cases. The law permitted photos or illustrations of money only for philatelic, numismatic, educational, historical, or newsworthy purposes in articles, books, journals, newspapers, or albums. But it generally did not permit those reproductions for advertising purposes. Furthermore, permitted reproductions had to be in black and white and less than three-fourths or more than one and one-half the size of the original. (In addition, the negative and plates used in making the reproductions had to be destroyed after their final authorized use.) Despite the warnings, Time, Inc. continued to use photos or illustrations of money in its magazines.

The front cover of the February 16, 1981, issue of Sports Illustrated *carried a photographic color reproduction of $100 bills pouring into a basketball hoop to illustrate an article concerning a bribery scandal in amateur basketball. When the Secret Service became aware of the cover, an agent informed Time's legal department that the illustration violated federal law and that it would be necessary for the Service to seize all plates and mate-*

rials used in connection with the production of the cover. The agent also asked for the names and addresses of all the printers who prepared the cover and requested an interview with a member of Time's management.

Ten days later, Time filed suit against the secretary of the treasury and the director of the Secret Service seeking a declaratory judgment that the provisions of federal law restricting its ability to use photos of money were unconstitutional.

The case reached the United States Supreme Court. The Court ruled that the purpose requirement contained in the law—which permitted reproductions of currency for philatelic, numismatic, educational, historical, or newsworthy purposes—was unconstitutional under the First Amendment to the United States Constitution because it discriminated on the basis of content; for example, the government could not constitutionally be in the position of determining whether some proposed use was "newsworthy." But the Court upheld the color and size limitations, finding that they served the government's interest in preventing counterfeiting.

After the Supreme Court's decision, the federal laws affecting the use of reproductions of money, postage and revenue stamps, and any other obligation or security of the United States government, were amended by Congress. Now, even advertisers can use the image of United States currency in their ads, but, generally speaking, the pictures only may be in black and white and they must meet the size requirements upheld by the Court. Violation of these rules is a felony.

▌Content Regulations in Federal Law

In addition to the rules on currency reproductions, a vast number of federal and state laws restrict the content of ads. Some of these regulations are rather well known, some are obscure, but all can lead to litigation costs and potential civil or criminal liability. Here is a short summary of what some of the federal statutes prohibit:

- Anyone who uses the coat of arms of the Swiss Confederation (consisting of an upright white cross with equal arms and lines on a red ground) or any simulation of the coat of arms as a trademark, on a commercial label, or in an ad is subject to a fine of not more than $250 and imprisonment of not more than six months.

- A bank that is not a member of the federal reserve system may not falsely advertise that it is a member; similarly a bank that does not have its deposits insured by the Federal Deposit Insurance Corporation may not advertise that it does.

- No business may use the words "Federal Bureau of Investigation" or the initials "FBI" in any ad in a manner reasonably calculated to convey the impression that the FBI approves, endorses, or authorizes the ad.

- It also is unlawful to knowingly use the Smokey the Bear or Woodsy the Owl characters, or the slogan, Give a Hoot, Don't Pollute, without the government's consent.

- Debt collection agencies and detective services may not use the words "national," "federal," or "United States," the initials "U.S.," or any emblem, insignia, or name in an ad for the purpose of conveying the false impression that the ad is from a department, agency, bureau, or instrumentality of the United States or in any manner represents the United States.

- No one may use the great seal of the United States or the seals of the president or vice-president of the United States or United States Senate in any ad for the purpose of conveying, or in a manner reasonably calculated to convey, a false impression of sponsorship or approval by the United States government or by any department, agency, or instrumentality of the government.

▮ State Content Regulations

State laws regulating or prohibiting the content of particular kinds of advertisements are just as diverse. Many were enacted for reasons long lost to history. Here is a short summary of a few particularly interesting rules from New York:

- No business may use a simulated check in an advertisement unless the document bears the phrase "This is not a check" diagonally printed in clear and conspicuous type on the front.

- It is unlawful to use, for advertising purposes or for purposes of trade, the name, symbol, device, or other identification of any nonprofit corporation, association, society, or organization organized exclusively for religious, benevolent, humane, charitable, educational, hospital, patriotic, fraternal, or veterans purposes without having first obtained the written consent of the entity.

- New York law regulates the use of the words "linen," "pure linen," or "all linen" on collars and cuffs.

- No business in New York, without express authority from the secretary general of the United Nations, may use in an ad the name or abbreviation of the United Nations, or any official emblem or other official insignia of the United Nations.

- No person may use the title "doctor" in making representations for the purpose of inducing, or which are likely to induce, the purchase of drugs or other goods or services intended to diagnose, treat, mitigate, prevent, or cure any human disease or physical condition unless that person obtained a degree from an institution of higher education authorized by law to confer doctoral degrees in the state where the institution is located.

Are these kinds of rules enforceable? The Supreme Court was persuaded that the color and size limitations contained in the federal statutes restricting the right to reproduce currency were constitutional in the case filed by Time; a similar argument probably can be made that all of these rules serve a valuable government interest. (These questions should be kept in mind for chapter 17.) But perhaps the law relating to the ultimate American symbol—the American Flag—can shed light on the validity of these other advertising restrictions.

▮ The American Flag Cases

In 1989, the Supreme Court ruled that a Texas statute criminalizing the desecration of venerated objects, including the United States flag, was unconstitutional as applied to an individual who had set an American flag on fire during a political demonstration. The Texas law provided that "[a] person commits an offense if he intentionally or knowingly desecrates . . . [a] national flag," where "desecrate" was defined to mean to "deface, damage, or otherwise physically mistreat in a way that the actor knows will seriously offend one or more persons likely to observe or discover his action."

The Court ruled that the protester's flag burning was conduct "sufficiently imbued with elements of communication to implicate the First Amendment." It then found that Texas's interest in protecting the flag's symbolic meaning could not justify the infringement on the demonstrator's First Amendment rights.

After the Supreme Court's decision in that case, Congress passed the Flag Protection Act of 1989. That law provided in relevant part that whoever knowingly mutilated, defaced, physically defiled, burned, maintained on the floor or ground, or trampled upon any United States flag "shall be fined . . . or imprisoned for not more than one year, or both." (The law excluded any conduct relating to the disposal of a flag after it became worn or soiled.)

After the law was passed, certain individuals were prosecuted for knowingly setting fire to several United States flags; some did so on the steps of the United States Capitol while protesting various aspects of the government's domestic and foreign policy and others did so to protest the law's passage. These cases also reached the Supreme Court.

The government argued that the Flag Protection Act was different from the Texas law that the Supreme Court had invalidated because it did not target conduct on the basis of the content of its message—the law proscribed conduct (other than disposal) that damaged or mistreated a flag, without regard to the actor's motive, intended message, or the likely effects of the conduct on others. By contrast, the government argued, the Texas law expressly prohibited only those acts of physical flag desecration "that the actor knows will seriously offend" onlookers.

The Court rejected the government's argument and found this law unconstitutional as applied in these cases. The law, it said, suppressed expression out of concern for its likely communicative impact and therefore was not permitted under the Constitution.

The case was a victory for proponents of so-called "political" speech, which is speech that intends to set forth a political statement; political speech may be compared with "commercial" speech (such as advertisements), which traditionally has been granted less protection than political speech (although the First Amendment nowhere distinguishes the two).

Indeed, in its decision striking down the Flag Protection Act, the Supreme Court specifically noted that it was not ruling on the validity of laws regulating commercial exploitation of the image of the United States flag. However, the Court did rule on that issue more than 85 years ago.

That case involved the validity of a Nebraska law entitled "An act to prevent and punish the desecration of the flag of the United States." Among other things, it prohibited placing any "word, figure, mark, picture, design, drawing, or any advertisement of any nature, upon any flag, standard, color, or ensign, of the United States of America." It expressly excepted, however, from its operation any publication in which a representation of the flag was printed "disconnected from any advertisement."

When the Nebraska attorney general found a bottle of beer upon which, for purposes of advertisement, a United States flag was printed, he went into action. The defendants were found guilty by a jury and ordered to pay a $50 fine and the costs of the prosecution.

In its 1907 decision, the Supreme Court said that it could not "hold that any privilege of American citizenship or that any right of personal liberty was violated by a state enactment forbidding the flag to be used as an advertisement on a bottle of beer." That use, it said, "tends to degrade and cheapen the flag in the estimation of the people, as well as to defeat the object of maintaining it as an emblem of National power and National honor." It concluded that "no one can be said to have the right, secured by the Constitution, to use the country's flag merely for purposes of advertising articles of merchandise."

Although the Supreme Court in its decision overturning the Flag Protection Act specifically stated that it was not resolving the issue of commercial uses of the flag, it is hard to believe that the Court's 1907 decision would stand today. Indeed, the flag now is used for many commercial purposes.

Perhaps the proof that using the flag in advertising is constitutional comes from a very recent decision by the U.S. Trademark Office that, at least a decade or so ago, would have seemed rather startling.

The Trademark Office granted a Massachusetts artist the right to trademark his logo of a waving-in-the-breeze condom containing the stars and stripes of an American flag. The artist's company, the Old Glory Condom Corp., sells its red, white, and blue "condoms with a conscience" in packages using that logo and a statement that protecting lives by safe sex is patriotic.

▌A Final Word

What should advertisers make of the kinds of restrictions still on the books that are discussed in this chapter? Perhaps the bottom line is that where advertisements are not misleading (for example, a bank should not claim to be a national insured bank when it is not) and where they do not use familiar icons (such as the United Nations name or building) without permission, advertisers have a great deal of freedom.

FIVE SUITS OVER VIOLATIONS OF SPECIFIC STATUTES

1. A real estate broker that formed a corporation under the name U.S.I.A. Homes, Inc., advertised individual houses for sale in several newspapers. In one ad, it gave its name as USIA HOMES; a second ad was headed "U.S.I.A. HOMES" in large letters, followed by text advertising a property for sale, and ending, in type less than one-fifth the size of the headline, "NON GOV'T AGENCY Local Agent Specializing in Gvt Approved VA, FHA Mtgs." The government filed suit, asserting that the letters USIA were the initials for the United States Information Agency and that use of those letters in the name of a private corporation, especially one in the real estate field, would tend to lead the public to believe that the company was in some way associated with the federal government.

The government asked the court to compel the company to change its name or to include with it in type of equal size a disclaimer of government agency, and the court agreed. It said that because of the likelihood of public confusion over the corporate name and the false suggestion of some association with the federal government, and the absence of any valid reason for using in the name the familiar initials of a well-known federal agency wholly unrelated to the company's business and affairs, "it must be concluded that continued use of the corporate name as presently used is fraudulent and enjoinable." (United States v. U.S.I.A. Homes, Inc., 409 F.Supp. 483 (E.D.N.Y. 1976).)

2. After Personality Posters Mfg. Co., Inc., began selling a poster of a smiling girl dressed in the well-known green uniform of the Junior Girl Scouts with her hands clasped above her protruding, clearly pregnant abdomen and the caveat "Be Prepared" next to her hands, the Girl Scouts of the United States of America filed suit. Among the Girl Scouts' contentions: the poster violated a federal law relating to the incorporation of the

Girl Scouts that granted it "the sole and exclusive right" to have, and to use, in carrying out its purposes, its emblems and badges, descriptive or designating marks, and words or phrases. The court ruled, though, that the purpose of the federal statute that incorporated the Girl Scouts was "only to protect the public and the Girl Scouts from the confusing . . . use of [the Girl Scouts'] symbols by those who might compete with it in its normal purposes and endeavors." The law was not intended to protect the Girl Scouts "from the lampooning use of its name, motto and insignia." Personality Posters was not a competitor, the court said, ruling in its favor. (Girl Scouts of USA v. Personality Posters Mfg. Co., 304 F.Supp. 1228 (S.D.N.Y. 1969).)

3. When Linmark Associates decided to sell real estate it owned in the township of Willingboro, New Jersey, it listed the property with a real estate agent. To attract interest, Linmark placed a For Sale sign on the lawn. Willingboro, however, limited the kinds of signs that could be erected on land in the township. It prohibited the posting of real estate For Sale and Sold signs in an attempt to stem what the township perceived as the flight of white homeowners from a racially integrated community. The United States Supreme Court ruled, however, that the regulation was unconstitutional. The primary defect was that the regulation acted to prevent residents from obtaining certain information. The Court said that that information, which pertained to sales activity in Willingboro, was of vital interest to Willingboro residents because it affected "one of the most important decisions they have a right to make: where to live and raise their families." The Willingboro council sought to restrict the free flow of that data because it feared that otherwise homeowners would make decisions inimical to what the council viewed as the homeowners' self interest and the corporate interest of the township: they would choose to leave town. But the Court said that "[i]f dissemination of this information can be restricted, then every locality in the country can suppress any facts that reflect poorly on the locality, so long as a plausible claim can be made that disclosure would cause the recipients of the information to act 'irrationally.'" (The Court said that in invalidating the law, it did not leave Willingboro defenseless in its effort to promote integrated housing. The township remained free to continue the "process of education" it had already begun; it could give widespread publicity—through Not for Sale signs or other methods—to the number of white citizens remaining in Willingboro. And it could create inducements to retain individuals who were considering selling their homes.) The Court concluded that the Willingboro ordinance, which impaired "the flow of truthful and legitimate commercial information" was constitutionally infirm. (Linmark Associates, Inc. v. Willingboro, 431 U.S. 85 (1977).)

4. After San Francisco Arts & Athletics, Inc. incorporated in 1981, it began to promote the "Gay Olympic Games," using those words on its letterhead and mailings and in local newspapers. The games were to be a nine-day event to begin in August 1982 in San Francisco; the Arts & Athletics group expected athletes from hundreds of cities in this country and from all over the world. A relay of more than 2,000 runners was expected to carry a torch from New York City across the country to San Francisco; the final runner would enter a stadium with the "Gay Olympic Torch" and light the "Gay Olympic Flame."

To cover the cost of the planned games, the Arts & Athletics organization sold T-shirts, buttons, bumper stickers, and other merchandise bearing the title Gay Olympic Games. However, Congress has granted the United States Olympic Committee the right to prohibit certain commercial and promotional uses of the word "Olympic" and various Olympic symbols. In late December 1981, the executive director of the committee wrote to the Arts & Athletics group, informing it of the existence of the law and requesting that it terminate use of the word "Olympic" in its description of the planned games. The committee then filed suit, and the case reached the United States Supreme Court. The Supreme Court, in a decision rejecting all of the contentions of the Arts & Athletics organization, ruled that the language and legislative history of the law indicated that Congress intended to grant the committee exclusive use of the word

"Olympic" and that the statute was enforceable. (San Francisco Arts & Athletics, Inc. v. United States Olympic Committee, 483 U.S. 522 (1987).)

5. A Clearwater, Florida, ordinance prohibited businesses from flying more than two flags without a permit. Dimmitt Chevrolet, Inc., which displayed 23 American flags at its dealership, sued the city, contending that the ordinance violated the First Amendment. The court found that the city's major concern was that display of the flag by commercial entities in a manner that called attention to their businesses would cause people to believe "that the flag does not stand for nationhood and national unity, but instead for commercial gain and gimmickry"; the city also sought to avoid visual clutter and preserve the community's esthetics. The court rejected the city's goals, finding that the government may not proscribe expressive conduct "simply because society finds the idea itself offensive or disagreeable" and that the ordinance as written was "a far greater restriction upon First Amendment interests than is essential to further the City's interest in avoiding visual clutter and preserving esthetics." It then ruled that the ordinance violated the dealership's First Amendment right to display the flag. (Dimmitt v. Clearwater, 782 F.Supp. 586 (M.D. Fl. 1991).)

Checklist on Laws Regulating Advertising Content

✓ Numerous federal laws prohibit or restrict the kinds of things that advertisers can say in their ads. The American flag and other similar symbols or emblems typically fall into the regulated category.

✓ State laws also prohibit or restrict advertisements; enforcement of those rules by state prosecutors is another potential burden of which advertisers should be aware.

✓ Many of these kinds of restrictions have been and will continue to be upheld by the courts. For example, the United States Supreme Court has upheld a ban on the full-color, full-size reproduction of money.

✓ The fact that America's ultimate symbol—the American flag—now graces a brand of condoms suggests, however, that advertisers have gained substantial freedom over the years.

✓ The best advice: advertisements should not be misleading (for example, a bank should not claim to be a national insured bank when it is not) and should not use familiar icons (such as the United Nations name or building) without permission.

16
TELEMARKETING AND "JUNK" FAXES

■ The Telemarketing Dilemma ■ State Telemarketing Restrictions
■ Consumer Protection? ■ A Final Word

Responding to constituent complaints about intrusive "junk" faxes tying up fax machines and costing money, the Connecticut legislature several years ago passed a bill to deal with the apparent problem. Sensing an opportunity because then-governor William O'Neill had not indicated whether or not he would sign the bill into law, opponents of the bill went into action.

They began bombarding the governor, via fax, with form letters objecting to the bill. Hundreds of faxes were sent to the governor's fax machine—unfortunately preventing his office from learning about possible flooding in the state from the state's Office of Emergency Management.

Declaring that the unwelcome faxes "brought home" the need for the legislation, the governor signed the bill.

■ The Telemarketing Dilemma

Is telemarketing an affordable method of advertising for businesses? Or is it an unconscionable invasion of privacy that should be prohibited at all costs—notwithstanding any possible constraints from the First Amendment. The answer is that it is, in some people's view, both.

The use of telephone and facsimile machines for advertising and marketing purposes is one of the greatest marketing advances of the past quarter century. Telemarketers rang up $435 billion in sales in 1990; furthermore, millions of businesses (and homes) now use fax machines. Today, phones and faxes can reach virtually everyone with a job, a home, or some money.

So where's the problem? The answer may be, paraphrasing something the comic strip character Pogo once said, that "we have met the enemy and it is us." If no one is home during the day, call at night—even though people may be eating dinner or babies may be sleeping. If one salesperson can make a dozen calls an hour, get an automatic dialer that can make 1,500 a day—even though it may be difficult or impossible for people to disconnect the automatic dialer and regain use of their phone line until the recorded message is over. If fax machines are still so new that people always read their faxes, send them a menu from a deli or a Chinese restaurant—even though the other delis and Chinese restaurants (and Japanese restaurants and pizza places and bakeries) have done the same thing.

Yes, telemarketing is important and yes, it does provide a good service to people who may not be able to get out of the house, but many people believe it also has led to abuses. Hence, federal and state legislators have taken it upon themselves to try to solve the "problem."

▌State Telemarketing Restrictions

Dozens of states from Arizona to Wyoming now regulate telemarketing in general or the use of automatic telephone dialing systems in particular. In some cases, those regulations amount to a virtual ban on calls for commercial purposes; other simply require registration by users of automatic dialers.

The Florida statute is rather comprehensive. It creates a "no sales solicitation calls" list on which consumers with residential or mobile phones or pagers can be placed for an initial $10 charge plus an annual $5 assessment. Telephone solicitors (including automatic dialing or recorded message devices) may not make any unsolicited sales calls to those phone numbers (except in connection with the sale of real estate). Generally speaking a call is not unsolicited if it is made in response to an express request of the person called; primarily in connection with an existing debt or contract, payment, or performance of which has not been completed at the time of the call to any person with whom the telephone solicitor has a prior or existing business relationship.

The Florida law says that a sale by a telemarketer to a consumer (other than for certain sales regulated under other sections of Florida law) is not valid or enforceable against the consumer unless it meets all of the following requirements. The contract:

- Must be reduced to writing and signed by the consumer
- Must comply with all other applicable laws and rules

- Must match the description of goods or services described in the telephone solicitation

- Must contain the name, address, and telephone number of the seller, the total price of the contract, and a detailed description of the goods or services sold

- Must contain, in bold, conspicuous type, immediately preceding the signature, the following statement: "You are not obligated to pay any money unless you sign this contract and return it to the seller"

- May not exclude from its terms any oral or written representations made by the telephone solicitor to the consumer in connection with the transaction

Furthermore, the Florida law prohibits the use of automatic dialing systems unless they also have live messages, but only if the calls are made or messages given solely in response to calls initiated by the persons to whom the automatic calls or live messages are directed. Calls also are permitted to numbers selected for automatic dialing that have been screened to exclude any subscriber on the "no sales solicitation calls" list or any unlisted telephone number.

Violation of the Florida telemarketing law can be expensive—courts may impose civil penalties of up to $10,000 per violation. In addition, private parties that successfully bring suit also may recover their attorney's fees, which can be a substantial incentive for private litigation.

In 1989 Texas also added a law regulating automatic dialing machines—and unsolicited faxes. It provides that automatic dialing devices may not be used for the purpose of making a sale if the person making the call or using the device knows or should have known that the called number is a mobile telephone. The reasoning? The mobile telephone owner will be charged for that specific call and the called person has not given consent to make such a call to the person calling or using the device, or to the business for which the person is calling or using the device.

Furthermore, it prohibits faxes for the purpose of a solicitation or sale "for which the person or entity receiving the transmission will be charged," unless that person has given prior consent. (It is unclear if the "will be charged" test can be satisfied by being obligated to pay for the cost of the fax paper or requires something else.)

Oregon has a junk fax statute that does not contain a "will be charged" standard. It simply states that a person who receives unsolicited advertising material for the sale of any property or services by fax may give the sender of the fax written notice to discontinue further such transmissions; the faxer is then prohibited for one year from sending unsolicited advertising material by fax.

Rhode Island's junk fax law is even more straightforward: it says that any person who uses a machine that electronically transmits facsimiles of unsolicited advertising material for the sale of any real estate property, goods, or services shall be guilty of a misdemeanor and shall be punished by a fine of not more than $200 for each occurrence. (Perhaps surprisingly, given the breadth of its fax law, Rhode Island does not forbid automatic dialing systems; it requires that they create a disconnect signal within five seconds after the called party hangs up; failure to comply subjects the violator to a fine of not more than $200.)

Unless all states have the same rules, though, it is possible that none of the states' rules can be effective—companies may be able to avoid the more stringent rules simply by moving to a different state. Congress, therefore, stepped into the fray.

▌ Consumer Protection?

In 1991 Congress passed the Telephone Consumer Protection Act in an attempt to regulate automatic telephone dialing systems. That law has been challenged in the courts; resolution of the constitutional issues the law raises may require a decision by the United States Supreme Court, which could be years away. Nonetheless, the basics of that law are important as a guide for what Congress thought wrong with telemarketing.

The Telephone Consumer Protection Act defines an automatic telephone dialing system as "equipment which has the capacity (A) to store or produce telephone numbers to be called, using a random or sequential number generator; (B) to dial such numbers." The act prohibits calls to emergency telephone lines, to patient or guest rooms in hospitals, and to paging services and cellular phones.

Furthermore, it prohibits the use of any automatic dialer to "initiate any telephone call to any residential telephone line using an artificial or prerecorded voice to deliver a message without express consent of the called party," subject to exceptions promulgated by the Federal Communications Commission (FCC) including for tax-exempt businesses and automatically dialed calls without a commercial purpose. In rules the FCC enacted under the law, all such telephone solicitations to residential phones are prohibited unless the calling party has "instituted procedures for maintaining a list of persons who do not wish to receive telephone solicitations."

▮ A Final Word

Several years before the United States Supreme Court ruled that commercial speech was entitled to the protection of the First Amendment, it upheld the validity of a junk mail law that permitted recipients to "require that a mailer . . . stop all further mailings." That case arose in the context of sexually provocative advertisements, and the Court's concern with morality and minors undoubtedly contributed to its decision.

Are telemarketing restrictions and prohibitions likely to be upheld? Clearly, a phone call is more intrusive than a letter; on the other hand, business-to-business telemarketing would not seem to implicate the same privacy concerns that business-to-consumer telemarketing raises.

Telemarketing groups have in recent years acknowledged the challenge of making all telemarketers more responsible. Future decisions by legislatures and the courts may well rest on how well these groups succeed.

FIVE TELEMARKETING CASES

1. Several years ago, Donald Urbanski was charged with violating a Suffolk County, New York, law regulating the solicitation of funds on behalf of law enforcement organizations. The law said that no law enforcement officer, law enforcement affiliated organizations, or professional fund-raiser "may solicit funds or contributions by use of the telephone for or in behalf of any law enforcement affiliated organization or law enforcement department within the geographical area of Suffolk County." Urbanski claimed that the law was applied in a discriminatory manner because it was not applied against other kinds of sales representatives, such as telemarketers selling newspaper subscriptions. But the court said that the law served the legitimate public concern "of ensuring integrity within the police department." The court quoted from a decision by former United States Supreme Court justice Oliver Wendell Holmes in a decision upholding the constitutionality of a police regulation prohibiting officers from soliciting money or any aid, on any pretense, for any political purpose whatever. Justice Holmes said in that case that there was nothing in the constitution "to prevent the city from attaching obedience to this rule as a condition to the office of policeman, and making it part of the good conduct required. The petitioner may have a constitutional right to talk politics, but he has no constitutional right to be a policeman." The court then upheld the Suffolk law, noting that it only restricted the means of soliciting funds and did not absolutely prohibit it. (People v. State D.A. Investigators, 428 N.Y.S.2d 144 (D.Ct. Suffolk Co. 1980).)

2. In July 1980, Michael Haubrich, a sales representative of Diamond Source Limited, contacted Randy Bonn by telephone and asked him whether he might be interested in investing in gemstones. Haubrich then met with Bonn at Bonn's house, where they discussed investment in the gemstone market. Bonn later claimed in a lawsuit he filed against Haubrich that Haubrich presented literature on rubies, claimed that rubies were a "hot selling thing on the market," and stated that the value of rubies would appreciate between 20 percent and 30 percent in the first year. Haubrich allegedly told Bonn that he could resell the ruby to him or any other gem company in the United States without a problem.

Bonn purchased a ruby from Haubrich for $5,049.20. Bonn received the stone in September 1980 and, approximately one week later, gave it to Haubrich to have it authenticated. Haubrich supplied Bonn with another ruby in November 1980, claiming that the first one had been lost in transit. He also provided a written appraisal valuing the stone at $13,130. According to Bonn, Haubrich stated the ruby had a resale value of between $8,000 and $9,000 and that this stone was better than the first one. But when Bonn could not resell the ruby through Haubrich and Diamond Source Limited, he filed suit under a Wisconsin statute prohibiting false advertising.

At trial, his expert jeweler testified that the ruby had a wholesale value of $700 and a resale value of 10 percent to 20 percent less than $700. He also testified that there was very little, if any, appreciation in the value of rubies between July 1980 and December 1981. The trial court dismissed Bonn's suit, finding that because Haubrich had not advertised to obtain his contact with Bonn, Bonn could not sue Haubrich under the false advertising law. But an appellate court reversed the decision, rejecting Haubrich's contention that coverage under that statute was limited to transactions involving media advertising in the first instance. It said the purpose of the law was to protect consumers from untrue, deceptive, or misleading representations made to promote the sale of a product. "Untruths, deceptions or misleading representations are no less harmful when they follow an initial telephone contact than a media advertisement," the court stated. Accordingly, it concluded that "the fact that Bonn was initially contacted by telephone rather than by media advertisement is not controlling." (Bonn v. Haubrich, 366 N.W.2d 503 (Wis. App. 1985).)

3. After North Carolina amended its law to provide that any "professional solicitor who solicits by telephone contributions for charitable purposes or in any way compensates another person to solicit by telephone contributions for charitable purposes shall be guilty of a misdemeanor," the Optimist Club of North Raleigh and Joseph A. Page, a professional solicitor who solicited funds for charitable purposes by telephone, filed suit. They contended that the law impermissibly foreclosed a mode of communication that was protected by the First Amendment and interfered with rights of professional solicitors to earn a livelihood. The government contended that it did not infringe on any constitutionally protected rights but simply posed a reasonable restriction on the manner in which charitable solicitations were conducted. It noted that charities were permitted under the law to conduct their own telephone solicitation campaigns and that professional solicitors could be hired to conduct, manage, or consult on a particular solicitation campaign. Finally, the government stated, the law permitted anyone to solicit contributions in person or through the mail, because the law imposed no restriction on those activities. Therefore, it argued, the law protected the public and only limited the manner in which charitable solicitations were conducted.

However, the court rejected the government's contention that the law was narrowly tailored to prevent fraud by regulating the kind and manner of charitable solicitations; it concluded that the total ban on telephone solicitations infringed on the First Amendment rights of professional solicitors and had a substantially restrictive effect not only on the solicitors' right to communicate but also on the ability of charitable organizations to conduct different kinds of solicitation campaigns. (Optimist Club of North Raleigh, N.C. v. Riley, 563 F.Supp. 847 (E.D.N.C. 1982).)

4. When the South Central Bell Telephone Company began considering offering local Dial-It service (for instance, sports scores, horoscopes, and soap opera updates) in the New Orleans area, it began having discussions with Carlin Communications, Inc., as a potential Dial-It subscriber. Carlin apparently knew from the inception of these discussions that South Central Bell would not permit operation of a Dial-It line similar to Carlin's High Society Hotline in New York, which transmitted sexually explicit messages. After South Central Bell received authorization to provide local Dial-It service, Carlin gave the company a list of programs that it said it intended to put in operation; they were (1) Info Line—976-2727; (2) Quiz Line—976-9467; (3) Telesports—976-4444; (4) News Line—976-2626; and (5) Hope Line—976-4673. However, the day it initiated its first Dial-It service in the New Orleans area, Carlin went to court to restrain South Central Bell from limiting the content of its programs. A Carlin representative provided the judge with a transcript of a message being played over Carlin's New York line and testified that Carlin intended to use that message or something similar to it in New Orleans—but the court found that it was patently obscene and therefore devoid of constitutional protection; it denied Carlin's request for an injunction.

Two days later, a South Central Bell employee dialed the Carlin number and heard a message essentially similar to the one the court had declared obscene. At 2:00 P.M. that day, after giving Carlin one hour's notice, South Central Bell disconnected Carlin's Dial-It service. Carlin, which claimed the transmission of the obscene message was a clerical error, went back to court for an order requiring South Central Bell to restore the service. A lower court ordered South Central Bell to reinstate Carlin's service, but that was not a complete victory for Carlin. A Louisiana state court of appeal said that "should Carlin ever again transmit a message which [South Central Bell] deems to be obscene, [South Central Bell] is authorized to disconnect Carlin's Dial-It service." (Carlin Communications, Inc. v. South Central Bell Telephone Co., 461 So.2d 1208 (Ct. App. Louisiana 1985).)

5. What can happen to fraudulent telemarketers? Just ask David E. Williams, the operator of World Wide Factors, Ltd. World Wide sold advertising specialty items through telemarketing and conducted sham prize giveaway promotions. It would inform consumers that they had won a substantial prize, require consumers to pay a processing fee, and advise them that if they bought products from World Wide the prize would be exempt from income tax. However, consumers never received the promised prizes, only the opportunity to purchase goods. Williams pleaded guilty to conspiracy, mail fraud, and wire fraud. He agreed to discontinue all telemarketing sales, to liquidate and dissolve World Wide, to pay $942,773 in restitution to 12,995 customers, and to pay $324,661 to 1,034 consumers who filed complaints with the Postal Inspection Service. Then, the Federal Trade Commission (FTC) filed a civil suit against World Wide and Williams seeking to freeze all of World Wide's and Williams' assets for distribution to consumers.

The court entered a temporary restraining order freezing those assets, except for an allowance for Williams's living expenses, attorney fees limited to the rate of $90 per hour, and other minor expenses. Furthermore, the court ordered Williams to transfer foreign funds to an institution in the United States and it appointed a special master to determine which of World Wide's and Williams's disbursements were necessary and reasonable. World Wide appealed to the U.S. Court of Appeals for the Ninth Circuit. The appellate court essentially upheld the lower court's decision, finding that the FTC has authority to freeze assets under federal law and that courts may limit or even deny amounts from frozen assets to be used for attorney fees. (FTC v. World Wide Factors, Ltd., 873 F.2d 1235 (9th Cir. 1989).)

Telemarketing Checklist

✓ Phones and faxes are big business . . . and they also are big ways of selling by business. But the telemarketing industry has a public relations problem on its hands. The question: Is telemarketing a boon to the economy or an invasion of privacy?

✓ Numerous state legislatures, and Congress, have enacted laws restricting or prohibiting certain forms of telemarketing. They generally seek to regulate automatic dialing machines and unsolicited faxes.

✓ Unfortunately, many of the laws are rather vague. For instance, it is sometimes not certain exactly what constitutes "prior consent" to receive an ad by fax. Some telemarketers have argued that a business that lists a fax number on its business card has given prior consent to receive unsolicited faxes.

✓ Furthermore, some (or perhaps most) of the laws may be unconstitutional because a complete ban on only one form of communication may not be permitted. Existing technology or expected technological developments may allow automatic dialing systems to meet people's objections.

✓ As other advertisers have learned, the key to avoiding regulation and to staying within any applicable law is to go as far as possible—but no further—than common sense and good taste dictate. And when a legal restriction is enacted, respected telemarketers should carefully analyze it to determine whether to fight it.

17

COMMERCIAL SPEECH

▌The New Commercial Speech Doctrine
▌Laws or Rules Limiting Commercial Speech
▌Central Hudson's Four-Part Test ▌The Casino Case
▌A Final Word

More than 50 years ago, the owner of a United States Navy submarine that he exhibited for profit prepared and printed a handbill to solicit visitors for a stated admission fee. However, when he attempted to distribute the handbill in New York City, the police told him that he had to stop. They said that he was violating Section 318 of the Sanitary Code, which forbade distribution in the streets of commercial and business advertising matter; he was told, though, that he could distribute handbills solely devoted to "information or a public protest."

The submarine's owner then prepared a two-sided handbill; on one side was a revision of the original with the reference to an admission fee deleted. On the other side was a protest against the actions of a city department in refusing to allow him to use facilities at a city-owned pier. The police said that distribution of the two-sided bill also was prohibited, although they said that a bill containing only the protest would not violate the law. He then brought suit seeking an injunction prohibiting the city from interfering with his distribution of the handbill.

In its 1942 decision in this case, the United States Supreme Court recognized that the streets are proper places for communicating information and disseminating opinion and that the government could not unduly burden or proscribe that right.

However, the Supreme Court said, "the Constitution imposes no such restraint on government as respects purely commercial advertising."

How times have changed.

Today, the Supreme Court recognizes that "commercial speech" is entitled to protection under the First Amendment of the Constitution. Even now, though, advertisements, marketing communications, trade dress, and other forms of commercial speech are not considered as "pure" and "worthy" of First Amendment protections as political or religious speech, debates over government policies, and other things not painted with any sort of commercial brush.

Nonetheless, the good news for marketers is that the kinds of restrictions on advertisements and other forms of commercial speech that are discussed in various chapters in this book must undergo First Amendment analysis; in years gone by, they all simply would have been upheld on their face. Because of this change in the law, fewer complete prohibitions and less restrictive limitations tend to be placed on marketers now than in the past and those that are, or are considered (such as a complete ban on tobacco advertising), always seem to bring forth a debate on First Amendment issues.

▎ The New Commercial Speech Doctrine

In 1975 the notion of commercial speech unprotected by the First Amendment all but passed from the scene when the Supreme Court reversed a criminal conviction for violation of a Virginia statute that made the circulation of any publication to encourage or promote an abortion in Virginia a misdemeanor. That case arose when a newspaper editor had published in his newspaper an advertisement noting the availability of legal abortions in New York. The Court rejected the contention that the publication was unprotected because it was commercial. In announcing the availability of legal abortions in New York, the ad "did more than simply propose a commercial transaction. It contained factual material of clear 'public interest.'" Furthermore, the advertisement related to activity—abortion—with which, at least in some respects, the State could not interfere, based on the Supreme Court's 1973 decision in *Roe v. Wade*. Because of that, the Court said that it did not have to decide the "precise extent to which the First Amendment permits regulation of advertising that is related to activities the State may legitimately regulate or even prohibit."

The following year, the Supreme Court clearly resolved the question of whether there is a First Amendment exception for "commercial speech"—and it ruled that there is not.

In that case, a woman who suffered from diseases that required her to take prescription drugs on a daily basis, a consumer group, and the Virginia State AFL-CIO challenged a portion of a Virginia law that provided that a pharmacist licensed in Virginia was guilty of unprofessional conduct if the pharmacist "publishes, advertises or promotes, directly or indirectly, in any manner whatsoever, any amount, price, fee, premium, discount, rebate or credit terms . . . for any drugs which may be dispensed only by prescription." They contended that prescription drug consumers would greatly benefit if the prohibition were lifted and advertising freely allowed. The Virginia State Board of Pharmacy contended, though, that the advertisement of prescription drug prices was outside the protection of the First Amendment because it was commercial speech.

In its decision, the Supreme Court noted that advertising is dissemination of information as to who is producing and selling what product, for what reason, at what price. "So long as we preserve a predominantly free enterprise economy, the allocation of our resources in large measure will be made through numerous private economic decisions." The Court said that it was a matter of public interest that those decisions, in the aggregate, be intelligent and well informed. "To this end, the free flow of commercial information is indispensable."

The justifications for an advertising ban consisted principally of maintaining a high degree of professionalism on the part of licensed pharmacists; the state board contended that the aggressive price competition that would result from unlimited advertising would make it impossible for the pharmacist to supply professional services in the compounding, handling, and dispensing of prescription drugs. Those services are time consuming and expensive, it noted; if competitors who economized by eliminating them were permitted to advertise their resulting lower prices, the more painstaking and conscientious pharmacist would be forced either to follow suit or to go out of business. The board also claimed that prices might not necessarily fall as a result of advertising. "If one pharmacist advertises, others must, and the resulting expense will inflate the cost of drugs." Furthermore, the board contended that advertising would lead people to shop for their prescription drugs among the various pharmacists who offered the lowest prices, "and the loss of stable pharmacist-customer relationships will make individual attention—and certainly the practice of monitoring—impossible." Finally, the board said that advertising would damage the professional image of the pharmacist. Price advertising would reduce the pharmacist's status "to that of a mere retailer" and the profession would no longer be able to attract highly talented people.

The Supreme Court said that the strength of those proffered justifications was greatly undermined by the fact that high professional standards, to a substantial extent, were guaranteed by the close regulation to which pharmacists in Virginia were subject. The State's protectiveness of its citizens, the Court said, rested in large measure on "the advantages of their being kept in ignorance." It noted that the advertising ban did not prevent the cutting of corners by the pharmacist who was so inclined; the only effect the advertising ban had on that person was "to insulate him from price competition and to open the way for him to make a substantial, and perhaps even excessive, profit in addition to providing an inferior service."

The Court said that there was an alternative to the highly paternalistic approach. "That alternative is to assume that this information is not in itself harmful, that people will perceive their own best interests if only they are well enough informed, and that the best means to that end is to open the channels of communication rather than to close them." The choice between these alternatives, the Court noted, was not for the Virginia legislature or for the Supreme Court to make. "It is precisely this kind of choice, between the dangers of suppressing information, and the dangers of its misuse if it is freely available, that the First Amendment makes for us," the Court stated. It said that Virginia was free to require whatever professional standards it wished of its pharmacists; but "it may not do so by keeping the public in ignorance of the entirely lawful terms that competing pharmacists are offering."

∎ Laws or Rules Limiting Commercial Speech

Though now subject to First Amendment protection, commercial speech is still accorded a lesser protection than other forms of constitutionally guaranteed expression. Some forms of commercial speech regulation are permitted. In a 1980 decision, the Supreme Court set forth a four-part test to determine whether a particular restriction on commercial speech is permitted.

The case arose from events in 1973, when the New York Public Service Commission ordered electric utilities in the state to cease all advertising that "promot[ed] the use of electricity." The order was based on the commission's finding that the interconnected utility system in New York did not have sufficient fuel stocks or sources of supply to continue meeting all customer demands for the 1973–1974 winter.

Three years later, when the fuel shortage had eased, the commission requested comments from the public on its proposal to continue the ban on promotional advertising. The Central Hudson Gas & Electric Corporation opposed the ban on First Amendment grounds. After reviewing the public comments, the commission extended the prohibition in a policy statement issued on February 25, 1977.

The policy statement divided advertising expenses into two broad categories: promotional, which it said was advertising intended to stimulate the purchase of utility services; and institutional and informational, which was a broad category inclusive of all advertising not clearly intended to promote sales. The commission declared all promotional advertising contrary to the national policy of conserving energy. The order permitted "informational" advertising designed to encourage "shifts of consumption" from peak demand times to periods of low electricity demand.

Central Hudson challenged the order in state court, arguing that the commission had restrained commercial speech in violation of the First Amendment. The order was upheld by the trial court and at the intermediate appellate level; New York's highest court also affirmed, finding little value to advertising in "the noncompetitive market in which electric corporations operate." It said that because consumers "have no choice regarding the source of their electric power," promotional advertising of electricity could not contribute to society's interest in "informed and reliable economic decision making." It concluded that the governmental interest in the prohibition outweighed the limited constitutional value of the commercial speech at issue. Central Hudson appealed to the United States Supreme Court.

The Court noted that a number of its prior decisions in the commercial speech area had recognized that commercial speech—expression related solely to the economic interests of the speaker and its audience—was entitled to First Amendment protection. But, it said, there was a common sense distinction between speech proposing a commercial transaction, which occurs in an area traditionally subject to government regulation, and other varieties of speech. The Constitution, it said, affords a lesser protection to commercial speech than to other constitutionally guaranteed forms of expression.

The First Amendment's concern for commercial speech is based on the informational function of advertising. Consequently, the Court stated, there can be no constitutional objection to the suppression of commercial messages that do not accurately inform the public about lawful activity. Accordingly, it said that the government may ban forms of communication more likely to deceive the public than to inform it and also may ban commercial speech related to illegal activity.

❚ Central Hudson's Four-Part Test

However, the Court found, if commercial speech is neither misleading nor related to unlawful activity, the government's power is more circumscribed. The Court then set forth a four part test for analyzing commercial speech restrictions:

1. Courts first must determine if the commercial speech is protected by the First Amendment. For commercial speech to come within that provision, it at least must concern lawful activity and not be misleading.

2. Then courts must analyze whether the asserted governmental interest in restricting commercial speech is substantial.

3. If the commercial speech is protected by the First Amendment and if the government's interest is substantial, the courts then must determine whether the regulation directly advances the governmental interest asserted.

4. Finally, the courts must analyze whether the regulation is more extensive than necessary to serve the government's interests.

In the *Central Hudson* case, the Court noted that the commission did not claim that the proposed advertising was either inaccurate or that it related to unlawful activity. Because electric utilities competed with suppliers of fuel oil and natural gas in several markets, such as those for home heating and industrial power, the Court said that the fact that electric utilities had a monopoly over a product was insufficient reason to conclude that their advertising was not commercial speech. Even in a monopoly market, the Court said that it would generally assume that the willingness of a business to promote its products reflected a belief that consumers were interested in the advertising.

The commission presented two justifications for the ban on promotional advertising. The first concerned energy conservation. It argued that the state's interest in conserving energy was sufficient to support suppression of advertising designed to increase consumption of electricity. The second was based on the commission's concern that promotional advertising would increase demand and result in higher overall rates. The Court said that energy conservation and the state's concern that rates be fair and efficient both represented substantial governmental interests.

The Court then turned to the third part of the analysis. It said that the impact of promotional advertising on the equity of Central Hudson's rates was highly speculative; "conditional and remote eventualities simply cannot justify silencing [Central Hudson's] promotional advertising."

However, it found that the state's interest in energy conservation was directly advanced by the commission's order. There is an immediate connection between advertising and demand for electricity, the Court said. "Central Hudson would not contest the advertising ban unless it believed that promotion would increase its sales." Thus, the Court found a direct link between the state interest in conservation and the commission's order, and turned to the fourth issue: whether the commission's complete suppression of speech ordinarily protectible by the First Amendment was no more extensive than necessary to further the State's interest in energy conservation.

Central Hudson insisted that but for the ban, it would have advertised products and services that used energy efficiently. These included the "heat pump," which both the commission and Central Hudson acknowledged to be a major improvement in electric heating, and the use of electric heat as a "backup" to solar and other heat sources. In the absence of authoritative findings to the contrary, the Supreme Court said that it "must credit as within the realm of possibility the claim that electric heat can be an efficient alternative in some circumstances."

The Court said that the commission's order reached all promotional advertising regardless of the impact of the touted service on overall energy use. But the energy conservation rationale, it said, could not justify suppressing information about electric devices or services that would cause no net increase in total energy use. In addition, it said, the commission made no showing that a more limited restriction on the content of promotional advertising would not adequately serve the state's interests; for example, the commission could have attempted to restrict the format and content of Central Hudson's advertising by requiring that ads include information about the relative efficiency and expense of the offered service, both under current conditions and for the foreseeable future. The Court therefore found that the total ban on promotional advertising violated the First Amendment.

▋ The Casino Case

The Supreme Court issued a troubling 5–4 opinion in 1986, troubling, that is, to proponents of commercial speech. It stemmed from a 1948 law in Puerto Rico that legalized certain forms of casino gambling in licensed gambling rooms to promote the development of tourism. The law also prohibited gambling rooms from advertising or otherwise offering their facilities to the public of Puerto Rico.

Regulations enacted under that law barred gambling parlors from advertising to the public in Puerto Rico and, in addition, prohibited the use of the word "casino" in matchbooks, inter-office and/or external correspondence, invoices, brochures, menus, elevators, lobbies, flyers, telephone books, and directories, and on lighters, envelopes, napkins, glasses, plates, banners, paper holders, pencils, bulletin boards, and any hotel object that could be accessible to the public.

After the Condado Holiday Inn Hotel and Sands Casino was fined for violating the rules, it filed suit seeking a declaratory judgment that the law and regulations impermissibly suppressed commercial speech in violation of the First Amendment.

The lower court interpreted the advertising restrictions as prohibiting local advertising addressed to residents of Puerto Rico but not advertising addressed to tourists even though those ads might incidentally reach the attention of residents. It then upheld the restrictions.

Ostensibly applying the four-part test in Central Hudson, the United States Supreme Court ruled that the Puerto Rico law and regulations (as interpreted by the Puerto Rico court) did not violate the First Amendment.

It said that the particular kind of commercial speech involved in the case, namely advertising of casino gambling aimed at the residents of Puerto Rico, concerned a lawful activity and was not misleading or fraudulent. The government of Puerto Rico had an important goal in restricting the ads—reducing demand for casino gambling by the residents of Puerto Rico. The Court said that the Puerto Rico legislature's interest in the health, safety, and welfare of its citizens constituted a substantial governmental interest.

Then, the Court found that the restrictions directly advanced the government's asserted interest—even though other forms of gambling such as horse racing, cockfighting, and the lottery were permitted to be advertised to the residents of Puerto Rico. The Court said "In our view, the legislature's separate classification of casino gambling, for purposes of the advertising ban, satisfies the third step of the Central Hudson analysis."

It also ruled that the restrictions satisfied the fourth step of the Central Hudson analysis because they were no more extensive than necessary to serve the government's interest.

The Casino argued that the ban was unconstitutional, citing cases in which the Supreme Court had struck down a ban on any "advertisement or display" of contraceptives and another in which it had reversed a criminal conviction based on the advertisement of an abortion clinic. But the Court said that there was a crucial distinction between those cases and the casino advertising case. In the two cases cited by the casino, the underlying conduct that was the subject of the advertising restrictions was constitutionally protected and could not have been prohibited by the government; in the casino case, however, "the Puerto Rico Legislature surely could have prohibited casino gambling by the residents of Puerto Rico altogether." In the Court's view, "the greater power to completely ban casino gambling necessarily includes the lesser power to ban advertising of casino gambling."

▌A Final Word

The Court's decision in the casino case has been greatly analyzed and criticized. Did it intend to set forth a standard that, while citing Central Hudson, goes beyond Central Hudson to permit virtually unlimited government regulation of commercial speech on the theory that if the conduct to which the speech related could be banned the commercial speech could be regulated?

One of the most recent Supreme Court commercial speech decisions since the casino case struck down a Florida ban on in-person solicitation of business clients by certified public accountants. The eight-justice majority decision relied on the Central Hudson analysis and never even mentioned the casino case (although Justice Sandra Day O'Connor's dissenting opinion did). It may be that the rationale espoused in the casino case that made it so troubling will be limited to those few areas (such as gambling and alcohol consumption) where morality concerns overwhelm constitutional analysis.

FIVE ATTORNEY ADVERTISING CASES

To a large extent, the changes in the law relating to commercial speech over the past two decades have coincided with, and perhaps even been driven by, changes in the attitude of professionals about marketing. Lawyers, accountants, and physicians, among others, now recognize that marketing is crucial to the development of their practices and many of them have been pushing the limits in an attempt to reap all possible benefits. For experienced business marketers, the issues in the attorney advertising cases that have reached the United States Supreme Court may seem silly—how could in-person solicitation of a customer or illustrations in ads be a problem?—but they have provoked arguments and dissension in the professions. Here is a survey of five Supreme Court cases dealing with attorney advertising issues:

1. In 1974 Arizona attorneys John R. Bates and Van O'Steen opened a law office in Phoenix. Their aim was to provide legal services at modest fees to persons of moderate income who did not qualify for governmental legal aid. To achieve this end, they decided they would accept only routine matters, such as uncontested divorces, uncontested adoptions, simple personal bankruptcies, and changes of name, for which legal costs could be kept down by extensive use of paralegals, new office equipment, and standardized forms and offices procedures. Because Bates and O'Steen set their prices so as to have a relatively low profit on each case they handled, they depended on substantial volume to make a living. To attract new clients, they decided to place an advertisement in a Phoenix daily newspaper that stated that they were offering "legal services at very reasonable fees" and that listed their fees for certain services. The president of the Arizona State Bar Association filed a complaint and a committee recommended that the lawyers be suspended from the practice of law for not less than six months; the board of governors of the State Bar recommended only a one-week suspension for each lawyer.

The United States Supreme Court noted that the case was *not* about advertising claims relating to the quality of legal services, which, it said, probably were not susceptible of precise measurement or verification and, under some circumstances might well be deceptive or misleading to the public, or even false. It also said that the case did *not* involve "the problems associated with in-person solicitation of clients—at the hospital room or the accident site, or in any other situation that breeds undue influence—by attorneys"; activity of that sort, the Court said, "might well pose dangers of overreaching and misrepresentation not encountered in newspaper announcement advertising." It said that the heart of the dispute was whether lawyers may constitutionally advertise the prices at which they perform certain routine services.

The Arizona Bar argued that these kinds of ads would "tarnish the dignified public image of the profession"; were inherently misleading because legal services are so individualized with regard to content and quality as to prevent informed comparison on the basis of an ad; would have an adverse effect on the administration of justice by stirring up litigation; would increase the overhead costs of the profession, resulting in increased fees to consumers; and would harm particularly unsophisticated members of the public who might be unable to protect themselves from misleading or deceptive advertising by lawyers. But the Supreme Court found that none of these justifications permitted the suppression of all lawyer advertising and ruled that lawyers may not be prevented from truthfully advertising the availability and terms of routine legal services. (Bates v. State Bar of Arizona, 433 U.S. 350 (1977).)

2. On February 13, 1974, a lawyer heard about an automobile accident in which Carol McClintock, a young woman with whom the lawyer was casually acquainted, had been injured. He called her parents, who informed him that their daughter was in the hospital; he said that he might visit her there and her mother asked that he first stop by at her home. During the lawyer's visit with the McClintocks, they explained that their daughter had been driving the family car on a local road when she was hit by an uninsured motorist. Both Carol and her passenger, Wanda Lou Holbert, were injured and hospitalized. In response to the McClintocks' expression of apprehension that they might be sued by Holbert, the lawyer explained that state law precluded that kind of suit. When he suggested to the McClintocks that they hire a lawyer, Mrs. McClintock said that the decision would be up to Carol, who was 18 years old and would be the beneficiary of any successful claim. The lawyer then went to the hospital, where he saw Carol lying in traction in her room. After a brief conversation about her condition, he told Carol he would represent her and asked her to sign an agreement, which provided that he would receive one-third of her recovery. She did so. With a possible suit against the McClintocks' insurance company in mind, the lawyer also saw Wanda, who also was 18, and persuaded her to allow him to represent her. Both Carol and Wanda later discharged the lawyer and filed complaints against him with the Grievance Committee of the local bar association.

The case reached the Supreme Court of Ohio, which found that he had violated prohibitions against solicitation and ordered that the lawyer be indefinitely suspended. The lawyer argued before the United States Supreme Court that his solicitation of the two young women as clients was indistinguishable for purposes of the First Amendment from the advertisement the Court upheld in the *Bates* case, but the Supreme Court disagreed and upheld the Ohio court's judgment. The U.S. Supreme Court ruled that in-person solicitation of professional employment by a lawyer did not stand on a par with truthful advertising about the availability and terms of routine legal services. "The facts in this case present a striking example of the potential for overreaching that is inherent in a lawyer's in-person solicitation of professional employment," it concluded. (Ohralik v. Ohio State Bar Association, 436 U.S. 447 (1978).)

As an aside: The Supreme Court ruled on April 26, 1993, that a Florida rule that prohibited certified public accountants from engaging in "direct, in-person, uninvited solicitation" to obtain new business clients violated the First Amendment; it said that the government had less of an interest in banning personal solicitation by accountants than by lawyers— for instance, unlike a lawyer, who is trained in the art of persuasion, a C.P.A. is trained in a way "that emphasizes independence and objectivity, not advocacy." (Edenfield v. Fane, No. 91-1594, 1993 U.S. LEXIS 2985 (April 26, 1993).)

3. After the Supreme Court's decision in the *Bates* case, the Missouri Supreme Court revised its lawyer advertising regulations. The revised rule said that lawyers may publish ads containing 10 categories of information: name, address and telephone number; areas of practice; date and place of birth; schools attended; foreign language ability; office hours; fee for an initial consultation; availability of a schedule of fees; credit arrangements; and the fixed fee to be charged for certain specified "routine" legal services. An addendum to the rule stated that lawyers could describe their practice in one of two ways. First, they could say either "General Civil Practice," "General Criminal Practice," or "General Civil and Criminal

Practice." Second, they could use one or more of a list of 23 areas of practice, including "Family Law" and "Probate and Trust Law." When a lawyer with a new practice took out some advertisements in local newspapers and in the yellow pages, he included information that was not expressly permitted by the Missouri rule. For example, the ads said that he was licensed in Missouri and Illinois; that he was "Admitted to Practice Before THE UNITED STATES SUPREME COURT"; and that he practiced in areas other than those 23 listed in the addendum to the rule—he said he practiced "personal injury" and "real estate" law instead of "tort law" and "property law" as the rule required. He was charged with unprofessional conduct and the Missouri Supreme Court issued a private reprimand.

In its decision, the United States Supreme Court summarized what it said was the commercial speech doctrine in the context of advertising for professional services: "Truthful advertising related to lawful activities is entitled to the protections of the First Amendment. But when the particular content or method of the advertising suggests that it is inherently misleading or when experience has proved that in fact such advertising is subject to abuse, the States may impose appropriate restrictions." Finding that none of the truthful information in the lawyer's ads was inherently misleading, the Supreme Court then reversed the Missouri Supreme Court's decision. (In re R.M.J., 455 U.S. 191 (1982).)

4. In 1982 an Ohio lawyer ran an ad in 36 newspapers publicizing his willingness to represent women who had suffered injuries resulting from their use of the Dalkon Shield Intrauterine Device. The ad featured a line drawing of the Dalkon Shield accompanied by the question, "Did you use this IUD?" The ad said that the IUD was alleged to have caused serious injuries and included the name, address, and phone number of the lawyer's firm. The ad was successful in attracting clients—the lawyer received more than 200 inquires and he initiated lawsuits on behalf of 106 of the women who contacted him as a result of the ad. The ad, however, also aroused the interest of the Office of Disciplinary Counsel, which charged him with a number of disciplinary violations—including that the ad violated the prohibition against illustrations in advertisements by attorneys. The United States Supreme Court rejected that contention, however. It said that the use of illustrations or pictures in advertisements serves important communicative functions: "It attracts the attention of the audience to the advertiser's message and it may also serve to impart information directly." Accordingly, the Court ruled that commercial illustrations are entitled to the First Amendment protections afforded verbal commercial speech. It found that the illustration was an accurate representation of the Dalkon Shield and had no features that were likely to deceive, mislead, or confuse the reader. Because Ohio failed to present a substantial governmental interest justifying the restriction on illustrations and to demonstrate that the restriction vindicated that interest through "the least restrictive means available," the Court ruled that the lawyer could not be disciplined for use of the illustration in the ad. (Zauderer v. Office of Disciplinary Counsel, 471 U.S. 626 (1985).)

5. A Kentucky lawyer asked the Kentucky Attorneys' Advertising Commission for permission to send the following solicitation letter to homeowners who had foreclosure suits filed against them:

> It has come to my attention that your home is being foreclosed on [date]. If this is true, you may be about to lose your home. Federal law may allow you to keep your home by ORDERING your creditors to STOP and give you more time to pay them. You may call my office anytime from 8:30 A.M. to 5:00 P.M. for FREE information on how you can keep your home. Call NOW, don't wait. It may surprise you what I may be able to do for you. Just call and tell me that you got this letter. Remember, it is FREE, there is NO charge for calling.

The Commission, as well as the Kentucky Bar Association's ethics committee and the Kentucky Supreme Court, declined to approve the letter. Though acknowledging that it had upheld an in-person ban on solicitation, the United States Supreme Court ruled that the First Amendment protected written efforts to bring in new clients whether directed to a specific group in a newspaper ad or to individuals in personalized letters.

"Kentucky could not constitutionally prohibit [the lawyer] from sending at large an identical letter opening with the query, 'Is your home being foreclosed on?' rather than his observation to the targeted individuals that 'It has come to my attention that your home is being foreclosed on.'" The Court concluded that the person who received the letter would not feel any more "overwhelmed" than by seeing a newspaper's ad. "Like print advertising, [the lawyer's] letter—and targeted, direct-mail solicitation—generally poses much less risk of overreaching or undue influence than does in-person solicitation." (Shapero v. Kentucky Bar Association, 108 S.Ct. 1916 (1988).)

Commercial Speech Checklist

✓ Without doubt, commercial speech—expression related solely to the economic interests of the speaker and its audience—is now entitled to First Amendment protection.

✓ However, the United States Supreme Court has clearly indicated that commercial speech is entitled to less First Amendment protection than other forms of speech, such as speech relating to political or religious matters. The extent of protection afforded to commercial speech still is the subject of numerous lawsuits and is an evolving concept.

✓ Commercial speech that is truthful and not misleading is seen as the most worthy form of commercial speech.

✓ Complete prohibitions are the kinds of regulations most subject to challenge; however, even restrictions on the time, place, or manner of advertisements must meet the four-part test set forth by the Supreme Court in the *Central Hudson* case.

✓ Under that test, commercial speech that is truthful and not misleading may be regulated only if the government has a substantial interest in doing so; if the interest is directly advanced by the regulation; and if the regulation is no more extensive than necessary to serve the government's interest.

GROWING PROBLEMS WITH STATES' RIGHTS

❚ States' Rights ❚ Little FTC Acts ❚ State Violations
❚ Federal Preemption ❚ A Final Word

Bestline Products, Inc. distributed and sold household cleaning products it manufactured through an organization comprised of a very large number of distributors in three categories. The local distributors, whose function was to make direct sales to the consuming public, purchased Bestline products from direct distributors or general distributors.

The next level above the local distributor was the direct distributor. The direct distributor purchased products from Bestline and sold them either to local distributors or directly to the public.

The top position in the Bestline distribution system was the general distributor. To become a general distributor, a direct distributor was required to recruit another direct distributor and to either recruit a second new direct distributor or "create" an additional volume of $5,000 in one calendar month by selling to local distributors or to the consuming public at retail. In addition, to become a general distributor, the direct distributor was required to pay $600 to Bestline Products for a general distributor school— that the direct distributor was not required to attend.

Apparently, the method by which the recruitment of new distributors was accomplished included a regular schedule of so called "opportunity meetings" and "D and G (direct and general) meetings" that were staged by Bestline but financed in part by monthly charges made to direct and general distributors. Bestline established the format for these meetings and scripts were provided for the guidance of those conducting the meetings.

The opportunity meetings were evening meetings. They included a general introductory narrated filmstrip presenting the Bestline product line and a similar presentation explaining the "golden opportunities" that participation in the Bestline program offered. In the movie, a woman described her experience as a local distributor. She then introduced her direct distributor. He described himself as having no college education or special training and stated that he was "just getting by" before becoming a Bestline distributor. He claimed that becoming a Bestline direct distributor was the greatest thing ever to happen to him and stated that if a direct distributor had "just" 10 local distributors, each of whom did "only" $700 volume per month, the resulting profit was $630 per month. The direct distributor introduced a general distributor who explained that the general distributor received an eight percent commission for his services in training and supervising direct and local distributors. He said a general distributor who "only" had four direct distributors, each of whom had an organization of 10 local distributors doing $700 volume per month, would earn $2,240 per month. He opined that the earning capacity of a general distributor seemed "unlimited."

While the numbers today may seem low, nearly 20 years ago they were rather high; indeed, according to a complaint filed by the California attorney general under a number of California laws against Bestline, they were too good to be true. The attorney general contended that Bestline and an affiliated company had operated "their marketing program by means of making numerous false and misleading representations at 'opportunity meetings' and at other meetings to which the members of the public are invited." Among the specific misrepresentations charged were descriptions of the Bestline marketing program as offering to prospective distributors the expectation of a large annual income as a result of their recruiting additional distributors who would in like fashion bring in further recruits;

giving nonrepresentative examples of income generated in various levels of distributorships; and making misstatements relating to the ease with which additional distributors could be obtained and relating to the level of retail sales.

The trial court found that Bestline had violated the law, and entered a permanent injunction comprehensively prohibiting it from operating a marketing program consisting of a chain scheme or engaging in any other of the deceptive practices the court found to have existed.

Then, the court ordered Bestline to make restitution and assessed civil penalties against the company in the amount of $1 million. The power of the state court to assess a $1 million penalty was upheld on appeal.

▌States' Rights

In the late 1960s and early 1970s, individuals and businesses across the country lamented what they viewed as the improper growth in the power of the federal government. "States' rights," a battle cry from the Civil War era, became a new rallying point.

As many have said through the ages, though, people should be careful what they wish for—they may get it.

The decline in the power of the federal government during the Reagan and Bush years created a vacuum that did not go unfilled. As Bestline saw, state government has moved into the breach.

There are two legal systems in this country—a federal system, under which Congress, the president, and the United States Supreme Court operates, and a state system, comprised of the state and local governments of all 50 states (as well as the District of Columbia and various territories of the United States).

At the least, this means that marketers have to comply with two sets of rules—the federal rules and the state rules. But state laws are not uniform. Theoretically there may be more than 50 different varieties of rules on a particular issue.

▮ Little FTC Acts

State attorneys general over the past decade have tended to focus on consumer protection, environmental, and antitrust legal issues. Generally speaking, though, the most important of the state laws marketers must consider are known as the little FTC acts. These laws, enacted by all 50 states and the District of Columbia, are modeled on the Federal Trade Commission Act and generally prohibit "unfair methods of competition and unfair acts or practices." In addition to the fact that they are enforceable by state governments, they commonly authorize consumers—and competitors—to bring suit, unlike the federal law; some even permit courts to award punitive damages as well as double or treble compensatory damages; and most provide that a prevailing plaintiff may be awarded attorney's fees.

While compliance with the terms of the FTC Act often is a complete defense to an action under a little FTC act for unfair or deceptive practices, the mere fact that a marketer's actions may be subject to the federal law does not mean that state action is prohibited. Indeed, as the General Motors Corporation learned a number of years ago, conduct that the Federal Trade Commission seemingly blessed can still lead to liability under state law.

▮ State Violations

On February 17, 1977, James F. Gour purchased a 1977 Oldsmobile Delta 88 Royale from Daray Motor Co., Inc. for $8,122.65. The car had been manufactured primarily by the General Motors' Oldsmobile Division; the engine, however, had been manufactured by General Motors' Chevrolet Division. The engine, designated by GM as an LM1 engine, had been substituted for the similar L34 engine manufactured by Oldsmobile.

Gour was an "Oldsmobile man" with a fondness for and familiarity with that particular make that had developed over a period of 20 years. During that time, he had owned six other Oldsmobiles, all similar to the one he purchased from Daray. Gour, employed as a district manager for an insurance company, had to drive extensively and had come to depend on and trust Oldsmobiles to meet his driving needs.

Gour would not have bought the car had he known of the substitution of the engines, but he did not know. There apparently was nothing on the car or in the documents that he viewed at the time of the sale that indicated to him the true source of the car's engine. The sales invoice contained only the notation, "Engine, 350 V-8 4BBL." Although the window sticker bore GM's code name, LM1, Gour did not know what it meant. Furthermore, the engine's air cleaner bore an eye-catching, red and black on silver decal that read Oldsmobile 350.

Gour filed suit against Daray and GM, alleging that they had violated the section of the Louisiana Unfair Trade Practices and Consumer Protection Law that declared unlawful "[u]nfair methods of competition and unfair or deceptive acts or practices in the conduct of any trade or commerce."

GM argued that its actions were exempt from the provisions of the Louisiana little FTC act because its conduct had been sanctioned by the FTC. It said that several years earlier the FTC had complained of GM's advertising automobile replacement parts as "genuine Chevrolet parts" when they were manufactured by outside vendors rather than by any division of GM. The FTC alleged that that advertising was false and deceptive. After a hearing, though, the FTC dismissed the complaint, holding that the parts were as much genuine parts as those made in General Motors' own plant, because they were made according to its specifications and tested, approved, and warranted by it.

The court in Gour's case said that it saw "a great deal of difference between replacement parts, used for maintenance purposes, and a major component part of a new car, such as the engine." It found GM's argument that its activities were sanctioned by federal law "untenable," and then ruled in Gour's favor.

▌Federal Preemption

On occasion, however, states go too far and interfere with federal laws or regulations. When that occurs, their actions may be deemed "preempted" by the federal rules under a provision of the Constitution that gives such federal rules priority. The United States Supreme Court recently decided just such a case.

Prior to 1978 the Federal Aviation Act gave the Civil Aeronautics Board (CAB) authority to regulate interstate air fares and to take administrative action against certain deceptive trade practices. It did not, however, expressly preempt state regulation and contained a "saving clause" providing that "[n]othing . . . in this chapter shall in any way abridge or alter the remedies now existing at common law or by statute, but the provisions of this chapter are in addition to such remedies." As a result, states were able to regulate intrastate airfares (including those offered by interstate air carriers) and to enforce their own laws against deceptive trade practices.

In 1978, however, Congress, determining that maximum reliance on competitive market forces would best further efficiency, innovation, and low prices, as well as variety and quality of air transportation services, enacted the Airline Deregulation Act. To ensure that the states would not undo federal deregulation with regulation of their own, the law included a preemption provision prohibiting the states from enforcing any law "relating to rates, routes, or services" of any carrier. The law retained the CAB's previous enforcement authority regarding deceptive trade practices (which was transferred to the Department of Transportation when the CAB was abolished in 1985) and it also did not repeal or alter the saving clause in the prior law.

In 1987, the National Association of Attorneys General, an organization whose membership included the attorneys general of all 50 states, various territories, and the District of Columbia, adopted air travel industry enforcement guidelines containing detailed standards governing the content and format of airline advertising, the awarding of premiums to regular customers (so called "frequent flyers"), and the payment of compensation to passengers who voluntarily yielded their seats on overbooked flights. These guidelines did not purport to "create any new laws or regulations" applying to the airline industry; rather, they claimed to "explain in detail how existing state laws apply to airfare advertising and frequent flyer programs."

Despite objections to the guidelines by the Department of Transportation and the FTC on preemption and policy grounds, the attorneys general of seven states sent a memorandum to the major airlines announcing that "it has come to our attention that although most airlines are making a concerted effort to bring their advertisements into compliance with the standards delineated in the . . . guidelines for fare advertising, many carriers are still [not disclosing all surcharges]" in violation of the guidelines. The memorandum said it was the signatories' purpose "to clarify for the industry as a whole that [this practice] is a violation of our respective state laws on deceptive advertising and trade practices."

A few months later, after receiving a formal notice of intent to sue from the attorney general of Texas, several airlines filed suit in federal district court seeking an injunction restraining Texas from taking any action to regulate their rates, routes, or services, or their advertising and marketing of their rates, routes, or services. The case reached the United States Supreme Court in 1992.

Texas argued that the federal law only preempted states from actually prescribing rates, routes, or services, but the Supreme Court disagreed. The Court noted that the guidelines regulated print advertisements of fares, imposed restrictions on broadcast advertisements of fares, and even required that billboard fare ads clearly and conspicuously state that "substantial restrictions apply" if there were any material restrictions on the fares' availability. It said that the guidelines also required that an advertised fare be available in sufficient quantities to "meet reasonably foreseeable demand" on every flight on every day in every market in which the fare was advertised; if the fare would not be available on that basis, it had to contain a "clear and conspicuous statement of the extent of unavailability." Other sections of the guidelines required that the advertised fare include all taxes and surcharges; the round-trip fare had to be disclosed at least as prominently as the one-way fare when the fare was only available on round-trips; and the words "sale," "discount," or "reduced" were prohibited unless the advertised fare was available only for a limited time and was substantially below the usual price for the same fare with the same restrictions.

The Court said that it could not avoid the conclusion that these aspects of the guidelines "relate to" airline rates. They established binding requirements as to how tickets may be marketed if they are to be sold at given prices. Under state laws, the Court said, many violations of these requirements would entitle consumers to file suit for an airline's failure to provide a particular advertised fare. Furthermore, the Court noted, "It is clear as an economic matter that state restrictions on fare advertising have the forbidden significant effect upon fares."

Texas argued that the states were not compelling or restricting advertising but instead merely preventing the market distortion caused by "false" advertising, but the Court rejected that claim as well. "All in all, the obligations imposed by the guidelines would have a significant impact upon the airlines' ability to market their product, and hence a significant impact upon the fares they charge."

The Court then ruled that the fare advertising guidelines were preempted by federal law and not enforceable.

▌A Final Word

The Supreme Court's decision in the airline case is probably one rather limited to its facts and is unlikely to serve as the basis for too many other decisions invalidating state regulations of advertising or marketing.

But the decision does show one way out of the "states' rights" problem for marketers—a single federal regulation (as manufacturers hope to achieve in the products liability area), can avoid the mishmash of competing state laws.

FIVE CASES OF STATES' RIGHTS

1. An advertisement placed in a local newspaper by Brian McNamara for his business, TV Rentals, offered color television sets and stereos to consumers. The ad stated in part, "Why buy when you can rent? Color TV and stereos. Rent to own! Use our Rent-to-own rental plan and let TV Rentals deliver either of these models to your home." Carolyn Murphy called McNamara the next day and signed a contract that stated that she could have a color television set for weekly payments of $16 and that she would be entitled to keep it if she made 78 successive payments (and paid a $20 delivery charge) totaling $1268. Murphy was not informed that the retail sale price for the same set was $499.

Murphy agreed to the contract because she had been persuaded through the advertisement that she could obtain the ownership and use of the television set without establishing credit. After making payments for six months, she noticed a newspaper article that criticized the lease plan and realized the total amount she would be required to pay for the television. She stopped making payments and consulted an attorney, who filed suit under Connecticut's Unfair Trade Practices Act, which, unlike the Federal Trade Commission Act, specifically permits individuals to bring suit. Relying on Federal Trade Commission rulings interpreting the FTC Act and on other state court decisions and statutes, the court ruled that "an agreement for the sale of consumer goods entered into with a consumer having unequal bargaining power, which agreement calls for an unconscionable purchase price, constitutes an unfair trade practice under the [Connecticut law]." (Murphy v. McNamara, 416 A.2d 170 (Sup. Ct. Conn. 1979).)

2. In the early 1970s, the United Farm Workers of America filed suit under a number of California laws, including the law prohibiting unfair or fraudulent business practices, against several California businesses charging that they wrongfully used the union's tradename and trademark—a black eagle emblem—and seeking an injunction and compensatory and punitive damages. The court said that "while it is true that the damages suffered by the labor organization whose rights have been infringed upon by such practices as are alleged here may be difficult to measure, that very real damage may [afflict] the union and its members is readily apparent." A company that usurped a union label could divert business away from a manufacturer who had an agreement with a particular union to employ only its members, possibly resulting in loss of employment by union members, the court said. It added that if goods falsely bearing a union label were shoddily made, the union could suffer financial loss to its commercial standing and financial position. Finally, the court said that a wrongful appropriator of a union label could profit by the wrongful use in that it might increase the sales of its products. The court concluded, therefore, that the union was entitled to bring suit seeking compensation for its losses, if any. In addition, it said that the union could seek punitive damages from the defendants as well. (United Farm Workers of America, AFL-CIO v. Superior Court, County of Kern, 120 Cal. Rptr. 904 (Ct. Appeal 5th Dist. 1975).)

3. For a number of years, Green Acres Trust, Inc., which operated two mortuaries, and Green Acres Memorial Gardens, Inc., which owned and operated a cemetery, marketed instruments styled "debentures" in denominations of $250 that could be redeemed at the time of the owner's death for application of the proceeds to the cost of funeral and burial services. Neither the debentures nor the Green Acres salespeople were registered with the Arizona Corporation Commission, which had informed Green Acres in 1961 that it was entitled to an exemption from registration requirements. However, in 1975, the Corporation Commission issued an order prohibiting Green Acres from selling debentures unless the salespeople and the debentures were registered under the state's securities act. The attorney general then filed a complaint against the companies. Green Acres argued that the attorney general could not bring suit under the state's consumer fraud law because it was subject to the state's securities act and to the state's prearranged funeral plan legislation—in essence, Green Acres' argument was analogous to those made by businesses that federal law preempts state power over their actions. However, an Arizona appellate court ruled that the attorney general could bring a consumer fraud suit against Green Acres notwithstanding the other two state laws. It said that the scope of the Consumer Fraud Act was not limited by the existence of the Board of Funeral Directors and Embalmers, which had a broad range of duties but limited resources with which to provide comprehensive consumer protection. "The fact that our Consumer Fraud Act may, in some instances, be cumulative with respect to other penal and remedial provisions available to public prosecuting authorities does not make it inapplicable," the court concluded. (People ex rel. Babbitt v. Green Acres Trust, 618 P.2d 1086 (Ct. App. Arizona 1980).)

4. Norman Garland, a Mobil credit card holder since 1967, purchased products from Mobil's dealers from July 11, 1969, to November 10, 1969, and charged the purchases on his credit card. Each monthly statement he received indicated that "payment [was] due on receipt of this statement." Each monthly statement also contained the legend that past due amounts may incur a monthly service charge at 1.5 percent. Prior to July 11, 1969, Mobil in fact imposed a service charge of 1.5 percent on a credit card customer in each consecutive month in which the balance owed by the customer was 60 days past due and amounted to $10 or more. On July 11, 1969, apparently as a result of a meeting (at Mobil's request) between Mobil officials and representatives of the Federal Reserve Board and the Federal Trade Commission, Mobil temporarily discontinued the levy of all late payment charges on its cardholder accounts and decided to refund all such charges levied between July 1 and July 11. From July 11 to August 22, Mobil levied no charges of any kind on cardholder accounts. On August 22, 1969, Mobil initiated a practice of imposing a single "late payment charge" upon a credit customer who owed $25 or more for more than 90 days. The delinquent customer's credit was terminated and a request made for the return of his credit card when this late payment charge was imposed. No notification was issued to customers regarding this change in credit practice. An additional unpublicized change was effected on February 5, 1970, from which date Mobil discontinued the practice of refunding late charges upon the reinstatement of credit that had been terminated. Finally, on October 1, 1970, Mobil revised its credit card system and, with notice, began assessing a finance charge of stated percentages on outstanding minimum monthly balances.

Garland contended in Count 1 of a lawsuit he filed against Mobil that Mobil had extended to Garland and others similarly situation "consumer credit" under an "open end credit plan" as defined in the federal Truth in Lending Act without disclosing to Garland or others the information required by the act to be disclosed in periodic open-end billing statements. Count 2 alleged that Mobil had violated the Illinois Uniform Deceptive Trade Practices Act by maintaining the legend on its bills that past due accounts would incur a service charge when in fact no service charge was being imposed for many past due balances and no monthly service charge for past due balances of $25 or more from August 22, 1969, to October 1, 1970. The court rejected Garland's claim under the Truth in Lending Act, finding that Mobil was not covered by that law. However, it said that the fact that Mobil used the legend that past due accounts might incur monthly service charges could have created a "likelihood of confusion or misunderstanding" proscribed by the Illinois Little FTC Act and that it could be liable for damages under that statute. (Garland v. Mobil Oil Corp., 340 F.Supp. 1095 (N.D. Illinois 1972).)

5. After Qantel Corporation terminated the distributorship it had given to Computer Systems Engineering, Inc., Computer Systems filed suit. It alleged that Qantel had violated the Massachusetts Little FTC Act because it had made false representations to Computer Systems with respect to the computer software it was selling on its behalf. The trial court ruled in favor of Computer Systems and awarded it more than $2 million in lost profits and more than $250,000 in attorney's fees. (Computer Systems Engineering, Inc. v. Qantel Corp., 740 F.2d 59 (1984).)

States' Rights Checklist

✓ The decline of the influence of the federal government—or at least the perception of a decline—during the Reagan and Bush years led to a vacuum that many states and state attorneys general filled.

✓ For marketers of national products, that may not have been good news. Different rules and laws enacted by 50 different state legislatures conceivably pose a very difficult compliance burden.

✓ Over the past few years, state attorneys general, competitors, and consumers have filed suits against marketers and manufacturers in increasing numbers relying on state laws modeled after the Federal Trade Commission Act.

✓ The broad provisions of these little FTC acts—which prohibit unfair or deceptive trade practices—make many different kinds of business decisions subject to challenge.

✓ Federal law may, on occasion, preempt enforcement of little FTC acts and state rules that conflict with federal standards, but, as a practical matter, there are probably many more instances when that will not be the case. Without uniform federal legislation, marketers may never be able to return to those "difficult" times of the 1960s when federal government influence was deemed so pervasive, and so invasive.

19

CAN THE MEDIA REFUSE YOUR AD (AND WHAT ABOUT ERRORS)?

▌A Right to Commercial Access?
▌A Right to Be Charged Equal Rates? ▌Errors in Ads
▌A Final Word

In the fall of 1972, Pat Tornillo, the executive director of the Florida Classroom Teachers Association, was a candidate for the Florida House of Representatives. After the Miami Herald *printed two editorials critical of his candidacy, he demanded that the paper print his replies defending the role of the Classroom Teachers Association and the organization's accomplishments for the citizens of Dade County. The paper declined and Tornillo brought suit.*

Tornillo's lawsuit was premised on Florida's "right of reply" law, which provides that if a candidate for nomination or election is assailed regarding his personal character or official record by any newspaper, the candidate has the right to demand that the newspaper print, free of cost to the candidate, any reply the candidate wants to make to the newspaper's charges. The reply has to appear in as conspicuous a place and in the same kind of type as the charges that prompted the reply, provided it does not take up more space than the charges. Failure to comply with the law, which was enacted in 1913, constitutes a first-degree misdemeanor.

The Florida Supreme Court determined that the law was constitutional, finding that it enhanced and did not abridge free speech and that it furthered the broad societal interest in the free flow of information to the public. The paper appealed to the United States Supreme Court.

Tornillo and others argued that the government had an obligation to ensure that a wide variety of views reach the public. They said that at the time the First Amendment was ratified in 1791, the press was broadly representative of the people it was serving. While many of the newspapers were intensely partisan and narrow in their views, the press collectively presented a broad range of opinions to readers. Entry into publishing was inexpensive; pamphlets and books provided meaningful alternatives to the organized press for the expression of unpopular ideas and often treated events and expressed views not covered by conventional newspapers. A true marketplace of ideas existed in which there was relatively easy access to the channels of communication.

"Access advocates," as the United States Supreme Court called them, contended that although newspapers of the late twentieth century were superficially similar to those of 1791 the press now was in reality very different from 200 years ago. Newspapers "have become big business"; there are far fewer of them to serve a larger literate population; and competing newspapers have been eliminated in most large cities. The result of these vast changes, they contended, was to place in a few hands the power to inform the American people and shape public opinion. They said that the First Amendment's interest in the public being informed was in peril because the "marketplace of ideas" was a monopoly controlled by the owners of the market.

The Supreme Court rejected those contentions. It said that while a responsible press is an undoubtedly desirable goal, "press responsibility is not mandated by the Constitution and like many other virtues it cannot be legislated."

The Court stated that the Florida law operated as a command in the same sense as a statute or regulation forbidding a newspaper to publish a specified matter. Governmental restraint on publishing, the Court said, need not fall into familiar or traditional patterns to be subject to constitutional limitations on governmental powers. The Florida statute intruded into the function of editors, the Court ruled, and therefore violated the First Amendment. "The choice of material to go into a newspaper, and the decisions made as to limitations on the size and content of the paper, and treatment of public issues and public officials—whether fair or unfair— constitute the exercise of editorial control and judgment." Governmental regulation of this "crucial process" cannot be exercised consistent with First Amendment guarantees of a free press, the Court concluded.

(It should be noted that in 1973—the year before the Supreme Court recognized that commercial speech was entitled to First Amendment protec- tion—the Supreme Court ruled that a newspaper could be restrained from placing help wanted advertisements in columns designated by sex. The Court said the ads were not entitled to First Amendment protection be- cause they were "classic examples of commercial speech." Would the Court so rule today and permit government regulation of the content of a news- paper, at least in the context of sexually discriminatory classified advertis- ing? Probably yes, despite the recent commercial speech cases, because the social value of nondiscriminatory ads would be deemed to outweigh the value of absolute nongovernmental involvement in the media. This case shows that there are exceptions to all legal rules, including the First Amendment.)

▌ A Right to Commercial Access?

If a candidate for election to a political position cannot force access to the press in the middle of an election, is there hope for a business that wants to purchase an advertisement? As Muriel Diamond learned in a case she filed several years ago against the publisher of the *Star*, the answer is no.

Through a media consultant, Diamond submitted an order for an advertise- ment for her antismoking pamphlet to run in an issue of the *Star*. She said she was informed, though, that the *Star* would be unable to run the ad because its antismoking nature would offend the tobacco companies who were major ad- vertisers in that paper. The publisher denied having a policy not to accept antismoking ads; it said it rejected her ad because it had no space. She then filed suit against the publisher under the federal antitrust laws.

The court ruled that the unilateral decision of a business not to deal with a particular customer, even if motivated by an attempt to please another party, was not a violation of the Sherman Antitrust Act. Finding she had no right of access, it then dismissed her complaint.

▌A Right to Be Charged Equal Rates?

The ability of the media to be free from government control also extends to advertising pricing issues.

In one case, newspaper publishers went to court seeking to invalidate a Florida law requiring newspapers to charge political candidates the lowest local advertising rate. A violation of that law exposed newspapers to a fine of $10,000 and forfeiture of their right to do business in the state.

The publishers asserted that they charged political candidates under the same advertising rate schedule that they used for commercial and other advertisers. That contract rate schedule was based on the volume of the customers' advertising, the lineage requested by the advertiser, the location of the advertisement in the newspapers, whether special art work or printing techniques were required, and other considerations. They contended that the political advertising rate statute imposed an unconstitutional restraint upon freedom of the press because it singled out the press for discriminatory economic regulation.

The court said that the legislature's effort in seeking to make news media advertising available to candidates of whatever degree of financial backing was laudable. However, it said that notwithstanding how commendable the purpose, the Supreme Court had "consistently struck down statutes which restrain the content of the publication." The court ruled that the fact that the restraint created by the Florida statute was aimed at revenue rather than content did "not insulate it from the constraints of the First Amendment."

▌Errors in Ads

If publishers cannot be forced to accept an ad, can they at least be required to compensate for errors they make in doing their job, much as other businesses have to do? The answer is yes, subject to certain limits.

A number of years ago, Stewart E. Wilson operated a tax service in Bogalusa, Louisiana, known as the Reliable Service Co. He purchased an ad in the yellow pages that he wanted to read as follows:

Tax Service

Income–Sales Tax—FICA

And All Small Business

Tax Service

Bookkeeping and Accounting

Dial 735-5318

Reliable Service Co.

223 Memphis Bogalusa, LA

When the ad was published, it was all correct—except for one thing. It was headlined "Taxi Service" rather than "Tax Service."

Wilson filed suit against the phone company for damages in the amount of $5,000 for harassment, annoyance, and interruptions to his regular business occasioned by calls for taxi service resulting from the erroneous ad; $5,000 for loss of a year of anticipated advertising value of the yellow pages; and $1,000 for cost of advertising through other media.

The phone company admitted the error in the ad but denied that any damages resulted therefrom; in any event, it said that if Wilson could prove damages, he was limited by the contract to recovering the cost for the advertising. The court agreed and awarded Wilson $87.

Wilson appealed and the appellate court upheld the lower court's ruling. The provision in the contract limiting liability was valid, it found, noting that other courts have similarly upheld the validity of limiting liability in an amount not to exceed the charges for the advertising.

Not every court that has faced the issue has so ruled, however.

In one case, an insurance agent who had contracted to place ads in the yellow pages, but whose ads were not published, filed suit against the phone company for damages. The phone company relied on the limitation of liability provision contained in the contract it signed with the insurance agent, but the court ruled that it was an unreasonable term that should not be enforced. "The parties to this suit are not in positions of equal bargaining power," the court said. "It is common knowledge that [the] yellow pages is the only directory of classified telephone listings freely distributed to all the telephone subscribers" in the insurance agent's locale. Under the circumstances, the court found that the insurance agent "had the option of agreeing to the offered terms or doing without advertising in the yellow pages. There being no competing directory or means of communicating with the same audience of potential customers except possibly at prohibitive (and by comparison totally disproportionate) cost, doing without in this case was not a realistic alternative."

▌A Final Word

Advertisers have virtually no ability to force the media to accept their ads and, under the majority rule as stated in the paradigmatic yellow pages' cases, little ability to recover more than minimal damages for errors in ads that are published. What can advertisers do? Place ads and market products in available avenues; keep as close an eye as possible on marketing communications that do make it out the door; correct problems as they appear; and move on to the next one.

FIVE CASES OF ACCESS AND AD ERRORS

1. In January 1970, the Business Executives' Movement for Vietnam Peace filed a complaint with the Federal Communications Commission charging that Washington, D.C., radio station WTOP had refused to sell it time to broadcast a series of one-minute spot announcements expressing the organization's views on Vietnam. WTOP, in common with many, but not all, broadcasters, followed a policy of refusing to sell time for spot announcements to individuals and groups who wished to expound their views on controversial issues. WTOP took the position that because it presented full and fair coverage of important public questions, including the Vietnam conflict, it was justified in refusing to accept editorial advertisements. WTOP also submitted evidence showing that the station had aired the views of critics of the government's Vietnam policy on numerous occasions.

Four months later, the Democratic National Committee (DNC) filed with the Federal Communications Commission (FCC) a request for a declaratory ruling that "under the First Amendment to the Constitution and the [Federal] Communications Act, a broadcaster may not, as a general policy, refuse to sell time to responsible entities such as the DNC, for the solicitation of funds and for comment on public issues." The FCC rejected the contentions of the Business Executives' Movement for Vietnam Peace and the DNC that "responsible" individuals and groups had a right to purchase advertising time to comment on public issues without regard to whether the broadcaster had complied with the fairness doctrine. A federal circuit court of appeals reversed the FCC's decision, holding that a "flat ban on paid public issue announcements is in violation of the First Amendment, at least when other sorts of paid announcements are accepted." The case reached the United States Supreme Court, which recognized that the broadcast media pose unique and special problems not present in the traditional free speech case because, unlike other media, broadcasting is subject to an inherent physical limitation—broadcasting frequencies are a scarce resource that must be portioned out among applicants. Nonetheless, the Court upheld the FCC's decision. "For better or worse, editing is what editors are for; and editing is selection and choice of material," it said. It concluded that it would not impose a constitutional right of access on the broadcast media. (Columbia Broadcasting System, Inc. v. Democratic National Committee, 412 U.S. 94 (1973).)

2. When contacted by a representative of the South Central Bell Telephone Company a number of years ago, Donald K. Butcher, a chiropractor, contracted for his name to be placed in the yellow pages under "CHIROPRACTORS DC" exactly as it appeared in the yellow pages the year before:

"BUTCHER DONALD K DC

Chiropractic Physician

Evangeline Chiropractic Clinic

Hours 8 A.M.–6 P.M. Mon-Fri

Saturday 9 A.M.–2 P.M.

Fiesta Village Shopping Center

4414 Johnston *981-2937*

Contrary to Dr. Butcher's agreement with South Central Bell, however, his name did not appear in the directory as contracted for. At trial, Dr. Butcher attempted to prove that the omission of the listing cost him approximately $26,000; he reasoned that he had 136 new patients directly attributable to referrals from the prior phone book and only 33 new patients during the comparable period when his name was omitted from the phone book; because the average fee for each new patient was $192.25 less $1.50 for costs of X-ray film, he argued that he sustained a net loss of $19,647.25. He further argued that 36 percent of his new patients were referred by old patients. Therefore, in addition to the 103 patients that he said he lost from telephone referrals, he said he lost 36 percent of 103 patients, or 37 patients, resulting in an additional loss of $7,057.75.

The trial court found that South Central Bell did breach the contract it had with Dr. Butcher by failing to list him as he wanted to be listed and ruled that he was entitled to some damages. But it awarded him only $1,500, and he appealed. The appellate court said that it was a "well-recognized fact" that the income of professionals fluctuates from year to year. Therefore, it said, it was difficult to calculate the damages to which Dr. Butcher was entitled with any degree of certainty. However, it noted that his contractual rights were clearly violated and said he was entitled to be compensated for his losses. Therefore, it affirmed the trial court's decision awarding him $1,500. (Butcher v. South Central Bell Telephone Co., 398 So.2d 197 (Ct. App. Louisiana 1981).)

3. In the early 1970s, Allen Wholesale Supply contracted with Southern Bell Telephone & Telegraph Co. for advertising in the yellow pages section of its telephone directory. In printing the directory, though, the phone company erroneously inserted in one of Allen's ads the telephone number and street address of its main competitor. Allen filed suit against the phone company, alleging that it had willfully and maliciously changed the ad or that, in the least, its conduct amounted to gross negligence. The phone company sought to limit its liability based on a provision in the contract that stated that the phone company's liability on account of errors in or omissions of an ad "shall in no event exceed the amount of charges for the advertising which was omitted or in which the error occurred." The court found that at most the phone company's conduct constituted an unintentional mistake and ordered judgment in favor of the phone company. (Allen v. Southern Bell Telephone and Telegraph Co., 285 So.2d 634 (D.Ct. App. Florida 1973).)

4. In 1975 a professional engineering firm that went by the name of McClure Engineering Associates, Inc., wanted to place advertisements in the yellow pages. The ads were important for the firm because at the time it was ethically precluded from any other kind of advertising. The ads failed to appear and McClure sued the phone company, seeking more than $45,000 in damages. The trial court granted judgment to McClure—but limited its recovery to $271.70, which was the price of the advertising, plus certain litigation costs. McClure appealed, arguing that the contract clause that limited the liability of the phone company should not be enforced because a monopoly existed in the solicitation of yellow pages advertising. The Supreme Court of Illinois, over the dissent of one justice, upheld the liability limitation, however. It specifically relied on the "many decisions in other jurisdictions which recognize that yellow pages advertising is a nonregulated activity, refuse to find unconscionable bargaining, and uphold the exculpatory clauses used in such contracts." (McClure Engineering Associates, Inc. v. Reuben H. Donnelley Corp., 447 N.E.2d 400 (Sup. Ct. Illinois 1983).)

5. Even two lawyers could not convince a court that the failure of the phone company to run their yellow pages ad entitled them to recover substantial damages. In that case, the law firm of Woloshin & Tenenbaum had inadvertently been omitted from the yellow pages of the phone book. The court said that the listing agreement "was entered into on one side by two lawyers with experience in the drafting and interpretation of contracts, and I am satisfied that there is no good reason why they should have been outbargained when they contracted for yellow pages listing." The court then upheld the contract's provisions limiting the phone company's liability "to an amount not exceeding the monthly charges for advertising and listing" provided for in the contract. (Woloshin v. Diamond State Telephone Co., 380 A.2d 982 (Ct. Chanc. Delaware 1977).)

Access and Error Checklist

✓ Advertisers do not have a right to access to the media; they simply have no right to force unwilling publishers to accept their ads. Courts have ruled that the First Amendment forbids government from forcing content (advertising or otherwise) on the media.

✓ The media can be held liable, as other kinds of businesses are, for their errors, though. Therefore, a publisher can be required to pay an advertiser's damages for a mistake in an ad.

✓ Typically, however, publishers include language in their contracts limiting their liability for advertising errors.

✓ These kinds of limitations have almost universally been upheld by the courts.

✓ Only if an advertiser can persuade a court that exceptional reasons exist, for instance, that the publisher had an unfair bargaining position or monopoly power, might a court invalidate the limitation on liability provisions contained in these kinds of contracts.

20.

PRODUCT LIABILITY

■ Duty to Warn ■ Postsale Warnings ■ A Final Word

On August 12, 1978, Christopher Billsborrow, an employee of Welmetco, Ltd., inhaled or was otherwise exposed to trichloroethylene vapors while cleaning a degreasing tank using Neutri solvent and died.

The Neutri solvent had been manufactured by Dow Chemical, which sold it to Pride Solvent Chemical Company, Inc. Pride then sold the solvent to Welmetco and the Eastern Salkover Metal Processing Corporation, which occupied the same premises.

After Billsborrow's death, his widow filed a lawsuit containing various claims against Dow and other companies. She contended that Dow had failed to provide any or adequate warnings to the ultimate consumers or users of the solvent. Dow asked the court to dismiss the claims against it.

Dow contended that it sold the solvent "in bulk" to Pride, affixed warning labels to all bulk shipments, and provided Pride with extensive safety literature, labels, and warnings regarding the use, handling, and application of the solvent, and that Pride was obligated to furnish all warnings and literature it received from Dow to its customers. Pride, Dow contended, was a "responsible intermediary" and Dow could not be held liable for any failure on its part to provide adequate warnings to Welmetco.

The court refused to dismiss the claims against Dow. Among other things, the court said that there was a question of fact as to the adequacy of the warning provided by Dow to Pride. Although it recognized that

Dow had provided a warning, it said that the adequacy of the warning must be "commensurate with the risk of harm and level of potential of such harm." That, the court said, was a question for the jury.

▌Duty to Warn

The law of product liability is a vast amalgam of cases, rules, and statutory provisions. Whether brought under a negligence or strict tort liability theory, a products liability claim usually alleges a defect in either the manufacture, design, or warning of a product. For marketers, one of the most important provisions of product liability law is the duty to warn. That may affect what companies can put on labels, mention in their advertising, and explain to sales reps and customers.

Though a product may be flawlessly made, it may be deemed defective if it is unreasonably dangerous to place the product in a user's hands without a suitable warning. Where a warning is required, it must be reasonably readable and apprise a consumer exercising reasonable care under the circumstances of the existence and seriousness of the danger sufficient to enable the consumer to protect against the danger.

Manufacturers, suppliers, and distributors are required under the law to give warning of latent dangers in inherently dangerous products or risk the imposition of liability. The duty to warn of latent dangers extends to the original or ultimate purchasers of the product, to employees of those purchasers, and to third persons exposed to a foreseeable and unreasonable risk of harm by the failure to warn.

Theoretically, a consumer buys a product after evaluating the risks in its use. But courts recognize that consumers are not on an equal footing with manufacturers who are in a unique position to know the specific risks involved. The courts' imposition of a duty to warn involves a balancing test that weighs the seriousness of potential harm to the consumer against the costs to the manufacturer. Because the cost of providing warnings is often minimal, the balance usually weighs in favor of an obligation to warn. Once a warning is given, the focus shifts to the adequacy of the warning.

Warnings must clearly alert the user to avoid certain unsafe uses of the product that would appear to be normal and reasonable. Furthermore, the degree of danger is a crucial factor in determining the specificity required in a warning. To be adequate, the warnings must be commensurate with the risks involved in the ordinary use of the product. Here are certain other factors that courts examine to determine the adequacy of a warning:

- The adequacy of a warning depends on the nature of the product and the context in which it is used.

- An adequate warning is one that is understandable in context and conveys a fair indication of the nature and extent of the danger to a reasonably prudent person.

- The sufficiency of a warning is dependent upon both the language used and the impression that the language was calculated to make upon the mind of the average user of the product.

- Courts also examine the location and conspicuousness of the warning and the method in which the warning is communicated to the ultimate user.

- Of critical importance is whether the warning sufficiently conveys the risk of danger associated with the product and is qualitatively sufficient to impart the particular risk of harm.

A warning may be inadequate when the magnitude of the potential harm requires more. For example, in one case a caution to use charcoal only in ventilated areas was found inadequate to warn of the risk of burning charcoal indoors. In another case, the word "flammable" affixed to a product was deemed inadequate when the real danger of the product was in its explosive characteristics. In another, a warning that a hammer face might chip if struck against another hammer, hardened nails, or other hard objects, possibly resulting in eye or other bodily injury, was found insufficient without an additional warning that the hammer, once chipped, must be discarded. Yet a different court deemed a label containing the caution "vapor may be deadly" insufficient to convey the particular danger that may cause death.

Here is a short summary of several other cases that have dealt with the adequacy of warnings:

- A warning affixed to an aerosol paint can was found inadequate in the absence of instructions for safe disposal.

- A warning not to use a product near a flame was found insufficient to warn of the danger from a pilot light behind a closed door.

- A warning that "continuous driving over 90 miles per hour" requires using high-speed capability tires was found inadequate when the manufacturer knew that the tires were designed for a maximum operating speed of 85 miles per hour.

- A warning to keep floor tile adhesive away from a flame was found insufficient to warn the user of the danger of working near a pilot light.

▎Postsale Warnings

Although a product may be reasonably safe when manufactured and sold and involve no then-known risks of which warnings need be given, risks thereafter revealed by user operation and brought to the attention of the manufacturer or vendor may impose upon one or both a duty to warn.

The notice to a manufacturer or vendor of problems revealed by use of the product that will trigger a postdelivery duty to warn appears to be a function of the degree of danger that the problem involves and the number of instances reported.

One case arose on June 8, 1974, when Irvin Cohen was driving his 1973 Chevrolet Malibu. He had purchased the car from Kinney Motors in October 1972 and had driven the car approximately 12,000 miles during the 18 months between the time it was delivered to him new on December 22, 1972, and June 8, 1974. During that period, he had experienced no difficulty with the acceleration system of the car.

On June 8, though, seeking to parallel park on the west side of East 49th Street in Brooklyn, New York, Cohen brought the car to a stop on that side and put it in reverse when, according to him, the car shot backward at high speed and could not be stopped although he had his foot on the brake. The car proceeded backward in an arc some 70 feet to the east side of the street, through an open space on that side where it jumped the curb, stopping only when it hit the wall of a building. The car crushed Astor Cover, who was walking along the east sidewalk at that point, against the wall by the car. His injuries forced him to have one leg amputated above the knee and to use a brace on the other.

Cover and his wife filed suit against Cohen, Kinney Motors, and General Motors, the manufacturer of the car, alleging, among other things, a failure of duty to warn. Apparently, after Cohen had purchased the car, General Motors had sent a technical service bulletin to its dealers acknowledging that "[s]ome 1973 passenger cars . . . may exhibit an erratic idle speed and slow return to idle." The court ruled that General Motors could be held liable if it had failed in its continuing duty to warn of the problem it acknowledged in that bulletin.

▎A Final Word

For many years, there has been talk about revamping the product liability system in the United States. That still appears quite a while away.

Therefore, the product liability rules remain important. The most significant, as they affect marketers and advertisers, is the duty to warn. Even if a product is produced in the most careful manner possible, a manufacturer or seller of that item must warn users of inherent, nonobvious dangers. Failure to do so can result in significant liability.

FIVE WARNING CASES

1. When Frances Ann McLaughlin was six years old, she was visiting her uncle and aunt in West Deering, New Hampshire. While bathing in Whittemore Lake, she almost drowned. She was carried from the lake in an unconscious condition. The local lifeguard administered first aid. After the Bennington Volunteer Fire Department arrived, two men removed a resuscitator and some blankets from the truck. They placed the resuscitator over McLaughlin's mouth, and a woman who identified herself as a nurse wrapped her in blankets. Realizing that more heat was needed to revive McLaughlin, the firefighters returned to their truck and obtained some boxes containing M-S-A Redi-Heat Blocks. They removed the blocks from their containers, activated them, and turned them over to the nurse. The nurse proceeded to apply several of them directly to the child's body under the blankets. Subsequently, she began to heave about and moan. At that point, she was taken, still wrapped in blankets, to a doctor's car and placed on the back seat. The heat blocks had fallen out from under the blankets. After a short stay at the doctor's office, McLaughlin was taken home. That evening, she developed blisters about her body. Doctors determined that she was suffering from third-degree burns, and she was taken to Peterborough Hospital, where she underwent extensive treatment.

The heat blocks had been manufactured by the Catalyst Research Corporation for the Mine Safety Appliances Co., packaged in Mine

Safety's cardboard container at Mine Safety's plant, and sold and distributed by Mine Safety to industrial houses and government agencies and departments for use in emergencies. The heat blocks actually were small magnesium blocks that were activated by raising the spring lever on the block, inserting a loaded cartridge therein, then permitting the spring lever to close and strike the cap of the cartridge, causing the firing pin to ignite the chemical enclosed in the cartridge and to create the heat. The block was covered in its entirety by a red woolen insulating material called "flocking," which appeared and felt like a blanket or flannel covering. Tests made upon the device indicated that the block attained a high surface temperature of 204 degrees Fahrenheit within two minutes after triggering in one case and a high of 195 degrees Fahrenheit within three minutes after triggering in another case. In both cases, after 39 minutes, the blocks retained a temperature of 138 degrees.

Affixed to each block on top of the flocking was an oval-like label containing the trade name of the block, and Mine Safety's name. Mine Safety sold the blocks and cartridges in cardboard containers that contained instructions for use. Among the instructions was the following: "Wrap in insulating medium, such as pouch, towel, blanket or folded cloth." When the heat blocks that the firefighters had applied to McLaughlin had been sold to the department, Mine Safety's representative had demonstrated their proper use. The representative warned that the heat blocks were to be covered with a towel or some other material to keep them from coming into contact with the skin.

McLaughlin filed suit against Mine Safety, seeking to recover damages for the burns she suffered when the heat blocks had been applied to her body. She contended that Mine Safety had failed adequately to warn the public of the danger involved in the use of the blocks and to properly "instruct" ultimate users as to the proper application of the blocks. After a jury trial in favor of McLaughlin, the case reached the New York Court of Appeals. The Court said that the jury could have found that a hidden or latent danger existed in the use of the blocks, or at least that the form and design of the product itself, together with the printing on the container, could have mislead ultimate users as to the need for further insulation. "The blocks were dressed in 'flocking' and appeared to be insulated, and the bold lettering on the containers revealed that the blocks were 'ALWAYS READY FOR USE' and 'ENTIRELY SELF CONTAINED,'" the court said. Thus, the jury could have found that the instructions did not amount to a warning of the risk at all, and that it was foreseeable that the small print instruction might never be read, and might be disregarded even if read. The court nonetheless reversed the judgment in favor of McLaughlin, finding that whether Mine Safety had furnished ample warning was irrelevant because the cause of McLaughlin's burns may have been attributable to the firefighter. If he not only had the means to warn the nurse but prevented any warning from reaching her by taking the blocks out of their container, the court said that Mine Safety should not be held liable. (McLaughlin v. Mine Safety Appliances Co., 11 N.Y.2d 62 (1962).)

2. Before his vasectomy, Stanley Cooley purchased a 6-ounce plastic container of Nair and applied the lotion on his scrotal area in preparation for surgery. After the vasectomy, Cooley experienced a severe infection that eventually disintegrated his scrotum and caused a prolapse of his testicles. He was hospitalized for more than a month and he required reconstruction of his scrotum by application of a plastic mesh and a skin graft from his left thigh. In a lawsuit he filed against Carter-Wallace, Inc., the company that produces and distributes Nair, he alleged that as a result of using Nair he had a permanent scar and hormonal deficiency and had suffered much pain, anxiety, and embarrassment. The back of the container of Nair including the following:

Warning: Irritation or allergic reaction may occur with some people, even after prior use without adverse effect. Therefore, test before each use by applying Nair on a small part of the area where hair is to be removed. Follow directions and wait 24 hours. If skin appears normal, proceed. Do not use on irritated, inflamed, or broken skin. Keep away from eyes. Should Nair touch the eyes, wash thoroughly with lukewarm water. Rinse

*with boric acid solution and if irritation occurs, consult your phy-
sician. Keep out of reach of children. Nair lotion can be used on
legs, arms, face, anywhere except . . . Eyes, nose, ears or on breast
nipples, perianal (sic) or vaginal/genital areas.*

Cooley acknowledged that he had read this label and was concerned
about the exception for vaginal/genital areas. The court nonetheless found
the warning to be inadequate. Carter Wallace, the court said, did not warn
of the specific risks involved if Nair were applied to the genital area. The
label stated only that "irritation or allergic reaction may occur with some
people." It ruled that the warning was such "that a prospective user could
fairly assume that any possible adverse effect of the product would be
mild, whereas the product was actually capable of producing serious and
permanent injury." It concluded that the warning was not "fully descriptive and complete" or "adequate." (Cooley v. Carter-Wallace, Inc., 478
N.Y.S.2d 375 (4th Dept. 1984).)

3. On July 4, 1974, Mark Brown was electrocuted while operating a
Craftsman portable electric circular saw to cut large tree limbs into
smaller pieces of firewood. At the time of his death, the saw was connected to an electrical outlet on the exterior of the Brown residence by
two extension cords. One of these extension cords was a three-prong
grounded cord manufactured by the Coleman Cable and Wire Co. This
extension cord had several cuts in the insulated casing that resulted in the
exposure of frayed conductors; the cuts had been covered with tape.
Brown's widow filed a product liability suit against Coleman, as well as
the manufacturer and retailer of the saw. Among other things, she
contended that the extension cord was defective because Coleman had
failed to issue a warning as to its use when the cord was damaged or improperly repaired. The court rejected her claim. It said that a manufacturer could be held liable when its product was in a condition not contemplated by the ultimate consumer and was dangerous to an extent
beyond that which would be contemplated by the ordinary consumer
who purchased it, with the ordinary knowledge common to the community as to its characteristics. Thus, it said, a product containing an obvious

hazard is generally considered neither defective nor unreasonably dangerous "and therefore there is no duty to warn of such dangers." In this case, it ruled, the cord was a simple thing of universally known characteristics. "Surely every adult knows that if an electrical extension cord is cut or frayed a danger of electrical shock is created." It concluded that as a matter of law Coleman had no duty to warn of the danger of electrical shock. (Brown v. Sears, Roebuck & Co., 667 P.2d 750 (Ct. App. Ariz. 1983).)

4. In September 1973 26-year-old Carole D. MacDonald obtained from her gynecologist a prescription for Ortho Novum contraceptive pills, manufacturer by the Ortho Pharmaceutical Corporation. As required by the then-effective regulations promulgated by the United States Food and Drug Administration (FDA), the pill dispenser she received was labeled with a warning that "oral contraceptives are powerful and effective drugs which can cause side effects in some users and should not be used at all by some women" and that "[t]he most serious known side effect is abnormal blood clotting which can be fatal." The warning also referred MacDonald to a booklet that she obtained from her gynecologist, and that was distributed by Ortho pursuant to FDA requirements. The booklet contained detailed information about the contraceptive pill, including the increased risk to pill users that vital organs such as the brain may be damaged by abnormal blood clotting. The word "stroke" did not appear on the dispenser warning or in the booklet. MacDonald's prescription was renewed at subsequent annual visits to her gynecologist. The prescription was filled annually.

On July 24, 1976, after using the pills for approximately three years, MacDonald suffered an occlusion of a cerebral artery by a blood clot, an injury commonly referred to as a stroke. The injury destroyed approximately 20 percent of her brain tissue and left her permanently disabled. Testifying in the suit she and her husband filed against Ortho, MacDonald stated that, during the time she used the pills, she was unaware that the risk of abnormal blood clotting encompassed the risk of stroke and that she would not have used the pills had she been warned that stroke was an associated risk. The jury found that MacDonald's injury was caused by Ortho's pills and that Ortho had failed to give MacDonald sufficient warnings of the dangers. However, the trial court reversed that ruling and the case reached the Massachusetts Supreme Judicial Court. Among other things, Ortho argued that its warnings complied with FDA labeling requirements and that those requirements preempted or defined the bounds of state law duty to warn. But the Judicial Court disagreed. It said that the regulatory history of the FDA requirements belied any objective to cloak them with preemptive effect. The court said that it was persuaded that, "in instances where a trier of fact could reasonably conclude that a manufacturer's compliance with FDA labeling requirements or guidelines did not adequately apprise oral contraceptive users of inherent risks, the manufacturer should not be shielded from liability by such compliance." Thus, it concluded, even if Ortho had complied with FDA requirements, the jury nonetheless could have found that the lack of a reference to stroke breached Ortho's state law duty to warn. (MacDonald v. Ortho Pharmaceutical Corp., 475 N.E.2d 65 (Mass. 1985).)

5. In early 1974 John Morrell and Company manufactured a Hooper 1000 meat packaging machine through its Hooper Engineering Division. That March it sold the machine to the Conti Packaging Company through the Cryovac Division of W. R. Grace & Co., the exclusive distributor of products manufactured by Morrell's Hooper Division. About a year and a half later, Hooper, Inc. was incorporated and, on October 24, 1975, it purchased some of the assets of Morrell's Hooper Engineering Division. It continued the manufacture of the Hooper 1000, together with other equipment and machinery. It also reached an agreement with Cryovac for Cryovac to continue distributing the Hooper 1000. On July 14, 1979, Julian Radziul was cleaning the Hooper 1000 in the Conti plant in which he worked when he was injured. He then filed suit against Cryovac, the distributor of the machine, and a Cryovac employee who was responsible for training Radziul on the machine and for its maintenance and repair. In addition, he filed suit against Hooper for "failure to warn." Hooper asked the court to dismiss the failure to warn claim, noting that it had nothing to do with the original manufacture or sale of the machine that injured Radziul. But the court refused to do so. It noted that a successor corporation does not generally assume liability for the actions of its predecessor. But, it said, there may be a time when the relationship between a successor corporation and a preexisting customer is sufficient to create a duty to warn. Among the factors to consider: succession to a predecessor's service contracts, coverage of the particular machine under a service contract, service of that machine by the purchaser corporation, and a purchaser corporation's knowledge of defects and of the location or owner of the machine. The facts in this case, the court stated, were sufficient to require that a jury decide whether Hooper had an obligation to warn Conti of potential defects in and possible improvements in the safety features of the Hooper 1000 that might have made it safer. (Radziul v. Hooper, Inc., 479 N.Y.S. 2d 324 (Sup. Ct. Monroe Co. 1984).)

Warning Checklist

✓ A products liability lawsuit usually alleges a defect of some sort in the product. For marketers and advertisers, one of the most important provisions of product liability law is the duty to warn.

✓ Though a product may be flawlessly made, it may be deemed defective if it is unreasonably dangerous to place the product in a user's hands without a suitable warning.

✓ Where a warning is required, it must be reasonably readable and apprise a consumer exercising reasonable care under the circumstances of the existence and seriousness of the danger sufficient to enable the consumer to protect against the danger.

✓ Once a warning is given, the focus shifts to the adequacy of the warning. Warnings must clearly alert the user to avoid certain unsafe uses of the product that would appear to be normal and reasonable.

✓ The sale of a product does not end a seller's duty. Although a product may be reasonably safe when manufactured and sold and involve no then known risks of which warnings need be given, risks thereafter revealed by user operation and brought to the attention of the manufacturer or vendor may impose upon one or both a duty to warn.

CUSTOMER RELATIONS

21

FORMING A CONTRACT

▮ The Uniform Commercial Code
▮ Writings to Satisfy the Statute of Frauds
▮ Exceptions to the Statute ▮ The Merchants' Exception
▮ A Final Word

According to Lawrence Wallach, on January 7, 1987, Michael Collins, a sales representative for the Donzi Marine Corporation, met Wallach at a boat show and offered him a Donzi dealership that would allow Wallach the right to purchase, market, and sell Donzi's products exclusively in the Long Island, New York, area for one year.

Wallach and the company he formed, Wallach Marine Corporation, contended that they accepted this oral offer and gave Donzi a $50,000 check, which Wallach understood to be the fee requested by Donzi, a builder of light speed boats, for the right to do business as a Donzi dealer and franchisee.

Subsequently, Wallach said that he and his corporation placed orders with Donzi for 21 boats at a cost to them of $775,000 and received 10 boats at a cost of $383,614; they also allegedly acquired interests in two boatyards for more than $1 million.

In a lawsuit he later filed against Collins and Donzi, Wallach contended among other things that Donzi breached the oral dealership contract by terminating it to enter into a dealer and franchise agreement with a competitor who would pay Donzi a higher fee or agree to purchase more boats.

Donzi contended that any dealership agreement it may have had with Wallach was unenforceable because it was not in writing. Donzi admitted that Collins had conversations with Wallach in December 1986 and on January 7, 1987, relating to the formation of Wallach Marine and its becoming a Donzi dealership. But, Donzi emphasized, on January 9, 1987, Wallach sent it a dealership application that contained only a bank reference and Wallach's address and phone number—all of the other requested information was left blank. The application stated that it created no obligation in the absence of a signed dealer sales contract, which never existed. Accordingly, Donzi asked the court to dismiss Wallach's breach of contract claim.

In its decision, the court relied on a provision of New York law that states that a contract for the sale of more than $500 in goods is not enforceable unless it meets three conditions:

1. There must be some writing sufficient to indicate that a contract for sale has been made between the parties.

2. The writing must be signed by the party against whom enforcement is sought.

3. The writing must specify a quantity of goods to be sold.

This law is the modern version of the Statute of Frauds. It is intended to protect individuals and businesses from being forced to litigate the existence of oral agreements—a difficult, and often unfair, version of "he said, I said."

The court in the Donzi case ruled that the law applied to franchise and dealership agreements, which obviously involve the sale of goods. Then, noting that Wallach and his corporation had alleged that the products they were to purchase from Donzi were for more than $500 and that they sought to rely on an alleged oral agreement, it ruled that Wallach's breach of contract claim had to be dismissed.

❚ The Uniform Commercial Code

The Statute of Frauds relied on by the court in the Donzi case is contained in the New York version of the Uniform Commercial Code (UCC). The UCC is a relatively uniform law that has been enacted by most states across the country; it governs virtually all aspects of the sale of goods, including one of the first questions that marketers, sales representatives, and other business people must think about: How is a contract formed?

Significantly, the UCC's Statute of Frauds does not state that an oral contract is unenforceable. Contracts may be made orally and oral contracts may be enforceable.

The Statute of Frauds simply requires some writing setting forth enough information (especially with respect to quantity) to allow a court to rule that a contract may have been made; at that point, the party seeking to enforce the contract or sue for its breach has the ability to attempt to prove that an oral agreement was made.

Courts recognize that businesspeople often make oral contracts. Therefore, they do not want the Statute of Frauds to be used to interfere with contracts that do exist; they only want it to protect businesses from false assertions that a contract had been formed. Thus, the writing requirement can be met by papers other than one single document that looks like a contract, has small print, and was prepared by a team of lawyers. The fact that the Statute of Frauds can be met through the integration of several documents, each of which alone might not be sufficient to meet the three requirements of the statute, was discussed in a recent decision by the U.S. Court of Appeals for the Fifth Circuit.

❚ Writings to Satisfy the Statute of Frauds

Certina USA, Inc., a watch manufacturer headquartered in Lancaster, Pennsylvania, sold its watches through the efforts of a traveling salesforce consisting of Certina's salaried employees and independent representatives paid on a commission basis. Gerald Murff was a Certina representative whose sales territory included Mississippi. Migerobe, Inc., a Mississippi corporation that owned and operated jewelry counters in McRae's department stores located throughout the southeastern portion of the United States, had, on occasion, purchased watches from Murff.

In the summer of 1987 Migerobe contacted Murff to notify him that Migerobe would be interested in buying Certina watches if Certina decided to sell a large portion of its inventory at reduced prices. Migerobe suspected that Certina might make such an offer because another retailer had decided to stop carrying the Certina line of watches and Migerobe believed that this would create a backlog of inventory for the manufacturer. In fact, Certina had decided to institute a special promotion to eliminate its inventory as a result of a corporate decision to withdraw its watches from the United States market.

Migerobe was hoping to acquire the Certina watches so that they could be used as "door-busters" for an after-Thanksgiving sales promotion. Door-busters, or loss leaders, are items offered at a low price that are designed to increase the traffic flow through a store and thereby increase the sales of nonadvertised items. Murff became aware that Migerobe was planning to use the watches in this special after-Thanksgiving promotion.

In a letter dated September 14, 1987, Murff responded to Migerobe's request. He indicated that he was pursuing a special price on the Certina inventories on Migerobe's behalf and that he would keep the company informed of his progress. At the time, Murff was attempting to negotiate a special discounted price with Certina's vice-president of retail sales, William Wolfe. On October 21, 1987, Wolfe provided Murff with a list of watches from Certina's inventory that Murff could offer to Migerobe at a price of $45 each. Murff scheduled an October 29 meeting with Migerobe to present the offer.

Murff met with Migerobe on October 29 and during the course of the day made several phone calls to Certina's home office to verify the number of watches in Certina's inventory and to secure specific payment terms. After a full day of negotiating for particular quantities and styles as well as payment terms and a shipping date, Migerobe agreed to purchase more than 2,000 Certina watches at a price of $45 each. Murff phone Certina's office one final time to report the sale, and Wolfe's administrative assistant recorded it on a Certina order form.

However, on November 4, 1987, Certina's national accounts manager, Don Olivett, called Migerobe to say that Certina would not ship the watches that it had ordered on October 29. The president of Certina, John Gelson, later explained that the order was rejected because the offered price was lower than that offered to other customers and he feared that the offer might constitute a violation of the Robinson-Patman Act, the federal law that regulates price discrimination. Migerobe then filed suit for breach of contract against Certina and, after a five-day trial, a jury awarded it $157,133.00. Certina appealed, arguing that Migerobe had failed to submit writings sufficient to satisfy the Statute of Frauds.

The court noted that a "writing" for the purposes of the Statute of Frauds may consist of separate writings, connected together by express reference to each other or internal evidence of their unity, connection, or relation. The signed writing need not refer explicitly to the unsigned writing; they will be integrated if the signed writing makes at least an implied reference to the other writing.

In this case, the court found that the integration of two signed documents and one unsigned document tended to show that Migerobe and Certina had made a contract for sale.

The first signed document was a memorandum from Wolfe to Certina's chief financial officer, R. B. Oliver. It stated in part that "Jerry Murff has been authorized to sell" Certina watches to Migerobe at a special $45 price. Wolfe explained that "Murff's commission on this sale has been set at three percent so that our net selling price is $43.65." Certina claimed that the purpose of this memorandum was to solicit authorization from Oliver so that Wolfe could go ahead with the Migerobe offer. But, the court noted, Certina's president—not Oliver—ultimately determined that the sale should be rejected. Moreover, it said, the language Wolfe used in the memorandum did not support Certina's interpretation that the memorandum was simply a request for authorization; the only mention of authorization occurred in the past tense, indicating that Murff had already been authorized to make the sale.

The second writing was a memorandum to several Certina employees from Charles Westhaeffer, the person at Certina in charge of inventory control. Westhaeffer's handwritten note announced that a new "promotion code has been set up to cover a special order from Migerobe." The court found that the note served as further confirmation that a transaction had taken place between Certina and Migerobe. It added that Westhaeffer's note contained the same promotion code, "03," that was found on the Certina order form that had been completed by Wolfe's administrative assistant.

A writing that was not signed by Certina but that the court found pertinent was the Certina order form, which listed the quantity, styles, and prices of the watches Migerobe ordered. The order form contained other information that, the court found, tended to connect it with the Wolfe and Westhaeffer memos, such as the customer name, "Migerobe," the promotion code, "03," the name of the sales representative, "Murff," and the initials of Charles Westhaeffer, dated "10/30," the same date on which he sent out his signed memo. The court ruled that the "connection among these three documents was sufficiently strong to justify their integration into a writing that would satisfy the Statute of Frauds." It then affirmed the jury's finding of a breach of contract by Certina and upheld its $157,133 award to Migerobe.

∎ Exceptions to the Statute

There are a number of exceptions to the Statute of Frauds. For instance, if a party against whom enforcement of a contract is sought admits in court papers or testimony that it made a contract, the contract will be enforceable (at least to the extent of the quantity of goods admitted) even though there is no writing. A contract also is enforceable notwithstanding the Statute of Frauds with respect to goods that have been received and accepted by the buyer or for which payment has been made by the buyer and accepted by the seller. The law allows these two exceptions because it is rather clear that a contract has been made in each of these cases.

There are two other exceptions to the Statute of Frauds that are quite significant. The first permits an oral contract to be enforced, even when not evidenced by a writing, if the goods were to be specially manufactured for the buyer, were not suitable for sale to others in the ordinary course of the seller's business, and the seller, before receiving any notice of repudiation from the buyer and under circumstances that reasonably indicated that the goods were for the buyer, substantially began their manufacture. Several years ago, the Supreme Court of Virginia issued a decision that helps to explain these requirements.

In 1977 Kern's Bakery of Virginia, Inc., operated a bakery in Lynchburg and R-P Packaging, Inc., of Columbus, Georgia, was a manufacturer of cellophane wrapping material that Kern's used in packaging its product. In late 1977, Kern's decided to change its system for the packaging of cookies it produced in its Lynchburg plant from a tied bread bag to a tray covered with printed cellophane wrapping. Kern's plant manager discussed the proposed change with R-P's representative and furnished R-P with several trays filled with cookies to enable R-P to take measurements to determine the appropriate size for the cellophane covering. In addition, Kern's asked R-P to design appropriate artwork to be printed on the cellophane wrapping.

On December 28, 1977, Kern's plant manager gave R-P's representative a verbal "order" for cellophane wrap, which was transmitted to R-P's home office. On January 4, 1978, R-P prepared and mailed to Kern's a written acknowledgement of the order that contained specifications, delivery instructions, order date, and quantity. The word "later" was typed in the space provided for the contract price. The sale price, $13,375.11, was subsequently supplied. The symbol "W/A" was written in the space titled "acknowledgment date;" it apparently stood for "will advise," which in company parlance meant that R-P did not have approval from the customer to proceed. The following was typed at the bottom of the acknowledgment form: "Produce printing plates per artwork sent to Frank Tarpley, but first send photostats with color stripe to customer for approval before etching."

On January 3, 1978, the day before R-P's acknowledgment form was issued, Kern's sold all of its assets in Lynchburg to the Flowers Baking Company of Lynchburg, Inc. without notice to R-P. R-P's acknowledgement, of course, arrived at the Lynchburg plant after Flowers had assumed control.

R-P sent a sample unprinted roll of the cellophane wrapping to the Lynchburg plant to be run on the plant's packaging equipment as a test for size. Although Flowers performed no such test, the plant manager, who had worked for Kern's and was still operating the plant for Flowers, advised R-P's representative in mid-February that the material was satisfactory and said, "Proceed with the order." On the following day, R-P's representatives met with Flowers' Lynchburg manager to discuss the proposed "artwork." The manager approved it, except for an agreed change of name from Kern's to Flowers, and requested that the material be produced and shipped as soon as possible.

Flowers received the printed wrapping material about March 27, 1978. However, contending that the material was too short to fit the trays and that the printing was not centered, it returned the material to R-P. R-P then filed suit for the purchase price of the packaging material and was awarded judgment against Flowers. Flowers appealed, contending that R-P's claim was barred by the Statute of Frauds.

The Virginia Supreme Court first found that R-P and Kern's had no contract to which Flowers could be bound as a successor to Kern's because "the words and conduct of R-P and Kern's were entirely tentative and were inconsistent with an intention to contract" at all times prior to January 3, 1978, when Kern's was replaced by Flowers. Throughout that period, the court said, Kern's was awaiting R-P's proposal, which was to be based upon R-P's measurements of the cookie trays that Kern's had provided. Kern's also was awaiting R-P's design of the artwork, which was to be submitted for Kern's approval. For its part, R-P made no proposal until after Kern's had left the scene, submitted no artwork for approval, sent no cellophane for testing, and quoted no price. When it issued its January 4 proposal, R-P took no steps to fill the "order" and denied any intention to do so until its customer had approved the artwork design.

However, the court found, there was a contract between R-P and Flowers that could not be barred by the Statute of Frauds even though there was no writing signed by Flowers sufficient to comply with the statute. The court stated that R-P manufactured the cellophane wrapping material to the size required by Flowers' containers and imprinted it with Flowers' name and unique artwork. Those factors, the court concluded, took R-P's claim against Flowers out of the Statute of Frauds.

▌ The Merchants' Exception

A second significant exception to the Statute of Frauds relates only to businesses (and not to, say, a sale by a business to a consumer). On certain conditions, this "merchants' exception" permits one business to send a writing within a reasonable time confirming the existence of a contract to another business; if the recipient of the writing does not object within 10 days, the Statute of Frauds is deemed satisfied.

Before the enactment of the UCC, a seller who entered into an oral agreement with a buyer and who sent the buyer a signed memorandum confirming their agreement could have the agreement enforced against itself but could not enforce it against the buyer. If the market fluctuated in the buyer's favor, the buyer could enforce the agreement against the seller. Conversely, if the market was unfavorable the buyer could refuse to perform because the oral agreement could not be enforced against it. The merchants' exception contained in the UCC remedies this situation by declaring that both parties can be bound unless one communicates objections to the other within 10 days from receipt of a written confirmation.

This exception to the general Statute of Frauds rule can be very costly, as the Gestetner Corporation, a distributor of a line of office equipment including stencil duplicators, discovered several years ago.

In January 1984, Anthony J. Casella, the president of the Case Equipment Company, began experimenting with stencil duplicators to develop a process using sublimation dyes as ink to produce full-color heat transfers for application to garments, metal, and acrylics. The use of sublimation dyes as ink overcame the color fading problem common in other heat transfers. Casella found that Gestetner's stencil duplicators, with some modification, were suitable for use with the sublimation ink he had developed. He called his process "Subli Color" printing.

That spring, Casella met with Gestetner's regional sales manager and inquired whether Gestetner would establish Case as an independent dealer and give it the sole right to market modified Gestetner stencil duplicators as part of Case's color transfer process. Although the parties had no written contract, Gestetner began to sell stencil duplicators, parts, and supplies to Case.

On September 11, 1984, Case's patent lawyer wrote to Gestetner's national sales manager that Case reserved its domestic and foreign patent rights in the Subli Color process. The letter also stated that Case looked forward "to its continuing role as exclusive dealer for Gestetner in the field of use of full-color and multicolor sublimation transfer printing." Gestetner's national sales manager forwarded the letter to Gestetner's president, who directed that no response be made to it.

At first, things went well. But starting in the fall of 1984, the relationship between the parties began to sour. Case claimed that it had received defective products that it could not sell and refused to bring its past due account current. Gestetner refused to ship further products. Then, on May 29, 1985, Gestetner brought suit for goods sold and delivered and not paid for. Case counterclaimed, alleging that Gestetner had breached their contract because it had failed to provide equipment to Case in a timely fashion.

After trial, Gestetner was awarded judgment against Case in the amount of $63,779.80. But although Gestetner claimed that Case's breach of contract claim should be barred because there was no writing sufficient to satisfy the Statute of Frauds, the jury returned a verdict for Case on that counterclaim in the amount of $225,600. Gestetner appealed.

The court rejected Gestetner's Statute of Frauds defense. It ruled that the September 11 letter from Case's patent lawyer to Gestetner (noting, among other things, Case's "role as exclusive dealer for Gestetner") met the UCC's requirements of the exception to the Statute of Frauds because, "[b]etween merchants, failure to answer a written confirmation of a contract within ten days of receipt is tantamount to a writing . . . and is sufficient against both parties." Noting that Gestetner had begun to sell stencil duplicators to Case in the spring of 1984, the court said that a letter dated September 11 of that year met the "reasonable time" requirement contained in the exception to the statute of frauds.

▍A Final Word

A contract can be formed in any manner sufficient to show the agreement of the parties. Thus, oral agreements and agreements evidenced by conduct of the parties both may be enforceable.

But the law requires that the parties intend to form a contract before it will find that a contract exists. Thus, to avoid being bound by letters of intent or drafts of other kinds of documents, businesses often insert language that clearly states that they do not intend to be bound until the execution of a formal, complete contract.

The point of the law relating to contract formation and the Statute of Frauds is that the courts seek to discover what the parties have agreed to, if anything. However, subjective intent that is belied by objective actions will not necessarily win out. Care is required, therefore, at all stages of contract negotiations.

FIVE CONTRACTS, OR NO CONTRACTS?

1. As a result of long-distance telephone conversations between Jack Skjonsby, a representative of Dataserv Equipment, Inc., and Ron Finerty, an employee of Technology Finance Group, Inc., regarding the possible purchase by Technology of certain IBM computer "features" that Dataserv had previously purchased in Canada, Dataserv sent a proposed form of contract to Technology on September 6, 1979. Dataserve's proposed contract included a section that provided for installation of the features by Indepth, a third party. The contract also provided that it was "subject to acceptance by the seller . . . and shall only become effective on the date thereof" and that it was made "subject to the terms and conditions included herein and Purchaser's acceptance is effective only to the extent that such terms and conditions are conditions herein. Any acceptance which contains conditions which are in addition to or inconsistent with the terms and conditions herein will be a counter offer and will not be binding unless agreed to in writing by the Seller."

On October 1 Finerty wrote Skjonsby that three changes "need[ed] to be made" in the contract, one of which was the deletion of the Indepth clause. The letter closed with, "Let me know and I will make the changes and sign." Two of the changes were thereafter resolved, but the resolution of the Indepth clause remained in controversy. Later in October 1979 Dataserv offered to accept, in substitution for Indepth, any other third-party installation company Technology would designate. Technology never agreed to this. On November 8, 1979, by telephone Dataserv offered to remove the Indepth clause from the contract form. Technology responded that it was "too late," and that there was no deal. On November 9, Finerty called Dataserv and informed it that "the deal was not going to get done because they'd waited until too late a point in time." However, by telex dated November 12, 1979, Dataserv informed Technology that the features were ready for pickup and that the pickup and payment should be no later than November 15, 1979. On November 13, 1979, Finerty responded by telex stating, "[S]ince [Dataserv] had not responded in a positive fashion to [our] letter requesting contract changes . . . its offer to purchase was withdrawn on 11/9/79 via telephone conversation with Jack Skjonsby. Ten to fifteen days prior, I made Jack aware that this deal was dead if Dataserv did not agree to contract changes prior to the 'Eleventh Hour.' " On June 19, 1980, Dataserv sold the features to another party for $26,000; it then sought a judgment against Technology for the difference between the price it received for the features and the contract price it had negotiated with Technology.

The court said that the critical issue was whether Dataserv rejected Technology's October 1 counteroffer. It noted that Dataserv responded to that counteroffer by agreeing to delete two of the three objectionable clauses, but insisting that the third be included. "By refusing to accept according to the terms of the proposal," the court said, "Dataserv rejected Technology's counteroffer and thus no contract was formed." Dataserv's so called "acceptance," when it offered to delete the Indepth clause on November 8, was "without any legal effect whatsoever, except to create a new offer which Technology immediately rejected." (Dataserv Equipment, Inc. v. Technology Finance Leasing Corp., 364 N.W.2d 838 (Ct. App. Minn. 1985).)

2. The Barber & Ross Co. was in the business of purchasing millwork products, including doors, from manufacturers, preparing them for installation in new homes, and selling them to new home builders, primarily in Virginia. In 1982 Barber & Ross began purchasing flush doors and six-panel doors from Lifetime Doors, Inc., a door manufacturer. In 1983 a sales representative for Lifetime apparently approached Barber & Ross to urge it to shift all its door purchases to Lifetime so as to constitute Lifetime its exclusive supplier. The sales rep provided Barber & Ross with sales literature that offered prospective purchasers the opportunity to join Lifetime's VIP Club. These writings promised new purchasers "continuous production availability . . . in full proportion to monthly needs" that would ensure that purchasers could "order flexible quantities" in shipments of a "desired number." The president of Barber & Ross allegedly then obtained an oral commitment from Lifetime that Lifetime would supply Barber & Ross's requirements of four truckloads of six-panel doors each month, in return for which Barber & Ross would purchase doors exclusively from Lifetime.

In July, however, Lifetime allegedly instituted an allocation system for its customers that tied the number of six-panel doors a customer could purchase to the number of flush doors that the customer bought. Then, in September 1983, the parties terminated their relationship. In the lawsuit that followed, Lifetime contended that it ceased shipping doors to Barber & Ross when Barber & Ross stopped paying its bills for past shipments. Barber & Ross's president testified that Lifetime refused to ship further quantities of six-panel doors to Barber & Ross after Barber & Ross threatened to file suit to challenge the allocation system. The jury found in favor of Barber & Ross on its claim that Lifetime had breached the requirements contract between the parties, but on appeal Lifetime contended that the alleged contract was unenforceable under the Statute of Frauds. The U.S. Court of Appeals for the Fourth Circuit found, though, that the written sales brochures given by Lifetime to Barber & Ross met the requirements of the Statute of Frauds. The court ruled that they met the signature requirement because the Lifetime Doors trademark appeared on the documents "and that was sufficient to authenticate the documents." The court also ruled that the brochures stated a sufficient definite quantity for purposes of the Statute of Frauds because they referred to meeting a purchaser's needs. It then upheld the jury's breach of contract award against Lifetime. (Barber & Ross Co. v. Lifetime Doors, Inc., 810 F.2d 1276 (4th Cir. 1987).)

3. According to Bazak International Corp., a textile merchant, Karen Fedorko, the marketing director of Mast Industries, Inc., met with Tuvia Feldman, Bazak's president, on April 22, 1987. Fedorko offered to sell Feldman certain textiles that Mast was closing out, and the two negotiated all the terms of an oral agreement except price. The next day, they agreed on a price of $103,330. Fedorko told Feldman that Bazak would receive written invoices for the goods the following day and that the textiles would be delivered shortly thereafter. When no invoices arrived, Feldman contacted Fedorko, who allegedly assured him that everything was in order and that the invoices were on the way.

However, on April 30, 1987, Fedorko had Feldman come to the New York City offices of Mast's parent company where, following Fedorko's instructions, Feldman sent five of Bazak's own purchase orders (which it generally used to reflect sales to its customers) by Telecopier to Mast's Massachusetts office with a notation on the bottom of the forms that stated, "As prisented [sic] by Karen Fedorko." That same day Feldman received written confirmation of Mast's receipt of the orders. Mast made no objection to the terms set forth in the Telecopied purchase orders, but it never delivered the textiles despite Bazak's demands; Bazak filed suit for breach of contract. Mast then moved to dismiss the contract claim, contending that the only writings alleged in Bazak's complaint—the purchase orders sent by Bazak to Mast and Mast's confirmation of receipt of the purchase orders—were insufficient to satisfy the Statute of Frauds.

The case ultimately reached the New York Court of Appeals. That court ruled that the purchase orders did not have to contain express language stating that they were "confirming" the existence of a prior agreement to be sufficient to comply with the merchants' exception to the Statute of Frauds. It also found that although the purchase orders were generally used by Bazak to record sales it made as a seller and not as a buyer, they were sufficient to defeat Mast's Statute of Frauds defense and to allow Bazak to proceed to trial on its breach of contract claim against Mast. (Bazak International Corp. v. Mast Industries, Inc., 73 N.Y.2d 116 (1989).)

4. In 1981 the Funston Machine and Supply Company purchased two drilling rigs from Cox Engineering, Inc. that it then resold. Then, contending that Funston had orally agreed to purchase two additional rigs but had failed to do so, Cox filed suit against Funston. Cox introduced evidence in court that it had forwarded two invoices to Funston making reference to ten percent down payments on the two additional rigs and that Funston had received those invoices but had not objected to them within 10 days of receipt. The court was faced with the question of whether the invoices were sufficient written confirmation of an underlying oral agreement to come within the UCC's merchants' exception to the Statute of Frauds. It ruled that they were because they afforded a basis for believing that the parties had reached a real agreement. The court then rejected Funston's Statute of Frauds defense. (Cox Engineering, Inc. v. Funston Machine and Supply Co., 749 S.W.2d 508 (Ct. App. Tex. 1988).)

5. In the 1970s and early 1980s, a manufacturing process of the Eastman Kodak Company generated a liquid waste stream of zinc chloride solution that Kodak converted into zinc hydroxide sludge; it then paid chemical waste handlers to remove the sludge to a landfill. In December 1981 Madison Industries, Inc., a zinc salt manufacturer, offered to purchase Kodak's zinc chloride solution for 10 cents per pound of zinc. In early 1982 Madison began removing the zinc chloride solution from Kodak's Rochester plant. On February 22, 1982, Kodak forwarded a draft agreement under which it proposed that the sale and transportation arrangement continue for a one-year period. The next month, Madison suggested an alternate pricing scheme based upon a concentration of zinc chloride ranging from 30 percent to 46 percent. In response, Kodak forwarded a second revised agreement on April 15, 1982, that incorporated Madison's suggested alternate pricing scheme and changed the term of the contract from one to three years.

The agreement went through a number of additional drafts and changes, including one that provided that "Madison shall have the right of first refusal to purchase any zinc hydroxide in Kodak's possession." Then, with one additional change added requiring Kodak to guarantee that its sludge would be 40 percent zinc, Madison executed the contract on September 16, 1982. Kodak, however, did not sign the agreement because it knew that its sludge could not consistently contain 40 percent zinc. Nonetheless, Madison continued to receive zinc hydroxide sludge from Kodak until October 12, 1984. On that date, Kodak advised Madison that it would no longer supply zinc hydroxide to it.

Madison filed a breach of contract action against Kodak, contending that the letter and contract executed by Madison and returned to Kodak on September 16, 1982, confirmed and embodied a prior oral agreement between the parties sufficient to comply with the merchants' exception to the Statute of Frauds. The court found that the merchants' exception did not apply to this transaction because it was not a sale to which the UCC applied. Rather, the alleged agreement provided only a "right of first re-fusal" or an "open-ended option" to Madison; it merely required Kodak, if and when it decided to sell, to offer its zinc to Madison at a stipulated price. Finally, the court ruled that the purported agreement was unen-forceable under the general Statutes of Frauds contained in New Jersey law, which, like the general Statute of Frauds contained in the law of most other states, makes certain unwritten contracts unenforceable and does not include a merchants' exception similar to that contained in the UCC. (Madison Industries, Inc. v. Eastman Kodak Co., 581 A.2d 85 (Sup. Ct. N.J. 1990).)

Contract Formation Checklist

✓ The Uniform Commercial Code (UCC), a relatively uniform law adopted by virtually all states across the country, governs the sales of goods.

✓ Under the UCC, oral sales agreements may be enforceable. However, con-tracts that are not in writing must comply with the Statute of Frauds.

✓ The UCC's Statute of Frauds states that a contract for the sale of more than $500 in goods is not enforceable unless there is a writing signed by the party against whom enforcement is sought that indicates that a contract was made and that specifies a quantity of goods to be sold.

✓ The UCC contains a number of exceptions to the Statute of Frauds, including one for specially manufactured goods.

✓ The merchants' exception is a second significant exception to the Statute of Frauds. Generally speaking, it prohibits a business from raising the Statute of Frauds defense if it received a written confirmation of the alleged contract and failed to respond within 10 days.

22

FILLING IN GAPS AND AVOIDING TRAPS IN SALES CONTRACTS

▮ Is There an Intention to Make a Contract?
▮ Clarifying and Adding Contract Terms
▮ The UCC's Other Gap Fillers ▮ Requirements Contracts
▮ Battle of the Forms ▮ UCC Section 2-207 ▮ A Final Word

The Dura-Wood Treating Company and Century Forest Industries, Inc. were both in the business of treating cross-ties for industrial and commercial use when Dura-Wood contracted to supply a third party—the William A. Smith Company—with cross-ties. Thereafter, the manager of Dura-Wood, Clyde M. Norton, contacted a vice-president of Century Forest, Melvin H. Durham, by telephone. During that conversation they discussed Dura-Wood's need for additional cross-ties to meet its contractual obligations to the Smith Company. Additionally, the two discussed Century Forest's capability to provide Dura-Wood with approximately 20,000 cross-ties at a price of $8.60 per tie.

Following the conversation, Norton sent a letter to Century Forest that stated, in its entirety: "Confirming our conversation, please enter our order of 20,000 6 X 8–8'6" No. 3 hardwood ties at $8.60 each. These are to be treated with creosote coal-tar solution. We will advise instructions just as soon as we get some releases on the job."

Century Forest did not respond to this letter in writing. However, communications between the two companies continued. In fact, because Dura-Wood's need to fulfill its contractual obligation to the Smith Company was delayed, Century Forest indicated that Dura-Wood should let it know "when the ties were going to be needed."

After the Smith Company informed Dura-Wood that it needed the cross-ties, Dura-Wood telephoned Century Forest. At this time, Norton learned that Durham was no longer employed by Century Forest. As a result, Norton talked to S. Harry Kerr, who was in charge of sales for Century Forest.

Norton claimed that he was told by Kerr that due to an increase in the cost of ties, Century Forest would not be able to ship Dura-Wood's order and would have to cancel it. Dura-Wood then decided to manufacture the ties internally; it also filed a breach of contract suit against Century Forest.

Century Forest contended that it had not reached a sales contract with Dura-Wood because essential terms were left out, including the specifications the cross-ties were to meet. But the court, relying on various provisions of the Uniform Commercial Code (UCC), disagreed.

▌ Is There an Intention to Make a Contract?

Under the UCC, a contract may be enforceable even though one or more terms have been left open if the parties intended to make a contract. (See chapter 21 for more on the Uniform Commercial Code.)

The court in the Dura-Wood case found substantial evidence to support the conclusion that there was a "meeting of the minds" between Dura-Wood and Century Forest and, thus, the requisite intent to enter a contract. Both Norton and Durham testified that they spoke to each other about Dura-Wood's need for cross ties and Century Forest's willingness to supply them. When asked by the court to describe the conversation, Norton testified:

> *I told him I wanted to buy the 20,000 cross-ties at the price of $8.60 that he was selling cross-ties for, and that we would go ahead and take the 20,000 cross-ties. And he said okay, we will supply. In fact, I asked him initially if they would take half the order [of Smith Company's 50,000 cross-ties] and he said no, I won't take half of it. I said well, will you take 20,000. He said yes, we'll take 20,000. At that point, I confirmed that we were going to purchase 20,000 cross-ties from him.*

Durham's rendition of the conversation's substance is strikingly similar. He testified that the two men discussed the fact that Century-Forest was unable to supply 25,000 ties, or half of the Smith Company order, but could supply 20,000. According to Durham, they also discussed the size of the cross ties. In Durham's words:

> *So, we had a specific number of ties, a specific quantity of ties. These ties were stacked on trips of 30 ties to the bundle, and if we could treat these ties dry, we had a definite price and a definite quantity that we could have sold the ties for. This is the lot we were talking about.*

The court found further evidence that the parties intended a contract. Norton's letter to Durham was dated the same day both Norton and Durham testified they discussed the sale of the cross ties. Additionally, Durham testified the letter expressed, in general terms, the substance of the discussion he had with Norton. Finally, Century Forest filled out a "phone order form" that stated 20,000 #3 MHW ties had been "sold to" Dura-Wood.

Having found that the parties had an understanding regarding what was to be bought and sold, the court turned to whether the contract was enforceable although certain terms were indefinite or had been omitted. For that analysis, the court turned to UCC Section 2-204, which states that an agreement for sale may be enforced even though one or more terms are left open. A number of other UCC sections explain just what to do in those cases.

▌Clarifying and Adding Contract Terms

Norton's note to Durham did not set out the date of delivery. The court noted, though, that UCC Section 2-309 fills in that gap; it provides that the time for shipment or delivery under a contract if not agreed upon "shall be a reasonable time."

Norton's note also failed to specify a place for delivery. But UCC Section 2-308 states that "[u]nless otherwise agreed . . . the place for delivery of goods is the seller's place of business."

Century Forest contended that the portion of the note from Norton that stated that "[t]hese are to be treated with creosote coal tar solution" was too indefinite to form a contract because there was no evidence from Dura-Wood as to what mixture of oil was to be used or what amount of oil the ties were to be treated with.

But the court rejected this contention, as well. It said that Durham testified that he and Norton had discussed treatment of the cross-ties. Durham stated, "I'm sure that when I discussed it with him, I told him—if I give him a price of $8.60, which is what we did, I told him that would be for seven pounds 60-40." Durham explained that the reference to seven pounds was a description of how many pounds of oil per cubic foot of pressure would be applied and that 60-40 meant 60 percent creosote and 40 percent coal-tar.

Accordingly, the court found that an enforceable contract with terms that could be determined had been formed and that Dura-Wood was entitled to damages for breach of that contract by Century Forest.

▌ The UCC's Other Gap Fillers

Under the UCC, contracts may be valid even when the exact time the parties reach an agreement is uncertain. Furthermore, as Century Forest learned, a court has the power to uphold an agreement even if the agreement does not expressly deal with what inarguably are crucial terms. Parties even may be bound to a contract although the buyer believes one set of terms apply and the seller contends that another set apply.

Once the parties are deemed to have reached an understanding or agreement, the UCC sets forth rules that help nail down the terms. It has standard provisions that can be incorporated into contracts when necessary. It resolves conflicts between buyers and sellers. And it also has rules to determine whether a buyer's terms, or a seller's terms, should govern.

Here is a short list of certain "gap filler" provisions in addition to those relied on by the court in the Dura-Wood case

- The UCC provides that parties may reach a valid sales agreement even though the price is not settled. If nothing is said as to price, the price is left to be agreed by the parties, and if they fail to agree, the price is to be fixed in terms of some agreed market or other standard as set or recorded by a third person or agency and if it is not so set or recorded, the price is deemed a reasonable price at the time for delivery.

- If a contract does not indicate the specifics of delivery, the UCC requires all goods called for by the contract must be tendered in a single delivery.

- Unless otherwise agreed, payment is due at the time and place at which the buyer is to receive goods.

- Unless excluded or modified, a warranty that the goods shall be merchantable is implied in a contract for their sale if the seller is a merchant with respect to goods of that kind. (To be merchantable, goods, among other things, must be fit for the ordinary purposes for which such goods are used.)

The UCC also validates contracts that measure the quantity by the output of the seller or the requirements of the buyer. In those cases, the quantity of goods refers to the actual output or requirements "as may occur in good faith, except that no quantity unreasonably disproportionate to any stated estimate or in the absence of a stated estimate to any normal or otherwise comparable prior output or requirements may be tendered or demanded." The "good faith" requirement implicit in enforceable requirements contract—and so often discussed with respect to other sections of the UCC—was analyzed recently by Judge Posner of the U.S. Court of Appeals for the Seventh Circuit.

▌Requirements Contracts

That case involved the Empire Gas Corporation, a retail distributor of liquefied petroleum gas, better known as propane, and the American Bakeries Company, which operated a fleet of more than 3,000 motor vehicles to serve its processing plants and bakeries.

American Bakeries became interested in the possibility of converting its fleet to propane, which at the time was one-third to one-half less expensive than gasoline. It entered into discussions with Empire Gas that resulted in an agreement in principle. Empire Gas sent American Bakeries a draft of its standard guaranteed fuel supply contract that would have required American Bakeries to install a minimum number of conversion units each month and to buy all the propane for its converted vehicles from Empire Gas for eight years. American Bakeries rejected that contract and Empire Gas prepared a new one, which the parties executed.

The executed contract was "for approximately three thousand [conversion] units, more or less depending upon requirements of Buyer, consisting of Fuel Tank, Fuel Lock Off Switch, Converter & appropriate Carburetor & Small Parts Kit" at a price of $750 per unit. American Bakeries agreed "to purchase propane motor fuel solely from Empire Gas Corporation at all locations where Empire Gas had supplied . . . dispensing equipment as long as Empire Gas Corporation remains in a reasonably competitive price posture with other major suppliers." The contract was to last for four years.

However, American Bakeries never ordered any equipment or propane from Empire Gas. Apparently within days after signing the contract, American Bakeries decided not to convert its fleet to propane. It gave no reason for that decision.

Empire Gas brought suit against American Bakeries for breach of contract and won a jury verdict for $3,254,963, representing lost profits on 2,242 conversion units (the jury's estimate of American Bakeries' requirements) and the propane fuel that the converted vehicles would have consumed during the contract period. American Bakeries appealed. Judge Posner said the issue was whether or not a requirements contract was "essentially a buyer's option, entitling him to purchase all he needs of the goods in question on the terms set forth in the contract, but leaving him free to purchase none if he wishes provided that he does not purchase the goods from anyone else and is not acting out of ill will toward the seller."

The court said that possibility—that a requirements contract was a form of a buyer's option—was one extreme. It also said that the other extreme was to interpret requirements contracts as committing the buyer to go through with whatever project generated an estimate of required quantity no matter what happened over the life of the project except those exceptional events that would excuse performance under the doctrines of impossibility, impracticability, or frustration. It rejected both interpretations.

The court decided that the essential ingredient of good faith in the case of a buyer's reduction of its estimated requirements was that it cannot arbitrarily declare its requirements to be zero. At a minimum, the court said a buyer cannot reduce its requirements motivated solely by a reassessment of the balance of advantages and disadvantages under the contract to the buyer. It simply needs a better reason than that—just how good, the court said, is something to be decided at another time.

▌Battle of the Forms

In addition to filling in gaps in contracts, the UCC also attempts to resolve what has been referred to as the "battle of the forms." This often occurs when a seller's confirmation order contains different terms than a buyer's purchase order or a buyer's form contains terms that differ from those included in the seller's offer. One rather typical case involved a lawsuit filed by the Valley Sheet Metal Company, a corporation engaged in the business of installing metal roofing systems, against the Reynolds Metals Company, a supplier of aluminum roofing materials and other aluminum products.

On November 20, 1986, Valley was awarded the roofing subcontract for the San Jose Convention Center in San Jose, California. Thereafter, Valley requested a bid from Reynolds on 3003 Aluminum to be used in roofing the convention center. Valley's estimating manager sent a copy of the specifications for the metal roofing material to Reynolds' field sales representative. Reynolds responded by providing Valley with the product description and data sheet for 5010 Aluminum, a potential substitute and less expensive roofing material. The information it sent Valley concerning 5010 Aluminum stated that there were no special handling requirements for the material.

On April 28, 1987, Valley issued its purchase agreement for 50 coils of 5010 Aluminum. Valley's form indicated in part as follows:

5. The Seller agrees:

5.1 To repair or replace at the construction site at the Seller's expense, all defects of material or workmanship in the material
. . . .

5.4 To indemnify Valley and the Prime against and hold harmless from any and all loss, damage, expense, attorneys' fees and liability incurred on account of any breach by the Seller of any of the Seller's obligations under this Agreement . . . .

5.6 That the material shall conform to the requirements of Valley's contract with Prime which are applicable to the material or, if Valley's Contract with Prime does not have such requirements, that the material shall be of the quality specified herein or of the best grades of their respective kinds if no quality is specified and shall be fit for the purposes intended . . . .

9. Additional Provisions:

No variance from terms herein will be accepted by Valley Sheet Metal Co. unless such variance is approved in writing."

On May 19, 1987, Reynolds sent an acknowledgement and sales order to Valley that provided in part as follows:

Our acceptance is expressly conditioned on your agreement to the terms and conditions on the front and reverse sides of this Sales Order. YOU WILL BE DEEMED TO HAVE AGREED TO SUCH TERMS AND CONDITIONS, AND, IN RELIANCE THEREON, THIS SALES ORDER WILL BE PLACED IN SCHEDULE UNLESS WRITTEN NOTICE OF ANY ERRORS OR OBJECTIONS TO THIS SALES ORDER IS RECEIVED BY US WITHIN 10 DAYS FROM THE DATE SHOWN BELOW.

2. WARRANTIES. As to its products at the time of shipment, Seller warrants good title, freedom from defects in material and workmanship and conformance to its standard specifications and those stated on the front of this Order. SELLER MAKES NO OTHER WARRANTIES, EXPRESS OR IMPLIED, WRITTEN OR ORAL, INCLUDING, BUT NOT LIMITED TO,

WARRANTIES OF MERCHANTABILITY OR FITNESS FOR ANY PARTICULAR PURPOSE.

3. LIMITATION OF LIABILITY. SELLER'S EXCLUSIVE LIABILITY FOR THE BREACH OF ANY OF ITS WARRANTIES SHALL BE TO REPLACE NONCONFORMING PRODUCTS AT THE ORIGINAL POINT OF DELIVERY, TO REPAIR NONCONFORMING PRODUCTS OR TO REFUND BUYER'S PURCHASE PRICE FOR THE NONCONFORMING PRODUCTS, WHICHEVER OPTION SELLER SELECTS. SELLER'S LIABILITY FOR ANY LOSS OR DAMAGE ARISING OUT OF OR RESULTING FROM OR IN ANY WAY CONNECTED WITH THIS ORDER SHALL NOT EXCEED BUYER'S PURCHASE PRICE FOR THE PARTICULAR PRODUCT OR SERVICE UPON WHICH SUCH LIABILITY IS BASED, REGARDLESS OF WHETHER SUCH LIABILITY ARISES IN CONTRACT . . . OR OTHERWISE. IN NO EVENT SHALL SELLER BE LIABLE TO BUYER FOR LOSS OF PROFITS OR REVENUE OR FOR ANY INCIDENTAL, CONSEQUENTIAL, SPECIAL OR PUNITIVE DAMAGES . . . .

4. PAYMENT TERMS . . . . Buyer agrees to pay . . . seller's reasonable costs of collection, including, but not limited to, reasonable attorneys' fees.

After Valley received Reynolds's confirmation, neither party attempted to communicate with the other regarding their forms despite the fact that their forms differed in a number of ways.

Reynolds delivered the 5010 Aluminum coils to Valley in September 1987 and Valley paid Reynolds for the full invoiced amount of $200,988.17. Valley inspected the materials for shipment damage and, finding none, stored the coils in their packing materials outside under a tarp. Valley's use of the coils was delayed, however, from October 1987 to July 1988 because of delays in the convention center construction project. When Valley began work on the job site in July 1988, it discovered that the 5010 Aluminum coils were badly water stained and would have to be replaced.

Valley informed Reynolds of the water damage by letter dated August 1, 1988. Reynolds denied responsibility on September 1. Valley obtained replacement materials and filed suit, claiming breach of express and implied warranties and negligence.

▍UCC Section 2-207

The battle of the forms is addressed by Section 2-207 of the UCC. That section provides rules of contract formation in cases in which the parties exchange forms but do not agree on all the terms of their contracts.

One on the principles underlying Section 2-207 is neutrality. If possible, courts interpret Section 2-207 to give neither party to a contract an advantage simply because it happened to send the first or, in some cases, the last form. Before the UCC was adopted, the "mirror image" rule required that offer and acceptance completely match; as a result, the party that "fired the last shot" often was given the advantage because the other party was deemed to accept its terms when it performed the contract. But the UCC did away with this result by giving neither party the terms it attempts to impose unilaterally on the other.

Section 2-207 provides that a definite and timely expression of acceptance or a written confirmation that is sent within a reasonable time operates as an acceptance even though it states terms additional to or different from those offered or agreed upon, unless acceptance is expressly made conditional on assent to the additional or different terms. The additional terms are to be construed as proposals for addition to the contract. Between merchants, the terms become part of the contract unless the offer expressly limits acceptance to the terms of the offer; they materially alter the contract; or notification of objection to them has already been given or is given within a reasonable time after notice of them is received.

Section 2-207 also provides that conduct by both parties that recognizes the existence of a contract is sufficient to establish a contract for sale although the writings of the parties do not otherwise establish a contract. In that case, the terms of the particular contract consist of those terms on which the writings of the parties agree, together with any supplementary terms incorporated under any other provision of the UCC.

The court in the Valley case found that the parties' conduct recognized the existence of a contract. Under Section 2-207, the contract terms include those terms upon which the parties' forms agreed, specifically, the express warranties of good title, freedom from defects in material and workmanship, conformity with standard specifications, and recovery of attorney's fees under specified circumstances. The parties' forms conflicted with regard to further express warranties, implied warranties, and limitation of liability provisions, so the court found that the provisions contained in the forms on those topics "drop out of the contract." It concluded that some of the gap fillers in the UCC may have provided additional warranties and remedies for breach of those warranties.

▌A Final Word

To paraphrase Calvin Coolidge, the business of the UCC is to see to the business of America. It tries very hard to allow contracts to be enforced; old rules—such as those that used to require that documents be "sealed" to be enforceable—are out the window.

By resolving disputes and filling in blanks, the UCC intends to enforce deals whenever and wherever possible. Accordingly, marketers, salespeople, and other business executives must recognize that, when dealing with customers, words, as well as actions, matter.

A COUPLE OF GAPS AND A FEW TRAPS

1. By the mid-1980s Advent Systems Limited, a company that produced computer software, had developed an electronic document management system that was able to transform engineering drawings and similar documents into a computer data base. In June 1987, Advent and the Unisys Corporation, a computer manufacturer, signed two agreements under which Advent agreed to provide the software and hardware making up the document systems to be sold by Unisys in the United States. Advent was obligated to provide sales and marketing material and manpower as well as technical personnel to work with Unisys employees in building and installing the document systems.

In December 1987 Unisys ended its relationship with Advent, having decided, in the throes of a restructuring, that it would be better served by developing its own document system. Advent filed suit, contending that Unisys had breached the contract, and a jury awarded it more than $4 million on that claim. Unisys then appealed, contending that the contract was one for the sale of goods and unenforceable under the UCC because it lacked an express provision on quantity. The appellate court first ruled that the UCC applied to computer software transactions; it next turned to the quantity issue. The court said that the parties obviously had been aware that they were entering a new speculative market and that some uncertainty was inevitable in the amount of sales Unisys could make and the orders it would place with Advent. Consequently, it recognized, the agreements did not state the quantity of goods involved in "absolute terms." In effect, the court said, the parties arrived at a "non-exclusive requirements contract." The court noted that other courts have upheld exclusive requirements contracts with indefinite quantity terms based upon their recognition that the UCC requires in all contracts good faith performance by the parties. Finding "no reason in logic or policy to differentiate" between an exclusive requirements contract and a nonexclusive requirements contract, it concluded that the same rules should apply. (Advent Systems Ltd. v. Unisys Corp., 925 F.2d 670 (3d Cir. 1991).)

2. Offen, Inc., and Rocky Mountain Constructors, Inc. had an oral agreement for the purchase and sale of petroleum products. Offen delivered the products to Rocky Mountain, together with delivery tickets. The tickets stated that an 18 percent interest rate and attorney's fees would be charged in the event collection actions became necessary. Invoices Offen mailed after delivery contained similar language in boldface type. However, Offen and Rocky Mountain had not discussed these terms. After Offen filed a collection action against Rocky Mountain, it obtained judgment and was awarded 18 percent interest and attorney's fees. Rocky Mountain appealed the award of interest and fees.

The appellate court noted that the invoices constituted written confirmation of the terms orally agreed to earlier by the parties. Because the parties had not discussed late charges or attorney's fees, the provisions on the invoices relating to these items were additional terms within the meaning of Section 2-207 of the UCC. The appellate court noted that, between merchants, additional terms in a written confirmation to which the other party does not object become part of the contract unless the terms "materially alter" the contract. It found that Rocky Mountain had not objected to the additional terms and then ruled that they did not materially alter the contract. (Offen, Inc. v. Rocky Mountain Constructors, Inc., 765 P.2d 600 (Ct. App. Colo. 1988).)

It should be noted that there is a conflict among the courts as to whether or not an additional term providing for the payment of attorney's fees materially alters a contract for purposes of UCC Section 2-207. For instance, the U.S. Court of Appeals for the Seventh Circuit, finding that such an unnegotiated clause in a written confirmation amounted to "an unreasonable surprise" to the other party, ruled that it materially altered a contract and was not enforceable. (Comark Merchandising, Inc. v. Highland Group, Inc., 932 F.2d 1196 (7th Cir. 1991).)

3. On December 24, 1984, Ben Diskin, the sole owner of the Massachusetts State Manufacturing Company, a business that purchased fabrics from wholesale suppliers, manufactured garments, and sold them to retail chain stores, met with representatives of J. P. Stevens & Co., Inc. to determine whether any Stevens fabrics were appropriate for his manufacturing needs. He found a "full-bodied, lofty all-wool flannel" that suited him and, according to Stevens, ordered 290 pieces of it. Diskin also requested that Stevens send him a 10-yard sample for further evaluation. Later that day, while he was still at the Stevens office, he wrote out a check payable to Stevens for the amount of $151,380 that he signed and dated December 31, 1984. On the reverse side, Diskin wrote the following: "In full payment for 290 pcs. flannel as per contract, less anti. to be figured upon billing. Final total subject to adjustment." After receiving the check, Stevens sent Diskin its standard form sales contract, designated as a "confirmation." The form provided that it was given "subject to all of the terms and conditions on the face and reverse sides . . . including the provisions for arbitration."

After a dispute between the parties, Diskin filed suit against Stevens seeking $151,380 plus interest and costs; Stevens asked that the suit be enjoined so that the dispute could be arbitrated. The court found that Diskin's notation on the back of his check constituted a written offer to purchase Stevens' textiles and that Stevens's confirmation accepted that offer. It said because both parties were merchants, the arbitration clause in Stevens's confirmation was an additional term that became part of the contract unless it materially altered it. The court recognized that courts are divided as to whether arbitration clauses materially alter contracts. It ruled, however, that because both parties were familiar with the fact that it was a custom of the textile industry to resolve disputes by arbitration, the arbitration clause was not a material alteration of the contract and became a part of it. (Diskin v. J. P. Stevens & Co., Inc., 652 F.Supp. 553 (D. Mass. 1987).)

4. In 1982 Polyclad Laminates, Inc., a manufacturer of printed electronic circuit boards, began negotiations with VITS Maschinenbau GmbH to purchase a "custom-built thermal incinerator and vertical impregnating machine" manufactured by VITS. During the course of negotiations, VITS sent Polyclad one quotation on July 14, 1982, two additional quotations on January 26, 1983, and an order of confirmation on February 11, 1983. Each of these documents contained the following sentence, printed as a single paragraph, just above the signature line: "This quotation is subject to our conditions of sale and delivery no. LW 188 which please find enclosed." LW 188, a multi-page document prepared under the auspices of the United Nations Economic Commission for Europe, was entitled "General Conditions for the Supply of Plant and Machinery for Export." One provision stated "Any dispute arising out of the Contract shall be finally settled in accordance with the Rules of Conciliation and Arbitration of the International Chamber of Commerce by one or more arbitrators designated in conformity with those Rules."

On March 16, 1983, Polyclad sent VITS two purchase orders. Although those orders made no mention of arbitration, they both contained the following language: "The only terms and conditions that apply to this offer to purchase . . . are those set forth below, those preprinted on or added to the face of this purchase order and those which are contained in attachments or exhibits attached hereto or referenced herein: seller is hereby notified in advance that buyer takes exception to any and all changes, additions or deletions which seller may make to the terms contained herein." Significantly, one of Polyclad's March 16, 1983, purchase orders referenced the VITS order confirmation that contained the reference to form LW 188. Polyclad's purchase order did not object to any of the terms of form LW 188. On March 25, 1983, VITS sent a final order confirmation that again contained the sentence making reference of "no. LW 188."

In March 1987, a thermal incinerator designed, manufactured, sold, and installed by VITS at Polyclad's plant in Franklin, New Hampshire, overheated, causing a fire. Polyclad filed suit against VITS to recover damages related to the fire and VITS sought to enjoin the action pending arbitration. The magistrate to whom the issue was referred said that the case presented a classic "battle of the forms," but the district court disagreed. It said that reference to UCC Section 2-207 was not required because LW 188 was not introduced by VITS in an "expression of acceptance" to which Section 2-207 applied. Rather, the court said, "VITS made reference to LW 188 in the very first memorialization of the parties' discussions" and consistently referred to LW 188 in subsequent quotations and confirmations. Contrary to the magistrate's determination, the court found that LW 188 was a term contained in the offer, not a material alteration to the original agreement. Finding that Polyclad had accepted VITS offer, the court ordered the lawsuit stayed pending arbitration of the dispute. (Polyclad Laminates, Inc. v. VITS Maschinenbau GmbH, 749 F. Supp. 343 (D.N.H. 1990).

5. In 1977 Hartwig Farms, Inc., Donald and Maryanne Rizzuti, and Dale Anderson purchased blue tag certified Norgold seed potatoes from the Pacific Gamble Robinson Co. Blue tag certified seed potatoes are those that have passed field inspections and are certified by the North Dakota State Seed Department to be within specified disease tolerances, including a one percent tolerance for blackleg. However, when the potatoes Hartwig, the Rizzutis and Anderson planted came up, there was a 75 percent to 80 percent infestation for blackleg, resulting in crop loss.

They sued Pacific, alleging negligence and breach of express and implied warranties. Pacific, in turn, cross claimed against Tobiason Potato Co., from which Pacific had purchased the seed. The jury found, among other things, that Tobiason had breached the implied warranty of merchantability; it gave judgment to Pacific against Tobiason on its cross claim and Tobiason appealed.

On appeal, the court noted that Tobiason typically conducted most of its business by telephone. Seed brokers, such as Pacific, would call and order seed and would reach an oral agreement with Tobiason at that time. Tobiason would send a written confirmation of sale, which the broker would sign and return. The confirmation of sale did not contain any disclaimer of warranties. Tobiason would ship the seed at the time it was needed by the broker. The invoice that accompanied each shipment would contain a disclaimer. The disclaimer typically would state: "Tobiason Potato Co. gives no warranty, express or implied, as to description, variety, quality, or productiveness, and will not in any way be responsible for the crop." Tobiason argued on appeal that this disclaimer was effective to exclude the implied warranty of merchantability contained in the UCC.

The court disagreed, however. It noted that the UCC permits a seller to give warranties and also to limit or exclude them. Disclaimers, it noted, are not favored in the law; as a result, courts have added two conditions for effectiveness: a disclaimer must be explicitly negotiated or bargained for and it must set forth with particularity the qualities and characteristics being disclaimed. More important for purposes of this case, though, the court ruled that a disclaimer "that is made after a sale is completed cannot be effective because it was not a part of the bargain between the parties." Because the terms of the contract between Tobiason and Pacific had been finalized before Tobiason sent the invoice to Pacific, the court said that the disclaimer had not become part of the contract and was ineffective to exclude any warranty. (Hartwig Farms, Inc. v. Pacific Gamble Robinson Co., 625 P.2d 171 (Ct. App. Washington 1981).)

Gaps and Traps Checklist

✓ Under the UCC, a contract may be enforceable even though terms are left open, so long as the parties intended to make a contract.

✓ Furthermore, contracts may be valid even though the exact time the parties reached their agreement is uncertain.

✓ A number of sections of the UCC fill in contract gaps; the gaps can relate to issues as significant as price, quantity, time of shipment, time of payment, and warranties.

✓ The UCC also helps to resolve the "battle of the forms," which occurs when a purchaser's order form contains terms different from the seller's confirmation form.

✓ The UCC's contract provisions reward "good faith" and reasonableness. Of course, what the UCC regards as good faith may not be what every business in every situation would deem to be good faith. Where possible, therefore, sales forms should be drafted with the appropriate provisions of the UCC in mind and forms received in response should be reviewed for potentially objectionable terms.

FOB, FAS, AND OTHER SUCH TERMS

■ Important Acronyms ■ FOB ■ FAS ■ CIF and C & F
■ "Unless Otherwise Agreed" ■ A Final Word

After T.O.S. Industries, Inc. agreed to purchase 40 drilling rigs from the Ideco Division of Dresser Industries, Inc., Ideco began to manufacture them. Several months later, though, T.O.S. told Ideco that it did not need the rigs. Ideco told T.O.S., however, that it was too far along in the manufacture of six of the rigs to cancel the order and that T.O.S. would have to purchase these six.

Ideco sent invoices for the rigs to T.O.S. that stated that the goods were to be "held for shipping instructions" and that contained an FOB ("free on board") point of shipment term. T.O.S. did not pay Ideco and Ideco retained possession of the rigs.

In an attempt to obtain clear title to resell the rigs, Ideco stopped sending invoices for the six rigs to T.O.S. and executed a mutual release with T.O.S. whereby each party released the other from all contractual obligations arising from the sale. Approximately one month later, T.O.S. filed for reorganization under Chapter 11 of the federal bankruptcy code.

In T.O.S.'s bankruptcy, the Crocker National Bank, which held a security interest in T.O.S.'s assets, filed a complaint against Ideco asserting that it was entitled to the rigs. It contended that the rigs constituted T.O.S.'s inventory and were subject to its lien. T.O.S. also asserted a claim to the rigs.

Ideco contended that it had an interest in the rigs superior to any interest possessed by the bank or T.O.S. It noted that the Uniform Commercial Code (UCC) provides that a seller that retains title to goods retains a security interest in those goods; a security interest in goods obtained through continued possession by a seller for the purpose of securing the purchase price of the goods is a purchase money security interest; and a purchase money security interest is entitled to priority over other security interests so long as the seller continues possession of the goods. Thus, Ideco argued that so long as it retained possession of the rigs to secure payment by T.O.S., its security interest had priority.

The bank and T.O.S. argued, however, that while Ideco had retained physical possession of the rigs, T.O.S. had acquired "constructive possession" of them, which served to oust Ideco's security interest.

They noted that the UCC provides that, unless otherwise explicitly agreed, title to goods generally passes to the buyer when the seller completes his performance with reference to physical delivery of the goods. Delivery even may take place without moving the goods. The bank and T.O.S. argued that that occurred in this case—the notation on the rig invoices to "hold for shipping instructions" was proof that the intention of Ideco and T.O.S. was that title should pass to T.O.S. at the time the rigs were identified to the contract even without physical delivery of them.

The court rejected this contention, however. It said that it was clear that by incorporating an "FOB" term into the contract, the parties never agreed to transfer title other than by delivery. The UCC "makes clear that the FOB term is a delivery term . . . and that FOB point of manufacture indicates that the seller must place the rigs in the hands of a common carrier at the point of manufacture." Thus, the court ruled, the terms of the invoice obliged Ideco to deliver the rigs to a carrier. "Title, therefore, passes only when that delivery obligation is met."

The court concluded that Ideco's notation, "hold for shipping instructions," did not conflict with the FOB term because whenever a sales agreement contains an FOB term, except when the term is FOB destination, the buyer must provide the seller with any needed shipping instructions. The "hold for shipping instructions" notation, the court found, simply recognized the buyer's obligation of cooperation with the seller and did not effect transfer of title of the goods to the buyer.

▌Important Acronyms

FOB, FAS, CIF, C & F and other similar acronyms defined in the UCC can be very important provisions in sales contracts. As is clear from the Ideco case, they may help resolve questions of title. They also may determine which party bears the risk of loss of the goods. And they may make the difference between a profitable and unprofitable contract—a high shipping expense may eat up a small profit margin.

What follows is a short explanation of the principal shipping acronyms contained in the UCC.

▌FOB

FOB means "free on board." Unless otherwise agreed, the term FOB at a named place—even though used only in connection with a stated price—is a delivery term under which:

- When the term is FOB place of shipment, the seller must at that place ship the goods and bear the expense and risk of putting them into the possession of a carrier.

- When the term is FOB place of destination, the seller must at its own expense and risk transport the goods to that place and there deliver them to the buyer.

- When the term is either FOB place of shipment or FOB place of destination and a vessel, car, or other vehicle is named, the seller must also at its own expense and risk load the goods on board. If the term is FOB vessel the buyer must name the vessel.

▌FAS

The term FAS means "free alongside." (It is the reverse of "ex-ship," which means from the carrying vessel and requires delivery from a ship that has reached a place at the named port of destination where goods of the kind are usually discharged. In a contract with an ex-ship term, the risk of loss does not pass to the buyer until the goods leave the ship's tackle or are otherwise properly unloaded.) The UCC provides that unless otherwise agreed, the term FAS vessel at a named port, even though used only in connection with a stated price, is a delivery term under which the seller must:

- At its own expense and risk deliver the goods alongside the vessel in the manner usual in that port on a dock designated and provided by the buyer

- Obtain and tender to the buyer a receipt for the goods in exchange for which the carrier is under a duty to issue a bill of lading (a statement listing goods shipped)

Furthermore, the UCC imposes a duty on the buyer in connection with most contracts with an FOB or FAS term. Specifically, it requires that the buyer within a reasonable time give the seller any needed instructions for making delivery, including the loading berth of the vessel and, in an appropriate case, its name and sailing date. A seller may treat the failure of needed instructions as a failure of the buyer to cooperate, which would excuse the seller from any resulting delay in its own performance or would allow the seller to move the goods in any reasonable manner in advance of delivery or shipment.

▌CIF and C & F

According to the UCC, the term CIF, meaning "cost, insurance, freight," means that the price includes in a lump sum the cost of the goods and the insurance and freight to the named destination. The term C & F (or CF), meaning "cost and freight," means that the price includes cost and freight to the named destination but not insurance.

The CIF contract is a shipment contract with risk of subsequent loss or damage to the goods passing to the buyer upon shipment if the seller has properly performed all of its obligations with respect to the goods. Unless the parties otherwise agree, those obligations require the seller at its own expense and risk to:

- Put the goods into the possession of a carrier at the port for shipment and obtain a negotiable bill or bills of lading covering the entire transportation to the named destination

- Load the goods and obtain a receipt from the carrier (which may be contained in the bill of lading) showing that the freight has been paid or provided for

- Obtain a policy or certificate of insurance, including any war risk insurance, of a kind and on terms then current at the port of shipment in the usual amount, in the currency of the contract, to cover the same goods covered by the bill of lading and providing for payment of loss to the order of the buyer or for the account of whom it may concern (but the seller may add to the price the amount of the premium for any such war risk insurance)

- Prepare an invoice of the goods and procure any other documents required to effect shipment or to comply with the contract

- Forward and tender with commercial promptness all the documents in due form and with any endorsement necessary to perfect the buyer's rights

Buyers and sellers should note that the insurance called for in CIF contracts is intended to cover the value of the goods at the time and place of shipment and does not include any increase in market value during transit or any anticipated profit to the buyer on a sale by it.

Unless the parties otherwise agree, the term C & F has the same effect and imposes the same obligations and risks upon the seller as the term CIF except the obligation of insurance.

▌"Unless Otherwise Agreed"

Throughout the UCC, the parties to contracts or agreements have the right to make the terms of their agreements different from the UCC's provisions. As noted above, the UCC permits this in connection with FOB, FAS, CIF, and C & F terms. The significance of "unless otherwise agreed" can be seen from a case filed by Trans-Colorado Concrete, Inc. against the Midwest Construction Company.

On August 20, 1984, Trans-Colorado, a concrete manufacturing company, entered into an agreement with Midwest to supply materials and perform labor for Midwest in connection with bridge repair and replacement at Fort Carson, Colorado. The only contract documents were three pages detailing the awarded bid and the bidding schedule for Trans-Colorado's services and materials. On the building schedule, only one location—Ellis Street—was specifically mentioned as a delivery site. However, both parties also relied on a single invoice to determine the places of performance of the contract. The invoice simply stated "FOB job site."

In January 1985, Trans-Colorado began supplying concrete to Midwest at the location identified by the parties as the Ellis Chiles Road site. Around May, Midwest orally contacted Trans-Colorado and requested additional concrete to be delivered to other bridge projects south of the original site and a substantial distance away. Although the parties agreed that the price of the concrete would remain the same, they apparently never discussed the extra distance.

From then to the end of October 1985, Trans-Colorado billed Midwest for charges based on transportation distances further than the original delivery site at Ellis-Chiles Road. For close to eight months, Midwest paid all these bills promptly to take advantage of an early payment discount. In what was to be its last payment to Trans-Colorado, on a check dated January 3, 1986, Midwest deducted all distance charges it had paid since May and sent Trans-Colorado the reduced balance. Trans-Colorado filed suit to recover that deducted amount. It argued that the place of performance under the contract was modified by subsequent conduct or agreement of the parties and that payment of distance charges became part of the contract between the parties as a result of their conduct.

As the court noted, the contract mandated that Trans-Colorado deliver the concrete "FOB job site." The court said while it was apparent from the bidding schedule that the first delivery site must have been the Ellis-Chiles Road site, and that under the UCC Trans-Colorado was responsible for transportation costs to that location, the subsequent "agreement between the companies to deliver elsewhere formed an otherwise agreement." In the court's view, the course of performance between the parties, under which Midwest paid for the additional transportation costs for a substantial time after the modification, comprised extrinsic evidence that demonstrated that new delivery terms had been agreed to and relied upon.

The court, finding that no express terms of the agreement negated the ability of the parties to modify the contract, concluded that Trans-Colorado was "correct in stating that the contract was subsequently interpreted by both parties so as to allow for extra transportation costs."

▌A Final Word

All businesspeople who negotiate contracts for the sale of goods should understand the meaning of these UCC terms. They affect the obligations of buyers and sellers and have the potential to alter the bottom line profitability of almost any transaction. Although they provide a welcome shorthand when used properly, used improperly they can be dangerous.

FIVE ABBREVIATED DISCUSSIONS

1. After Phillips Puerto Rico Core, Inc. agreed by telephone to buy 25,000 to 30,000 metric tons of naphtha from Tradax Petroleum, Ltd. that was located in Skikda, Algeria, a confirming telex specified that the sale was to be C & F Guayama, Puerto Rico, and that shipment was to be made between September 20–28, 1981. The agreement incorporated the International Chamber of Commerce 1980 Incoterms, a set of standardized terms for international commercial transactions that defined a C & F contract as one in which the seller arranged and paid for the transport of the goods but the buyer assumed title and risk of loss when the goods passed the ship's rail in the port of shipment. Tradax nominated the Oxy Trader, an integrated tub barge, as the vessel for the journey and, after determining that the Trader would fit in the Puerto Rico berth and was available at the correct times, Phillips accepted the nomination. The Trader arrived at Skikda for loading on the afternoon of September 20, 1981, and the naphtha was completely loaded by the early morning of September 24; at 10:30 that morning the ship embarked for Puerto Rico.

The Trader's voyage to Puerto Rico was cut short the following day when it was detained by the Coast Guard at Gibraltar for an inspection. Tradax relayed word of the delay to Phillips, which telexed back on October 1 that October 15 was the last acceptable delivery date. Tradax objected to Phillips's attempt to specify a delivery date; its position was that it sold the naphtha under a shipment contract, not a destination contract, and that, as seller, it had ceased to be responsible for the goods when it transferred the goods to the carrier for shipment. On October 7, Tradax received word that the Trader might have a latent defect, that the authorities were not letting the Trader proceed, and that the naphtha cargo would have to be transshipped. Tradax relayed this message to Phillips, which replied that it was reserving the right to cancel the contract if delivery did not occur within 30 days. Tradax reiterated its claim that its responsibility ended at the time of shipment and notified Phillips that it would present the shipping documents for payment of the contract price the following day. Phillips instructed its Puerto Rico office not to make payment if Tradax tendered the documents.

Shortly afterward, Tradax informed Phillips that the Trader would be at Lisbon for the transshipment and that Phillips should make arrangements accordingly. Phillips thereafter terminated the contract due to the "unseaworthiness" of the Trader and an "unreasonable delay" in performance. Tradax sold the naphtha to a third party and filed a claim against Phillips to recover its losses of approximately $1 million. The court said that as a C & F seller, Tradax had two duties: to deliver the naphtha to an appropriate carrier with which it had contracted for shipment and to tender proper documents to Phillips. Phillips in return was contractually obliged to pay for the naphtha when presented with the shipping documents by Tradax.

The court noted that it was undisputed that after Tradax loaded the naphtha on the Oxy Trader and presented Phillips with the shipping documents, Phillips had refused to pay for the cargo. Phillips contended that Tradax had not adequately performed its contractual duties, but the court rejected Phillips's position. The court noted that the relevant provision in the 1980 Incoterms requires that a C & F seller contract for the carriage of goods "in a seagoing vessel . . . of the type normally used for the transport of goods of the contract description." Although the Oxy Trader, an integrated tug barge, was of novel design in that the tug and the barge were married together, the court said that this feature did not disqualify the Trader as a ship that might "normally" be used for transport. The court added that there was no basis for concluding that Tradax should have known before the ship left port that the Trader was likely to have a problem because the defect in the Trader was a latent one. Accordingly, the court ruled that Tradax was entitled to judgment against Phillips for more than $1 million. (Phillips Puerto Rico Core, Inc. v. Tradax Petroleum, 782 F.2d 314 (2d Cir. 1985).)

2. When the tomatoes that William D. Branson, Ltd. had contracted to ship CIF Bridgetown, Barbados, arrived in Bridgetown, the buyer inspected them, found them to be spoiled, and shipped them back to Branson. Branson then filed suit against the Tropical Shipping & Construction Co., which had transported the tomatoes. Tropical argued, though, that the buyer in Bridgetown—not Branson—was the proper party to bring suit because, under a CIF contract, title and risk of loss pass to the buyer upon shipment if the seller has properly performed all of its obligations with respect to the goods. The court agreed that the buyer would have been the proper party to file suit against Tropical except that the contract indicated that payment was not to occur against tender of the required documents but rather was to await arrival of the tomatoes themselves. Because the buyer never accepted the shipment of the tomatoes from Branson, the court found that the buyer did not have an action against Tropical for the price of the tomatoes. Instead, it ruled that Branson (or the insurance company to the extent that it had paid Branson for its losses) was the proper party to file suit. (William D. Branson, Ltd. v. Tropical Shipping & Construction Co., Ltd., 598 F. Supp. 680 (S.D.Fl. 1984).)

3. Several years ago, Donald E. Barliant, the owner of two bookstores in Chicago, filed suit against the Follett Corporation alleging that Follett had overcharged for its shipments of books. Specifically, Barliant claimed that the terms of sale, published in Follett's catalogs and order forms and consistent with the custom and usage in the industry, were

FOB seller's warehouse in Chicago and that Follett had breached those terms by charging "BKPST TRANS-INS" without notifying its customers. The BKPST charge reflected the fourth class book rate charged by the postal service; the TRANS charge was an estimate of the cost of the shipping carton and the paper filler, plus the cost of shipping; and the INS charge was the insurance charge, a flat 20 percent charge that was added to each shipment.

The court ruled, though, that Barliant failed to prove that Follett's transportation and insurance charges were contrary to industry custom. Furthermore, it said that even if trade usage was contrary to Follett's practice, the course of dealings between Barliant and Follett—Barliant had paid 24 invoices without objection that included a BKPST TRANS-INS charge—"superceded any industry custom." It then ruled that Follett had not breached its contract or committed fraud. (Barliant v. Follett Corp., 483 N.E.2d 1312 (App. Ct. Ill. 1985).)

4. The contract between the Fertilizer Corporation of America and P.S. International, Inc. provided that P.S. would sell 10,000 metric tons of di-ammonium phosphate at $180 (U.S. currency) per metric ton to Fertilizer on terms FOB Gabes, Tunisia. The parties did not specify a date for delivery and did not explicitly contract that time was of the essence. Rather, the agreement provided for shipment within 45 days after P.S. received a letter of credit from Fertilizer. Although P.S. received the letter of credit November 30, 1987, it was later amended to extend its validity until February 23, 1988, and to permit shipment by February 2, 1988.

On three separate occasions, Fertilizer presented vessels (as it was required to do as the buyer) with lay days in January, but P.S. was unable to confirm before the ships were lost to other business. Finally, the vessel *M/V Securitas* was booked with lay days of January 19-25, 1988. However, on January 25, P.S. was informed that the *Securitas* was delayed because of rain and was not expected to arrive in Gabes until January 27. Then, on January 28, P.S. told Fertilizer that it would not supply the goods under the agreement but it offered to supply them at $215 (U.S.

currency) per metric ton. Fertilizer filed a breach of contract action against P.S.

Because the contract had failed to specify an exact time for delivery and because the parties apparently did not consider time to be of the essence, the court turned to the UCC's gap-filling provisions to determine the date of delivery. Under those rules, Fertilizer was required to present its vessel for shipment "within a reasonable time." It said that neither P.S. not Fertilizer could unilaterally set the date for delivery. It then found that presenting a ship within three days of January 25 was reasonable considering the factual circumstances of the case and the difficulties inherent in ocean transport. Thus, the court concluded, when P.S. stated on January 28 that it would not supply the goods to Fertilizer, it breached the contract. (Fertilizer Corp. of America v. P.S. International, Inc., 729 F. Supp. 837 (S.D. Fla. 1989).)

5. On November 6, 1986, Bomar Resources, Inc. agreed to purchase 11,700 long tons (plus or minus 10 percent) of steel scrap from Camden Iron & Metal, Inc.; the shipping term was FOBS.T. Vessel Camden, New Jersey. FOBS.T. is a common maritime variation of the standard FOB contract in which the seller also agrees to "stow and trim" the cargo, that is, prepare the cargo and the vessel's holds to ensure efficient, safe loading. At some point in that month, Bomar apparently advised Camden Iron of its nomination of the ship *M/V Kalli* to transport the steel scrap. It turned out, however, that Camden was unable to load the steel scrap on that ship because of the ship's size and strength limitations. Camden then filed suit against Bomar for breach of contract. The court found that a seller's obligation to load goods on board a ship under a contract with an FOBS.T. shipping term was "not an absolute one"—a buyer must tender a reasonable vessel. The unreasonableness of the *Kalli*, both as to its structure and physical condition, led to the court's conclusion that Bomar had breached the contract. (Camden Iron & Metal, Inc. v. Bomar Resources, Inc., 719 F. Supp. 297 (D.N.J. 1989).)

Acronym Checklist

✓ Businesspeople who negotiate contracts for the sale of goods must understand the meaning of, and responsibilities imposed by, acronyms defined in the Uniform Commercial Code (UCC) and the other bodies of law that regulate commercial transactions.

✓ FOB, FAS, CIF, C & F, and various forms of these terms impose certain obligations on sellers.

✓ Similarly, though, these terms may impose duties on buyers—in certain cases, for instance, buyers may have to designate a ship for the seller to be able to comply with its duties.

✓ These acronyms may determine whether the seller or buyer in a particular transaction bears the risk of loss of goods; as a result, they may make the difference between a profitable and an unprofitable contract.

✓ Significantly, the UCC does permit parties to "otherwise agree" about the meaning of these terms; one should never do that, though, without understanding how the UCC defines them in the first place.

WHEN A SELLER'S GOODS DON'T MEET SPECS

■ The Right to Reject ■ Seller's Instructions ■ Seller's Right to Cure
■ Measuring Damages ■ A Final Word

When a shortage developed several years ago of a particular kind of microprocessor, known as model no. 8748, the E. F. Johnson Company, a Minnesota-based manufacturer of two-way taxi radios, could not obtain it from its usual sources. It then contracted to purchase the microprocessors from Integrated Circuits Unlimited, Inc., an electronic components distributor. In March 1984 Johnson placed three purchase orders with Integrated: WO4746 for 2,500 UPD8748 microprocessors at $85 each; WO4747 for 2,500 D8748H microprocessors at $87.50 each; and WO4750 for 1,100 D8749 microprocessors at $120 each.

Between March 21, 1984, and April 13, 1984, Integrated delivered to Johnson 1,709 UPD8748 microprocessors pursuant to purchase order number WO4746, about 70 percent of the total order. The deliveries were made in four shipments. Johnson received shipments containing 130 and 150 on March 21 and 22 respectively, for which it gave Integrated payment in full of $23,800.00 on March 30. It subsequently received 829 on April 11 and 600 on April 13. Between March 23 and April 7, Johnson received all 1100 ordered under purchase order WO4750, for which it paid in full.

On April 24 Johnson sent Integrated a letter rejecting the 130 parts from the March 21 WO4746 shipment based on tests indicating that the devices were of substandard quality. The letter said that Johnson's accept-

able quality level—the number of devices that could be defective without rendering the entire shipment unacceptable—was one percent. It attached a memorandum summarizing results of laboratory tests in which six of the devices, or 4.6 percent, had failed. The next day Johnson sent Integrated a similar letter regarding the WO4750 units. It stated that out of 115 devices tested 113 had failed, and offered their return for credit. The attached memorandum summarizing the test results indicated that devices tested at a standard temperature failed at a 2.6 percent rate. All tests were conducted by an independent laboratory.

On May 8 Johnson sent Integrated an itemized list of almost 2,000 parts that it wished to return based on the laboratory tests. Not all of these parts had been individually tested. Rather, the rejections were premised on the laboratory test results previously summarized in the memoranda it had sent to Integrated. These results were based on tests of a sampling of each kind of device. Under separate cover, Johnson also sent to Integrated 18 samples of the rejected devices so Integrated could conduct its own tests, and it issued debit memoranda for the value of these parts.

From May until August, Johnson wrote and called Integrated repeatedly requesting authorization to return the rejected parts; Integrated declined to accept the returns and continued to press for payment of its invoices. Johnson informed Integrated on August 15 that it was returning the rejected parts "no matter what." It shipped them back to Integrated, debited Integrated's account $170,450.00 (the value of the rejected parts less the 18 samples previously sent back and debited), and withheld payment on two Integrated invoices for $51,000 and $109,725, a total of $160,725.00. The parts were returned to Johnson, which then held them for Integrated's account. Integrated thereafter filed suit against Johnson for the $160,725 it claimed it was owed.

▌The Right to Reject

The Uniform Commercial Code (UCC) contains numerous provisions setting forth the rights and duties of sellers and buyers of goods. For example, sellers have the duty to timely deliver goods that meet the specifications of the contract—and the right under certain circumstances to attempt to cure a nonconforming tender of goods. The failure of a seller to perform its obligations authorizes a buyer to take a number of different steps. Under certain conditions, these include the right to reject the goods; the right to revoke an acceptance of goods; and the ability to purchase "cover" to substitute for the goods the buyer was to receive from the seller. Correspondingly, buyers in certain cases must fulfill certain duties imposed on them by the UCC with respect to rejected goods.

The court that issued a decision in the Johnson case recognized that a buyer is entitled under the UCC to reject goods that fail to conform to the contract. It noted that the failure rate of the parts Johnson tested at standard temperatures was greater than the acceptable industry rate of less than one percent. The court found that Johnson had tested an adequate sample of the microprocessors before deciding to reject them and that, though the sampling was not scientifically randomized, it selected parts to test without bias. Therefore, the court said, it was reasonable for Johnson to conclude that the remaining untested devices were similarly defective without sending all of them to a laboratory for expensive testing.

Under the UCC a seller is entitled to sue for the price of goods sold if the buyer accepted the goods or failed to effectively reject the goods. The court found that not only did Johnson have the right to reject the parts it sought to return to Integrated, it rejected them in an effective manner because it rejected them within a reasonable time after delivery and provided timely notification to Integrated of its concerns.

A buyer must have time to test complex electronic parts, the court recognized. In this case, it ruled that the testing by the independent laboratory retained by Johnson "was prompt and thorough." Then, immediately after learning that the test results had revealed excessive flaws in the microprocessors, Johnson notified Integrated of the results and of its intention to reject the parts. "Less than two weeks later, it sent [Integrated] an itemized list of parts being rejected. Its letter of May 8 satisfied the requirements of [the UCC] that the buyer set forth the nature of the defect with sufficient particularity to allow the seller to cure it."

The court also said that the fact that Johnson took temporary physical possession of the microprocessors and even used some of them before rejecting them "did not mean that it accepted them" because the UCC provides that acceptance of goods does not occur until a buyer has had a reasonable opportunity to inspect them.

Furthermore, it found that Johnson had not waived any rights by paying for the microprocessors after it had rejected them. "The payments represented an effort on the part of Johnson to resolve the dispute amicably."

Finally, the court noted that Johnson's actions with respect to the microprocessors following its rejection were proper. The UCC requires that a buyer "hold rejected goods with reasonable care at the seller's disposition for a time sufficient to permit the seller to remove them." The court said that Johnson fulfilled that duty by holding the microprocessors in storage, during which time they remained in good condition without physical deterioration while it unsuccessfully sought authorization from Integrated to return them. Nor was Johnson required to resell the rejected parts; having received no instructions from Integrated with respect to disposition of the parts after it gave notice of rejection, it was not required to take any further action. Integrated, the court concluded, would have been able to sell them far more readily than Johnson, which had no ready access to the seller's market for these components.

▌Seller's Instructions

The obligations of a buyer with respect to rejected goods were analyzed in somewhat more detail in a decision by the U.S. Court of Appeals for the Fourth Circuit. Believing that a substantial percentage of the handles that it purchased from Pic-Air, Inc. were defective, T & S Brass & Bronze Works, Inc. offered to return the ones it could not use and to charge Pic-Air for the costs of sorting or to allow it to sort them itself. Pic-Air at first notified T & S that the "slight imperfections" in the handles did not justify rejection and that it did not authorize T & S to sort the handles. It later acknowledged that improper packaging had caused scratches on some of the handles and asked T & S to return those it deemed defective; it said that it then would determine whether or not any needed to be replaced. However, it expressly refused to pay the costs of sorting the handles and T & S did not return any of them. In the lawsuit between Pic-Air and T & S that followed, Pic-Air sought payment of the contract price.

Although the court found that more than 10,000 handles were defective, Pic-Air argued that T & S's failure to return them constituted an acceptance of the goods or waiver of its claim that they were defective. It also argued that T & S's failure to return the handles prevented Pic-Air from curing the defects and that its failure should block T & S from objecting to the defects.

The court noted that upon rejecting goods a buyer must "hold them with reasonable care at the seller's disposition for a time sufficient to permit the seller to remove them." T & S's invitation to Pic-Air to inspect and sort the goods at T & S's facility "fulfilled T & S's immediate obligation to the seller," the court said. Consequently, it found that T & S's failure to return the goods upon rejecting them was not acceptance or waiver.

Moreover, noting that the UCC provides that a buyer has a security interest in rightfully rejected goods to the extent of any expense of inspection, the court said that T & S was entitled to retain the defective handles after sorting them from the acceptable handles because T & S held a security interest in the handles for the costs of inspecting and sorting them.

T & S's duty to "follow any reasonable instructions received from the seller with respect to the goods" was subject to its security interest for inspection costs; indeed, Pic-Air's instructions were not "reasonable" without its agreement to indemnify T & S for its expenses. Consequently, the court ruled that T & S rightfully rejected the defective handles and did not lose the right to object to their defects by refusing to return them.

▌ Seller's Right to Cure

The UCC provides that a seller may cure a nonconformity in two cases. If the time for the seller's performance has not yet expired, the seller may notify the buyer of its intent to cure and may then cure within the time of performance specified in the contract. If the time for performance has passed, the seller's right to cure is limited. The seller must reasonably believe at the time it tendered the goods that they would be acceptable; after learning of the nonconformity, the seller must within a reasonable time notify the buyer of its intent to substitute conforming goods. Upon satisfying these two requirements, the seller may then have a reasonable further time to substitute conforming goods.

In the Pic-Air case, the court ruled that the fact that T & S held the handles did not affect Pic-Air's ability to cure the defects because Pic-Air never unequivocally told T & S that it intended to cure. "Pic-Air cannot now insist on its right to cure, having never acknowledged the defects or promised to cure them."

▌ Measuring Damages

When a seller supplies, on time, goods under a contract that conform to the contract's terms and the buyer accepts the goods and pays for them, both sides are happy. When a seller breaches a contract, though, and the buyer suffers damages as a result, the UCC requires the seller to compensate the buyer. A Colorado appellate court recently explained one way to calculate a buyer's damages.

In that case, Smith-Wolf Construction, Inc. sought to bid on a subcontract with a general contractor to perform waterproofing services in conjunction with the construction of a tunnel. Before preparing its bid, Smith-Wolf had several conversations with Al Hood concerning Hood's waterproofing product Deckseal. During those talks, Hood represented and warranted that his product could be used to perform the work Smith-Wolf needed to perform with only two kettles to heat the product and that a crew of five, working with squeegees to apply the product, could waterproof about 13,500 square feet per day.

Relying on Hood's representations, Smith-Wolf prepared and presented a bid to the general contractor for a total of $153,995, which included an allowance for direct costs, an allowance for pro rata overhead costs (based upon a formula provided by Smith-Wolf's accountant), and a profit. Smith-Wolf's bid was accepted and Smith-Wolf and the contractor executed a contract using Smith-Wolf's bid figure as the contract price.

Smith-Wolf then paid Hood for all of the Deckseal product that it expected to use on the project. However, as Smith-Wolf began to use the product in the manner Hood suggested, it encountered several problems. The first Deckseal Hood supplied had hardened in its containers and could not be removed. In addition, it was impossible to heat the product to the necessary temperature with only two kettles, so Smith-Wolf needed three or four kettles and a crew of 10 or 11 to perform the work. Even so, during the first 30 days that Smith-Wolf worked on the project, it was able to waterproof less than 7,000 square feet per day (and on some days less than 3,000 square feet).

Smith-Wolf immediately informed Hood of the problems that it was encountering. Hood advised doing a number of things, such as mixing the Deckseal with paint thinner and preheating the cans containing the product. Smith-Wolf followed these suggestions, but they did not result in any substantial improvement in the product's initial utility.

About 30 days after Smith-Wolf first began using the Deckseal, Hood supplied additional Deckseal that had been produced some time after the date that the first batch had been manufactured. From the time that this material was furnished, Smith-Wolf was able to substantially increase its daily production—up to between 8,000 and 10,000 square feet per day; however, it continued to need three or four kettles and a crew of 10 or 11.

Altogether, Smith-Wolf used approximately 16,000 gallons of Deckseal supplied by Wolf at a cost of about $53,000. In addition, in the last few days of work, it used approximately 4,700 gallons of another material that it obtained from another supplier. With that product, it was able to achieve a daily production of work approximating the 13,500 square feet of area Hood had initially forecast, although it needed to use an increased number of kettles and workers.

In a lawsuit that Smith-Wolf filed against Hood, Smith-Wolf contended that its actual "cost" to perform its subcontract was $218,078, as contrasted with the $153,995 that it had received. The larger figure included actual direct labor and other costs and an allowance for additional overhead and for profit. The trial court found that 90 percent of the difference between these two figures (after adjustments for amounts owed to Hood by Smith-Wolf and for acknowledged credits due Smith-Wolf) represented the damages Smith-Wolf had incurred as a result of the failure of Deckseal to perform as Hood had warranted. (The court attributed the other 10 percent to other causes.)

The court noted that under the UCC, if a buyer that has accepted goods learns of their nonconformity and gives notice to the seller of that nonconformity, the buyer may recover the difference between the actual value of the goods and their value as warranted, as well as any incidental and consequential damages. Consequential damages include any loss resulting from general or particular requirements and needs of which the seller at the time of contracting had reason to know and which could not reasonably be prevented by cover or otherwise; the UCC provides, though, that a buyer cannot recover for those damages that reasonable actions on its part would have prevented.

Hood first argued that because Smith-Wolf did not "cover," that is, purchase goods to substitute for those that were to be provided by Hood, upon discovery of the defect in the Deckseal, Smith-Wolf could not recover any consequential damages for breach of warranty.

The court said that Smith-Wolf apparently did not attempt to cover by buying another product initially because Hood, upon notification of the defects, assured Smith-Wolf that following his suggestions would result in a defect-free product. In addition, having paid Hood for the full amount of Deckseal that was to be used, acquisition of a substantial amount of another product would have resulted in a financial hardship to Smith Wolf. In any event, the court ruled that a seller cannot rely upon a buyer's failure to acquire substitute goods for that seller's defective goods if the other goods were equally available for the seller to acquire and to provide to the buyer and actions on the seller's part could have reduced the buyer's damages.

Hood in addition claimed that Smith-Wolf was not entitled to any award based on increased overhead expenses. The court noted, though, that the

UCC specifically authorizes a seller in certain cases to collect "reasonable overhead" as an item of damages in the case of a contract breach by a buyer. The court ruled that recovery of overhead expenses also should be available to buyers. It said that if a company can establish that its overhead expenses over a period of time have borne a certain ratio to its variable expenses for labor and materials, and if the company can prove the amount of labor and materials allocable to a particular transaction, it could allocate to its overhead expenses that portion of the costs of labor and materials that overhead expenses have constituted in connection with other transactions. The court then overruled Hood's objection to Smith-Wolf's inclusion of overhead expenses in its damages claim.

▌A Final Word

The UCC favors reasonableness. It is only reasonable for a buyer to expect a seller to meet its commitment. It is only reasonable for a buyer to notify a seller if it believes the goods it received from the seller are defective. It is only reasonable to require that notice of defects be given within a reasonable time. It is only reasonable to allow a seller the right to cure defects—if the buyer will not be harmed. It is only reasonable to prohibit a buyer from relying on defects of which it did not give timely notice when a seller seeks payment for the goods. It is only reasonable to require that the buyer take reasonable care of the seller's goods before the seller can regain possession. It is only reasonable to require that a buyer make a reasonable effort to sell goods it rejected if they are perishable or threaten to decline in value. And on and on.

The UCC protects innocent buyers, but not if their unreasonable actions result in unnecessary harm to sellers. The UCC recognizes rights and imposes obligations on both buyers and sellers. However one might describe it, whatever one might call it, the fact of the matter is that the UCC favors—and rewards—commercial reasonableness.

FIVE SELLER SUITS

1. When Fertico Belgium, S.A. learned that the Phosphate Chemical Exports Association, Inc. could not deliver either of two shipments of phosphate fertilizer by the dates required under their contract, it took steps to cover by purchasing 35,000 tons of the same kind of fertilizer from a third party—at an additional cost of $700,000. Phosphate delivered the first shipment of 15,000 tons to Fertico late; because Phosphate had received payment for that shipment under a letter of credit Fertico had opened in its behalf, Fertico believed it had no commercially reasonable alternative but to take title to that shipment. Indeed, several months after the delivery, which was nonconforming because it was late, Fertico sold the 15,000 tons to another buyer, Janssens, and earned a profit of $454,000. Fertico then filed suit against Phosphate to recover the $700,000 loss it incurred on the cover. Phosphate contended, though, that Fertico's $700,000 loss should be offset by the $454,000 profit it made on the Janssens sale.

In its decision in this case, the New York Court of Appeals noted that Fertico was entitled to damages because its cover purchase was made in good faith, without unreasonable delay, and the fertilizer it purchased was a reasonable substitute for the Phosphate fertilizer. It then ruled that Fertico did not have to offset the profit it made on the Janssens sale. The court noted that Fertico, a trader, both bought and sold fertilizer. "It would be anomalous to conclude that had it not been for [Phosphate's] breach Fertico would not have continued its trade and upon such reasoning to counterpoise the profits from the Janssens sale against the damages arising from [Phosphate's] breach." The court concluded, over a vigorous dissenting opinion, that the profit Fertico made on the sale of goods such as fertilizer, of which the supply in the market is not limited, "should not therefore be deducted from the damages recoverable from [Phosphate]." (Fertico Belgium, S.A. v. Phosphate Chemicals Export Ass'n, Inc. 70 N.Y.2d 76 (1987).)

2. Intending to use them in a beautification project for the City of Albuquerque, New Mexico, Garcia Tree & Lawn, Inc. contracted to purchase 985 spreading juniper bushes from Oda Nursery, Inc. Oda shipped the bushes to Albuquerque in March 1982 and they were inspected by one of Garcia's employees; a city official also examined them sometime between their arrival and the time they were planted. For four months following delivery the bushes remained in their five-gallon shipping containers. Garcia watered and fertilized them throughout that time. Finally, it planted the junipers, but within several months some of them had begun to die. Garcia removed nearly 700 of them and discovered that they were root-bound. On December 8, 1982, Oda filed suit against Garcia for payment; Garcia answered the complaint on February 25, 1983, contending that it was not obligated to pay Oda because the bushes had been defective. Oda contended that that was the first notice it had received regarding any defects in the bushes.

In its decision in this case, the Supreme Court of New Mexico noted that the UCC requires that a buyer that rejects goods must notify the seller of its rejection within a reasonable time after delivery or tender of the goods. Furthermore, the UCC says that an effective rejection because of defects in the goods requires the buyer to tell the seller of all defects in the goods ascertainable by reasonable inspection so that the seller has the opportunity to cure them. The court found that Garcia had not notified Oda of any problems with the bushes before Oda had filed suit. Garcia's answer to Oda's complaint, which notified Oda of its contention that the bushes were defective, was "clearly unreasonable," the court concluded. (Oda Nursery, Inc. v. Garcia Tree & Lawn, Inc., 708 P.2d 1039 (N.M. 1985).)

3. In April 1985 Haralambos Fekkos purchased a Yammar model 165D, 16 horsepower diesel tractor and various implements from the Lykins Oil Company. When Fekkos attempted to use the tractor for the first time, he discovered it was defective. Among other things, it apparently had a dead battery that required jump starts, overheated while pulling either the mower or tiller, and was missing a water pump and safety shields over the muffler and the power takeoff. After stopping payment on his check, Fekkos spoke with Lykins's manager, service manager, and sales representative; they told him they would have the tractor picked up. Fekkos then placed the tractor with the tiller attached in his front yard at the edge of the lawn as near as possible to the front door without driving it into the landscaped area closest to his house. He left the tractor on the lawn because his driveway was broken up for renovation and the garage was inaccessible, and because the tractor had to be jump started by Lykins's employees when they picked it up.

On May 1, 1985, at 6:00 A.M., Fekkos discovered that the tractor had been stolen, although the tiller had been unhitched and was still in his yard. Lykins picked up the remaining attachments that evening and then sought payment for the tractor from Fekkos. The court said that under the UCC, when a buyer has taken possession of goods, rejects them, and retains possession, liability can be imposed on the buyer if the goods are lost, stolen, or destroyed if the buyer fails to exercise reasonable care for the goods' preservation until such time as the seller removes the goods. In this case, the court ruled Fekkos's actions were reasonable under the circumstances and he did not breach his duty to use reasonable care to hold the tractor until Lykins retrieved it. Therefore, it said, the loss should be shouldered by Lykins. (Lykins Oil Co. v. Fekkos, 507 N.E.2d 795 (Ct. Com. Pl. Ohio 1986).)

4. The telephone order Edward Roth placed on behalf of his companies with the George A. Milton Can Company called for one truckload of cans consisting of 17,000 Walker DOT 3 brake fluid cans, 12,000 Walker carburetor cleaner cans, 20,000 Walker gas octane cans, and 20,000 Morak brake fluid cans, and another truckload of all Walker DOT 3 brake fluid cans. When Milton found that it did not have 17,000 Walker DOT 3 brake fluid cans in made-up stock at the time of shipment, it shipped an additional 9,000 Morak brake fluid cans and an additional 9,000 Walker gas octane cans to complete the truckload. The excess cans were noted on Milton's invoice, which was stamped "received," and on a packing list signed by a person who worked for Roth. Furthermore, Roth apparently agreed that his businesses would pay for the extra Morak and Walker cans. They did not pay, though, and Milton filed suit.

The trial court held that Milton could only recover for the 40,000 cans Roth had actually ordered, not the 58,000 cans that Roth had received. It said that "under the facts and circumstances of this case, where the shipment of the additional amount was for your convenience and without confirmation or approval by the purchaser, I do not think that you can overship and then put the burden on the customer to say, 'I didn't order that many.' I don't think the Uniform Commercial Code so requires." Milton appealed and the appellate court reversed the lower court's decision. The appellate court noted that under the UCC, where goods or the tender of delivery fail in any respect to conform to the contract, the buyer may reject the whole, accept the whole, or accept any commercial unit or units and reject the rest. It said that an excess in quantity of goods delivered is a nonconformity that the buyer has a duty to reject within a reasonable time after their delivery or tender; failure of a buyer to make an effective rejection operates as an acceptance of the goods. Here, Roth had been put on notice of the nonconformity of the shipment. Accordingly, the court ruled that Roth's companies were obligated to pay Milton for the full amount of cans delivered. (Van Dorn Co. v. Future Chemical and Oil Corp., 753 F.2d 565 (7th Cir. 1985).)

5. The purchase orders Oxford Industries, Inc. submitted to Texpor Traders, Inc. provided that Texpor would sell to Oxford first grade 100 percent French terry or knit cotton sweatshirts. Texpor understood that the garments were to be resold by Oxford to top quality department stores and speciality retail stores and boutiques. However, many of the sweatshirts Texpor delivered were materially defective and nonconforming to the requirements of the contract. When Texpor filed suit to collect payment from Oxford, Oxford asserted that it had properly rejected the sweatshirts and that it was entitled to recover the profit it would have made on the resale. The court said that it was entitled to recover the $61,036.40 it paid for the first shipment; cancel the second shipment and be excused from paying $36,612; and recover consequential damages amounting to lost profits from confirmed customer orders in the amount of $111,112.78. The court emphasized that the sweatshirts were not fungible; they were a special order, part of a line of clothing that Oxford was attempting to develop. Because the goods in both shipments it received from Texpor were nonconforming; because the goods from the first shipment were delivered very close to Oxford's commercial deadline; and because the goods from the second shipment were delivered late, the court said "Oxford could not possibly cover or in any way recoup its loss." (Texpor Traders, Inc. v. Trust Company Bank, 720 F. Supp. 1100 (S.D.N.Y. 1989).)

Buyer's Rights Checklist

✓ The Uniform Commercial Code (UCC) contains numerous provisions setting forth the rights and duties of sellers and buyers of goods.

✓ Sellers have the duty to timely deliver goods that meet the specifications of the contract—and the right under certain circumstances to attempt to cure a nonconforming tender of goods.

✓ The failure of a seller to perform its obligations authorizes a buyer to take a number of different steps. Under certain conditions, these include the right to reject the goods; the right to revoke an acceptance of goods; and the ability to purchase cover to substitute for the goods the buyer was to receive from the seller. Correspondingly, buyers in certain cases must fulfill certain duties imposed on them by the UCC with respect to rejected goods.

✓ A buyer may be entitled to recover lost profits and other forms of significant damages resulting from a seller's breach of a contract.

✓ The watchword of the UCC is reasonableness—buyers and sellers that act in a commercially reasonable manner can expect to see their losses limited.

WHEN A BUYER BREACHES

▌ Kinds of Breaches ▌ Seller's Remedies ▌ Resale Rules ▌ Damages
▌ A Final Word

Following a series of trans-Atlantic telephone and telex communications, the Afram Export Corporation reached an agreement with Metallurgiki Halyps, S.A., a Greek steel company, for the purchase by Metallurgiki of 15,000 tons of clean shredded scrap metal, at $135 per ton, F.O.B. Milwaukee. Metallurgiki apparently intended to use the scrap to make steel for shipment to Egypt under a contract it had with an Egyptian buyer.

Afram prepared the scrap for the contract in Milwaukee. After inspecting the scrap, an agent for Metallurgiki said that the scrap was clean but told Afram that Metallurgiki would not accept it because the price of scrap had fallen. Metallurgiki indeed did not accept the scrap. Afram sold the scrap to other buyers and filed suit in the United States; it was able to obtain a judgment against Metallurgiki for breach of contract.

▌ Kinds of Breaches

A buyer can breach a sales contract in a number of ways. It may wrongfully reject goods; wrongfully revoke its prior acceptance of goods; fail to make a payment due on or before delivery; or indicate in advance of the seller's performance that it will not comply with part or all of the contract.

What's a seller to do? When a buyer defaults, it has to deal with two principal issues: what to do with the goods the buyer does not want, and how to make itself "whole" notwithstanding the buyer's breach.

▌ Seller's Remedies

The Uniform Commercial Code (UCC) has provisions that deal with both of these issues. Generally speaking, the UCC provides that following a buyer's breach a seller may

- Withhold delivery of goods
- Stop delivery of goods that are in the hands of a shipper
- Resell the goods and recover damages from the breaching buyer based on the price it receives
- Recover damages for nonacceptance
- Sue the buyer for the price

▌ Resale Rules

Sellers may resell goods at public or private sales. They may sell the goods as a unit or in parcels and at any time and place and on any terms—but every aspect of the sale, including the method, manner, time, place, and terms, must be commercially reasonable.

Where the resale is at a private sale, the seller must give the buyer notification of its intention to resell.

Where the resale is at a public sale, it must be made at a usual place or market for public sale if one is reasonably available and, except in the case of goods that are perishable or threaten to rapidly decline in value, the seller must give the buyer reasonable notice of the time and place of the resale. Furthermore, if the goods are not to be within the view of those attending the sale, the notification of sale must state the place where the goods are located and provide for their reasonable inspection by prospective buyers. The UCC is quite clear that the seller may buy the goods at a public resale.

Furthermore, the UCC provides that the seller is not accountable to the buyer for any profit it makes on any resale.

▌ Damages

The damages provisions of the UCC are designed to put a seller in the same position it would have been in had its buyer not breached the contract. They permit a seller's damages to be calculated in different ways, depending on the circumstances.

First, the seller may resell the goods and recover the difference between the contract price and the resale price, plus incidental damages, assuming the resale is accomplished in a commercially reasonable time. An aggrieved seller must mitigate damages by resale if feasible.

If an aggrieved seller fails to resell in a commercially reasonable time, then its damages can be calculated as the difference between the unpaid contract price and the market price of the goods at the time and place of tender, plus incidental damages.

If that amount is inadequate to put the seller in as good a position as performance would have done, then damages may be calculated by awarding the seller its lost profit, including reasonable overhead and incidental damages.

In addition, a seller also may sue for the price of the goods, plus incidental damages, if the seller is unable after reasonable effort to resell them at a reasonable price or the circumstances reasonably indicated that that effort would have been unavailing.

The method courts use to determine the measure of a seller's damages was analyzed recently in a decision by a New York trial court. In that case, the Tesoro Petroleum Corporation asserted that it had contracted to sell approximately 10 million gallons of gasoline to a group of buyers at a price of $1.30 per gallon. After Tesoro notified the buyers of the name of the ship that was going to deliver the gasoline, the buyers told Tesoro that they would not accept the gasoline because they had no binding contract. While the loaded vessel was proceeding to New York, Tesoro negotiated the sale of the cargo on board to petroleum company Esso Sapa in Argentina, for a price of $1.10 per gallon.

Tesoro contended that because of a sudden sharp drop in price, the value of the gasoline at the time of the buyers' alleged breach was between $.75 and $.80 per gallon and that, although it resold the product for $1.10 per gallon, its recovery should not be limited to the actual loss it suffered from the buyers' alleged breach ($.20 per gallon plus incidentals) but rather that it was entitled to recover the difference between market price and contract price. If it could prevail on that theory, it would recover at least $3 million in excess of its actual contractual loss (10 million gallons times the difference between the $1.10 resale price and the $.80 market price).

The court looked to the UCC to resolve the issue. It noted that Section 2-706 of the UCC states that a seller that resells goods in good faith and in a commercially reasonable manner may recover the difference between the resale price and the contract price together with certain incidental damages (less expenses saved as a result of the buyer's breach). On the other hand, Section 2-708 states that the measure of damages for nonacceptance or repudiation by a buyer is the difference between the market price at the time and place for tender and the unpaid contract price together with certain incidental damages (less expenses saved as a result of the buyer's breach).

The court found that if Tesoro's damages were measured in accordance with Section 2-706, Tesoro would be receiving the benefit it reasonably expected when it entered into the alleged contract with the buyers. However, granting it the approximately $3 million additional recovery under Section 2-708 "would result in a windfall which cannot be said to have been in the contemplation of the parties at the time of their negotiations."

According to the court, the situation would be different if Tesoro's sale were from its inventory and it lost an opportunity to sell to Esso Sapa, if it had already contracted to sell gasoline to Esso Sapa, or "perhaps even if it was then actually engaged in negotiations for trades in this type of gasoline." Noting that Tesoro had made no such claim, it ruled that Section 2-706 should apply.

▌A Final Word

Getting a signature on a sales contract is not the end of a marketer's concerns—the seller must deliver, the goods must conform, and the buyer must accept and pay for them. That can be a long and difficult process even in the best of times. But a buyer's breach can cause significant problems to the seller.

The UCC intends to put the seller in the position it would have been in had the buyer complied with its agreement; thus, the seller is entitled to all of the economic benefits of its contract—but, as the court made clear in the Tesoro case, probably not more than that.

What should sellers do when buyers breach? Think clearly, be aware of the various options, act in a commercially reasonable manner, and try to recover as much as possible as quickly as is reasonable.

FIVE BUYER BREACHES

1. In the lawsuit filed by the North American Foreign Trading Corporation against DMS, Inc., in which North American alleged that DMS had failed to purchase all of the 164,968 items that it had agreed to buy, North American asked the court to determine the prejudgment interest to which it would be entitled if it succeeded on its claim. North American contended that DMS had agreed to purchase 164,968 units of its product in minimum monthly installments of 15,000 units at a cost of $12 per unit and that DMS had provided a $100,000 deposit to be applied to the last shipment. North American said that it made four 15,000 shipments, for which it was paid, but that DMS then canceled the contract.

It took North American nearly three years to sell the goods in bulk to a single purchaser at a price of $11 per unit. When North American filed suit, it still had DMS's $100,000 deposit. The court ruled that, if successful on its breach of contract claim, North American would be entitled to recover interest at the statutory interest rate on the full contract price (less the $100,000 deposit) from the date of DMS's breach until the time at which it could reasonably have resold the goods with reasonable effort for a reasonable price. The court said that if it found the nearly three-year delay until resale to be unreasonable, North American would be entitled to interest on its damages based on the difference between the contract price and the market price at the time of the breach or some reasonable time thereafter or on its lost profit. (North American Foreign Trading Corp. v. Direct Mail Specialist, 697 F. Supp. 163 (S.D.N.Y. 1988).)

2. One of the products manufactured by National Controls, Inc. was the model 3221 electronic microprocessor technology load cell scale, which it designed to interface with a cash register for use at check-out stands. National sold the 3221 to cash register manufacturers, also known as original equipment manufacturers, or OEMs. After Commodore Business Machines had purchased several 3221s from National, it placed an order by telephone for an additional 900 scales over the phone; representatives from the two companies agreed on the quantity, price, and delivery schedule. As it usually did, Commodore gave National its own purchase order number; in a departure from previous practice, though, it also mailed its purchase order to National. National prepared a sales order, entered the Commodore purchase number on it, mailed a copy to Commodore, and sent a copy to its Florida manufacturing facility, which began to manufacture the units. Commodore accepted only the first 50 scales and did not accept or pay for the remaining 850 units. National then resold those 850 units to an existing OEM customer and filed suit, contending that it was a "lost volume seller" entitled to recover the loss of profit it would have made on the sale of the 850 units to Commodore.

The court found that it was undisputed that at the relevant times National's manufacturing plant was operating at approximately 40 percent capacity; that production of the 900 units did not tax that capacity, and that the plant could have more than doubled its output of 3221s and still have stayed within its capacity. It therefore found the evidence sufficient to find that National had the capacity to supply both Commodore and the OEM customer to which it had sold the 850 units Commodore had rejected and that had there been no breach of contract by Commodore, National would have had the benefit of both the original contract and the resale contract. Accordingly it ruled that National was entitled to its lost profits on the contract with Commodore. (National Controls, Inc. v. Commodore Business Machines, Inc., 209 Cal. Rptr. 636 (Ct. App. 1985).)

3. The Apex Oil Company was obligated to deliver 315,000 gallons of no. 2 heating oil meeting the specifications of the New York Mercantile Exchange in New York Harbor to The Belcher Company of New York, Inc. and Belcher New Jersey, Inc. The Merc's specifications required that oil delivered in New York Harbor have a sulfur content no higher than 0.20 percent. Apex asked Belcher whether Belcher would take delivery of 190,000 barrels of oil in Boston in partial satisfaction of its obligation, and Belcher agreed. The oil arrived in Boston Harbor on February 9, 1982, and on the next day the ship began discharging its cargo at Belcher's terminal. Initial tests showed the oil contained 0.28 percent sulfur, in excess of the New York Harbor specifications (but within the 0.30 percent range for Boston). A second test Belcher performed after 141,535 barrels had been pumped indicated that the oil contained 0.22 percent sulfur, within the range of tolerance for oil containing 0.20 percent sulfur. Nevertheless, Belcher refused to resume pumping.

Apex contacted another customer to which it was scheduled to deliver oil later in the month and sold it the 48,000 barrels of oil remaining in its ship. For some time, Apex asked Belcher to take delivery of the 48,000 barrels still owing under the contract but Belcher refused. Almost six weeks after Belcher's breach, Apex then "identified" 48,000 barrels of oil as relating to the Belcher contract, sold them to a third party for approximately 13 cents per gallon less than Belcher had agreed to pay, and filed suit against Belcher for breach. The court said that Apex's delay of nearly six weeks between Belcher's breach and its "resale" was "clearly unreasonable." The purpose of a resale is to allow the court to determine a seller's damages so that it may be put in the position it would have been on the date of the breach had the buyer complied with the contract. But in a market, such as the oil market, that had rapid price fluctuations, the court ruled that the delayed resale could not properly be used to calculate Apex's damages. (Apex Oil Co. v. Belcher Co. of New York, Inc., 855 F.2d 997 (2d Cir. 1988).)

4. After a tenant defaulted on its real estate lease with Samson Bandimere, Bandimere took possession of the property, some equipment, and about three dozen 55-gallon barrels of chemicals on the property to offset past due rent. Another ex-tenant told Bandimere that he probably had "an EPA problem" with the barrels. Seeking to sell the equipment and barrels in one lot, Bandimere contacted the president of Jelen and Son, Inc., a company that specialized in the purchase and resale of mining equipment. Jelen examined the items on Bandimere's property and agreed to exchange a compressor Bandimere wanted for the materials, equipment, and barrels on the property and $3,500. An invoice Jelen prepared, which Bandimere signed, reflected the trade of a compressor for mining equipment, 13 55-gallon barrels of concentrate and chemicals with open tops, and $3,500.

Bandimere loaded the barrels, many of which were still leaking and open, on two flatbed trucks and he and an employee drove to Jelen's property to deliver them. The fire marshall happened to notice the trucks with liquid splashing out of the barrels; he investigated and determined that they contained acid and potassium cyanide, which, when combined, produce hydrocyanic acid, a deadly gas. The fire marshall impounded the trucks and barrels. Jelen refused to accept any barrels containing chemicals or hazardous materials and the authorities determined they were Bandimere's responsibility. He agreed to pay all costs associated with the cleanup and then filed suit against Jelen, contending that it was Jelen's refusal to accept the barrels that had caused him to incur the cleanup costs. The Supreme Court of Colorado ruled that Bandimere could not recover from Jelen his cleanup costs because those costs did not arise as a result of Jelen's refusal to accept delivery of the chemicals but instead were incurred as a result of Bandimere's improper storage, handling, and transportation of the hazardous waste. (Jelen and Son, Inc. v. Bandimere, 801 P.2d 1182 (Colo. 1990).)

5. In October 1982 a salesperson for Midwest Precision Services, Inc., an industrial machinery distributor based in Illinois, met with employees of PTM Industries Corporation, a machine shop business located in Westfield, Massachusetts. They discussed PTM's possible purchase of Midwest's computer-driven industrial metal grinder. During those discussions, Midwest tentatively offered to customize the machine to suit PTM's needs for $345,500. PTM then discussed financing the transaction with the Shawmut Bank of Boston, N.A. They agreed that Shawmut would purchase the machine from Midwest and lease it to PTM for five years, after which PTM could buy it from Shawmut for one dollar. The purchase order Shawmut sent to Midwest stated, among other things, that Shawmut would pay Midwest $345,500 for the machine but that it would have no liability and could cancel the purchase order unless within 90 days Midwest had delivered the machine and Shawmut had received from PTM a "signed acceptance certificate" acknowledging receipt of the machine in good condition and requesting payment of Midwest's invoice.

Midwest modified the machine to meet PTM's requirements and shipped it. Upon inspection, however, PTM complained to Midwest that the machine was damaged and declared that it would not accept delivery. Midwest made repeated offers to cure any damage, irrespective of its nature or cause, but PTM steadfastly rejected Midwest's proposals. Then, 101 days after Shawmut had issued the purchase order, Shawmut notified Midwest that it was canceling their agreement; Midwest filed suit against Shawmut and PTM. A jury found that Shawmut had breached its contract with Midwest and Shawmut appealed, arguing that it was a mere financing agent, not the buyer, and that it could not held liable for breach of contract.

The U.S. Court of Appeals for the First Circuit rejected Shawmut's contentions. It noted that the purchase order issued by Shawmut to Midwest, which said it was the "complete and exclusive statement" of the agreement between Shawmut and Midwest, contained promises by both sides (Shawmut's promise to pay and Midwest's promise to deliver); duties on both sides (Shawmut's duty to pay and Midwest's duty to deliver); and rights on both sides (Midwest's right to payment and Shawmut's right to deliver). Nothing in the agreement expressly stated that Shawmut and Midwest had no rights under the contract as against each other. Indeed, the appellate court said, all indications were to the contrary—including language that stated that Midwest's express warranties in the purchase order were enforceable directly by Shawmut or PTM. (Midwest Precision Services, Inc. v. PTM Industries Corp., 887 F.2d 1128 (1st Cir. 1989).)

Buyers' Breaches Checklist

✓ Buyers can breach sales contracts by wrongfully rejecting goods; wrongfully revoking their prior acceptance of goods; failing to make a payment due on or before delivery; or indicating in advance of the seller's performance that they will not fulfill some or all of their duties.

✓ When a buyer defaults, a seller has to deal with two principal issues: what to do with the goods the buyer does not want, and how to make itself "whole" notwithstanding the buyer's breach.

✓ The most common seller's remedies are to withhold delivery of goods; stop delivery of goods that are in the hands of a shipper; resell the goods; and sue for nonacceptance or for the contract price.

✓ The damages provisions of the UCC are designed to put a seller in the same position it would have been in had its buyer not breached the contract.

✓ The UCC permits a seller's damages to be calculated in a few ways, depending on the circumstances. They include the difference between the contract price and the resale price; the difference between the unpaid contract price and the market price of the goods at the time and place of tender; and, in certain cases, even lost profits.

THE LAW ON LEASES

▌ Leasing Goods ▌ UCC Article 2A ▌ Risk of Loss
▌ Liens on Leased Goods ▌ Leases in Bankruptcy ▌ Aircraft Leases
▌ A Final Word

In July 1973 Anthony and Grace Cucchi leased a burglar alarm system from the Rollins Protective Services Company that Rollins installed in the Cucchis' home. Anthony Cucchi and a Rollins sales representative signed an installation service contract that provided that the Cucchis would pay $500 for installation of the burglar alarm system and a $15 monthly fee for service and maintenance. The contract also stated that the security system remained Rollins's property, that the Cucchis should refrain from damaging the system, and that, upon termination of the lease, the Cucchis would return the system to Rollins. Additionally, the contract limited Rollins's liability for all loss or damage resulting from the failure of the system to properly operate or perform to $250.

The Cucchis paid Rollins to install the burglar alarm system and Rollins installed it in their home. For more than 10 years, Rollins regularly maintained and serviced the Cucchis' system and the Cucchis made regular monthly payments for service and maintenance charges.

Then, on February 2, 1984, the Cucchis' home was burglarized and approximately $36,000 in valuables was taken. Grace Cucchi recalled activating the burglar alarm system before she left her home on the day of the burglary. Subsequent testing indicated that the system was operating only intermittently.

On October 30, 1985, the Cucchis filed suit against Rollins seeking damages for the loss of their property. They contended among other things that Rollins had breached express and implied warranties of merchantability and fitness for intended use and that Rollins had been negligent in manufacturing, installing, repairing, and servicing the burglar alarm system. Rollins denied the allegations of liability and asserted various defenses to the claims, including that the Cucchis' action was barred by the applicable statute of limitations and that any damages were limited to $250 by the express limitation of damages provision of the written contract.

At trial, Anthony Cucchi testified as to the representations Rollins' salesperson made in July 1973. Cucchi said the salesperson had stated that the system was "state of the art" and "almost unbeatable."

The trial court found sufficient evidence of an express oral warranty from Rollins to the Cucchis to the effect that the burglar alarm system would provide safety. The jury then returned a $30,000 verdict in favor of the Cucchis. In 1990 the case reached the Supreme Court of Pennsylvania, which was forced to decide the law that applied to Rollins's lease of the burglar alarm system to the Cucchis.

▌Leasing Goods

Every year in this country, businesses and consumers lease billions of dollars worth of personal property as diverse as automobiles and industrial equipment. Leasing is big business and is often used as the means of financing the acquisition of capital goods. Indeed, businesses often lease their goods to reach virtually the same result as a sale. The essence of both kinds of transactions is the same—the lessee/buyer acquires the right to use certain goods and the lessor/seller transfers the right to use those goods. However, there are differences, especially relating to the transfer of title, the risk of loss, financial considerations, taxes, and the effect of a lease compared with a sale in the event of one party's bankruptcy.

Up until recently, the leasing of property other than real estate (which is subject to its own rules and which is outside the scope of this book) was governed by a conglomeration of rules and laws. These included court decisions, the general legal principles underlying those rulings, the law relating to real estate leases (applied by analogy), Uniform Commercial Code (UCC) Article 2 (relating to the sale of goods), and UCC Article 9 (dealing with secured transactions).

In the late 1980s, however, the UCC was amended to include a proposed Article 2A to govern leases of personal property. By 1993, Article 2A had been adopted by approximately two dozen states. Although it has some significant differences from Article 2, Article 2A is based on UCC Article 2. And so it should be, given that many of the assumptions underlying Article 2 are equally applicable to conventional leases:

- Parties to both of these kinds of transactions frequently act without counsel.

- The agreement of the parties to these kinds of transactions is often oral or evidenced by scant writings.

- The obligations between the parties to these transactions are bilateral.

The Pennsylvania legislature had not adopted Article 2A by the time the Cucchis' case reached the Pennsylvania Supreme Court. Thus, the court had to determine what law to apply to the Cucchis' lease.

It noted that UCC Article 2 did not by its terms apply to contracts for the lease of goods but dealt with sales, contracts for sale, sellers, and buyers. Article 2 defined a sale as "the passing of title from the seller to the buyer at a price." Because the Rollins's burglar alarm system was only leased to the Cucchis and was intended to be returned to Rollins upon termination of the agreement, the court said that Article 2 was not strictly applicable to the transaction.

However, the court said, courts have extended Article 2 to leases, albeit somewhat inconsistently. It then ruled that selected provisions of Article 2 should be applied to transactions involving the lease of goods on a case by case basis, considering the nature of the lease, the language, purpose, and intent of the particular UCC provision under consideration, "and the practicality of applying the particular provision" to the particular lease.

The court then held that Article 2's warranty provisions should apply to the conventional leasing of goods. It said that lessees such as the Cucchis relied on express and implied representations of lessors as to the quality, merchantability, and fitness of goods to the same extent and in the same manner as buyers relied on similar representations by sellers. The court found further support for applying the Article 2 warranty provisions to leases because Article 2A essentially adopts the sales warranty provisions of Article 2 to lease transactions.

However, the Pennsylvania Supreme Court rejected Rollins' contention that the Statute of Limitations contained in Article 2 should apply to the Cucchis' suit. Generally speaking, with respect to a sale of goods, a breach of warranty occurs when the goods are tendered. Under Article 2, buyers must file suit within four years after the breach of warranty occurs. Thus, Rollins contended, the Cucchis' suit should have been dismissed under the Statute of Limitations.

But the Pennsylvania Supreme Court noted that Article 2A accommodated the respective interests of a lessor and a lessee somewhat differently from the way Article 2 handled buyers and sellers. Article 2A eliminated Article 2's "tender of delivery" as the usual event that began the running of the four-year Statute of Limitations. Under Article 2A, warranties were assumed to be made for the future performance of the leased goods. The court then held that the express and implied warranties Rollins made extended to the future performance of the burglar alarm system and that the Cucchis had four years from discovering any breach of warranty from which to bring suit. Accordingly, it upheld the jury award in their favor.

▌ UCC Article 2A

Many of the provisions of Article 2A are similar to provisions in Article 2. Article 2A contains its own Statute of Frauds, which is quite similar to the Article 2 Statute of Frauds. To be enforceable, a lease must be in writing and signed by the party against whom enforcement is sought, if the total payments to be made under the lease (excluding payments for options to renew or buy) are $1,000 or more. (Note that the Article 2 Statute of Frauds requires a writing for a sale of goods of $500 or more.) Article 2A contains exceptions similar to those contained in Article 2 for goods specially manufactured or for goods received and accepted by the lessee.

Leases, like sales contracts, may be created under Article 2A even though the moment of agreement is undetermined and even though one or more terms may be left open.

In addition, as Rollins discovered in the lawsuit filed by the Cucchis, lessors may create express and implied warranties and that fact is recognized by Article 2A, much as it is recognized for sales by Article 2. Article 2A states that express warranties by a lessor are created as follows:

- Any affirmation of fact or promise made by the lessor to the lessee that relates to the goods and becomes "part of the basis of the bargain" creates an express warranty that the goods will conform to the affirmation or promise.

- Any description of the goods that is made part of the basis of the bargain creates an express warranty that the goods will conform to the description.

- Any sample or model that is made part of the basis of the bargain creates an express warranty that the whole of the goods will conform to the sample or model.

Lessors need not use words such as "warrant" or "guarantee" or even intend to create a warranty for a warranty to be created. As with sales of goods, warranties for leased property may be created in advertisements, brochures, and catalogs, and orally by salespeople.

In addition, lessors (other than lenders under finance leases) impliedly warrant that the goods subject to a lease are "merchantable," which means that they:

- Pass without objection in the trade under the description in the lease

- In the case of fungible goods, are of fair average quality within the description

- Are fit for the ordinary purposes for which goods of that kind are used

- Run, within the variation permitted by the lease, of even kind, quality, and quantity within each unit and among all units involved

- Are adequately contained, packaged, and labeled as the lease may require

- Conform to any promises or affirmations of fact made on the container or label

Furthermore, as with sales contracts, a lessor that has reason to know of any particular purpose for which the leased goods are required and that the lessee is relying on the lessor's skill or judgment to select or furnish goods impliedly warrants that the goods will be fit for that purpose.

Article 2A also provides for additional warranties by lessors that go beyond Article 2 warranties. For instance, implicit in a lease is a warranty by the lessor that for the lease term no person will hold a claim to or interest in the goods arising from an act or omission to act of the lessor that will interfere with the lessee's use of the leased goods.

Article 2A also requires that a disclaimer of the warranty of merchantability be conspicuous and in writing, as is the case for a disclaimer of the warranty of fitness. Article 2A also generally provides that to exclude or modify the implied warranty of merchantability, fitness, or against interference or infringement, the language must be in writing and conspicuous.

▌ Risk of Loss

Except in the case of a finance lease, the lessor retains the risk of loss. However, the parties can change that rule by agreement, as often occurs. For instance, if the lease requires or authorizes the goods to be shipped by carrier and it does not require delivery to a particular destination, the risk of loss may pass to the lessee when the goods are duly delivered to the carrier.

▌ Liens on Leased Goods

Because a lessor continues to have an interest in the leased goods, the Article 2A provisions concerning liens on leased goods are quite important.

Article 2A first deals with what are commonly referred to as "mechanic's liens." It states that if a person in the ordinary course of his or her business furnishes services or materials with respect to leased goods, a lien upon those goods that are in the possession of that person for those services or materials has priority over any interest of the lessor or lessee under the lease unless the statute or rule of law creating the lien otherwise provides.

In other cases, as a general rule, Article 2A states that a lessor has priority over a creditor of the lessee.

By the same token, a lessee has priority over a creditor of the lessor, unless the creditor held a lien on the goods before the lease became enforceable or the lessee did not give value and receive the goods without knowledge of the creditor's security interest. However, a lessee in the ordinary course of business takes the lease free of a security interest in the goods created by the lessor even though the lessee may know it exists. Special rules apply in the case of a lessor's creditor's security interest in the leased goods to cover future advances by the creditor.

▌ Leases in Bankruptcy

Suppose a business or individual that has leased goods files a petition for relief from creditors and enters bankruptcy. What happens to the goods and the lease? The federal bankruptcy code has special provisions dealing with leases.

Under the bankruptcy code, a debtor has the right to terminate a prebankruptcy lease if, in its business judgment, it decides that doing so would be in its best interest. The other party to the lease has a claim against the debtor for its damages that is deemed a prepetition claim and that must share in the debtor's assets with other prepetition creditors.

The bankruptcy code also permits a debtor in bankruptcy to continue a prebankruptcy lease notwithstanding that it was in default of the lease before entering bankruptcy so long as the lease had not been terminated by bankrutpcy. To do so, it must cure, or provide adequate assurance that it will cure, any pre bankruptcy defaults; compensate, or provide adequate assurance that it will promptly compensate, the other party to the lease for any actual pecuniary loss resulting from the default; and provide adequate assurance that it will meet all future obligations under the lease.

Leases often contain provisions that declare that a party's bankruptcy is a default under the lease. These kind of so-called *ipso facto* provisions are ineffective under the Bankruptcy Code.

The bankruptcy code also has special provisions regarding assignments. A party to a lease that enters bankruptcy generally may assign its rights under the lease to another party notwithstanding prohibitions in the lease forbidding assignment. To do so, the debtor must cure any defaults and the assignee must provide the other party to the lease with adequate assurance of future performance.

▌ Aircraft Leases

The bankruptcy code provides special protection to lessors of aircraft, aircraft engines, propellers, appliances, or spare parts, as defined in Section 101 of the Federal Aviation Act of 1958, that are leased to a debtor that is an air carrier operating under a certificate of convenience and necessity issued by the Civil Aeronautics Board. In those cases, lessors are entitled to repossess their equipment unless the debtor cures all defaults relating to the leases within 60 days of filing for bankruptcy. (The same protection is available to secured creditors holding purchase money equipment security interests in these kinds of equipment.) Congress included these provisions in the bankruptcy code to induce businesses to extend substantial amounts of credit to the airline industry, and it has succeeded. However, there has been frequent litigation over exactly what the provisions mean. For instance, does it apply only to a "true" lease (yes) or may it also apply to a transaction in the form of a lease but that actually is a security interest? (No.) Does it apply to all leased aircraft and related equipment or only to new aircraft and related equipment? (The courts are divided on this.) Does it apply to lease extensions and renewals? (Probably yes.) Does it apply if a debtor was not certified at the time of the transaction but thereafter became certified? (Probably not.)

Despite these issues, manufacturers and other airline suppliers have found these provisions of the bankruptcy code very helpful in airline bankruptcies;

in addition, they also have provided leverage to these creditors in connection with prebankruptcy financial restructurings.

❙ A Final Word

Now that Article 2A of the UCC has been drafted and become law in a number of states, the law on leasing has been clarified. Article 2A contains provisions for leases that are often analogous to those contained in UCC Article 2 relating to sales contracts, but often with a twist to reflect the special nature of a lease.

The importance of leases to today's economy also can be seen from the special lease provisions contained in the federal bankruptcy code. Lessors and lessees should conduct their lease negotiations with these two bodies of law well in mind.

FIVE LEASING CASES

1. About two years before Ludlum Enterprises, Inc. entered bankruptcy, the American Industrial Leasing Company leased it certain restaurant and kitchen equipment; it did not record or file the lease with any government filing office. In Ludlum's bankruptcy, American claimed that it was the owner of the equipment but Ludlum's bankruptcy trustee disagreed. The trustee contended that the lease violated a Florida law that provided that "any loan of goods" that the borrower possessed for two years "shall be taken, as to the creditors . . . to be fraudulent" and the "property shall be with the possession, unless such loan . . . [was] declared by will or deed in writing proved and recorded." The U.S. Court of Appeals referred to three other court decisions that, in the context of statutes substantially identical to the Florida law, construed them to exclude leases of goods. Then, finding "a significant difference" between a loan and a lease, it ruled that the Florida law did not apply to leases and upheld American's claim. (In re Ludlum Enterprises, Inc., 519 F.2d 997 (5th Cir. 1975).)

2. The Armstrong Equipment Company, indebted to the Clark Equipment Company in an amount exceeding $1.8 million, granted Clark a security interest in its heavy road building equipment and parts. However, Armstrong leased much of the equipment to others located in the states of Alabama, Florida, Georgia, Mississippi, and Tennessee. The security agreement required Armstrong, upon a default, to assemble and make available to Clark the property subject to its lien. Armstrong defaulted and Clark filed suit, seeking a court order requiring Armstrong to assemble the equipment for Clark. The case reached the U.S. Court of Appeals for the Fifth Circuit, which ruled that a federal court could order Armstrong to obtain the equipment for Clark notwithstanding that the equipment was located in several different states and notwithstanding that it might be leased to others. (Clark Equipment Co. v. Armstrong Equipment Co., 431 F.2d 54 (5th Cir. 1970).)

3. On November 14, 1980, A. Moneim Ramadan signed a lease with the Hastings Capital Corporation for a computerized energy management system for his office building in Gainesville, Florida. The unit was manufactured by a subsidiary of Hastings and was installed by a Gainesville heating and cooling company. Hastings claimed the system would reduce the building's electricity consumption. Before Ramadan executed the lease, Equico Lessors, Inc. conducted a credit check on Ramadan after Hastings approached Equico about a future assignment of the yet to-be executed lease. Equico also set the financial terms of the lease.

Within days after Ramadan signed the lease, Hastings assigned the lease to Equico by executing a preprinted assignment clause that named Equico as the assignee. Hastings also assigned Ramadan's personal guarantee of the lease to Equico by executing a preprinted assignment clause, which again named Equico as assignee. The lease contained a waiver of defenses clause as to any assignee of the lease. The clause provided that an assignee would be free of all defenses or claims Ramadan, as lessee, may have against Hastings, as lessor.

Unfortunately, the leased equipment failed to perform and repeated attempts to repair it were unsuccessful. According to Ramadan, the system not only failed to save any energy, it resulted in greater energy use. One year after signing the lease, Ramadan had the equipment removed by the installer and he stopped making lease payments. Hastings went out of business. Equico then brought suit against Ramadan for the balance of the payments due on the lease. Ramadan raised the defense of misrepresentation and counterclaimed for breach of warranty. The court noted that the Uniform Commercial Code contains a provision that validates waiver of defenses clauses in contracts or leases. The purpose of this provision is to treat an assignee of a contract or lease as a holder in due course of a negotiable instrument; it is intended to facilitate financing of transactions by insulating an innocent or unknowing purchaser of the contract or lease from disputes over the underlying transaction. Waiver of defense clauses reduce the risk to assignees in taking such assignments and thereby encourage the financing of transactions by assuring a market for those wishing to assign contracts and leases.

However, because of the great protection such a clause gives an assignee, such as Equico, it is only valid when the assignee gives value to the assignor, in good faith, and without knowledge of a defense or claim. Ramadan claimed that Equico and Hastings had such a close connection that Equico should not be permitted to rely on the waiver of defenses clause. Ramadan pointed out that Equico supplied preprinted forms for the lease between Hastings and Ramada, the lease and personal guarantee contained preprinted assignment clauses naming Equico as assignee, and Equico conducted a credit check on Ramadan before he executed the lease. He also noted that Equico had taken assignments of approximately 30 leases from Hastings in the past with a total value of $250,000. The court emphasized, though, that Ramadan had produced no evidence of a standing agreement that Hastings would assign to Equico all the leases it executed or that Equico agreed to take all assignments from Hastings. Furthermore, the court said, Ramadan introduced no evidence that Equico had knowledge of Hasting's performance guarantee. It then ruled that Equico could benefit from the waiver of defenses clause contained in the lease and was entitled to judgment against Ramadan for payments under the lease. (Equico Lessors, Inc. v. Ramadan, 493 So.2d 516 (D.Ct. App. Florida 1986).)

4. On November 11, 1974, the Scotti Commercial Co., a muffler franchisor, and Finger Lakes Motors, Inc., a car dealer, signed an equipment lease as part of a 10-year "exclusive" dealership, trademark, and licensing agreement. The agreement stated that Scotti would provide training, management consulting, sales materials, and the products and equipment necessary to be a Scotti dealer in return for payments from Finger Lakes. The lease contained a commercial assignment clause that provided for a waiver of defenses. It stated, "The obligations of the Lessee hereunder shall not be subject, as against any such transferee or assignee, to any defense, setoff or counterclaim available to Lessee against Lessor and that the same may be asserted only against Lessor. Scotti assigned the lease to a bank on September 8, 1976.

After Finger Lakes defaulted, the bank filed suit to collect the balance due and owing under the lease. Finger Lakes defended on the ground that Scotti had entered into the contract for the express purpose of fleecing it; the bank argued, though, that the waiver of defenses clause blocked Finger Lakes from raising such a defense and it asked the court for summary judgment. The court that issued a decision in the case said that Finger Lakes would have been blocked from raising that defense if the bank could have shown that it paid Scotti for the lease in good faith and without notice of any claim or defense by Finger Lakes and thus was a holder in due course of the lease. But because the bank had failed to provide evidence to that effect, the court rejected its motion and ordered the case to proceed to trial. (Chase Manhattan Bank, N.A. v. Finger Lakes Motors, Inc., 423 N.Y.S.2d 128 (Sup. Ct. Ontario Co. 1979).)

5. Many years ago, the Hawkins Construction Company entered into a contract with Swift and Company under which Hawkins agreed to construct a ham canning facility for Swift in Omaha. Hawkins needed a substantial amount of scaffolding equipment for the job and investigated as to availability, cost, and similar factors. It saw a pamphlet published by the Waco Scaffold and Shoring Company describing the various kinds of scaffold components it manufactured and stating that the "Waco HI-LOAD shoring equipment is designed to safely carry working loads up to 20,000 pounds per panel. This is twice the load capacity of conventional steel scaffolding." Hawkins then described the project and the purposes for which the equipment was to be used to the Matthews Company, Inc. and provided Matthews with blueprints of the job.

In time, Hawkins received back from Matthews a series of drawings prepared by Waco showing the recommended scaffolding configuration for Hawkins' plant's construction. Thereafter, Hawkins agreed to lease Waco equipment from Matthews and began work on the project. During the roof deck cement pour, a portion of the roof deck collapsed. Nobody was injured, but Hawkins suffered more than $30,000 in damages, and it filed suit against Matthews and Waco, contending that the scaffolding had been defective. Matthews urged that, as a "mere lessor" of the scaffolding it could not be held liable to Hawkins, but the Supreme Court of Nebraska disagreed. Finding that the pamphlet constituted an express warranty and that Matthews had supplied the pamphlet to Hawkins, the court ruled that it could be held liable to Hawkins for the damages it suffered when the scaffolding collapsed. (Hawkins Construction Co. v. Matthews Company, Inc., 209 N.W.2d 643 (Sup. Ct. Nebraska 1973).)

Leasing Checklist

✓ Billions of dollars worth of leases for personal property are signed every year in this country. Now, in many states, a single body of law governs those kinds of leases—Article 2A of the Uniform Commercial Code.

✓ Many of the provisions of UCC Article 2A for leases are based on UCC Article 2 provisions for sales contracts.

✓ Article 2A covers matters as diverse as lease formation, a lessor's express and implied warranties, who bears the risk of loss of leased goods, and the damages available upon breach by a lessee or a lessor.

✓ In addition, the federal bankruptcy code contains provisions relating to leases. A debtor in bankruptcy may continue a prebankruptcy lease even if it had been in default so long as it cures the default and meets the law's other requirements. It also may assign the lease under certain conditions.

✓ A lease is a valuable method of marketing property; manufacturers that lease goods should be well aware of the rules contained in Article 2A and the bankruptcy code with respect to leases.

PROTECTION WITH SECURITY INTERESTS

■ Secured Financing ■ Financing Statements ■ Priority
■ Lease or Security Interest ■ A Final Word

In August 1980 the Interfirst Bank of Abilene, N.A. extended two lines of credit to the Ted Evans Equipment Company, which sold and leased various kinds of equipment to retail customers in the Abilene, Texas, area. At that time, Evans was a sole proprietorship operated by Ted Evans, Sr. In connection with the loans from Interfirst, Evans executed several security agreements that granted the bank a security interest in Evans's inventory, including inventory it acquired after the time it signed the agreements.

The bank gave notice of its security interest by filing properly executed UCC-1 financing statements with the Texas secretary of state.

In September 1980 Evans became a distributor for Lull Manufacturing, a manufacturer of heavy construction and material handling equipment. Thereafter, Evans formed a corporation, although it continued to use the same name. The bank made no change in the UCC-1 filings following Evans's incorporation.

Ted Evans, Sr. died on May 27, 1982, but the company continued in business. On June 14, Ted Evans, Jr. ordered a forklift from Lull, which Lull delivered to Evans on July 8, 1982.

Significantly, as it turned out, Lull did not have any security agreement with Evans to cover the forklift and did not bother to investigate whether any other creditor might have a security interest in it.

On July 15, 1982, Evans defaulted on its obligations to Interfirst and the bank repossessed all of Evans' inventory, including the Lull forklift. Lull contacted the bank and asked that the forklift be returned. The bank claimed a security interest in the lift and refused to relinquish possession to Lull. Lull, apparently with the aid of the Evans family, removed the forklift from Evans's locked premises but without the bank's consent. The bank then filed suit against Lull for conversion and was awarded judgment against Lull. The court found that the bank's security interest in the forklift was superior to any claim that Lull may have had.

▌Secured Financing

The court in the Lull case noted that Lull, as the seller of the forklift, could have protected its interests—it could have obtained a purchase money security interest in the forklift that would have been superior to the bank's rights in Evans's property. But Lull did not sell to Evans on a secured basis, and that led to its losses.

Security interests are governed by Article 9 of the Uniform Commercial Code (UCC). Banks typically extend credit on a secured basis; businesses often neglect to do so. Certainly not every trade supplier can demand that every customer grant it a security interest, but more should consider insisting on that than do.

Article 9 has very basic requirements for creating a valid and enforceable security interest in property as diverse as goods, instruments, accounts, inventory, and equipment. First, a creditor needs a security agreement, which is an agreement signed by the debtor that grants a security interest to the creditor in certain described collateral.

For the security agreement to be enforceable, it must "attach." Attachment occurs after the debtor has granted the creditor a security interest, the secured creditor has given value, and the debtor has rights in the collateral. Thus, if a debtor signs a security agreement in favor of a creditor with respect to the debtor's existing inventory, the security agreement will attach as soon as the creditor gives value—extends credit—to the debtor.

A security agreement that has attached is enforceable between the debtor and creditor and may provide the creditor with certain rights in the collateral against other creditors that have knowledge of its security interest. But to attempt to ensure its priority, the creditor must "perfect" its security interest.

Generally speaking, there are two ways a security interest may be perfected. The first way is for the creditor to retain possession of the collateral. The second, and more common way, is for the creditor to file one or more financing statements in the appropriate state or local filing offices. The financing statements provide a record that creditors may examine to determine whether or not a debtor's assets are encumbered. A creditor that examines the filings and sees that a creditor's assets are not encumbered may then decide to extend credit on a secured priority basis or an unsecured basis; if on an unsecured basis, it must be aware of the risk of another creditor becoming secured and gaining priority in the debtor's assets.

▌Financing Statements

The UCC contains a number of rules regarding financing statements, including where and when financing statements must be filed and what they must include. For instance, it provides that a financing statement is sufficient if it includes:

1. The name and address of both the creditor and debtor

2. A statement indicating the types, or describing the items, of collateral

3. The debtor's signature

The goal of UCC financing statements is to provide notice to other creditors; therefore, a misspelling that results in a misfiled financing statement might doom a creditor's security interest. On the other hand, courts permit rather broad statements of collateral because they believe that a creditor that sees such a financing statement will be put on notice to make further inquiry.

In one case, Dillard Ford, Inc., a Ford dealership, entered into an inventory financing agreement with the Ford Motor Credit Company. Under the agreement, Ford Credit promised to loan Dillard money to purchase new and used cars for its inventory. This inventory financing agreement included a security agreement that granted Ford Credit a security interest in various assets owned by Dillard.

Under the financing agreement, Ford Credit advanced Dillard the funds it needed to buy cars to fill its inventory. When Dillard sold a car, it would pay off the inventory financing loan on that car. Under the revolving line of credit provisions of the agreement, Dillard would simultaneously take out another loan to buy another car to restock its inventory.

Ford Credit also participated in consumer retail financing. The financing agreement created a dealer proceeds withheld (DPW) account held by Ford Credit. Under the agreement, Ford Credit agreed to pay Dillard for consumers' notes in an amount equal to the notes' present value. Ford Credit would then place a portion of the money it owed the dealer into a special fund, called the DPW account, to cover the risk of consumers' defaulting on their loans. Whenever the fund rose above three percent of the balance on the outstanding consumer notes, Ford Credit would pay Dillard the surplus. When all of the notes were paid in full, Ford Credit agreed to refund any money left in the account to Dillard.

On August 31, 1983, Ford Credit discovered that Dillard had insufficient funds to cover two checks that Dillard had written to Ford Credit to meet its obligations under the inventory financing agreement. One of Ford Credit's managers went to Dillard and was told that Dillard either could not or would not cover the checks. The Ford Credit manager informed Dillard that he was suspending Dillard's inventory financing line of credit. Within days, Dillard entered bankruptcy and a bankruptcy trustee was appointed to liquidate its assets. The bankruptcy judge allowed Ford Credit to repossess all of Dillard's cars for which Ford Credit had provided inventory financing. After sale of the cars, Dillard still owed Ford $54,943. Ford Credit, meanwhile, held $36,283 in Dillard's name in the DPW account.

Ford Credit claimed that it had a security interest in the proceeds of the DPW account. The bankruptcy court ruled that Ford Credit did indeed have a security interest but that it had failed to perfect its security interest. The case reached the U.S. Court of Appeals for the Eleventh Circuit, where Dillard's bankruptcy trustee argued that Ford Credit had no security interest in the DPW account.

The Eleventh Circuit stated that for Ford Credit's alleged security interest in the DPW account to be valid against Dillard's bankruptcy trustee, its security interest had to attach to the property and had to be perfected.

The court noted that a security interest attaches when three conditions are met. First, the debtor (in this case, Dillard), must sign a security agreement that contains a description of the collateral. Second, the creditor (in this case, Ford Credit), must give value. Third, the debtor must have rights in the collateral.

The Eleventh Circuit found that the bankruptcy court had been correct when it concluded that Ford Credit had a security interest that attached to the DPW account. It noted that the financing agreement the parties had signed contained a description of the collateral in that it stated that Ford Credit had a security interest in the DPW account; Ford Credit gave value to Dillard when it financed its inventory; and Dillard had rights in the DPW account, albeit the rights were contingent on a number of conditions.

In addition, the court ruled, Ford Credit had a perfected security interest in the DPW account because it had filed a UCC-1 financing statement that stated that Ford Credit had a security interest in Dillard's "general intangibles" (a term that is defined in the Uniform Commercial Code as any personal property other than goods, accounts, chattel paper, documents, instruments, and money) and in other property Dillard owned. Although the bankruptcy court had ruled that this description of Ford Credit's collateral was too vague, the Eleventh Circuit said that it fulfilled the UCC's requirements.

It ruled that the financing statement's use of the term "general intangible" complied with the UCC's description of collateral requirement. The UCC allows a secured party to file a financing statement that describes the property only by its "type." The court said that it was clear that a type of collateral is, for example, goods, accounts, chattel paper, general tangibles, and the like. Under the notice filing system adopted by the UCC, "[l]ater creditors who find the broadly worded financing statement are expected to inquire into the exact terms of the security agreement by reading the agreement or obtaining assurances from the debtor or creditor." The circuit court then ruled that Ford Credit had a valid, perfected, and enforceable security interest in the DPW account.

▋ Priority

The UCC also has elaborate rules that set forth the priority of creditors in the same collateral. Generally speaking, secured creditors have priority over unsecured creditors; the first perfected secured creditor has priority over a later perfected secured creditor; and a perfected purchase money secured creditor has priority over other secured creditors. Different rules may apply for federal tax liens and for buyers in the ordinary course of business. However, not all buyers who contend that they are buyers in the ordinary course of business actually are.

In 1984 the Transamerica Commercial Finance Corporation and the Transamerica Fleet Leasing Corporation executed a floor plan financing agreement with Tom Wright, who was doing business as T & W Coach Sales. The agreement provided that Transamerica would finance T & W's purchase of vehicles for resale in exchange for a security interest in assets T & W then owned or thereafter acquired. Transamerica properly perfected its security interest in T & W's inventory by filing a financing statement with the secretary of state of Alabama.

From 1984 to 1988, Transamerica financed the purchase of many vehicles for T & W. The security agreement provided that, until the vehicles were sold by T & W, Transamerica had the right to hold in its possession the "certificate of origin" or the "manufacturer's statement of origin" relating to the vehicles purchased by T & W and financed by Transamerica.

In 1987 and 1988, T & W purchased five limousines and a hearse that Transamerica financed. Subsequently, T & W informed Transamerica that it had sold the six vehicles. Wright Leasing Company, which was owned and operated by Tom Wright and which had its place of business at the same address as T & W, purchased them. Although Transamerica knew of the existence of Wright Leasing, it did not know at the time that Wright Leasing had purchased the six vehicles.

Wright Leasing borrowed the money to pay T & W for the vehicles from the Union Bank & Trust Company. As indicia of ownership of the vehicles, Wright Leasing presented certificates of origin and the manufacturer's statements of origin for the vehicles to Union Bank; they did not contain any indication that the vehicles were subject to a security interest in Transamerica. Although Wright Leasing paid T & W for the vehicles, T & W did not pay Transamerica because of "cash flow problems." After Wright Leasing defaulted on its note payments to Union Bank, Union Bank repossessed the vehicles from Wright Leasing.

Transamerica then filed suit against Wright leasing. It contended that it had a prior security interest in the six vehicles. The case reached the Alabama Supreme Court.

Transamerica argued that it had a security interest in the vehicles notwithstanding their sale. It pointed to a section of the UCC that states that "[e]xcept where this article otherwise provides, a security interest continues in collateral notwithstanding sale, exchange or other disposition thereof unless the disposition was authorized by the secured party in the security agreement or otherwise, and also continues in any identifiable proceedings including collections received by the debtor."

Union Bank countered by citing an exception to that section, which states that a buyer in the ordinary course of business "takes free of a security interest created by his seller even though the security interest is perfected and even though the buyer knows of its existence."

The UCC defines such a buyer as a "person who in good faith and without knowledge that the sale to him is in violation of the ownership rights or security interest of a third party in the goods buys in ordinary course from a person in the business of selling goods of that kind." Transamerica conceded that if Union Bank could prove that Wright Leasing satisfied the elements of a "buyer in the ordinary course of business," then Wright Leasing was entitled to take the vehicles free of Transamerica's security interest.

However, the Alabama Supreme Court rejected Union Bank's contention that Wright Leasing was a buyer in the ordinary course.

Among other things, it found that Tom Wright, and therefore Wright Leasing, was aware that T & W had violated the Transamerica security agreement by stating to Transamerica months after the vehicles had been sold that they were still in T & W's possession. One dealer monthly inventory report that T & W prepared for Transamerica indicated that at that time all six vehicles were in T & W's possession even though T & W had transferred five of them to Wright Leasing. Thus, the court ruled, as to those five vehicles, Union Bank failed to prove that Wright Leasing was a buyer in the ordinary course; indeed, the court said, the evidence tended to prove that Wright Leasing was not a buyer in the ordinary course of business.

Finding that Union Bank also failed to prove that the sale of the sixth vehicle was not in violation of the Transamerica security agreement, the court rejected Union Bank's contentions that Wright Leasing was a buyer in the ordinary course. It then ordered judgment for Transamerica.

▌Lease or Security Interest

Instead of selling goods, businesses may lease them. Is a business that leases property obligated to take a security interest to protect itself? The answer is no if the lease is truly a lease; however, if the lease is a conditional sale contract, the lessor/seller should take a security interest or it risks the loss of its property if the lessee/buyer defaults. It therefore is essential that a business that calls its transactions with customers "leases" makes sure that they are in fact leases. The differences between a lease and conditional sale agreement were clearly set forth in a case between Ryder Truck Rental, Inc. and H. D. Sutton.

There, Sutton entered into a truck lease and service agreement with Ryder on February 28, 1983. In 1984, and again in 1986, Sutton leased additional vehicles from Ryder. In 1987 Sutton stopped making payments to Ryder under their agreement. Ryder then filed suit against Sutton and Sutton counterclaimed, alleging that the agreement was actually a conditional sale that was usurious. Sutton's counterclaim sought damages in the amount of twice the sum of the alleged interest paid by Sutton to Ryder under the agreement.

The jury found the contract was a valid lease agreement and returned a verdict for Ryder in the amount of $208,072.13. In addition, the trial court awarded Ryder attorney's fees in the amount of $53,256.50. Sutton appealed to the Supreme Court of Alabama.

The Alabama Supreme Court said that the presence of the following five factors indicate a conditional sale:

1. The lessor is a finance company.

2. The agreement puts all the risk upon the lessee.

3. The agreement provides the same remedies upon the lessee's default in the payment of rent that would be available to a conditional seller or to a mortgagee upon similar delinquency.

4. The agreement provides that the lessee will upon the lessor's request join the lessor in executing UCC financing statements and other assurances the lessor deems necessary for protection of the interest of the lessor in the equipment.

5. There is no appreciable residue in the lessor at the expiration of the lease.

In applying this analysis, courts have identified the absence of any appreciable residue in the lessor at the expiration of the lease as the "most fruitful single test" to distinguish a conditional sale from a lease. Thus, courts place great emphasis on the amount the lessee must pay to acquire title after all payments have been made.

The court applied these five factors in the Sutton case. It first noted that the lessor, Ryder, was not a finance company. It leased vehicles and provided other incidental services to its customers associated with the use of these leased vehicles; the "facts show that Ryder is a full service lease company, not a finance company."

The court also said that the facts showed that the agreement did not put all the risk upon the lessee, Sutton. Under the agreement, Ryder assumed the risk of repairs to the leased vehicles and agreed to replace or furnish substitute vehicles for those that became temporarily inoperable because of mechanical failure. The court noted that Ryder also procured and provided Sutton with liability insurance with combined bodily injury and property damage limits of $750,000 per occurrence. Ryder paid at least one claim on Sutton's behalf in which one of the leased vehicles was completely destroyed and the driver killed. In the court's view, therefore, "Sutton did not assume all the risk of loss under the agreement."

With respect to the third factor—whether the agreement provided the lessor with the same remedies upon default as available to a conditional seller or mortgagee—the court noted that upon a default, a secured creditor or mortgagee may declare all remaining payments due, repossess the property, sell it, and hold the debtor liable for any deficiency. The court said that the Ryder truck lease and service agreement provided that upon default, Ryder could repossess the vehicles and demand that Sutton purchase them. However, the court said, Ryder did not seek to enforce that remedy. Instead, it sought damages for the lease payments that were actually due and payable in addition to the early termination charges provided for under the contract.

Next, the court noted that the agreement contained no provision obligating Sutton to execute a financing statement or provide other assurances to protect Ryder's interest in the vehicles.

Finally, the court said that the facts clearly showed that Ryder retained an appreciable residual at the expiration of the lease and on each anniversary date of the lease when Sutton could exercise his option to purchase under the contract. The court found that at no time was the option price "nominal"; it at all times exceeded the fair market value of the vehicles.

The court then concluded that the lease was a valid lease agreement rather than a conditional sale.

▌A Final Word

Financing on a secured basis can protect creditors. If a debtor fails to pay its debts, the secured creditor may turn to the collateral in which it has a security interest for payment. Of course, creditors must comply with the UCC's requirements for attachment and perfection of a security interest; once they do so, they are likely to find it well worth the effort.

FIVE SECURITY INTEREST CASES

1. After Berryman Farms, Inc. executed a security agreement granting Bank Independent a security interest in the cotton it grew to secure a preexisting indebtedness, the bank filed financing statements in the Probate Court of Franklin County, Alabama, and with the secretary of state's office. Berryman Farms thereafter sold warehouse receipts representing the collateral to the Davis-Hunt Cotton Company. Berryman Farms failed to pay the bank in full from the proceeds of the sale and Davis-Hunt refused the bank's demand for it to pay the remaining debt. The bank then filed an action against Davis-Hunt to determine whether it had a valid perfected security interest in the Berryman Farms cotton that was superior to Davis-Hunt's rights.

The bank's security agreement described the collateral as "[a]ll farm supplies, farm products, crops, timber to be cut, and all natural increases thereof now or at any time hereafter located or growing on ASCS Farm No. S-2 in Franklin County, Alabama, and all such crops after they have been harvested." However, Davis-Hunt pointed out that a creditor with a security interest in crops must file a financing statement that includes the following information: "A financing statement covering . . . crops growing or to be grown . . . must show that it covers this type of collateral, must show that it is to be cross-indexed in the real estate mortgage records and must contain a description of the real estate. If the debtor does not have an interest of record in the real estate the financing statement must also show the name of a record owner." Davis-Hunt contended that the bank's financing statement was inadequate to perfect its security interest because it failed to show the name of the record owner of the real estate on which the crops were grown and because it failed to definitely describe the real estate on which the crops were grown. The bank conceded that its financing statement had minor errors but maintained that they were not misleading and that its statement substantially complied with the UCC's requirements.

The Supreme Court of Alabama ruled, though, that the bank's failure to show on the financing statement the name of the record owner of the real estate and that it was to be cross indexed in the real estate mortgage records was "fatal to perfection of its security interest." Those omissions, the court found, were more than a "minor error." The court then said that because the bank had failed to show that Davis-Hunt received the warehouse receipts representing Berryman Farms' cotton crop with knowledge of the bank's unperfected security interest, Davis-Hunt cut off the bank's unperfected security interest when it purchased the warehouse receipts for value. (Davis-Hunt Cotton Co., Inc. v. Bank Independent, 541 So.2d 5 (Alabama 1989).)

2. Sometime between 1970 and 1972, Peter J. Nikolaisen, the owner of Nikolaisen's Sunset 44 Restaurant, agreed that Siegfried Reinhardt, a well-known St. Louis artist and a close friend, could display and sell his art work at Nikolaisen's restaurant. They also agreed that Reinhardt could charge his food and drink purchases at the restaurant and pay later. In December 1978 Nikolaisen loaned $3,000 to Reinhardt that Reinhardt agreed to repay in full by June 30, 1979, or in monthly installments beginning on July 31, 1979. Reinhardt also orally agreed that the paintings in Nikolaisen's possession would serve as security for the repayment of the $3,000 loan and any outstanding debt he owed for food and drink. At the time of Reinhardt's death in October 1984, 45 of his paintings were on display at the restaurant. Sometime after Reinhardt's death, a representative of his estate asked Nikolaisen to return the paintings to the estate. Nikolaisen returned 41 of the 45 works; he held four paintings as collateral for what he said was a $7,693.17 debt. A representative of Reinhardt's estate then challenged his security interest.

The court noted that the UCC provides that an oral security agreement is enforceable where the collateral is in the possession of the secured party. The court also said that Nikolaisen was under no obligation to file a claim against Reinhardt's estate because he had a security interest in the art. State law provides that a creditor "may" surrender its security and be paid out of the assets of the estate but nothing in the law compels a creditor to surrender its security until it receives payment. (Reinhardt v. Nikolaisen, 775 S.W.2d 284 (Ct. App. Missouri 1989).)

3. On March 1, 1982, the Tascosa National Bank of Amarillo extended a loan to T & L Ventures, Inc., doing business as The Video Connection, in the amount of $30,006. T & L granted the bank a lien on certain of its assets and the bank filed a financing statement with the Texas secretary of state on March 4 that described the collateral as "[v]ideo software and hardware, computer games hardware and software, all inventory, furniture, fixtures of [T & L] located at Amarillo, Potter County, Texas." From time to time, the bank renewed the debt and extended additional funds to T & L, all secured by promissory notes and secured by the same collateral.

On March 7, 1982, the Borg Warner Acceptance Corporation executed and entered into an inventory security agreement with T & L that granted Borg-Warner a security interest in inventory purchased by T & L with proceeds of loans made by Borg-Warner. Borg-Warner perfected its security interest—which was a purchase money security interest—by filing a financing statement describing the collateral with the Texas secretary of state and by notifying the bank of Borg Warner's security interest in T & L's inventory. Following the perfection of its purchase money security interest, Borg-Warner began financing the acquisition of inventory by T & L under a floor-planning arrangement pursuant to which Borg-Warner purchased from vendors and paid directly to the vendors the invoice purchase price of inventory acquired by T & L for resale. Borg-Warner continued financing T & L through most of the spring of 1986.

T & L defaulted and, on May 11, 1986, the bank repossessed T & L's inventory and placed it in a warehouse. Borg-Warner demanded that the bank deliver the inventory to it but the bank refused. Borg-Warner filed suit against the bank alleging wrongful conversion of the inventory in which it said it held a purchase money security interest. While the suit was pending, the bank and Borg-Warner agreed to sell the inventory; net proceeds totaled approximately $140,000. The court that issued a decision in this case noted that the general rule of priority among conflicting security interests in the same collateral where both interests are perfected by filing is that the secured party who first files a financing statement prevails. However, it said that the UCC has a special rule for a purchase money security interest in inventory.

A purchase money security interest in inventory has priority over a conflicting security interest in the same inventory and also has priority in identifiable cash proceeds received on or before the delivery of the inventory to the debtor (in this case, T & L) if the purchase money security interest was perfected at the time the debtor received possession of the inventory; the purchase money creditor gave notice in writing to all other secured creditors who had filed financing statements covering the same kind of inventory before the date of filing by the purchase money creditor; the other secured creditors received any required notification within five years before the debtor received possession of the inventory; and the notification stated that the purchase money creditor expected to acquire a purchase money security interest in the debtor's inventory and described the inventory by item or type. Finding that Borg-Warner had complied with the UCC's requirements, the court ruled that it was entitled to priority in T & L's inventory. (Borg-Warner Acceptance Corp. v. Tascosa National Bank, 784 S.W.2d 129 (Ct. App. Texas 1990).)

4. In May 1985 Sam and Emily Ritter entered into a security agreement granting the NBD-Sandusky Bank a securing interest in their farm equipment. The security agreement also contained an "after-acquired property" clause covering equipment the Ritters purchased in the future. NBD filed a correlating financing statement on May 30, 1985. On July 23, Sam Ritter negotiated the purchase of certain pieces of farm equipment from the Laethem Farm Service Company to be financed by the John Deere Company. He executed a purchase order for one used John Deere model 6600 Diesel Combine, one set of new John Deere bin extensions, and one set of used float springs. He also agreed to rent a John Deere 16-foot Quick Tach platform with a view toward purchasing this additional piece of equipment. Ritter took possession of the farm equipment that same day.

On July 31, 1985, Ritter agreed to purchase the 16-foot Quick Tach platform and executed three documents, including a second purchase order covering the platform, the Model 6600 Combine, the bin extensions, and the float springs. He also signed a combination variable rate loan contract and security agreement stating that he was applying to John Deere for a loan to be used to finance the balance owed on the purchase order from Laethem. The agreement specified that "if this Loan Contract is accepted by Lender," Ritter promised to repay the amount loaned plus a finance charge and agreed to secure his indebtedness by granting John Deere a security interest in the equipment. Lastly, Ritter executed a correlating financing statement listing John Deere as the secured party, himself as the debtor, and the John Deere 6600 Combine with bin extensions and float springs, and John Deere 16-foot Quick Tach platform, as collateral.

On August 7, 1985, John Deere filed a fully executed financing statement covering the subject equipment with the Sanilac County Register of Deeds. On August 15, a representative of John Deere signed the loan contract and security agreement. In December 1985 the Ritters borrowed a total of $60,917.20 from NBD. Subsequently, the Ritters defaulted under their obligations to NBD and the bank filed suit against the Ritters, Laethem, and John Deere alleging that its perfected security interest in the equipment had priority over all competing claims. The trial court ruled that the bank had priority despite John Deere's claimed purchase money security interest because John Deere's purchase money security interest was not perfected until August 15, 1985, more than 20 days from July 23, 1985, the date on which Ritter received possession of the collateral, and thus lost the priority otherwise afforded it by the UCC.

The Michigan Supreme Court reversed that decision. It found no dispute that John Deere's security interest was a purchase money security interest because it was "taken by a [creditor] who by making advances or incurring an obligation gives value to enable the debtor to acquire rights in or the use of collateral [and] such value [was] in fact so used." The court said that John Deere's security interest was valid, perfected, and enforceable on August 7, when it filed the financing statement, well before August 15, the date a John Deere representative signed the documents. Thus, the court ruled that because John Deere perfected its purchase money security interest within 20 days from the date Ritter received the collateral, its purchase money security interest was entitled to priority over all competing claims. (NBD-Sandusky Bank v. Ritter, 471 N.W.2d 340 (Michigan 1991).)

5. On March 27, 1984, Reese M. Williams, the Reese M. Williams Trust, and Crystal Bar, Inc. (the "sellers") sold 200 shares of capital stock, liquor license no. RL-5877, business assets and inventory of Crystal Bar, Inc. to Cosmic, Inc. under a written contract. Cosmic made a $50,000 downpayment, assumed $40,468.58 of the sellers' debts, and promised to amortize the $164,531.42 balance due at 12 percent interest over 10 years. The sellers did not perfect a security interest in the assets they sold.

On December 18, 1984, Cosmic assigned the property it had acquired on March 27 to Virgil Hauff for $284,877.75; in addition, Hauff agreed to assume all of Cosmic's obligations under the March 27 agreement. However, Hauff failed to make the payments to the sellers required of Cosmic under the March 27 agreement that were due on the first day of August and September 1989. Furthermore, the Internal Revenue Service (IRS) claimed a lien on the property described in the March 27 and December 18 agreements for personal income taxes allegedly due from Virgil and Karen Hauff and for withholding and social security taxes the IRS claimed they owed.

The IRS sought to satisfy its lien from Hauff's assets, particularly the liquor license. The court noted that because the sellers had failed to properly file the required financing statements they had only an unperfected security interest in the liquor license. Because an unperfected security interest is subordinate to the rights of a lien creditor, the court said that the IRS lien was entitled to first priority. The court did state, though, that if the sellers had perfected their security interest they would have been protected from the IRS lien. (Crystal Bar, Inc. v. Cosmic, Inc., 758 F. Supp. 543 (D.S.D. 1991).)

Security Interest Checklist

✓ Unsecured creditors rely on a business's goodwill to be paid; secured creditors have something more—collateral. Indeed, creditors holding purchase money security interests have something even greater—the very goods that they sold to the debtor serve as collateral for payment of the debtor's obligations.

✓ The Uniform Commercial Code governs security interests. Under the UCC, creditors may take a security interest in all of a debtor's property, including its goods, instruments, accounts, inventory, and equipment.

✓ To begin with, a creditor that wants to be a secured creditor needs a security agreement, which generally is an agreement signed by the debtor that grants a security interest to the creditor in certain described collateral.

✓ For a security agreement to be enforceable against the debtor, the secured creditor must provide value to the debtor and the debtor must have rights in the collateral.

✓ To give a creditor priority over other creditors in the collateral, the secured creditor must perfect its security interest. It generally does so by filing one or more UCC-1 financing statements in the appropriate state or local filing offices. They are intended to provide notice to other creditors that the secured creditor has an interest in the debtor's collateral as described in the financing statement.

FINANCING TRANSACTIONS WITH LETTERS OF CREDIT

▌Structure of a Letter of Credit Transaction ▌ Strict Compliance
▌ Letters of Credit and Bankruptcy ▌ A Final Word

On April 23, 1981, Central Bank issued a document entitled "Irrevocable Commercial Letter of Credit No. 02408" in the amount of $4.5 million. The bank issued the credit at the request of its customer, United Machinery Services, Inc., in favor of the Philadelphia Gear Corporation, as beneficiary, to allow United Machinery to purchase goods from Philadelphia Gear.

The letter of credit provided that it could accommodate individual drafts from Philadelphia Gear in maximum amounts of $75,000 to a limit of $4.5 million. Each draft Philadelphia Gear presented under the credit was required to bear the notation "Drawn under Letter of Credit of Central Bank," and a copy of the letter of credit was to accompany each draft. In addition, the letter of credit conditioned payment upon presentation by Philadelphia Gear's intermediary, the Provident National Bank of Philadelphia, of an "inland bill of lading evidencing shipment of any of the above described units to United Machinery, Inc."

Sometime during the latter half of 1981, relations between United Machinery and Philadelphia Gear soured. United refused to pay for goods that it claimed it had not ordered; Philadelphia Gear, maintaining that it had delivered the goods pursuant to a contract, demanded payment. As a result of this dispute, Philadelphia Gear, through Provident, tendered six drafts on the letter of credit in late December 1981. Several days later,

Central decided that it would not pay the drafts and returned them to Provident with notice to that effect. The notice stated that the drafts were being returned "due to their non-compliance with the terms of the relevant credit." Philadelphia Gear then filed suit against Central for breach of contract, contending that Central had wrongfully dishonored its drafts. The case reached the U.S. Court of Appeals for the Fifth Circuit, which ruled that Philadelphia Gear was not entitled to payment of the drafts it presented because it knew that they were nonconforming.

▌Structure of a Letter of Credit Transaction

Letters of credit are near-mechanical forms of payment designed to facilitate commercial exchange at a relatively modest cost. A letter of credit transaction usually comprises three separate contracts.

First, the issuing bank enters into a contract with its customer to issue the letter of credit, which provides, among other things, that the customer will reimburse the issuer for proper payments the issuer makes under the letter of credit.

Second, there is a contract between the issuing bank and the party receiving the letter of credit, who is known as the beneficiary.

Third, there is a contract between the customer who obtained the letter of credit and the beneficiary, usually involving the sale of goods or the provision of some services.

Significantly, the obligations and duties created by the contract—the letter of credit—between the issuer and the beneficiary are completely separate from the underlying transaction, with absolutely no consequence given the underlying transaction unless the credit expressly incorporates its terms. As a consequence, the issuer's duty to pay is conditioned solely upon the letter of credit's terms, which usually only require that the beneficiary present facially conforming documents. Moreover, the issuer has no obligation to go beyond a facial examination of the documents tendered by the beneficiary in determining whether payment is warranted (and, indeed, it may incur liability if it does so). Most commonly, the issuer's promise to pay under a letter of credit is irrevocable. These features facilitate economic exchange because they can provide comfort to a seller of goods or services that it will be paid for them; the seller is able to rely on the financial standing of a bank rather than a business about which it may know very little.

Letters of credit are different from guarantees, although they serve a similar purpose. A true guarantee creates a secondary obligation whereby the guarantor promises to answer for the debt of another and may be called upon to perform once the primary obligor has failed to perform. Because a guarantee is ancillary to the underlying contract, a dispute as to the rights and obligations of a guarantor can only be resolved by a factual determination of the rights and obligations of the parties to the underlying contract. A bank that issues a letter of credit, however, creates a primary obligation as principal, not as an agent of its customer. Thus, on the issuance of a letter of credit, the bank assumes a primary obligation independent of the underlying contract to make payment from its own assets, not from the assets of its customer.

▌Strict Compliance

Because an issuer's duty to pay arises exclusively from the terms of the letter of credit, with no defenses beyond those terms, its liability turns on whether the beneficiary has performed in accordance with the terms and conditions contained in the letter of credit. The documentation necessary to support payment must conform exactly to the requirements of the letter of credit; otherwise, the issuer is entitled to refuse payment.

The doctrine of strict compliance is firmly grounded in commercial reality. In the event an issuer pays a draft that does not conform to the letter of credit, the issuer loses its right to reimbursement from its customer. In this event, the beneficiary's debt is satisfied and the customer escapes liability on both the underlying and letter of credit contracts while the issuer incurs a corresponding liability—without defense or recourse. A case that helps to illustrate the requirements of strict compliance was filed a few years ago by Exotic Traders Far East Buying Office against Exotic Trading U.S.A., Inc. and BayBank Boston, N.A.

That case stemmed from two sales contracts. In the first, Exotic Traders Far East (the "seller") agreed to sell Exotic Trading U.S.A. (the "buyer") 2,000 holsters. The total price was $2,200. The buyer's sales agent, Burton M. Kaufman, obtained an irrevocable documentary letter of credit from BayBank for $2,200. To obtain payment under the letter of credit, the seller was required to present a sight draft accompanied by the following documents:

1. A signed commercial invoice

2. A special U.S. Customs invoice

3. A packing list

4. An inspection certificate signed by the seller

5. A signed air waybill

6. A copy of a telex sent one day prior to shipment covering the holsters, FOB Seoul. The telex was required to state: the cost of goods, date of shipment, air waybill number, estimated date of arrival, airline, master air waybill number, and number of cartons.

The seller shipped the holsters on June 13, 1985; they arrived in the United States on June 14, 1985. The buyer sold the goods in transit to Intermark Trading, which took possession of them. Neither the buyer nor Intermark paid the seller for the goods.

On June 21, 1985, the seller made a demand for payment on the $2,200 letter of credit. Although the demand was accompanied by all the required documents, they varied in two aspects from the literal terms of the letter of credit: the telex required by the letter of credit was sent one day after shipment of the goods, rather than one day before shipment, and the commercial invoice indicated that the goods had been shipped FOB Korea, rather than FOB Seoul. Relying on these discrepancies, BayBank refused the demand for payment.

In September 1985, the seller agreed to sell the buyer 3,000 electronic stun guns for a total price of $30,000. Kaufman obtained an irrevocable documentary letter of credit from BayBank for $30,000; to obtain payment, the seller had to present essentially the same kind of documents as were required in the first transaction.

The seller shipped the stun guns on October 12, 1985; they arrived in the United States on October 14, 1985. The buyer again sold them in transit to Intermark, which took possession of them. Neither the buyer nor Intermark paid the seller for the goods.

On October 17, 1985, the seller made a demand for payment on the $30,000 letter of credit accompanied by all the required documents. Again, there were two discrepancies between the documents it presented and the literal terms of the letter of credit: the required telex was sent on the day of shipment, rather than one day prior to shipment, and the telex did not contain the cost of goods sold. Because of these discrepancies, Baybank refused the demand for payment.

The court that issued a decision in the seller's lawsuit against the buyer and the bank recognized that the law requires that a demand for payment comply strictly with the terms of a letter of credit. It said, however, that a bank may not reject a demand for payment on "the basis of a hypertechnical reading of a letter of credit."

It noted that in one decision, a court ruled that a bank was not justified in refusing to pay under a letter of credit that required a certificate that stated that "the goods were in conformity with the order" when the certificate it received said the goods were found "conforming to the conditions stipulated on the order-stock sheets."

In another decision, there were three discrepancies between the documents presented by the beneficiary and the terms of the letter of credit that the court said the bank could not rely on to deny payment. Those discrepancies were that the draft was drawn by Flagship Cruises, Inc. instead of Flagship Cruises, Ltd.; the draft did not contain a statement that it was in conjunction with certain collateral documents as required by the letter of credit; and the draft did not say it was drawn under "NEMNB Credit No. 18506" but rather simply identified "No. 18506." The court said that permitting the discrepancies was not a retreat "from rigorous insistence on compliance with letter of credit requirements . . . [but] recognizing that a variance between documents specified and documents submitted is not fatal if there is *no* possibility that the documents could mislead the paying bank to its detriment."

Relying on those two decisions, the court in the Exotic Traders case found that the discrepancies between the documents presented by the seller and the terms of the letters of credit were not sufficient to justify BayBank's refusal to pay. "None of the discrepancies in the presented documents could have misled anyone."

The court acknowledged that each telex was to be sent the day before the goods were shipped but that the holster telex was sent the day after the goods were shipped and the stun gun telex was sent the same day the goods were shipped. Nevertheless, both telexes indicated that they were received before the goods were due to arrive in this country. Consequently, the court said, BayBank knew that both telexes had served their intended purpose of notifying the buyer of shipment, so as to avoid the accrual of warehouse fees. "The fact that the telexes were sent a matter of hours late is, therefore, of no substantive significance."

The court also was not troubled by the fact that the commercial invoice for the holsters indicated that the shipment was FOB Korea rather than FOB Seoul and that the stun gun telex had failed to mention the cost of the goods because the other documents presented "clearly rectified these technical variances." It concluded that "[t]echnical inconsistencies between the documents presented and those specified under a letter of credit do not justify the undermining of an otherwise valid commercial transaction."

▌ Letters of Credit and Bankruptcy

One of the key advantages of a letter of credit to a seller is that the seller can rely on the bank's financial condition rather than the buyer's. This can be especially important if the buyer enters bankruptcy before paying for the goods; a seller with a letter of credit backing up the buyer's obligation need not be concerned because it can simply draw on the letter of credit notwithstanding the buyer's bankruptcy. Or is that prohibited?

A very small number of court decisions have allowed debtors in bankruptcy to interfere with a beneficiary's right to draw under a letter of credit. Typically, they do so on the theory that allowing a draw would be harmful to the debtor's bankruptcy estate because it would increase the fixed obligations of the debtor (namely, its obligation to reimburse the issuing bank for the amount of the draw) while providing no benefit to the debtor.

Fortunately, though, the vast majority of the courts that have decided whether an issuing bank may be prohibited from paying on a letter of credit merely because the bank's customer—the entity that requested the letter of credit—is in bankruptcy have recognized the independent nature of the issuing bank's obligation and have ruled that no injunction is permitted. A recent decision by the federal district court for the Southern District of New York illustrates the majority—and correct—rule.

That case arose from the decision by Latino Americano de Reaseguros, S.A., a Panamanian reinsurance company, to enter into contracts in 1984 and 1985 with the Insurance Corporation of Hannover by which Latino agreed to reinsure certain risks of Hannover. Latino backed up its obligations to Hannover with a letter of credit issued by Banco Cafetero, a Panamanian bank, for the benefit of Hannover.

On April 6, 1990, Latino went into statutory reorganization, a rough equivalent of bankruptcy, under the protection of the Panamanian National Reinsurance Commission. Alleging that Latino owed it more that $1.7 million as a result of breaching the reinsurance agreements, Hannover then filed suit against Banco Cafetero in California, seeking payment under the letter of credit. Hannover also brought suit against Latino in New York seeking to attach the assets of a New York trust Latino established for the protection of the rights of its policyholders and beneficiaries under New York insurance regulations.

On November 18, 1991, just before trial of the action in California, Latino filed an ancillary proceeding in bankruptcy court in New York. The New York bankruptcy court then issued orders enjoining Hannover from proceeding with its California action against Banco Cafetero as well as its action against Latino in New York. Hannover appealed to the district court.

The district court said that the bankruptcy court's order enjoining Hannover's action against Banco Cafetero was "based on an incorrect theory of law." Hannover's action against Banco Cafetero, the district court emphasized, was not brought against Latino nor against Latino's property. It said that Banco Cafetero's letter of credit was an irrevocable and unconditional promise on the part of Banco Cafetero to pay Hannover upon the presentation of specified documents. Hannover's action was against the bank, not Latino, and the money to be used in making the payment was the bank's money, not Hannover's.

Furthermore, the court said, the fact that the bank held Latino's collateral to secure the bank's extension of credit to Latino "has no bearing on the beneficiary's right to receive payment from the bank on the bank's contract." The court concluded that allowing Latino's bankruptcy to interfere with payment of clean, irrevocable letters of credit "would vitiate the purpose of such letters. Letters of credit are an ingenious device of international commerce. By interposing the bank between buyer and seller, as an independent party, they permit a seller to ship merchandise abroad with confidence that payment is guaranteed by a bank; and permit the purchaser to pay with the assurance that the payment will not be released to the seller unless the seller delivers proof of the shipment of the goods." The court recognized that one of the primary purposes of letters of credit is to relieve a seller/shipper from worry as to the purchaser's solvency because the seller looks not to the purchaser, but to the bank, for payment. "If the payment of letters of credit could be stayed, as here, merely because the account party had obtained the protection of a bankruptcy court, this would do incalculable harm to international commerce." It concluded that letters of credit "would no longer reliably perform the function they were designed for."

❙ A Final Word

A seller can be protected from a buyer's failure to pay by a properly drafted letter of credit. Well recognized and respected in the law, a letter of credit shifts the burden of payment to a bank—at least once the seller properly complies with the requirements of the letter of credit. Thus, assuming strict compliance (and the solvency of the issuing bank), letters of credit are as good as money in hand.

FIVE LETTER OF CREDIT CASES

1. A complaint filed by the Hendry Construction Company, Inc. against the Bank of Hattiesburg alleged that Hendry had an agreement with the Producers Marketing Association to renovate, refurbish, remodel, and construct certain improvements on land described in the contract; that Hendry sought financing and obtained a "letter of credit" from the Deposit Guaranty National Bank dated July 22, 1981; and that the letter of credit acted as confirmation to Hendry that when it met all conditions and after approval by the Farmers Home Administration, it would receive the amount set out in the letter. The July 21 "letter of credit" from Deposit Guaranty to Hendry stated:

> This letter is to advise you that the Producers Marketing Association (AAL) has applied to the Farmers Home Administration for a loan in the amount of $800,000 with Deposit National Bank of Hattiesburg acting as the lender to fund this loan. This application was approved by the Farmers Home Administration and Deposit Guaranty National Bank on April 29, 1981, subject to certain conditions that the Producers Marketing Association must meet in order for the loan to be funded. The Producers Marketing Association has a copy of this if you should desire to review these conditions that have to be met prior to loan closing. The Producers Marketing Association has asked us to set aside $275,000 for plant renovation under contract to your construction company. This letter will act as confirmation to you that when all conditions have been met and approval is granted by the Farmers Home Administration for us to fund the loan, a check in the amount of $275,000 will be made payable to Hendry Construction Company and Producers Marketing Association.

Hendry contended in his complaint that when he delivered the letter to the Bank of Hattiesburg, he relied on the Bank of Hattiesburg to obtain construction funds; that the bank advanced $138,543 and refused to make any further advances, disregarding the "letter of credit"; and that because the bank would not lend any more money, Hendry had difficulty in completing his construction contract and suffered $200,000 in damages.

The case reached the Supreme Court of Mississippi, which examined the "letter of credit" and found that it met "none of the requisites which would mandate finding this a 'letter of credit.'" It did not provide that Deposit Guaranty would honor drafts or other demands upon compliance with conditions specified in the letter. Indeed, the letter was not even addressed to the Hattiesburg Bank and there was no indication that the Hattiesburg Bank had ever agreed to rely upon the Deposit Guaranty letter or that it did rely on it. The court ruled that the motion by the Bank of Hattiesburg for summary judgment "should have been sustained." (Hendry Construction Co. v. Bank of Hattiesburg, 562 So.2d 100 (Mississippi 1990).)

2. On July 6, 1981, the First National Bank of Mason City, Iowa, issued a letter of credit on behalf of Carl Hankenson, doing business as Hank Oil Co., Inc., Clear Lake, Iowa. The letter of credit contained the following language: "This Commercial Letter of Credit shall remain in force for a period of six (6) months from August 5, 1981, and will be available to Conoco, Inc. on its sight draft for 100% invoice cost to be accompanied by a letter of demand from Conoco, Inc. and supported by commercial invoices." In addition, the letter of credit incorporated the provisions of the *Uniform Customs and Practice for Documentary Credits (1974 Revision)*, International Chamber of Commerce brochure no. 290, which provides that a letter of credit may be either revocable or irrevocable, and that absent clear indication of irrevocability, letters of credits are deemed revocable. The means by which irrevocability may be indicated are not spelled out in brochure no. 290; however, it does not require that the word "irrevocable" be used, only that the words "clearly indicate" that the letter is indeed irrevocable.

On November 12, 1981, First National revoked the letter of credit. The following day, Conoco presented its sight draft and supporting documents to the bank; the bank refused to make payment. Conoco then sued the bank for wrongful dishonor. First National argued that the language in the letter of credit relating to the fact that it would remain in force for a period of six months only designated an expiration date, and nothing more. The court rejected that position. It said that the letter of credit said that it "shall remain in force"; in addition to setting forth an expiration date, it clearly also required that the letter of credit remain effective until that date was reached. The court then ruled that the letter of credit had been irrevocable and that Conoco was entitled to judgment against the bank for wrongful dishonor. (Conoco, Inc. v. Norwest Bank Mason City, N.A., 767 F.2d 470 (8th Cir. 1985).)

3. When Dessaleng Beyene agreed to sell two prefabricated houses to Mohammed Sofan, a resident of the Yemen Arab Republic, Sofan attempted to finance the purchase through the use of a letter of credit issued by the Yemen Bank for Reconstruction and Development in favor of Beyene. The Yemen Bank designated the Irving Trust Company as the confirming bank for the letter of credit and Irving subsequently notified Beyene of the letter's terms and conditions. Beyene designated the National Bank of Washington as his collecting bank. After National sent Irving all of the documents required under the terms of the letter of credit, Irving telephoned National to inform it of several discrepancies in the documents, including the fact that the bill of lading listed the party to be notified by the shipping company as Mohammed Soran instead of Mohammed Sofan. Irving nonetheless undertook to request authorization from the Yemen Bank to pay the letter of credit despite the discrepancy; the Yemen Bank refused to provide the authorization, and Irving refused to pay Beyene.

Beyene filed suit against Irving, and the case reached the U.S. Court of Appeals for the Second Circuit. The court noted that the terms of a letter of credit generally require the beneficiary of the letter to submit to the issuing bank documents such as an invoice and a bill of lading to provide the buyer with some assurance that it will receive the goods for which it bargained and arranged payment. The issuing bank, or a bank that acts as confirming bank for the issuer, takes on an absolute duty to pay the amount of the letter of credit to the beneficiary so long as the beneficiary complies with the terms of the letter. To protect the issuing or confirming bank, the court said that this absolute duty does not arise unless the beneficiary strictly complies with the terms of the letter.

The court added that literal compliance is generally essential so as not to impose an obligation upon the bank that it did not undertake and so as not to jeopardize the bank's right to indemnity from its customer. It ruled that while some variations in a bill of lading might be so insignificant as not to relieve the issuing or confirming bank of its obligation to pay, the misspelling in the bill of lading of Sofan's name as Soran was a material discrepancy that entitled Irving to refuse to honor the letter of credit. The court said that this was not a case "where the name intended is unmistakably clear despite what is obviously a typographical error, as might be the case if, for example, 'Smith' were misspelled 'Smithh.' " Nor did Beyene contend that in the Middle East Soran would obviously be recognized as an inadvertent misspelling of the name Sofan. Furthermore, the court said, Sofan was not a name that was inconsequential to the document, because Sofan was the person to whom the shipper was to give notice of the arrival of the goods and the misspelling of his name "could well have resulted in his nonreceipt of the goods and his justifiable refusal to reimburse Irving for the credit." It then ruled against Beyene and in favor of Irving. (Beyene v. Irving Trust Co., 762 F.2d 4 (2d Cir. 1985).)

4. At the request of its customer, the Orion Manufacturing Company, the Penn Square Bank, N.A. issued an irrevocable standby letter of credit in the amount of $145,200 for the benefit of the Philadelphia Gear Corporation, one of Orion's suppliers. After Penn Square was declared insolvent by the comptroller of the currency and the Federal Deposit Insurance Corporation (FDIC) was appointed receiver, Orion presented eight drafts under the letter of credit to the FDIC. The FDIC disaffirmed "any and all" obligations under the letter of credit and stated that it would not honor any of drafts thereunder. Philadelphia Gear filed a lawsuit against the FDIC, and the case reached the U.S. Court of Appeals for the Tenth Circuit. The court first ruled that the letter of credit was an insured "deposit" within the meaning of federal law. It then stated that Philadelphia Gear, as the beneficiary of the letter of credit, was the depositor for purposes of entitlement to insurance proceeds from the FDIC. (Philadelphia Gear Corp. v. Federal Deposit Insurance Corp., 751 F.2d 1131 (10th Cir. 1985).

5. Since 1978, Barclay Knitwear Co., Inc. and its subsidiary Brooke Sweater Co., Inc., importers of men's and boys' wearing apparel, had successfully used King'swear Enterprises Ltd. and its principal, Amy Lee, as their agent in Taiwan. Barclay would negotiate directly with the local Taiwan manufacturers regarding the style, quality, and quantity of the merchandise it desired. It would pay for the goods by having a letter of credit issued to King'swear, which would then assign the credit to the specified local manufacturer. Barclay gave Amy Lee presigned blank inspection certificates and authorized her to sign them on Barclay's behalf once the goods were ready for delivery. In February 1985, Barclay entered into contracts with King'swear and other Taiwan manufacturers for the production of approximately 13,000 dozen men's and boys' sweaters, with payment to be made by irrevocable letter of credit. In all, Barclay caused six letters of credit to be issued, each naming King'swear as beneficiary.

One of the six, an assignable $209,650 letter of credit, was issued by National Westminster Bank, N.A. Barclay alleged that instead of transferring that letter of credit to the local manufacturers with whom Barclay had made arrangements, Lee, apparently in deep financial trouble, assigned them to manufacturers not known to Barclay. On March 9, 1985, King'swear assigned $180,000 available under National Westminster's letter of credit to Lucky Jewel Knitwear Corp., which, on April 25, 1985, applied in writing to the Bank of Communications to negotiate its draft for $180,000 under the letter of credit. After determining that the draft and the accompanying documents complied with the terms of the credit, the Bank of Communications negotiated the draft and applied $50,250.26 of the proceeds in payment to Lucky Jewel's loan indebtedness to it, $1,901.68 for banking charges, and the balance of $128,657.06 as a credit to Lucky Jewel's account at the bank. On the same day, the bank forwarded the draft, accompanied by the documents required by the letter of credit, to National Westminster for payment.

On May 13, National Westminster advised the Bank of Communications that it would not honor the draft because of a discrepancy in the documents. Barclay then went to court to obtain a temporary restraining order prohibiting National Westminster from honoring drafts drawn against the various letters of credit pending a hearing on its motion for a preliminary injunction. In support of its motion it asserted that it had been defrauded by its own agent—it said that Lee had assigned the letter of credit to Lucky Jewel, a manufacturer unknown to Barclay, to alter the specifications of Barclay's order and thus make the goods cheaper to produce. Barclay further alleged that Lee had submitted fraudulent documentation under the letter of credit, including an inspection certificate signed by Barclay, purportedly representing that the goods had been manufactured in accordance with contract specifications.

The court found that the Bank of Communications was entitled to payment notwithstanding Barclay's allegations of fraud because the Bank of Communications negotiated the draft under circumstances that made it a holder in due course, which is defined in the law as one who takes an instrument for value, in good faith, and without notice that it is overdue or has been dishonored or of any defense against or claim to it on the part of any person. Finding that the documents the Bank of Communications submitted with the draft strictly complied with the terms of the letter of credit, it rejected Barclay's contentions. (Barclay Knitwear v. King'swear Enterprises, Ltd., 533 N.Y.S.2d 724 (1st Dep't 1988).)

Letter of Credit Checklist

✓ A letter of credit is an independent obligation on the part of the issuer to make payments to the beneficiary upon presentation of required documents. It is separate and apart from the underlying contract between the applicant and the beneficiary. It also is distinct from the applicant's contractual obligation to reimburse the issuer for any payment it makes under the letter of credit.

✓ Though they serve a similar purpose, letters of credit are different from guarantees. A creditor is subject to defenses by a guarantor that a letter of credit issuer simply may not raise.

✓ A properly drafted letter of credit essentially can remove a seller's credit risk from a transaction.

✓ To obtain payment under a letter of credit, a beneficiary must strictly comply with all of the terms.

✓ The vast majority of courts rule that the bankruptcy of an applicant should not affect the independent obligation of the issuing bank to make payment under the letter of credit.

29

HANDLING CHECKS MARKED "PAID IN FULL"

▌Accord and Satisfaction ▌UCC Section 1-207 ▌States Split
▌A Final Word

A number of years ago, the Horn Waterproofing Company agreed to repair a leaking roof on a building owned by the Bushwick Iron & Steel Co., Inc. After two days of work, Horn concluded that the building needed a new roof and submitted a bill for the work it already had performed. Bushwick disputed the charge and Horn revised the bill down from $1,241 to $1,080.

Bushwick nonetheless remained unsatisfied with the charges and sent Horn a check for only $500. The check bore the following notation: "This check is accepted in full payment, settlement, satisfaction, release and discharge of any and all claims and/or demands of whatsoever kind and nature." Directly under that language, Horn printed the words "under protest," endorsed the check with its stamp, and deposited the $500 into its bank account.

Horn then filed suit against Bushwick, seeking $580 as the balance due on its revised bill. Bushwick moved for summary judgment on the ground that Horn's acceptance and negotiation of the check constituted an accord and satisfaction. The trial court rejected Bushwick's contentions, but an appellate court reversed. The case reached the New York Court of Appeals.

▌ Accord and Satisfaction

It has long been the general rule in most states across the country that if a debt or claim is disputed or contingent at the time of payment, the payment, when accepted, of a part of the whole debt satisfies the debtor's obligation. The theory underlying this common law rule of accord and satisfaction is that the parties entered into a new contract displacing all or part of their original one: The debtor made an offer to settle the dispute when it sent the creditor a check marked payment in full; the creditor had the right to accept the check with the proposed terms or to reject the offer by returning the check. Although it presented creditors with a rather difficult choice upon receiving partial payment from debtors—do they accept the check as payment in full or completely reject the check to be able to file suit for the amount to which they claim they are entitled?—the rule of accord and satisfaction generally was accepted as a legitimate and expeditious means of settling contract disputes. As one court stated, "The law wisely favors settlements, and where there is a real and genuine contest between the parties and a settlement is had without fraud or misrepresentation for an amount determined upon as a compromise between the conflicting claims such settlement should be upheld, although such amount is materially less than the amount claimed by the person to whom it is paid."

▌ UCC Section 1-207

Despite the general rule of accord and satisfaction, lawyers often have contended that Section 1-207 of the Uniform Commercial Code (UCC) should apply to "full payment check" cases. Section 1-207 states that "[a] party who with explicit reservation of rights performs or promises performance or assents to performance in a manner demanded or offered by the other party does not thereby prejudice the rights reserved. Such words as 'without prejudice,' 'under protest' or the like are sufficient."

Those that advocate application of Section 1-207 to "full payment check" cases recognize that a debtor, as the "master of its offer," has reason to expect that its check will either be accepted or returned. At the same time, though, they contend that a creditor has good cause to believe that it is fully entitled to retain the partial payment that rightfully belongs to it and is in its possession without having to forfeit its entitlement to whatever else it is due.

In the Horn case, the New York Court of Appeals agreed with those who advocate application of Section 1-207 to "full payment checks." It ruled that Horn had explicitly reserved its rights by endorsing the check below its notation "under protest" and that Bushwick's motion for summary judgment should have been denied.

▌States Split

One of the goals of the UCC is to attempt to introduce uniformity among the states with respect to commercial transactions. There is, however, perhaps no greater division among the states in any area of UCC law than with respect to the relationship of Section 1-207 to full payment checks.

Courts in the following states have ruled that creditors may reserve rights on full payment checks under Section 1-207: California, Delaware, Florida, Massachusetts, New Hampshire, New York, Ohio, Oregon, South Dakota, Texas, and West Virginia.

Courts in these states have come to the opposite conclusion: Alaska, Colorado, Connecticut, Nebraska, Maine, Utah, Virginia, Wisconsin, and Wyoming.

In other states, courts either have not ruled on the matter or there is a division among the courts of those states that has not yet been resolved at the state supreme court level. This area of law remains an expanding and developing area.

▌A Final Word

The categories of states listed above should be taken with more than a grain of salt. Indeed, there are several important reasons that a business that receives a check marked payment in full in, say, Florida, should not simply note that Florida is on the list where reservation of rights has been upheld, place a notation on the back of the check reserving rights, and cash it.

For one thing, laws change. States may have altered their rule regarding Section 1-207 and full payment checks since this book was published.

Second, it may not be clear what law applies. If a check comes from a business in a state that does not recognize reservation of rights to a business in a state that does, what happens? The law of the recipient's state may not be determinative.

Third, those states that permit reservation of rights under Section 1-207 clearly apply the rule to contracts for the sale of goods. But some may not apply it to contracts for the supply of services, to which the UCC generally is inapplicable; others may not apply it to transactions with consumers; finally, particular state laws may overrule Section 1-207 in particular cases, as noted in the Colorado Security Deposit Act case discussed below.

In this area, especially if the amount in excess of the amount of the full payment check is substantial, businesses (and individuals) would be particularly well advised to check with counsel before acting.

FIVE FULL PAYMENT CHECK CASES

1. Several years ago, AFC Interiors agreed with Nicholas DiCello, who was doing business as Ohio State Home Services, that AFC would perform certain interior decorating services for DiCello. AFC performed those services and purchased and delivered furnishings to DiCello; it then invoiced him. DiCello did not pay, however, and AFC filed suit. Thereafter, DiCello sent a letter to AFC stating that it was returning certain items that it no longer wanted pursuant to their oral contract and enclosing a check payable to AFC that contained the following notation on the back: "Payment in full for any and all claims."

A vice-president of AFC received the merchandise and the check but crossed out the notation on the back and inserted the words "payment on account." AFC then negotiated the check. DiCello contended that AFC's negotiation of the check amounted to an accord and satisfaction of the underlying debt; the case reached the Supreme Court of Ohio. The court ruled that AFC sufficiently reserved its rights against DiCello to collect the balance it alleged to be due by crossing out DiCello's notation on the back and substituting its own notation, "payment on account." (AFC Interiors v. DiCello, 544 N.E.2d 869 (Ohio 1989).)

2. When Joseph P. Sullivan, doing business as K & B Plumbing, received checks from Conant Valley Associates, Ltd. and Dennis Papa for less than he claimed was owing, he scratched out the words "complete and final payment" that Conant and Papa had written at the top of the back of the checks. Sullivan then deposited the checks and filed suit against Conant and Papa for the balance of what he claimed he was owed. The court noted that Section 1-207 of the UCC may protect a creditor from a debtor's defense of accord and satisfaction only if the creditor made an "explicit" reservation of rights. The court ruled that "mere scratching out of final payment conditions on a check followed by endorsement and cashing" is not the explicit and unambiguous reservation of rights required; further added words were necessary. (Sullivan v. Conant Valley Associates, 560 N.Y.S.2d 617 (Sup. Ct. Westchester Co. 1990).)

3. A contract between Air Van Lines, Inc. and Keystone Complex, a partnership between Jack Buster and Bill Lawrence, provided that Air Van Lines was to perform a moving job in Valdez, Alaska, for Keystone but that Keystone was to supply local laborers; a single Air Van Lines employee was to supervise the loading. Bill Reed, Air Van Lines's employee, arrived in Valdez on October 13, 1980. Reed considered the three local laborers provided by Keystone to be inexperienced. One of them quit after a day and a half. Reed allegedly called Lawrence in Anchorage and received authorization to bring two Air Van Lines's employees from Anchorage to finish the job. According to Reed, Lawrence told him to finish the job as soon as possible and the move was completed on October 19. Air Van Lines then sent Keystone a bill for $11,317.98, itemized as follows:

Van & labor, reg. rate	*$4,946.80*
Van & labor, overtime	*2,278.19*
Packing materials	*3,084.19*
Per diem & travel	*1,008.80*

Buster objected to the billing on the ground that he had not authorized Air Van Lines to use its own employees, nor had he authorized overtime. According to Buster, the total amount due on the basis of the original agreement was $4,355.56 for the van and labor, plus packing materials. Air Van Lines contacted Lawrence, who stated that Keystone would not pay the per diem and travel expenses of the two extra Air Van Lines' employees, nor would it pay the overtime charges. Air Van Lines offered to reduce its bill by $1,000, the approximate amount of the travel and per diem costs of the two extra men. Lawrence sent Air Van Lines a letter stating that Keystone still objected to paying overtime, and it wanted a further reduction of $2,278.19. The letter enclosed a check in the amount of $8,039.79, "as full and complete payment for all services, equipment and materials provided by your company." The check bore the notation, "Endorsement of this check constitutes a complete settlement of your claim." Air Van Lines endorsed the check without any reservation of rights. However, it later sent Keystone a letter stating that the payment had been applied to the debt and that it reserved its right to seek further sums. It then filed suit, and the case reached the Supreme Court of Alaska.

The court ruled that even if Section 1-207 of the UCC did apply to "full payment checks," Air Van Lines' attempted reservation of rights failed to comply with that section because it attached no reservation to the check at the time it cashed it. Air Van Lines "merely sent a letter subsequent to cashing the check purporting to reserve rights." Indeed, because the letter did not reach Keystone until after Air Van Lines had cashed the check, Keystone "never had the opportunity to consider whether to accept [Air Van Lines'] decision or stop payment on the check." (Air Van Lines, Inc. v. Buster, 673 P.2d 774 (Alaska 1983).)

4. In August 1978 Spyros Stanley and the Charleston Urban Renewal Authority entered into a written month-to-month lease for property located at 501-515 Summers Street in Charleston, West Virginia. Under the terms of the lease, Stanley agreed to pay the Authority rent of $600 per month; he used the property as a parking lot. In November 1982 the Authority exercised its prerogative and terminated the lease. The Authority informed Stanley that if he failed to surrender possession of the property by January 2, 1983, his continuing occupation would be construed as a day-to-day tenancy at a rental rate of $150 per day. Stanley did not surrender the property and, when the Authority sued him for possession, he filed a counterclaim alleging representations by the Authority over a number of years that he would be able to continue to enjoy possession.

In July 1983 the court ruled in favor of the Authority in its action for eviction and against Stanley on his counterclaim. The Authority then sought payment of the rent to which it claimed it was entitled. Stanley introduced evidence that he had tendered to the Authority the sum of $600 per month in one form or another for every month that he had remained in possession according to the following schedule:

Check Date	Amount
January 3, 1983	*$150.00*
January 4, 1983	*150.00*
January 5, 1983	*150.00*
January 6, 1983	*150.00*
February 20, 1983	*600.00*
March 15, 1983	*600.00*
April 20, 1983	*600.00*
May 16, 1983	*600.00*
June 20, 1983	*600.00*
July 15, 1983	*600.00*

The front of the January 6 check bore the legend "January rent in full." Stanley contended that the Authority scratched out the "in full" when it deposited the check. The checks for the subsequent months contained legends that stated only the month to which they corresponded, for example "April rent," "May rent," etc.

The Supreme Court of West Virginia rejected Section 1-207's application to a "full payment check" and ruled that the $600 that Stanley paid to the Authority in January was payment in full for that month's rent. It then said that the full payment legend on one check was not enough to permit it to infer that the other checks also had been tendered in full payment. Therefore, it returned the case to the lower court to determine if the other checks Stanley had tendered after January also had been offered and accepted as full satisfaction. Perhaps significantly, the dissenting Justice stated that he believed that Stanley's intent was clear. "The words 'February rent,' etc., indicated that the checks were offered in full settlement of the rental payments for the respective months . . . . [The Authority's] acceptance and use of the February through July checks should constitute an accord and satisfaction as a matter of law for the amounts due for those months." (Charleston Urban Renewal Authority v. Stanley, 346 S.E.2d 740 (West Virginia 1985).)

5. Within weeks of renting an apartment from Ian and Sandi Rosebrook, E. Peter Anderson and three other people were informed by officials of the City of Boulder that the building failed to meet the city's housing code standards; they were given 10 days to vacate. After they left, the Rosebrooks sent them an accounting of their security deposit, together with a partial refund. The $883.46 refund check had a restrictive endorsement on the back that stated, "Cashing of this check demonstrates agreement between [the tenants] and Ian & Sandi Rosebrook that this payment is full settlement of any and all monies owed to them jointly or individually by Ian & Sandi Rosebrook and precludes any efforts on their part to obtain further monies from us." When he received the check, Anderson crossed out the restrictive endorsement, wrote "I do not agree to above," endorsed the check, and cashed it. He advised the Rosebrooks in writing that he did not agree with the charges against him of $103 and requested a refund within seven days. When they failed to tender the remainder of the deposit, he brought suit against them in small claims court.

The case reached the Supreme Court of Colorado, which ruled that Section 1-207 of the UCC did not permit Anderson to reserve rights on a full payment check. However, it said that the Rosebrooks' attempt to force Anderson to waive his right to seek return of the remainder of the security deposit was prohibited by the Colorado Security Deposit Act, which voids a restrictive endorsement by which a landlord attempts to create a waiver of a tenant's right to legal recourse. (Anderson v. Rosebrook, 737 P.2d 417 (Colorado, 1987).)

Full Payment Check Checklist

✓ In the past, a creditor that accepted a check marked payment in full could not seek to collect any disputed balance it claimed it was owed, notwithstanding any notation it made on the check reserving its rights.

✓ In recent years, a number of states have relied on Section 1-207 of the Uniform Commercial Code to change that rule—although almost as large a number have refused to change it.

✓ To reserve rights to pursue a disputed balance in states in which it is permitted, a creditor that receives a check marked payment in full must explicitly indicate on the check that it is reserving its rights; to do so, it should use words such as "without prejudice" or "under protest."

✓ Even those states that permit reservation of rights under Section 1-207 may only allow it in connection with contracts for the sale of goods; thus, contracts involving provision of services may be subject to the common law rule of accord and satisfaction.

✓ For a number of reasons, including that laws change and that the state's law that applies to a particular transaction may not be evident to a nonlawyer, this area of law is particularly one that requires an attorney's counsel.

RECLAIMING GOODS FROM BANKRUPT BUYERS

▌Right to Reclamation ▌Demand ▌Receipt of Goods
▌Time of Demand ▌Competing Security Interest ▌A Final Word

On March 24, 1981, the Montello Oil Corporation, which was located in Dedham, Massachusetts, contracted to sell to Marin Motor Oil, Inc., which was located in Elmwood Park, New Jersey, 1,054,000 gallons of regular leaded gasoline at $0.9725 per gallon, FOB, New York Harbor, any day in April 1981. Marin agreed to pay Montello for the gasoline within one day after delivery and receipt by Marin of a certificate of inspection by an independent inspector as to the quality and quantity of gasoline.

In accordance with the contract, Marin called Montello on April 10, 1981, and arranged for a commercial barge to pick up the gasoline from Montello's terminal in New York Harbor. The barge arrived at the Montello terminal at 3:05 P.M. that same day and completed loading of the gasoline at 8:35 P.M. that evening. At 9:15 P.M. the barge departed Montello's terminal and proceeded to Cities Service Company's terminal in New Jersey, where Marin had storage rights under a terminalling agreement between Cities and Marin.

The barge arrived at Cities's New Jersey terminal at 10:30 P.M. on April 10 and began unloading into Cities's storage facility at 12:01 A.M. on April 11. The unloading took approximately 13 hours and was completed by 1:05 P.M. on April 11. On April 13 Marin received Montello's invoice in the amount of $1,032,570.35 and the independent inspector's certificate of compliance.

On April 16 Thomas McManmon, Montello's vice-president, went to Marin's office in Elmwood Park, New Jersey, and orally demanded payment of Montello's invoice or, in the alternative, return of the gasoline. On the same day, Montello filed suit against Marin in New Jersey Superior Court seeking a writ of attachment against all of Marin's assets and an injunction prohibiting Marin from reselling the gasoline Montello had sold it. The Superior Court entered a temporary injunction enjoining Marin from making any further sales and ordering Marin to place all proceeds from the sale of Montello gasoline into a segregated account. Montello served its state court complaint and the court order on Marin on April 20. On April 21, Marin filed a petition for reorganization under Chapter 11 of the bankruptcy code.

Many sellers in Montello's position might believe that a buyer's bankruptcy puts the nail in their coffin; that they have no recourse other than to await resolution of the Chapter 11 to collect all (or, more likely, only some) of the debt they are owed. That is not necessarily true, however.

At 11:04 P.M. of the day Marin entered Chapter 11, Montello, through its attorney, transmitted a demand for reclamation to Marin by telex through Western Union. The demand stated: "Pursuant to Section 546(c) of the Bankruptcy Code and pursuant to section 2-702 of the U.C.C., demand is hereby made upon you for the return and reclamation of all gasoline delivered to you 11 April, 1981."

Marin's bankruptcy court rejected Montello's reclamation request but, on appeal, the U.S. Court of Appeals for the Third Circuit ruled that Montello was entitled to reclamation.

▌Right To Reclamation

As Montello's telex indicates, the right of an unpaid seller to reclaim goods from a buyer in bankruptcy generally stems from Section 2-702 of the Uniform Commercial Code (UCC). That section states in pertinent part that where a seller discovers that a buyer has received goods on credit while insolvent, the seller may reclaim the goods upon demand made within 10 days after receipt.

Section 546(c) of the bankruptcy code recognizes the right of reclamation provided by UCC Section 2-702. It provides that a business that sells goods in the ordinary course of its business may reclaim those goods from a bankrupt buyer if the buyer received the goods while insolvent and the seller demands reclamation in writing before 10 days after the buyer received the goods. It is important to note that although Section 2-702 does not require a written demand, the demand must be in writing to comply with the bankruptcy code. (UCC Section 2-702 also waives the 10-day notice requirement if the buyer fraudulently misrepresents its solvency to the seller within three months prior to the receipt of the goods. However, this provision is not recognized by the bankruptcy code and thus has no effect where the buyer is in bankruptcy at the time the seller seeks reclamation.)

In addition, Section 546(c) states that the court may deny reclamation to a seller if it grants the seller a "priority" claim against the buyer in the buyer's bankruptcy or provides the seller with collateral to secure its reclamation claim. While neither a priority claim nor collateral necessarily are as good as getting the goods back, or being paid for them, each is certainly far superior to having a general unsecured claim against the buyer.

▌ Demand

In the Marin case, Montello contended that the complaint it filed in state court on April 16, in conjunction with the temporary restraining order issued by the state court against Marin, was sufficient to satisfy the demand requirement of Section 546(c). The Third Circuit rejected that argument, though, noting that Montello's right to reclamation was not mentioned in either Montello's complaint or the court's restraining order. The complaint sought only damages and a restraining order prohibiting Marin from "further sales of the gasoline heretofore delivered to it by [Montello] and/or directing that the proceeds of all such sales be held by [Marin] in a segregated account to be released upon direction of the Court." While the complaint sought attachment of all Marin's property, including the gasoline Montello had sold to Marin, the Third Circuit said that the attachment appeared to be designed to assure Montello that it would be able to recover any damages that it might be awarded when the case ultimately was decided. "Reclamation, on the other hand, is a separate remedy explicitly created by the U.C.C. to supplement a seller's right to other legal and equitable relief." It then ruled that the state court complaint was insufficient to satisfy Section 546(c)'s requirement of a written demand for reclamation.

▌Receipt of Goods

Montello argued that Marin did not "receive" the gasoline within the meaning of Section 546(c) until April 11, when the barge pumped the gasoline into Cities' storage terminal. Marin argued, though, that it received the gas on April 10, when Montello pumped it onto the barge that Marin had hired. The practical significance of this dispute was that the date of "receipt" is established by Section 546(c) as the day from which to begin counting the 10-day period within which the seller must make a written demand for reclamation. As the Third Circuit noted, if Marin was correct and "receipt" was deemed to have occurred on April 10, then regardless of whether Montello's telex demand was viewed as having been made on April 21, when it was sent, or April 22, when it was received, it was not made within the 10-day period provided for by Section 546(c).

The appellate court noted that there is no definition of "receipt" in the bankruptcy code but that UCC Section 2-103(1)(c) defines receipt of goods as "taking physical possession of them." Marin argued that it took possession of the gas when it was loaded on the barge because at that point, under the terms of the sales contract, "title" and risk of loss passed to Marin. But the Third Circuit noted that UCC Section 2-705 views goods given by a seller to a common carrier for delivery to a buyer as being in the possession of the common carrier, not the buyer, and gives the seller the right to stop delivery of the goods upon discovery of the buyer's insolvency. Accordingly, the court ruled that while the gasoline was physically on the barge, it was not in the physical possession of Marin. The court said that Marin had constructive possession only after the gasoline was delivered to Cities.

▌Time of Demand

Finally, the court in the Marin case examined whether Montello had made a "demand" within the meaning of Section 546(c) on April 21 when it sent the telex at 11:04 P.M. or whether a "demand" requires receipt by the buyer, in which case the demand was not made until April 22 when Marin turned on its telex machine and received the message.

The court noted that the bankruptcy code does not define what constitutes a "demand." Marin asserted that Congress's purpose in enacting Section 546(c) was to foster commercial certainty by establishing a flat 10-day receipt rule. It argued that such a rule would do the most to foster commercial certainty because it would allow Chapter 11 debtors and their creditors to know exactly what assets are available to satisfy the debtor's obligations.

The Third Circuit stated, though, that a "dispatch" rule would provide the greatest certainty because there can be very few disputes concerning whether the seller made a timely dispatch. The concept of dispatch is straightforward and the date of dispatch is easily measurable—for example, the court could simply look at the postmark date on the envelope or the electronically recorded date and time that a telex was sent. However, it said, a dispatch rule required that the method of communication the seller chooses be "commercially reasonable."

A receipt rule, on the other hand, would not involve courts in an inquiry into whether the method of communication the seller chose was reasonable. The only question would be whether the buyer received the demand within the 10-day period. However, the court said, applying a receipt rule in the modern world, where telex and other forms of electronic communication are the norm, would require the courts to become involved in a number of "conceptually difficult disputes concerning what constitutes receipt." It said that there was no doubt that Montello sent its telex demand at 11:04 on April 21. But, it asked, when did Marin receive the message? "Apparently, Marin's machine was not turned on between the time Montello sent the message and the next morning, but did the electrons that made up the message proceed along the wires and enter Marin's machine and wait there until the next morning? And would that be enough for receipt?" The court also wondered what would have happened if Marin's telex machine had been accidentally left on the day before; in that case, the court said, the message would have been visible on the screen in Marin's offices but no one would have been there to read it. Would that have been enough to constitute receipt? The court then concluded that a dispatch rule was more effective than a receipt rule and found that Montello's reclamation demand had been timely.

▌ Competing Security Interest

What if a seller supplies goods on credit to a buyer that has granted a second creditor a security interest in its property? As the American Saw & Manufacturing Company discovered, the supplier may come in second best because secured creditors generally are deemed to meet all the requirements for a good faith purchaser for value, as described in UCC Section 2-207, and thus have priority to the goods under that section.

Before the Bosler Supply Group, which did business under several names, including Tools and Abrasives, Inc., entered Chapter 11, American Saw had sold it certain goods on open account in the ordinary course of its business, as follows:

Date of Invoice and Shipment	Invoice Nos.	Amount
1/31/86	30418	$558.60
2/3/86	27868	26,434.32
	30469	247.20
	31136	1,236.31
2/5/86	27808	2,398.59
	27868-01	521.73
	30383	159.50
2/6/86	230801	294.10
	32092	161.33
	32573	106.65

Prior to these sales, Bosler Supply entered into an accounts receivable financing arrangement with the Manufacturers Hanover Commercial Corporation. To secure these loans, Bosler Supply granted the bank liens on and security interests in certain collateral, including its inventory. The bank perfected its security interest in the collateral by filing UCC financing statements in the offices of the secretary of state of Illinois and Wisconsin. When Bosler Supply entered Chapter 11, it was indebted to the bank in the approximate amount of $4,645,000, plus accrued interest and other costs and fees. American Saw delivered a written reclamation demand to Bosler Supply within 10 days of its receipt of the goods.

Within weeks after entering Chapter 11, Bosler Supply's assets were sold and the proceeds of the sale were paid to the bank, as a secured creditor, in full payment of Bosler Supply's indebtedness to it. Then American Saw asked the court to determine the status of its reclamation claim.

The court ruled that American Saw had no reclamation claim against Bosler Supply because the bank's superior lien to Bosler Supply's assets extinguished it. "No provision of the Bankruptcy Code or of the Uniform Commercial Code gives a reclaiming seller an administrative priority or substitute lien if the seller's reclamation rights are frustrated by the presence of a prior lien," the court said. It added that the fact that the bank had been paid in full did not reestablish American Saw's right to reclaim. "There is but one moment of truth under Bankruptcy Code [Section 546(c)]: that moment of truth is when American Saw attempts to assert its right to reclaim."

▍A Final Word

Significantly, the law is rather clear that the reclamation section of the bankruptcy code provides the exclusive remedy to an unpaid seller seeking to reclaim goods from a debtor in bankruptcy. A seller that fails to meet its requirements will be left only with an unsecured claim against the buyer and will be forced to stand in line with other similarly situated creditors.

FIVE RECLAMATION CASES

1. From July 21 to 29, 1988, the Jones Oil Company, Inc. sold the Intercity Oil Co., Inc. $22,444.21 worth of gasoline and fuel oil. On July 29 Jones learned that the Internal Revenue Service intended to levy on Intercity's assets to satisfy tax liens in the amount of $532,738.08. Jones immediately mailed Intercity a notice of reclamation and sent a driver to reclaim the gas and fuel oil. It was unable to do so, though, because Intercity's storage tanks were empty—Intercity had sold Jones's gas and fuel oil before Jones could physically reclaim them. Intercity voluntarily entered Chapter 7 of the bankruptcy code, which provides for liquidation, and Jones asserted that it was entitled to a priority claim in lieu of reclamation as provided by Section 546(c) of the bankruptcy code. Jones argued that a reclaiming seller's notice of reclamation created an obligation for a debtor to hold the goods for redelivery. It said that if a debtor breached this obligation by selling the goods to another party, the bankruptcy code must grant the seller an administrative priority or a lien. The court recognized that a seller might be entitled to an administrative claim or lien if a debtor received a reclamation notice, ignored it, and then disposed of the goods. However, it ruled that because a purchase by a good faith purchaser precluded a seller's reclamation claim under UCC Section 2-207 and because Intercity had sold Jones's products before Jones made any demand for reclamation, Jones was not entitled to any relief. (In re Intercity Oil Co., Inc., 122 B.R. 358 (Bankr. W.D. Wisconsin 1990).)

2. Flav-O-Rich, Inc. sold and delivered milk products and ice cream to Rawson Food Service, Inc., a retail food chain, daily between February 11 and February 19, 1986. The aggregate value of the delivered products was approximately $102,000. Rawson filed a petition under Chapter 11 of the bankruptcy code on February 19, 1986. The following day, Flav-O-Rich made a written demand for reclamation of the goods it had delivered to Rawson on or after February 11, 1986. When Rawson did not comply with the demand, Flav-O-Rich filed a reclamation action in the bankruptcy court; it sought either an order requiring Rawson to return the products or, in the alternative, an order granting it either an administrative priority or a lien on Rawson's unencumbered assets in an amount sufficient to satisfy its reclamation demand.

Following pretrial discovery, the parties stipulated that Flav-O-Rich's reclamation demand met the requirements of bankruptcy code Section 546(c), that Flav-O-Rich did not have to prove Rawson's insolvency, that Rawson had taken physical possession of the milk and ice cream products, and that Rawson did not comply with the reclamation demand. The parties also stipulated as to the value of the goods Flav-O-Rich sought to reclaim. At trial, Flav-O-Rich produced no evidence that Rawson was in possession of any of the goods it sought to reclaim when it received the demand for reclamation. Flav-O-Rich contended that the burden was on Rawson to prove that it did not have possession of the goods at that time, but the U.S. Court of Appeals for the Eleventh Circuit disagreed. It ruled that a seller has the burden of proving that a buyer had in its possession the goods at the time the buyer received the demand. Because Flav-O-Rich failed to present convincing evidence of possession, the court ruled that Flav-O-Rich's action should be dismissed. (In re Rawson Food Service, Inc., 846 F.2d 1343 (11th Cir. 1988).)

3. After Furniture Distributors, Inc. entered bankruptcy, three of its creditors filed reclamation motions. The bankruptcy court held a hearing and the creditors presented their case. When their attorney rested, the court noted, "If that concludes the evidence, unless I missed something, there is one essential piece of evidence that has not been submitted; and it would seem that, unless I've missed it, because I'm not going to reopen the evidence now to take new evidence, that there's a fatal gap here. I don't recall any evidence that was offered that Furniture Distributors, Inc. was insolvent on the date that the goods were shipped. Did I miss it? Was it there somewhere?" The creditors' attorney was unable to point to any specific evidence; indeed, the court found that the creditors had failed to prove the debtor insolvent using a balance sheet test (the sum of the debts exceed assets, at a fair valuation) or an "equity" test (the inability of the debtor to pay its bills as they come due). It then rejected the creditors' reclamation action. (In re Furniture Distributors, Inc., 45 B.R. 38 (Bankr. D. Massachusetts 1984).)

4. A number of years ago, the Kerr Pacific Milling Corporation agreed to sell 33,000 bushels of wheat to the Coast Trading Company. Coast then sold part of it to the Dallas Co-Op, which in turn sold it to the United Grain Corporation. Coast then directed Kerr to deliver that portion of the contract directly to United Grain by Union Pacific Railroad. Kerr shipped it pursuant to a nonnegotiable straight bill of lading. United Grain, in accordance with the custom of the trade, paid 90 percent of the purchase price to Dallas, which in turn paid it to Coast. Coast, however, paid nothing to Kerr. After the wheat was delivered to United Grain and unloaded from the rail car, United Grain paid the remaining 10 percent of the price to Dallas. When Kerr realized that Coast was insolvent, it made written demand upon Coast for reclamation of the wheat and advised United of its demand by mailgram. United admitted that Kerr had made a valid demand upon Coast to reclaim the wheat within 10 days after delivery as required by the UCC.

The court said that if the wheat actually had been delivered to Coast rather than to a third party, and if Coast had not resold it to a bona fide purchaser before it received Kerr's demand, Kerr would have been entitled to reclaim the grain. The court said that to uphold Kerr's position—that a good faith purchaser for value such as United Grain could not defeat the rights of a seller where delivery is made by the original seller to the last buyer in a predelivery chain of transfers—would create such uncertainty in the grain trade as to curtail transfer of goods other than by direct delivery from the buyer's immediate seller. Thus, it concluded, when United Grain "accepted delivery of the wheat and paid the full price, it was both a good faith purchaser for value and a buyer in the ordinary course and Kerr had lost its right to reclaim." (In re Coast Trading Co., Inc., 31 B.R. 663 (Bankr. D. Oregon 1982).)

5. From April 8, 1985, through April 15, 1985, while the Wheeling-Pittsburgh Steel Corporation was insolvent, the Bethlehem Steel Corporation sold on credit and delivered to Wheeling's Monessen, Pennsylvania, facility 2,249.83 tons of low volatile coal. The purchase price of the shipment was $105,854.50. In a process known as "coking," Wheeling blended 1,963.76 tons of the low-volatile coal with high-volatile coal, adjusted the mixture for bulk density and placed it into its coke ovens; there, the mixture underwent substantial chemical and other changes, producing such by-products as tar, ammonia sulfate, light oil, and the main product, coke. Wheeling entered Chapter 11 on April 16, 1985. Bethlehem filed a reclamation demand, with which Wheeling refused to comply, and subsequently manufactured the remaining 286.07 tons of coal into coke.

The court first ruled that where a supplier has sold and delivered raw materials on credit to an insolvent buyer and the raw goods have been manufactured into a finished product by the date it makes a written demand for reclamation, the supplier had no right to reclaim the finished product. Thus, it said, Bethlehem did not have a right of reclamation with respect to the 1,963.76 tons of coal that Wheeling had manufactured into coke as of the date Bethlehem made its written demand. As to the remaining 286.07 tons of coal, the court noted that on the date Bethlehem made its written demand for reclamation, that coal sat in Wheeling's inventory atop a pile of coal of like kind and grade that had been delivered by other sellers. It found that these 286.07 tons were reclaimable by Bethlehem even though they had been commingled with coal from other sellers. Because Wheeling had converted the coal into coke after receiving Bethlehem's reclamation demand, the court said that Bethlehem was entitled to an administrative priority claim in Wheeling's bankruptcy in an amount equal to the value of the coal as of the date Bethlehem sought reclamation, plus interest. (In re Wheeling-Pittsburgh Steel Corp., 74 B.R. 656 (Bankr. W.D. Pennsylvania 1987).)

Reclamation Checklist

✓ When a seller provides goods to a buyer on credit, it is taking a risk—the risk that it will not be paid. The Uniform Commercial Code and the federal bankruptcy code help to ameliorate that risk somewhat. Generally speaking, they permit an unpaid seller that makes a demand within 10 days of an insolvent buyer's receipt of goods to reclaim its goods.

✓ The bankruptcy code requires that the demand be in writing. It also is quite strict about the 10-day requirement, generally measured from the dispatch of the reclamation demand rather than receipt.

✓ In addition, to meet the requirements of the law, the buyer must be in possession of the goods when it receives the reclamation demand.

✓ The bankruptcy code permits the court to provide an administrative priority claim or a lien rather than reclamation; while not as good, they both are far superior to the alternative—a general unsecured claim against a debtor in bankruptcy.

✓ Significantly, both the UCC and the bankruptcy code provide that if the buyer has granted a security interest in its assets to another creditor, a seller's right of reclamation may be valueless. Sellers that worry about this risk ought to consider obtaining a security interest, letter of credit, or other form of protection.

SELLING TO CUSTOMERS IN BANKRUPTCY

■ Ten Questions and Answers about Bankruptcy
■ Administrative Priority ■ A Final Word

After the TransAmerican Natural Gas Corporation entered Chapter 11 in 1983, Toma Steel Supply, Inc., entered into a requirements contract with TransAmerican to sell it well casing. Under that contract, it sold TransAmerican approximately 1.5 million feet of casing, which TransAmerican used in conducting its business of well drilling, completion, and operation.

In the fall of 1985, TransAmerican experienced five successive well failures. Four of the wells contained casing supplied by Toma; the fifth contained casing supplied by another distributor.

Then, in August or September 1986, TransAmerican stopped paying Toma's invoices. Nevertheless, Toma continued to supply casing to TransAmerican, until the balance due reached $2,288,683.45 (nearly Toma's entire net worth).

Toma filed emergency motions with the bankruptcy court in February 1987 seeking to have its $2.3 million claim allowed as an "administrative expense" in TransAmerican's bankruptcy. TransAmerican objected.

The bankruptcy court held a hearing on March 11, 1987, on Toma's motions. TransAmerican asserted that Toma had provided no benefit to the estate because some of the casing Toma had supplied was defective and caused well failures and damages exceeding the balance TransAmerican owed Toma. At the conclusion of the hearing, the bankruptcy court found that Toma had satisfied its burden of proving that the expenses were reasonable and necessary for the preservation of the estate. It allowed Toma's administrative expense claim in full, ordered that TransAmerican pay Toma immediately, and directed Transamerican to pursue its claims for defective casing within 60 days. When TransAmerican failed to pay, Toma garnished its bank accounts.

After a hearing on June 15, the bankruptcy court ordered Toma to escrow $500,000 in an interest-bearing account to protect TransAmerican from third-party liens by Toma's suppliers. It further ordered Toma to assign to TransAmerican its interest under its product liability insurance policies to protect TransAmerican in the event that TransAmerican succeeded on its claim against Toma for damages allegedly caused by defective casings. The court released the unescrowed portion of the garnished amount, approximately $1.8 million, to Toma.

After the bankruptcy court denied its motion for a new trial, TransAmerican appealed the bankruptcy court's order to the federal district court. In the meantime, on September 4, 1987, the bankruptcy court entered an order confirming TransAmerican's plan of reorganization. The plan provided that each holder of an allowed administrative expense claim was to "be paid the full amount of such expense or claim when due (but not earlier than the consummation date) except to the extent the Bankruptcy Court orders otherwise." Toma's allowed administrative expense claim was not treated separately in the confirmation order.

On June 30, 1989, the district court vacated the bankruptcy court's orders on Toma's motions and remanded the dispute between Toma and TransAmerican back to the bankruptcy court. The bankruptcy court then denied Toma's administrative expense claim. It found that Toma had supplied defective casing to TransAmerican and that Toma had failed to prove that it had rendered a benefit to the estate. The court ordered Toma to *return the $1.8 million it had received in 1987 to TransAmerican. The district court, to which Toma appealed, affirmed the bankruptcy court's decision. The case reached the U.S. Court of Appeals for the Fifth Circuit in 1992.*

▌Ten Questions and Answers about Bankruptcy

Q1: What law governs bankruptcy cases?

A1: Virtually all business bankruptcies in the United States (and personal bankruptcies as well) are governed by the federal bankruptcy code. (Banks and insurance companies are not subject to the bankruptcy code but to other liquidation or reorganization statutes.)

Q2: How do businesses enter bankruptcy?

A2: A business may voluntarily file a petition for relief from creditors or it may be forced into involuntary bankruptcy by its creditors. Three creditors of a business that has at least a dozen creditors may petition the business into bankruptcy if they hold claims against the business aggregating at least $5,000 more than the value of any collateral, and if the debtor is generally not paying its debts as the debts become due, unless the debts were the subject of a bona fide dispute.

Businesses usually enter either Chapter 7 of the bankruptcy code or Chapter 11 of the bankruptcy code. A business in Chapter 7 will liquidate its assets and distribute whatever value those assets generate to its creditors and shareholders. Chapter 11, on the other hand, allows a company to reorganize and exit bankruptcy as an ongoing concern.

Q3: Why might a business enter bankruptcy?

A3: A business that enters Chapter 11 often has defaulted on its obligations to its lenders, has substantial past due trade debt, and may owe taxes to the local, state, and federal governments. In other words, there are more claims to the Chapter 11 company's assets than there are assets.

In the past decade, though, businesses have extended the traditional uses of the bankruptcy laws and have entered bankruptcy to deal with problems other than immediate financial problems. For instance, some businesses have entered bankruptcy seeking to develop a plan to deal with product liability claims, even though they were in default of none of their current financial obligations.

Q4: What happens when a company enters bankruptcy?

A4: The bankruptcy code provides for an automatic stay or injunction immediately upon a company's petition for relief that prohibits creditors from seeking to collect their debts through lawsuits, setoff, self-help, or otherwise. The automatic stay is intended to provide "breathing room" to a debtor in bankruptcy to allow it time to file schedules of creditors, negotiate with creditors, develop a plan of reorganization, and emerge from bankruptcy.

Q5: What role may creditors play in a customer's bankruptcy?

A5: Creditors have the ability to become very involved in a debtor's bankruptcy. Indeed, a debtor must file significant amounts of information with the bankruptcy court; reviewing this information might provide creditors with some competitive advantage.

Additionally, they may be able to join an official creditors' committee, which represents all unsecured creditors and negotiates with the debtor and other interested parties on their behalf for a plan of reorganization.

Q6: How successful are companies at reorganizing under the bankruptcy laws?

A6: There has been much discussion in recent years of the bankruptcy explosion. United States bankruptcy filings reached 971,517 in 1992, an all-time high. However, fewer than 70,000 of the filings were by businesses; most were by individuals seeking to discharge their debts. Some commentators have criticized business filings, contending that "only lawyers" get paid and that most of the Chapter 11 filings by businesses end up being converted to Chapter 7 and liquidating. While it is quite difficult for a company in Chapter 11 to successfully reorganize, the fact of the matter is that many companies do so. Studies have indicated that publicly held, well-capitalized companies have a better likelihood of emerging from bankruptcy than privately owned businesses; that may be because they have better capital, it may be because they have better management, or it may be a combination of factors. Businesses that intend to continue supplying goods to customers in bankruptcy should keep this in mind.

Q7: How do creditors get paid by companies in bankruptcy?

A7: The answer depends on the kind of claim that a creditor has. Creditors' claims may be divided into a number of categories. Unsecured claims are claims arising from the debtor's activities before it filed its petition for relief that are held by creditors that have no security. Secured claims are prepetition claims held by creditors with collateral. The bankruptcy code also recognizes other kinds of prepetition claims, such as claims for certain unpaid taxes and claims of employees for unpaid wages up to a certain amount.

Generally speaking, a secured creditor is in the best position when a company enters bankruptcy because it is entitled to get paid in full or to keep its collateral (or the value of its collateral). Unsecured creditors have to share in assets remaining after secured creditors and priority creditors obtain payment; unfortunately, they often seem to receive little if anything on their claims. Shareholders are entitled to value with respect to their stock only after all other creditors have been paid in full.

Q8: What is a "preference?"

A8: Not only may a creditor with an unpaid claim not be paid if the debtor enters bankruptcy, or be paid only a portion of the amount it is owed, but the creditor may have to return some payments it received before the debtor's bankruptcy. These payments are known as preferences.

Generally speaking, the bankruptcy code permits a bankrupt business or individual to recover certain payments made to creditors within 90 days of the debtor's bankruptcy if the payments were made on account of a then-existing debt by an insolvent debtor. Where a creditor is an insider of the debtor (such as an officer), the period is one year. There are numerous defenses to preference actions, including that the payments are made in the ordinary course of the debtor's and creditor's business with respect to a debt incurred by the debtor in the ordinary course of its business. The goal of the preference laws is to create a "level playing field" and to allow all creditors similarly situated to be treated the same; often times, though, the creditor charged with having received a preference feels that it is being persecuted rather than that it is contributing to a worthy cause.

Q9: May businesses operate in bankruptcy?

A9: When a business enters Chapter 11, its existing management generally continues to conduct the company's affairs. On occasion, a bankruptcy trustee may be appointed to operate a company in Chapter 11. But whether management or a trustee is operating a Chapter 11 debtor, the fact remains that the debtor needs to hire employees, purchase supplies, and otherwise continue in business. As Toma recognized after TransAmerican filed for bankruptcy, this can present a kind of opportunity for sellers.

Q10: But how do postpetition suppliers get paid?

A10: Businesses that sell goods or provide services to Chapter 11 debtors may be entitled to administrative priority claims for payment. Administrative priority claims are entitled to priority over prepetition unsecured claims and prepetition tax claims. It must be emphasized that holding an administrative claim does not ensure that a creditor will be paid—all too often a Chapter 11 company fails to reorganize because it is unable to pay its administrative claims in full as it is required to do under the bankruptcy code to reorganize. Thus, while supplying goods to a customer in bankruptcy may present a sales opportunity, and is something that should be investigated, it does not involve a sure fire way to make money.

The bankruptcy code recognizes administrative claims because Congress understood that to effectuate a successful reorganization, third parties had to be willing to furnish postpetition goods and services on credit. It knew that they might be unwilling to do so if they feared that their claims would not be paid, but Congress knew that requiring payment in advance or upon delivery would impede the debtor's business. Thus, it included a provision in the bankruptcy code that required that these kinds of claims be given priority. In the words of the bankruptcy code, priority is granted to claims for "the actual, necessary costs and expenses of preserving" the debtor's bankruptcy estate.

▌Administrative Priority

In the Toma case, TransAmerican argued that Toma's casing had not "preserved" its estate because it had been defective and led it to incur approximately $2.5 million in damages. But the Fifth Circuit rejected its argument. It said that the purpose of the administrative claim section of the bankruptcy code was "to determine whether the estate received a benefit—not whether the estate was harmed." The court noted that Toma had introduced evidence at the hearing, including copies of its invoices, that the cost of the entire casing string in each well was approximately $80,000 per well. Thus, the court said, invoices for allegedly defective casing totaled, at most, approximately $400,000 ($80,000 for each of the four failed wells, plus $80,000 for casing that it removed from another well).

In the Fifth Circuit's view, consideration of the damages allegedly caused by a small portion of the casing supplied by Toma was only part of the analysis. It said that the bankruptcy code also required consideration of the fact that Toma's willingness to undertake the risk of supplying goods to TransAmerican in bankruptcy enabled TransAmerican to continue conducting its business, as well as the fact that profits from wells in which Toma-supplied casing was successfully used were available for payment of prepetition creditors and enhanced the likelihood of a successful reorganization. The circuit court then ordered that the bankruptcy court's original orders regarding Toma's motions for administrative claim treatment be reinstated.

▌A Final Word

Bankruptcy is here to stay. While the 1990s may, ultimately, see a drop-off from the high number of filings of the early part of the decade, it seems clear that large numbers of businesses will continue to enter bankruptcy during the decade due to fraud and mismanagement, if not the economy. Suppliers that are able to evaluate a bankrupt's prospects may find a worthwhile opportunity in postpetition transactions with a bankrupt. Of course, they should keep the risks of non-payment firmly in mind.

FIVE BANKRUPT CUSTOMERS

1. On September 11, 1990, the Tate Cheese Company, Inc. delivered $10,925.65 worth of cheese to Crofton & Sons, Inc., which was insolvent on that date. On September 20, 1990, Crofton received a letter from Tate demanding that Crofton either immediately pay for the cheese or immediately return the cheese to Tate. The letter also stated that in the event Crofton neither paid for the cheese nor returned it, Tate would exercise its right to reclaim the cheese under the Uniform Commercial Code. On February 6, 1991, Crofton filed a voluntary petition for relief under Chapter 11 of the bankruptcy code. At that time, Crofton no longer had possession of any of the cheese that Tate had delivered, having sold the cheese in the ordinary course of its business following Tate's reclamation demand. Several months after Crofton's bankruptcy filing, Tate filed an action seeking payment of $10,925.65 as an administrative expense, which is a permitted alternative to reclamation. The court rejected its claim. It noted that Tate had made a timely, written reclamation demand on September 20. But, it said, for more than four and a half months prepetition and more than three months postpetition, Tate did nothing further. Because Tate failed to diligently assert its right to reclamation, the court ruled that it lost that right and therefore was not entitled to any administrative claim in lieu of actual possession of its cheese. (In re Crofton & Sons, Inc., 139 B.R. 567 (Bankr. M.D. Fla. 1992).)

2. The North American Printing Ink Company supplied ink to the Regensteiner Printing Company by shipping large steel containers, known as totes, fully loaded with ink. North American would bill Regensteiner after North American picked up the totes and determined how much ink Regensteiner had used. Between October 1989 and January 1990, North American delivered totes 122, 129, 121, and 119 to Regensteiner. On March 13, 1990, Regensteiner filed for Chapter 11. North American thereafter billed Regensteiner $23,901.35 for the ink it had consumed from totes 122, 129, 121, and 119. When Regensteiner did not pay that bill, North American filed a claim in the bankruptcy court seeking the payment as an administrative expense. The court rejected North American's claim. It stated that North American had fulfilled its contractual obligations by furnishing the ink to Regensteiner prepetition; it did not supply the ink to Regensteiner after it had entered bankruptcy. Thus, although it may have billed Regensteiner postpetition, it was not entitled to a postpetition administrative priority claim. (North American Printing Ink Co. v. Regensteiner Printing Co., 140 B.R. 474 (N.D. Illinois 1992).)

3. After Colortex Industries, Inc., a carpet manufacturer in Chatsworth, Georgia, filed a Chapter 11 petition on October 24, 1989, it requested that Varsity Carpet Services, Inc., Textile Coating, Ltd., and Chem-Tech Finishers, Inc. perform finishing services on a credit basis while Colortex operated in Chapter 11. Between October 26, 1989, and February 1, 1990, the three suppliers extended trade credit to Colortex for postpetition finishing services. On April 17, 1990, the bankruptcy court converted Colortex's Chapter 11 reorganization case to a Chapter 7 liquidation case. A couple of weeks later, the three suppliers filed a motion with the bankruptcy court requesting immediate payment of their administrative expense claims, which totaled approximately $45,000. They sought first administrative expense priority on the trade credit they had extended to Colortex during the time Colortex operated under Chapter 11 and on the interest accrued on that trade credit.

Colortex's bankruptcy trustee objected, noting that while the estate had $723,738 on deposit, payment of any administrative claims was premature because a number of outstanding Chapter 7 administrative expense claims and other Chapter 11 administrative expense claims against the Colortex estate had not been resolved. The bankruptcy court allowed the three suppliers' administrative expense claims but denied their claims for interest and for immediate payment. They appealed to the district court. The district court ruled that the suppliers were entitled to interest on the debt incurred by Colortex while it was operating under Chapter 11. It said that debts incurred during a reorganization were administrative expenses that ought to be paid on a current basis and "must bear interest if any creditor is to remain willing to do business with a debtor in reorganization." The district court then found that the bankruptcy court had not abused it discretion in deferring payment of the three suppliers' administrative claims because the suppliers had offered no definitive proof of the final amount of administrative expense claims. (If not all could be paid in full, they would have to be paid pro rata.) (Varsity Carpet Services, Inc. v. Richardson, 146 B.R. 881 (N.D. Georgia 1992).)

4. The proof of claim filed by the Telerent Leasing Corporation in the Cardinal Industries, Inc. Chapter 11 bankruptcy case asserted that Telerent was entitled to $4,468,739.71 administrative claim for unpaid postpetition lease payments, taxes, attorneys' fees, and costs, and an open account for parts and repairs. The charges arose from Telerent's lease of televisions and related equipment to various limited partnerships of which Cardinal or one of its subsidiaries was the general partner. At the time of the leases the partnerships owned and operated motels that provided the leased televisions for their guest rooms. Telerent argued that after Cardinal had entered Chapter 11, Telerent and the Cardinal Lodging Group, as agent for the partnerships, entered into a modification agreement relating to the various leases; Cardinal Industries, Inc. and Cardinal Industries Services Corporation also executed the modification agreement for certain purposes specified therein.

Telerent recognized that the leases affected by the modifications had not been executed by Cardinal Industries, Inc. on its own behalf but rather by limited partnerships in which Cardinal served as general partner. Telerent argued that by continuing to lease televisions to the partnerships after Cardinal Industries, Inc. filed its Chapter 11 petition, Cardinal's estate benefited from the modification even if the benefit was indirect. The court rejected its contentions, however. It found that Telerent had failed to establish any benefit to the Cardinal bankruptcy estate from the modification beyond a potential indirect or tenuous benefit to the partnerships from the continued leasing of television sets and equipment. The court said that Telerent offered no evidence to support its allegation that the leasing of television sets to the limited partnerships controlled by Cardinal Industries, Inc. was a necessary expense that benefited Cardinal Industries' estate. (In re Cardinal Industries, Inc., 151 B.R. 833 (Bankr. S.D. Ohio 1992).

5. Before Cardinal Industries, Inc. filed for protection from creditors under Chapter 11 on May 15, 1989, it had entered into two equipment leases with the Textron Financial Corporation: a lease for a CADD computer system and a lease for 35 trailers. On June 22, 1989, Textron asked the court to order Cardinal to assume and continue the equipment leases or to reject them and return the equipment to Textron. Cardinal rejected the trailer lease and CADD lease on August 9, 1989, and September 26, 1989, respectively. Textron contended that it was entitled to administrative priority for the two to three months between the time it asked the court to order Cardinal to assume or reject the trailer and CADD leases and the time Cardinal ultimately rejected them. The court recognized that a debtor must pay a lessor a reasonable administrative expense for actual use of property that benefited the bankruptcy estate during the pendency of its decision to assume or reject a lease. It noted, though, that Textron failed to prove that Cardinal had used the CADD system or the trailers during the postpetition period before rejection of the leases. Thus, it ruled, Textron had failed to satisfy its burden of proving that it was entitled to an administrative expense with respect to that equipment. (In re Cardinal Industries, Inc., 151 B.R. 838 (Bankr. S.D. Ohio 1992).)

Bankruptcy Checklist

✓ Bankruptcy is a fact of life. More bankruptcy petitions were filed in this country in 1992 than in any other year; it seems likely that numerous petitions will be filed for many years into the future.

✓ A customer that enters bankruptcy may present a supplier with an opportunity for significant profits because businesses that enter Chapter 11 of the bankruptcy code may continue to operate and thus continue to need suppliers.

✓ However, before a supplier contracts with a company in bankruptcy, it should evaluate the risk of nonpayment notwithstanding the fact that it will be entitled to an administrative priority claim for the value of its goods.

✓ A business in bankruptcy may continue its ordinary operations; to the extent that a particular supplier may be outside what, for the debtor, is the ordinary course, the debtor should obtain a court order authorizing the proposed transaction with the supplier in advance.

✓ The bankruptcy code has special laws relating to a seller's rights to reclaim goods from insolvent buyers in bankruptcy (see chapter 30). It also affords special protections to secured creditors (see chapter 27).

ESPECIALLY FOR MARKETING EXECUTIVES

32

THE RISKS OF WHITE COLLAR CRIME

❚ Criminal Liability ❚ Mail Fraud ❚ False Statements ❚ Other Crimes
❚ What to Do ❚ A Final Word

Hayes International Corp. operated an airplane refurbishing plant in Birmingham, Alabama. In the course of its business, Hayes generated certain waste products, including fuel that it drained from the fuel tanks on the planes on which it worked and paint and solvents from painting the aircraft with spray guns and cleaning the paint guns and lines.

L. H. Beasley was the Hayes employee responsible for disposal of hazardous wastes. In early 1981, Beasley orally agreed with Jack Hurt, an employee of Performance Advantage, Inc., that Performance would dispose of Hayes' wastes. Performance agreed to pay Hayes 20 cents per gallon for the valuable jet fuel Hayes drained from the planes and, at no charge, to remove other wastes from the Hayes plant including the mixture of paint and solvents. Performance was a recycler, and used the jet fuel to make marketable fuel. Performance transported wastes from Hayes on eight occasions between January 1981 and March 1982.

Beginning in August 1982, government officials discovered drums of waste generated by Hayes and illegally disposed of by Performance. The government found approximately 600 drums, deposited among seven illegal disposal sites in Georgia and Alabama. The waste was the paint and solvent that Performance had removed from Hayes. Some of the drums were simply dumped in yards, while others were buried.

The government indicted Hayes—and Beasley—on charges of violating the federal Resource Conservation and Recovery Act (RCRA). That law creates a cradle to grave regulatory scheme to ensure that hazardous wastes are properly disposed of. Generators of waste are required to identify hazardous wastes and use a manifest system to ensure that wastes are disposed of only in facilities possessing a permit.

The regulatory scheme sets forth two different methods of identifying a hazardous waste. A waste is hazardous if it appears on a list of wastes adopted by the Environmental Protection Agency. A waste also is hazardous if it possesses certain characteristics. The mixture of paint waste and solvent is a characteristic waste based on its ignitability. Performance did not have a permit.

After trial, Beasley and Hayes were convicted of eight counts of violating RCRA for "knowingly" transporting hazardous waste to a facility that did not have a permit. The case reached the U.S. Court of Appeals for the Eleventh Circuit.

Beasley and Hayes contended that they had not committed any "knowing" violation because they misunderstood the regulations. They also contended that they had not "known" that Performance did not have a permit. Finally, they contended that they had not committed a knowing violation because they believed that Performance was recycling the waste. The court rejected all of their arguments.

RCRA, the court said, is a public welfare statute involving a heavily regulated area with great ramifications for the public health and safety. The court said that it was completely fair and reasonable to charge those who choose to operate in this kind of area with knowledge of the relevant regulations. It ruled that "ignorance of the regulatory status is no excuse."

The court also ruled that, based on the evidence presented by the government, the jury could have found beyond a reasonable doubt that Hayes and Beasley knew that Performance did not have a permit.

Finally, the court said, the jury could quite reasonably have concluded based on the evidence that Beasley did not believe the waste was being recycled. "Beasley was directly told that the waste was being disposed of rather than recycled, and he nevertheless continued to ship waste to Performance," the court noted. It then ruled that the jury verdicts of guilty should be upheld.

▌Criminal Liability

The law is no more serious than when it gets down to criminal violations. Quite simply, this can mean jail; at the least, it can require payment of significant penalties that are not reimbursable through insurance and that are not payable by an employer. When a corporate employee, officer, or director breaks the law in the course of employment, the risks are real.

But just how serious is the risk? When the penalties are so severe, it would seem apparent that even a small probability of a great penalty presents a weighty problem. Now that the go-go 1980s have come and gone, the likelihood is that criminal prosecutions of employees (and their corporate employers) are only likely to increase.

Employees can commit a wide range of white collar crimes, ranging from the environmental violations for which Beasley was found guilty to prohibitions against bribery of foreign officials under the Foreign Corrupt Practices Act.

Two commonly used federal criminal laws served as the basis for criminal convictions stemming from a comprehensive criminal investigation conducted by the Antitrust Division of the United States Department of Justice into the practices of the river construction industry of the Mississippi River and its major tributaries.

On September 27, 1978, a grand jury of the Eastern District of Louisiana indicted much of that industry—10 individuals and 16 corporations. The indictment charged one count of conspiracy to restrain competition in violation of the Sherman Antitrust Act, 29 counts of mail fraud, and 24 counts of false statement. The charges related to an alleged bid-rigging scheme allegedly carried out by the industry between 1964 and 1978 for the allocation of river bank stabilization projects awarded by the United States Army Corps of Engineers.

▮ Mail Fraud

The federal mail fraud statute essentially condemns any scheme to defraud in which the mails are used. To convict of mail fraud, the prosecution must establish beyond a reasonable doubt, among other things, that the defendants participated in a "scheme or artifice to defraud" and that there was use of the mails "for the purpose of executing the scheme."

In the bid-rigging case, the U.S. Court of Appeals for the Fifth Circuit said that the government's evidence indicated a long-running scheme designed to circumvent competitive bidding procedures of the Corps of Engineer by "arranging" bids to allocate the river construction work. The government's principal witnesses were four river contractors who testified in detail regarding pre-bid allocation meetings over a period of years and in a number of cities including Omaha, Kansas City, St. Louis, Memphis, Vicksburg, and New Orleans. The operation of the scheme, the court said, remained consistent over the years; through face to face meetings or telephone conversations the river contractors would collectively agree on who would be awarded the Corps jobs. The other co-schemers were then given prices "to clear" or "to protect" and either submitted complementary bids or did not bid at all. The common goal—to allocate Corps of Engineers river construction work—remained constant throughout the scheme, the court said.

The mailings charged as the basis of the mail fraud counts were sent by the Corps of Engineers to contractors who obtained the allocated work. There were two kinds of mailings: "notices to proceed" that were sent to instruct a contractor to commence construction on a project and checks in payment for completed work. One defendant argued that the mailings were not sufficiently related to the scheme to defraud to support the convictions and that, further, the scheme did not "cause" those mailings. The court rejected those arguments.

The court said that it was "well settled" that use of the mails will support a mail fraud conviction if it is incident to an essential part of the scheme. The court recognized that the scheme defrauded the government of its right to depend upon the competitive process to allocate the jobs and to set the costs of those jobs. It said that the mailings from the government were crucial to the scheme—it "would have been meaningless, incomplete, and futile without final award and payment which were accomplished through the mail." Clearly, the court ruled, the mails were used "in furtherance" of the scheme.

▌ False Statements

To convict any defendant of making a false statement in violation of federal law, the government must prove beyond a reasonable doubt that the defendant knowingly made a false statement on a matter within the jurisdiction of a federal agency or department, that the false statement related to a material matter, and that the defendant acted willfully with knowledge of the falsity of the statement.

In the bid-rigging case, bidders made certain certifications on each bid submitted to the Corps of Engineers on river construction work. Among the certificates on the bids was the following: "The prices in this bid have been arrived at independently, without consultation, communication, or agreement, for the purpose of restricting competition, as to any matter relating to such prices with any other bidder or with any competitor." Two of the defendants contended that because of an allegedly misplaced comma following "agreement" the certification literally meant not that the bid was independently made to protect competition but that "the prices in this bid have been independently arrived at for the purpose of restricting competition." Accordingly, although they admitted making the statements, they contended that because the statement was not literally false it could not serve to support the false statement convictions. The court rejected that position. "Despite defendants' novel contention, the certification 'fairly read,' . . . stated that the bids were entered independently and not collusively. That statement was false and the defendants knew it."

▌ Other Crimes

Numerous federal and state laws are used to prosecute corporate executives for actions they take in the course of their business: mail fraud; wire fraud (involving use of the interstate phone lines); conspiracy; antitrust laws (especially with respect to bid-rigging, price-fixing, and customer allocation); federal securities laws, including insider trading rules; prohibitions against false statements to government officials; and environmental crimes. The list goes on and on: the federal Racketeer Influenced and Corrupt Organizations Act (known as RICO) is often used to prosecute business people, as well as mobsters and racketeers. Federal and state laws prohibit commercial bribery; violations can lead to criminal sanctions, civil fines and penalties, and, perhaps, a court order voiding the tainted contract. Indeed, in recent years, penalties for commercial bribery have increased—New York recently changed the crime of commercial bribery in the second degree to a Class A misdemeanor from a Class B misdemeanor; it raised commercial bribery in the first degree, which occurs when a bribe greater than $1,000 causes more than $250 in damage to the bribed employee's employer, from a misdemeanor to a felony. The penalties under the federal law prohibiting kickbacks in connection with government contracts have been raised recently, too.

▌ What to Do

There are five steps that businesspeople should keep in mind to protect themselves from criminal prosecution.

First, as a general rule, more disclosure is better than less disclosure and accurate disclosure to customers is essential. Is making a sale worth risking jail?

Second, because ignorance of the law may not be a defense, get legal advice when in doubt. Read newsletters that lawyers provide; go to seminars about the antitrust laws, RICO, and other aspects of white collar crime; ask questions.

Third, follow company rules regarding record retention. It is not a good thing to destroy a document right before it is subpoenaed by a federal grand jury, but it is less of a bad thing if the destruction occurred in the ordinary course.

Fourth, keep business and pleasure separate. For instance, avoid using office supplies and office workers for personal business; reject gifts that have a substantial value unless a supervisor has specifically granted permission in writing.

Finally, because of the severe nature of potential criminal prosecution, corporate executives should make sure to speak with their own lawyer—not just the company's lawyer—before talking with government investigators or appearing before a grand jury. It is a sign of nothing—other than intelligence—to refuse to speak with government investigators. They are not friends; they are doing a job.

▌ A Final Word

In recent years, federal and state governments seem to have expanded the number of areas to which corporate officers and directors may be subject to criminal liability—and thus jail or other severe criminal penalties. Perhaps just as important, criminal prosecutions against corporate officers and directors have skyrocketed. This may be a reflection on the 1980s "era of greed" or, perhaps less cynically, a desire on the part of government prosecutors to try to improve the actions of corporate America. Whatever the reason, the potential downside is quite real.

Criminal laws for the most part tend to make unlawful those things that moral people know are improper. If it feels wrong, don't do it. If it is an industry-wide "policy" and it feels wrong, change industries. Or accept the quite substantial risks.

FIVE CRIMINAL CASES

1. From the mid-1950s to 1962, when the federal government finally removed them from the market, John Andreadis (who also was known as John Andre) and Andreadis's Drug Research Corporation manufactured and sold Regimen tablets as a miracle weight-reducing drug. The tablets consisted of supplies of three pills: a green pill containing 22.5 mg. of benzocaine plus vitamins and minerals that was supposed to deaden the tongue and sense of taste; a pink pill containing 648 mg. of ammonium chloride and various vitamins that was supposed to act as a diuretic; and a yellow pill containing 75 mg. of phenyl propanolamine (PPA) that was supposed to act as an appetite depressant. Boxes of Regimen Tablets were sold over-the-counter in two sizes: a three dollar box containing 78 tablets, the so-called 10-day supply; and a five dollar box containing 156 tablets, a so-called 20-day supply.

In the beginning, Drug Research used mail-order advertising to sell Regimen Tablets. The advertising materials claimed that Regimen Tablets were a new "wonder drug for fat people" that made possible "no-diet reducing" and that without dieting, special eating, or giving up "the kinds of food you like to eat" the pills would cause "your body to lose weight the fastest acting way." Newspaper and magazine advertisements and television ads also claimed that Regimen Tablets made possible "no-diet" reducing or reducing "without dieting" and that the pills had been "clinically tested" or "proven clinically effective." In certain instances, Drug Research qualified these claims when a national magazine or television program refused to accept the Regimen Tablets copy as submitted, but Andreadis agreed to these changes grudgingly and ordered his advertising agency to retain the extravagant claims in the copy submitted to other media.

The federal government indicted Andreadis and his company for knowingly using either the mails or radio and television in interstate commerce in furtherance of an intentional scheme to defraud prospective purchasers of Regimen Tablets by false or fraudulent pretenses, representations, and promises in violation of the federal mail fraud and wire fraud statutes. The thrust of the government's case was that Andreadis and Drug Research intended to defraud consumers because their representations and statements were scientifically and factually false and yet they continued to include them in their ads for the product. Andreadis and Drug Research were found guilty of 16 counts of mail fraud, 27 counts of wire fraud, and conspiracy, and they appealed to the U.S. Court of Appeals for the Second Circuit. The Second Circuit upheld their convictions. It ruled that the government had presented sufficient evidence to support its claims that certain representations and statements found in most advertising for Regimen Tablets were scientifically and factually false, that Andreadis and Drug Research knew them to be false, and that despite this falsity and their knowledge of the falsity, they continued to include these representations and statements in their advertising. (United States v. Andreadis, 366 F.2d 423 (2d Cir. 1966).)

2. A New Jersey law stated that "whoever gives, offers or promises to an agent, employee or servant any gift or gratuity whatever, without the knowledge and consent of the principal, employer or master of such agent, employee or servant, with intent to influence his action in relation to his principal's, employer's or master's business," shall be guilty of a misdemeanor.

In the early 1920s, Edward Landecker, an employee of Richards Chemical Works, was indicted for violating that New Jersey statute. The government contended that Landecker offered and paid $100 to another employee of Richards Chemical to obtain a secret formula belonging to Richards Chemical that the company used in manufacturing silk goods. After Landecker was tried and convicted, he appealed to the Supreme Court of New Jersey. He argued, among other things, that the prosecutor did not show that Richards Chemical had been injured by Landecker's actions.

The court rejected his contentions. The test, it said, was whether the person who gave, offered, or promised the gift or gratuity did so with the intent denounced by the law. "Where that intent appears, it is quite immaterial whether its successful carrying out will be injurious to the business of the employer or not." The court concluded that the "legislative purpose . . . [was] to punish attempts to corruptly influence agents, employees, or servants with relation to the matters indicated in the body of the act; and proof that such attempt has been made is proof that the statutory provision has been violated." (State v. Landecker, 126 A. 409 (Sup. Ct. N.J. 1924).)

3. When a grand jury indicted the National Dairy Products Corporation for allegedly engaging "in a combination and conspiracy to eliminate price competition in the sale of milk in the Greater Kansas City market in unreasonable restraint of . . . trade and commerce, in violation of Section 1" of the Sherman Antitrust Act, it also indicted an officer of the company. The officer argued that the Sherman Antitrust Act did not apply to corporate officers acting in their official capacity and his indictment was dismissed by a federal district court judge.

The case reached the United States Supreme Court. Under Section 1, "[e]very contract, combination in the form of trust or otherwise, or conspiracy, in restraint of trade or commerce among the several States, or with foreign nations, is declared to be illegal." In addition, "[e]very person who shall make any contract, or engage in any combination or conspiracy declared . . . to be illegal shall be deemed guilty of a misdemeanor." Noting that corporate officers have been indicted under the Sherman Antitrust Act almost since it was first enacted in 1890, the Supreme Court ruled that a corporate officer was subject to criminal prosecution under Section 1 of the Sherman Antitrust Act "whenever he knowingly participates in effecting the illegal contract, combination, or conspiracy—be he one who authorizes, orders, or helps perpetrate the crime—regardless of whether he is acting in a representative capacity." (United States v. Wise, 370 U.S. 405 (1962).)

4. Between January 1983 and June 1987, Richard H. Liebo was vice-president in charge of the Aerospace Division of NAPCO International, Inc. located in Hopkins, Minnesota. NAPCO's primary business consisted of selling military equipment and supplies throughout the world. In early 1983 the Niger government contracted with a West German company, Dornier Reparaturwerft, to service two Lockheed C-130 cargo planes. After the Niger Ministry of Defense ran into financial troubles, Dornier sought an American parts supplier to qualify the Ministry of Defense for financing through the United States foreign military sales program. The foreign military sales program was supervised by the Defense Security Assistance Agency, an agency of the United States Department of Defense. Under the program, loans were provided to foreign governments for the purchase of military equipment and supplies from American contractors.

In June 1983, representatives from Dornier met with officials of NAPCO and agreed that NAPCO would become the prime contractor on the C-130 maintenance contracts. Under this arrangement, NAPCO would supply parts to Niger and Dornier, and Dornier would perform the required maintenance at its facilities in Munich. Once NAPCO and Dornier agreed to these terms, Liebo and Axel Kurth, a Dornier sales representative, flew to Niger to get the president of Niger's approval of the contract. In Niger, they met with Captain Ali Tiemogo, the chief of maintenance for the Niger Air Force. Liebo and Kurth allegedly told Tiemogo that they would make "some gestures" to him if he helped get the contract approved. Following Tiemogo's recommendation that the contract be approved, the president signed the contract.

Tahirou Barke, Tiemogo's cousin and close friend, worked for the Niger Embassy in Washington, D.C. Barke allegedly met Liebo in Washington in 1983 or 1984. According to Barke, Liebo said that he wanted to make a "gesture" to Captain Tiemogo and asked Barke to set up a bank account in the United States. With Barke's assistance, Liebo opened a bank account in Minnesota in the name of "E. Dave," a variation of the name of Barke's then-girlfriend, Shirley Elaine Dave. NAPCO allegedly deposited about $30,000 in the account; Barke apparently used some and gave a portion of the money to Captain Tiemogo. In August 1985, Barke allegedly informed Liebo that he was leaving for Niger to be married and that he and his wife planned to honeymoon in Paris, Stockholm, and London. Liebo allegedly offered to pay for his airline tickets as a gift. Liebo made the flight arrangements for Barke's return to Niger and for his honeymoon trip and paid for the tickets, which cost $2,028, by charging them to NAPCO's Diner's Club account.

In addition, over a two-and-a-half-year period beginning in May 1984, NAPCO made payments totaling $130,000 to three "commission agents." Using agents and paying them commissions on international contracts was an accepted business practice in third world countries. NAPCO issued commission checks to three "agents," identified as Amadou Mailele, Tiemogo's brother-in-law, Fatouma Boube, Tiemogo's sister-in-law, and E. Dave, Barke's girlfriend. At Tiemogo's request, both Mailele and Boube set up bank accounts in Paris. Neither Mailele, Boube, nor E. Dave, however, received the commission checks or acted as NAPCO's agent. Instead, these individuals were merely intermediaries through whom NAPCO made payments to Tiemogo and Barke. NAPCO's corporate president, Henri Jacob, or another superior of Liebo's apparently approved these "commission payments."

NAPCO received a total of three contracts from Niger. The parties signed one, in the amount of $1 million for the supply of spare parts and maintenance, on August 20, 1984. They signed another one, in the amount of $1.55 million, on August 2, 1985. To obtain foreign military sales program financing, NAPCO was required to submit a Contractor's Certification and Agreement with the Defense Security Assistance Agency. In the contractor's certification that NAPCO submitted in connection with the third Niger contract, Liebo certified that "no rebates, gifts or gratuities have been given contrary to United States law to officers, officials, or employees" of the Niger government. Liebo certified that NAPCO's commission agent under the contract was Amadou Mailele and that he would be paid $47,662. Liebo also certified that NAPCO paid no commissions or contingent fees to any agent to solicit or obtain the contract other than as identified in the certificate.

Liebo was indicted on 19 counts; after a three-week trial, the jury acquitted Liebo on all charges except the count concerning NAPCO's purchase of Barke's honeymoon airline tickets (under the Foreign Corrupt Practices Act) and the related count of making a false statement to a government agency. He appealed to the U.S. Court of Appeals for the Eighth Circuit. Liebo argued that his conviction under the Foreign Corrupt Practices Act should be reversed because there was insufficient evidence to show that he gave Barke the airline tickets "to obtain or retain business" and because there was no evidence to show that his gift of honeymoon tickets was done "corruptly." The appellate court said, though, that there was sufficient evidence that Liebo gave Barke the airline tickets to obtain or retain business. Tiemogo testified that the president of Niger would not approve the contracts without his recommendation. He also testified that Liebo promised to "make gestures" to him before the first contract was approved, and that Liebo promised to continue to "make gestures" if the second and third contracts were approved. Evidence established that Tiemogo and Barke were cousins and best friends. The court said that the relationship between Barke and Tiemogo could have allowed a reasonable jury to infer that Liebo made the gift to Barke intending to buy Tiemogo's help in getting the contracts approved. Indeed, the court noted, Tiemogo recommended approval of the third contract and the president of Niger approved that contract just a few weeks after Liebo gave the tickets to Barke. "Accordingly, a reasonable jury could conclude that the gift was given 'to obtain or retain business.'"

The court also ruled that there was sufficient evidence from which a reasonable jury could find that Liebo gave Barke the airline tickets "corruptly." For example, Liebo gave the airline tickets to Barke shortly before Niger approved the third contract. That evidence, together with undisputed evidence concerning the close relationship between Tiemogo and Barke and Tiemogo's important role in the contract approval process, was sufficient for a reasonable jury to find that Liebo's gift to Barke was given "corruptly," the court said. (The court did, however, order a new trial for Liebo on the basis of newly discovered evidence that indicated that NAPCO's president had approved the charge of the airline tickets to NAPCO's Diner's Club card. The court said that this may have indicated that Liebo acted at his supervisor's direction and therefore did not act "corruptly" by giving the tickets to Barke.) (United States v. Liebo, 923 F.2d 1308 (8th Cir. 1991).)

5. By 1976 more than 77,000 of the 86,000 lots that had been staked out on a 91,000-acre tract of land known as the Rio Rancho Estates, located in Sandoval County, New Mexico, had been sold, mostly to people living outside of New Mexico. Rio Rancho Estates, Inc., a wholly owned subsidiary of the AMREP Corporation, had purchased the property, located some 15 to 20 miles northwest of downtown Albuquerque, for $17.8 million; it received approximately $170 million for the 77,000 lots that it sold. However, as of 1976, only 1,700 lots on this 142-square-mile tract were occupied by homes. Moreover, most of the vacant lots were on unpaved roads and without utilities of any sort.

The United States government contended that the volume of sales and the disparity between Rio Rancho Estate's purchase price and selling price resulted in large measure from two fraudulent sales representations made by AMREP, Rio Rancho Estates, another AMREP subsidiary, and various of the companies' officers and directors, including a senior vice-president of sales. The first was that Albuquerque was "bursting at the seams" with people and was so situated geographically that it could grow only to the northwest through Rio Rancho. The second was that the purchase of a Rio Rancho lot would be a safe and profitable investment. After a jury convicted the defendants of 20 counts of mail fraud and of 5 counts of interstate land sale fraud, they appealed to the U.S. Court of Appeals for the Second Circuit. The appellate court noted that most of the sales after 1964 resulted from "slickly organized and carefully scripted promotional dinners and tours." The scripts, which all sales representatives were required to follow, emphasized that Albuquerque, "one of the fastest growing cities" in the country, had "one unique, serious problem." It was surrounded on three sides by mountains or government land so that its future growth could go in one direction only, i.e., "in the very path where Rio Rancho Estates is located."

The government introduced substantial evidence that these representations were untrue and that the defendants knew them to be untrue. For example, a planning report published by Albuquerque in 1964 stated: "Albuquerque has an abundance of vacant land available for urban development. Even the most optimistic growth projections would not utilize this land within the current century." The court then stated that declarations of opinion as to future events that the declarant does not in fact hold "may be found by a jury to be fraudulent." Furthermore, it said, declarations made with reckless indifference for the truth may be viewed in the same light.

The court then analyzed what the government said was the defendants' second fraudulent representation. The court said that because of Albuquerque's failure to expand to Rio Rancho and also because of the manner in which Rio Rancho itself was developed, there was an extremely limited resale market for Rio Rancho lots. It said the jury could have concluded from this that the purchase of these lots as a profitable investment was unwise and unwarranted. However, the defendants had told purchasers that "investment" was "truly the key, the theme" to the defendants' program, that it was a "land investment program" in which they could make a great deal of money, up to 25 percent a year on their investment. Opinions given with respect to anticipated profits "carry with them the representation that they are honestly held," the court said. The expression of an opinion not honestly entertained is a factual misrepresentation that could serve as the basis for a criminal conviction for fraud.

The court said that "where, as here, the proof shows that corporate officers participated in setting up a fraudulent sales program, trained and instructed the salesmen, prepared sales pitches widely and consistently used, and monitored the results thereof, the statements and representations made by the sales representatives in furtherance of the scheme are admissible against the officers." This is so, the court said, even though the sales representatives themselves were not participants in the fraudulent scheme. The court concluded that the active and knowing participation by the corporate officers in the fraud made them equally liable with the corporate defendants. (United States v. AMREP Corp., 560 F.2d 539 (2d Cir. 1977).)

White Collar Crime Checklist

✓ The 1990s are likely to see increased government interest in prosecuting white collar crimes. To paraphrase a federal government ad used in a different context, that could mean you!

✓ Even though acting on behalf of an employer, a corporate executive may be held liable for participating in a criminal act.

✓ Numerous and diverse federal and state laws can be used to impose criminal liability—possibly resulting in jail time and significant fines and penalties.

✓ Criminal laws to which corporate officers should pay particular attention include laws relating to mail fraud, wire fraud, antitrust, RICO, the environment, and commercial bribery.

✓ To protect oneself, corporate executives should recognize that it is better to disclose too much rather than too little; that they should take advantage of all opportunities to learn about the law and to discuss matters with counsel; that records should be disposed of properly; that they should avoid improperly benefiting from their employment; and that they should never speak to government investigators or appear before a grand jury without advice from their own lawyers.

33

THE RISKS OF PERSONAL LIABILITY

▌Personal Liability ▌Antitrust Liability ▌Breach of Duty
▌Corporate Fraud ▌Personal Guarantees ▌Securities Laws
▌Tax Liability ▌Costs of Suit ▌A Final Word

Alleging that a corporation known as Trail Bronc, Inc. had breached a contract to provide janitorial services at Warren Air Force Base in Wyoming, the United States government filed a breach of contract suit seeking to recover its damages against Trail Bronc—and against David E. Van Diviner and Harold E. Lipsmeyer, as "surviving officers" of the corporation.

After a trial, the district court entered judgment against all three defendants, finding them jointly and severally liable. It then amended its judgment by dismissing Lipsmeyer. Van Diviner appealed.

The U.S. Court of Appeals for the Tenth Circuit noted in the decision it issued on Van Diviner's appeal that a corporation is ordinarily regarded as a separate entity distinct from the individuals comprising it. Thus, personal liability cannot be imposed on an individual merely because the person is an officer or shareholder of a corporation.

The court stated that the contract was in the name of Trail Bronc, Inc. and was signed in the name of Trail Bronc, Inc. by Van Diviner. But that was insufficient to hold Van Diviner personally liable. "Unless otherwise agreed, a person making or purporting to make a contract with another as agent for a disclosed principal does not become a party to the contract," the court said.

The government also contended that Van Diviner had signed some letters to the government in his own name and thus should be deemed to have agreed to become liable on the contract. But the court rejected the government's contention that Van Diviner could be sued for breach of contract on the ground that he was an individual party to the contract, finding that he was not.

Finally, the government also argued that Van Diviner could be sued personally because he had disregarded the requirement that he keep his corporation separate from himself and thus Trail Bronc, Inc. and Van Diviner should be treated as the same entity.

Courts consider a variety of factors in determining whether to respect the corporate form:

- Whether the corporation is operated as a separate entity

- Commingling of funds and other assets

- Failure to maintain adequate corporate records or minutes

- The nature of the corporation's ownership and control

- Disregard of legal formalities and the failure to maintain an arms-length relationship among related entities

- Diversion of the corporation's funds or assets to noncorporate uses

Upon reviewing the evidence, though, the court found that Trail Bronc's corporate form should not be disregarded to allow the government to sue Van Diviner for breach of contract. While there was evidence that indicated that he did not always scrupulously maintain the distinction between himself and the corporation, the court found "no evidence that he commingled the corporation's funds with his own, distributed to himself corporate assets, misled the government or anyone, or otherwise misused or abused the corporate form in a way that would threaten injustice to the government."

❙ Personal Liability

As the Van Diviner case indicates, employees of corporations may not be held liable for every one of their employer's debts—indeed, avoiding personal liability is one of the major reasons that businesses incorporate. What the Van Diviner case does not show, though, is that there are numerous cases where corporate executives and officers may be held liable to third parties as a result of "doing their job" or with respect to debts or other obligations incurred by their employers. In recent years, the number of suits brought by third parties, competitors, former employees, and shareholders against corporate officers and directors has skyrocketed.

Many of the areas of law under which criminal liability may be imposed on corporate officers and directors also can serve as the basis for civil liability. What follows is a short summary of a number of important potential areas for liability.

❙ Antitrust Liability

More than 100 years ago, Congress passed the Sherman Antitrust Act of 1890. Fearful of monopolies and perhaps somewhat distrustful of big business, the law is the principal restriction on "restraints of trade" although other federal and state antitrust laws also prohibit certain actions, such as improperly "tying" the sale of one product to another and improperly discriminating among customers with respect to price. In addition to the Sherman Act's criminal provisions, which are discussed in chapter 32, the law also provides civil liability and permits successful plaintiffs to recover treble, or triple, damages from defendants.

Corporate officers are subject to liability for antitrust violations, such as price fixing and other anticompetitive practices, of their employers. Indeed, one New York judge has referred to antitrust liability as "an occupational hazard to the officers and directors of large corporations, as truly as falling from a ladder is an occupational hazard to a painter or carpenter."

❙ Breach of Duty

Corporate officers and directors must fulfill the obligations of their positions in good faith and must seek to benefit their corporate employers. When something goes wrong, they often are sued for breach of their "fiduciary duty" to their companies. A fiduciary is a person that has a special relationship of trust or confidence with another. A breach of fiduciary duty is a failure to meet that level.

The test by which actions of corporate officers and directors is measured is known as the business judgment rule. To the extent that executives act along the lines that other reasonable and similarly situated executives would act, the business judgment rule should protect them from liability.

▌Corporate Fraud

Corporate officers and directors generally may not be held individually liable for the conduct of their corporate employers, whether the conduct involves contract performance or fraud. However, they may be held liable if they have directly and actively participated in, or knowingly acquiesced in, their corporations' fraud or other wrongdoings.

▌Personal Guarantees

Ordinarily, when a corporation borrows money from a bank or acquires inventory, equipment, or other goods on credit from suppliers, only the corporation is liable; the corporation's officers and directors are not liable for these kinds of debts or corporate obligations.

However, especially in companies that are not public companies and that do not have widespread stock ownership (in other words, in privately owned companies), creditors—especially lenders—often insist that corporate executives give up this freedom from personal liability by agreeing to be liable for the corporation's debts. Executives relinquish that very valuable benefit when they personally sign guarantees agreeing that they may be held responsible for a particular corporate obligation in the event the corporation fails to meet it. On occasion, creditors may insist that these exectuives also put up collateral (such as their homes) to back up their guarantees. Executives faced with a creditor's request for a guarantee must examine it quite closely, because their net worth could be quite seriously impaired if something were to go wrong with the business.

▌Securities Laws

Corporate officers and directors of most large companies must be aware of the requirements of federal (and state) securities laws, from which civil (and criminal) liability may be imposed. Material misrepresentations in publicly filed documents, or the failure to disclose material information, can result in liability. Significant rules apply with respect to mergers, the sale of stock, and other securities-related transactions.

▌ Tax Liability

The Internal Revenue Code (IRC) provides that taxes required to be deducted by employers from the wages paid to employees under Section 3102(a) and 3402(a) of the IRC, such as withholding and Social Security taxes, "shall be held to be a special fund in trust for the United States." Thus, the withheld funds are commonly referred to as "trust fund" taxes.

If a corporation is unable to pay its trust fund taxes, the United States Treasury suffers the loss because the employees from whose wages the taxes were withheld are still credited with those amounts as if they had in fact been paid to the government. As a result, Congress has imposed personal liability on any officer or employee of a corporation who is responsible for the collection and payment of trust fund taxes who "willfully fails to collect such tax, or truthfully account for and pay over such tax, or willfully attempts in any manner to evade or defeat such tax or the payment thereof." These officers and employees are termed "responsible persons."

▌ Costs of Suit

Certainly, many corporations have director and officer liability insurance and many agree to indemnify officers and directors from costs associated with litigation arising from the course of their official conduct. However, that may not be enough. A corporate indemnity is only as good as the financial status of the corporation that has issued the indemnity; if it is insolvent or otherwise in difficult financial straits, the indemnity may be valueless. Similarly, director and officer liability insurance may provide little comfort when the insurer disclaims coverage if the alleged acts fit within exceptions to the policy—such as for environmental liabilities or intentional acts. Counsel fees in protracted litigation can run past six figures, a difficult nut for most executives to crack on their own.

▌ A Final Word

Corporate directors, officers, and employees may not necessarily be held liable for all debts or other obligations of their corporate employers—the corporate form generally protects them from that liability.

However, there are significant possibilities for the imposition of personal liability on corporate employees. Certain laws, including the environmental and tax laws, specifically provide for liability on individuals notwithstanding corporate formalities. In addition, employees who actively participate in, or knowingly acquiesce in, a corporation's wrongdoing may be held liable to injured third parties.

FIVE CIVIL CASES

1. L. B. Industries, Inc. contended in a lawsuit it filed that David Smith, a corporate director of Independent Power Developers, Inc., and his employer Control Data Capital Corporation, a minority shareholder of Independent Power, were liable for fraudulent misrepresentations allegedly made to L. B. Industries by William Delp, the president of Independent Power and Homestake Consulting and Investments, Inc. L. B. Industries acknowledged that neither Smith nor Control Data specifically directed, actively participated in, or knowingly acquiesced in Delp's alleged fraudulent activities but argued that they should be held liable for Delp's alleged wrongdoing because Smith, as one of Independent Power's corporate directors, had some degree of knowledge of Delp's activities.

Evidence at trial indicated that in December 1979, pursuant to a financing arrangement between Control Data and Independent Power, Control Data designated Smith to sit on Independent Power's three-member board of directors. From January 1980 through July 1981 Smith became increasingly concerned about the propriety of Delp's activities on behalf of Independent Power. At some point during that period, Control Data and Smith became aware that Independent Power was becoming unable to meet its contractual obligations. Smith continued to sit on the board of Independent Power until June 1982, and a subsidiary of Control Data continued to provide technological assistance to Independent Power until that date. However, at no point did Smith or Control Data ever specifically direct, actively participate in, or knowingly acquiesce in Delp's alleged fraudulent activities.

The federal district court granted summary judgment in favor of Smith and Control Data, ruling that their relationship to Delp's alleged fraudulent activities was too remote for them to be held liable. The case reached the U.S. Court of Appeals for the Ninth Circuit, which upheld the district court's decision. It ruled that because Smith and Control Data did not specifically direct, actively participate in, or knowingly acquiesce in the fraudulent activities that Delp allegedly engaged in as president of Independent Power, they could not be held liable to L.B. Industries. (L.B. Industries, Inc. v. Smith, 817 F.2d 69 (9th Cir. 1987).)

2. Claiming that she was fired in violation of the Age Discrimination in Employment Act, Yvonne Fletcher filed suit against Becky Loosen, her former boss, and the Wesley Medical Center, Inc., her former employer. She also asserted a claim for the "tort of outrage." Loosen and Wesley Medical asked the trial court to dismiss the tort of outrage claim. The court noted that the tort of outrage allows an injured party to sue one "who by extreme and outrageous conduct intentionally or recklessly causes severe emotional distress to another." The "extreme and outrageous" conduct of which Fletcher complained boiled down, the court said, to "nothing more" than that Loosen and Wesley Medical fired her ostensibly for legitimate reasons but actually because of her age. The court stated that the termination of an employee, whatever the secret motive underlying it, is the kind of event that happens every day; "such an act is not even a breach of modern-day business etiquette, much less an uncivilized barbarism." According to the court, quite a bit more—such as a stream of vulgar, racist invective, and threats of violence—must accompany a firing if it is to be deemed "outrageous." It then dismissed Fletcher's "outrage" claim. (Fletcher v. Wesley Medical Center, 585 F.Supp. 1261 (D. Kansas 1984).)

3. Arthur Jensen, Inc. was an Alaska corporation engaged in the housing construction business. Arthur Jensen owned over half of the corporation's stock and served as its president. The corporation became insolvent in 1980. Alaska Valuation Service conduced appraisals for Arthur

Jensen from the early 1970s until 1979. On July 19, 1979, Jensen ordered by telephone appraisals on five single-family homes. Alaska Valuation was to appraise these residences from plans and blueprints rather than from an actual inspection of the sites. Its president, Alfred Ferrara, who took the order, recorded it as being for Art Jensen. Alaska Valuation later sent invoices to "Art Jensen, Jensen Builders" at the corporation's Anchorage post office box address. Arthur Jensen, Inc. was not mentioned in Alaska Valuation's records until late 1979, when Jensen specifically informed Alaska Valuation of his company's corporate status. The appraisals Jensen ordered on July 19 were completed but never paid for.

In 1982 Alaska Valuation filed a complaint for $823 against Jensen personally in small claims court. Jensen admitted the amount of the debt but denied any personal liability. At trial, Ferrara testified that he had not been aware that Jensen had been doing business as a corporation until late 1979. He stated that his company's records had always shown Jensen as "Arthur Jensen, Jensen Builders" and that he had assumed that Jensen operated as a sole proprietorship. Jensen testified that he had always paid for appraisal services with his corporation's checks. He also testified that he placed signs with his corporation's name on each of the houses he built. He conceded, however, that Alaska Valuation completed the appraisals before he began construction on the houses. He testified that he could not think of anything other than the checks that might have put Alaska Valuation on notice that it was dealing with a corporation.

The small claims court concluded that "just writing checks after the fact to a bookkeeper" did not provide Alaska Valuation with adequate notice of Arthur Jensen's position as an agent of a corporation. It awarded Alaska Valuation $831, and Jensen appealed. Ordinarily, the Supreme Court of Alaska stated, officers of a corporation may not be held personally liable for contracts they make as agents of their corporation; however, they must disclose their agency and the existence of the corporation before they will be absolved from liability. The court then stated that it would not disturb the lower court's decision that Jensen's use of corporate checks did not provide Alaska Valuation with notice of his company's corporate status. (Jensen v. Alaska Valuation Service, Inc., 688 P.2d 161 (Sup. Ct. Alaska 1984).)

4. For many years, Shipowners & Merchants Tugboat Co., Ltd. and the Bay Cities Transportation Company were engaged in the ship assist and ship towing business on the San Francisco Bay and its tributaries. Both companies were substantially owned and controlled by the Crowley family; major decisions by the management of either company required the approval of Thomas B. Crowley, who was the principal officer of each of the companies. Beginning in about 1973, Crowley Maritime Corporation became the holding corporation of these companies and gradually undertook to provide various administrative services.

In the early 1970s, a six-month tug strike idled the Crowley companies' ship assist business. During the strike, other companies entered the ship assist business in the area, including the Murphy-Pacific Marine Salvage Corporation, which had acquired the use of seven tugs. Roger Murphy headed the ship assist operations for Murphy Pacific. After the strike was over, the Crowley companies resumed their operations and Murphy-Pacific began to suffer substantial losses in its ship assist operations and ultimately agreed to sell its tugs to the Crowley interests in June 1971. For some years before Murphy's entry into the ship assist business, the Crowley companies had a policy of refusing, except in emergencies, to provide service to a vessel that also was being assisted by tugs of another company. Thus, if a vessel had arranged for ship assist services with another tugboat company, and more tugs were required for the job than that company could furnish, Crowley would decline to furnish the additional tugs to work with the tugs of the other company. It gave as a reason for the policy the hazards of dividing responsibility in ship handling. (Other Crowley-controlled companies operating in Los Angeles harbor and Puget Sound, and other tugboat companies operating in New York harbor, did not adhere to such a policy.)

After Murphy-Pacific sold its tugs to Crowley, Murphy organized the Murphy Tugboat Company, which entered the ship assist business on San Francisco Bay with a single tug. It remained in business, acquiring additional tugs, until September 1975. Murphy then filed suit against Crowley and his companies, alleging that their policy of refusing to work with competitors effectively excluded Murphy from the large vessel segment of the ship assist market, where most of the demand for multi-tug jobs arose. Murphy contended that but for Crowley's exclusionary practice, its share of the large vessel market would have been equal to the 28 percent share it held of the small vessel market. A jury found that Crowley and his companies had engaged in a monopoly or an attempt to monopolize the market and awarded Murphy more than $700,000 in damages, including $180,000 from Thomas B. Crowley personally.

The defendants asked the court for judgment notwithstanding the verdict. The court noted that Thomas B. Crowley was at all material times his companies' chief executive officer with authority to exercise control over their operations. Individuals through whom a corporation acts and who shape its intentions can be held liable on a charge of attempted monopolization, the court stated. But, the court said, the evidence of Thomas B. Crowley's conduct did not sustain a finding that he participated in inherently wrongful conduct. "While he must be assumed, as chief executive officer, knowingly to have approved or ratified the policy of refusing to work vessels with competitors, that policy . . . cannot be said to be inherently wrongful." In the absence of evidence of knowing approval of inherently wrongful acts, the court said that he "cannot be held personally liable for the corporate defendants' violation of [the Sherman Antitrust Act]." (Murphy Tugboat Co. v. Shipowners & Merchants Towboat Co., Ltd., 467 F. Supp. 841 (N.D. California 1979).)

5. The Kentucky-Tennessee Light & Power Company brought suit against Henry D. Fitch, its former president, the Nashville Coal Company, and Justin Potter, its president, alleging that Fitch, in purchasing coal for the Light & Power Company, had accepted bribes from Potter and the Coal Company and that the three defendants thereby violated the Robinson-Patman antitrust law. Potter and the Coal Company paid the Light & Power Company $75,000 to settle. A jury then found that Fitch had received "compensation" from Potter or the Coal Company and it found that the Light & Power Company had been damaged in the amount of $58,788.01; the court trebled that sum, credited the $75,000, and entered judgment against Fitch. The court said that "[a]ny payment of compensation by a seller to an agent or representative of the buyer, except for services rendered, is prohibited and unlawful, whether the agent, in receiving the commissions, is acting in the transaction in behalf of the buyer, or merely for his own pocket." It upheld Fitch's liability under the antitrust law, finding "the payment of secret commissions to Fitch was an unfair trade practice, and obviously resulted in lessening competition in the sale of the coal to the Power Company." (Fitch v. Kentucky-Tennessee Light & Power Co., 136 F.2d 12 (6th Cir. 1943).)

Civil Liability Checklist

✓ Corporate directors, officers, and employees may not be held liable for every corporate act or every corporate liability or obligation; that is the primary reason that businesses incorporate.

✓ In numerous cases, however, the law specifically imposes liability on individuals notwithstanding the corporate form. These laws include federal and state environmental laws and federal tax withholding rules.

✓ Furthermore, employees who actively participate in, or knowingly acquiesce in, a corporation's wrongdoing may be held liable to injured third parties.

✓ Particular areas of concern include the antitrust laws (with the potential for treble damage awards); breach of fiduciary duty; corporate fraud; personal guarantees; and federal and state securities laws.

✓ Corporate employees that act in good faith, deal fairly with employees, suppliers, competitors, and other business contacts, and appropriately disclose material matters can limit the risks of being faced with personal liability.

KEEPING CONFLICT OUT OF COURT

▌ Dispute Resolution in the 1990s
▌ Forms of Alternative Dispute Resolution (ADR)
▌ Benefits of ADR ▌ Potential Disadvantage of ADR
▌ Some Organizations Involved in ADR Today
▌ When ADR May Be Appropriate for a Dispute ▌ A Final Word

On February 28, 1989, Byerly Johnson, Ltd., an agent for the Chilewich International Corp., an import-export firm based in New York, signed a contract with Raznoexport, the Soviet (now Russian) Foreign Economic Association, that obligated Byerly to supply footwear to Raznoexport. Section 10 of the contract contained an arbitration clause that required all disputes "which may arise out of or in connection with the present Contract . . . to be settled . . . by the Arbitration at the USSR Chamber of Commerce and Industry, Moscow, in accordance with the Regulations of the said Arbitration."

On July 27, 1989, Melvin Chilewich sent a letter to Antonio Filograna, chief executive officer of Filanto, S.p.A., an Italian company that manufactured and sold footwear, regarding its purchasing the goods it needed to fulfill the Russian contract. The letter stated, "Attached please find our contract to cover our purchase from you. Same is governed by the conditions which are enumerated in the standard contract in effect with the Soviet buyers, copy of which is also enclosed."

Filanto apparently sent Chilewich a letter that stated that it only agreed to several paragraphs in the Russian contract; it did not include the arbitration provision in that list. Chilewich claimed never to have received that letter.

Then, on March 13, 1990, Chilewich sent Filanto a merchant's memo for signature by both parties that confirmed that Filanto would delivery 100,000 pairs of boots to Chilewich at the Italian/Yugoslav border on September 15, 1990, and 150,000 pairs on November 1, 1990. Chilewich's obligations were to open a letter of credit in Filanto's favor prior to the September 15 delivery and another letter prior to the November delivery. The memo included the following provision: "It is understood between Buyer and Seller that [the Russian contract] is hereby incorporated in this contract as far as practicable, and specifically that any arbitration shall be in accordance with that Contract."

Filanto at that time did not sign or return the document. Nevertheless, on May 7, 1990, Chilewich opened a letter of credit in Filanto's favor in the sum of $2,595,600. The letter of credit mentioned the Russian contract, but only with respect to packing and labeling.

Again, on July 23, 1990, Filanto sent another letter to Chilewich that stated that it only agreed to several paragraphs in the Russian contract, not including the arbitration provision. That letter caused some concern on the part of Chilewich and its agents; a July 30, 1990, fax from Byerly Johnson, Chilewich's agent, to Chilewich mentioned Filanto's July 23 letter and stated that Johnson would "take it up" with Filanto during a visit to Filanto's offices the following week.

Then, on August 7, 1990, Filanto returned the memo that Chilewich had sent it in March; Filanto had signed it but appended a covering letter that purported to exclude all but three sections of the Russian contract.

That same day, Chilewich sent a telex to Byerly Johnson stating that Chilewich would not open the second letter of credit unless it received from Filanto a signed copy of the contract without any exclusions.

As the date specified in the merchant's memo for delivery of the first shipment of boots—September 15, 1990—approached, the parties evidently decided to make further efforts to resolve the issue. The chief executive officer of Filanto asserted that when he was in Moscow from September 2 through September 5, 1990, he met with Simon Chilewich. "Simon Chilewich, then and there, abandoned his request . . . and agreed with me that the Filanto Chilewich Contract would incorporate only the packing, shipment and delivery terms of the [Russian contract]."

However, Chilewich said that he "met with Mr. Filograna face to face in Paris during the weekend of September 14, 1990. During that meeting, I expressly stated to him that we would have no deal if Filanto now insisted on deleting provisions of the Russian contract from our agreement. Mr. Filograna, on behalf of Filanto, stated that he would accede to our position, in order to keep Chilewich's business."

On September 27, 1990, Filograna faxed a letter to Chilewich. The letter referred to "assurances during our meeting in Paris" and complained that Chilewich had not yet opened the second letter of credit for the second delivery, which it had supposedly promised to do by September 25. Chilewich responded by fax on the same day; his fax stated that he was "totally cognizant of the contractual obligations which exist" but that Chilewich had encountered difficulties with the Russian buyers and needed to "reduce the rate of shipments." It also denied that Chilewich had promised to open the letter of credit by September 25.

According to a lawsuit that Filanto later filed against Chilewich, Chilewich bought and paid for 60,000 pairs of boots but never purchased the 90,000 pairs of boots that comprised the balance of Chilewich's original order.

After filing the lawsuit, Filanto sent a letter to Chilewich dated June 21, 1991. The letter was in response to claims by Byerly Johnson that some of the boots that had been supplied by Filanto were defective. The letter expressly relied on a section of the Russian contract that Filanto had earlier purported to exclude.

Thereafter, Chilewich asked the court to enjoin Filanto's lawsuit pending arbitration; Filanto moved to enjoin arbitration or, alternatively, for an order that arbitration be held in New York rather than Moscow because of unsettled political conditions in Russia. The court, finding among other things that Filanto's July 21 letter was an admission by Filanto that its agreement with Chilewich incorporated the terms of the Russian contract, ruled that the parties had agreed to arbitrate disputes arising from their contract. It then ordered their dispute arbitrated in Moscow.

▌ Dispute Resolution in the 1990s

For the most part, disputes among businesses are resolved through negotiations. Traditionally, when negotiations fail, the parties turn to litigation. A lawsuit is court costs; it is attorneys' fees; it is executive time spent (or, as some might describe it, wasted); and it is damaged relationships. There may be a better way: alternative dispute resolution, or ADR.

There is a growing movement by courts and legislators to mandate ADR as an adjunct to, or substitute for, litigation. ADR was a primary recommendation of former Vice-President Dan Quayle's Council on Competitiveness. Furthermore, a large number of major corporations have already pledged to the Center for Public Resources that "in the event of a business dispute between our company and another company which has made or will then make a similar statement, we are prepared to explore with that other party resolution of the dispute through negotiations or ADR techniques before pursuing full-scale litigation."

▌ Forms of Alternative Dispute Resolution (ADR)

There are many different forms of alternative dispute resolution (ADR). Because all forms are subject to the agreement of the parties, existing methods can be altered to reflect individual concerns in particular instances. Here is a short description of the most widely used ADR techniques.

- *Mediation:* In mediation, a skilled neutral helps the parties themselves reach a mutually acceptable negotiated agreement. The mediator has no authority to make a decision to resolve the dispute. The mediator facilitates the parties' exploration of their interests and helps them to fashion a solution. In the process, the mediator often helps dispel extraneous factors that may impede settlement. The mediator may also help the parties evaluate the merits of their dispute, pointing out the weaknesses in each side's case and analyzing the risks inherent in litigation.

- *Mini-trial:* In a mini-trial, lawyers for both sides present summaries of their cases—much as they do in a closing argument before a judge—to a panel consisting of a "neutral advisor" and one "decision-maker" from each side. After the hearing, the decision-makers attempt to negotiate a settlement with the assistance of the neutral advisor, who both facilitates their negotiation and helps them evaluate their cases.

- *Private trial:* In a private trial, an independent attorney retained by the parties hears evidence and legal arguments presented by both sides and renders a decision that is the equivalent of a final trial court judgment, although it is not open for public review.

- *Arbitration:* Lawyers for each side present evidence, examine witnesses, and make arguments to one or more arbitrators. The arbitrators then make a binding ruling that decides the case. Arbitration can be either formal or informal, depending on the preferences of the parties or the contractual provision that brought them to arbitration. There are several variations of arbitration, including bracketed arbitration, which sets the parameters in which an arbitrator must rule.

While not every dispute may be amenable to ADR, ADR can be used to resolve disputes in a wide range of categories, including:

- Private antitrust actions
- Insurance coverage
- Breach of contract
- Intellectual property
- Construction
- Mergers and acquisitions
- Dealer/distributor
- Noncompetition agreements
- Employment
- Professional liability
- Financial transactions
- Real estate purchase/lease

- Insolvency

- Unfair competition

▌Benefits of ADR

There are numerous benefits to resolving disputes through ADR, including:

- *Cost:* ADR can result in the resolution of a dispute at a much lower cost than a full-fledged civil lawsuit.

- *Speed:* While a lawsuit may languish in courts for years, it is possible for an ADR process to be designed, scheduled, and completed in a matter of weeks. Quick resolution eliminates longstanding contingent liabilities and the distraction affecting those involved with the dispute.

- *Privacy:* For the most part, lawsuits that get to court become a matter of public record and can become public knowledge with adverse publicity. ADR proceedings involving private parties can be kept strictly confidential if the parties so desire.

- *Finality:* The resolution of a dispute by ADR usually ends the matter. For instance, mediation culminates in the signing of a settlement agreement, which is a binding contract; arbitration awards can be appealed to the courts only in extraordinary circumstances.

- *Flexibility:* The forms of ADR can be varied to suit the needs of particular controversies. Furthermore, ADR—and mediation in particular—permits creative settlements that work to the benefit of all parties.

- *Control:* Parties to a lawsuit have limited control over the case because of the uncertainties inherent in litigation and the workings of the court system. However, mediation and other non-binding ADR processes allow disputants to retain control over their dispute. If they are not able to reach agreement at the end of a mediation session, they can simply walk away.

- *Relationships:* When parties have ongoing dealings, a dispute can disrupt relationships. The collaborative nature of many ADR processes helps to preserve a commercial relationship that might otherwise be damaged by litigation.

▮ Potential Disadvantage of ADR

There is some thought that a company's willingness to support ADR suggests weakness. This is where the marketing or sales executive can play a large role.

During contract negotiations, a corporate executive can ask that an arbitration clause (or other clause requiring the use of ADR in the event of a dispute) be added to the contract. Thus, if a dispute occurs, the parties will already be contractually bound to try to resolve it through arbitration or ADR rather than through litigation and cannot suffer a loss of face. An arbitration clause might say, "Any controversy or claim arising out of or related to this contract, or a breach of this contract, shall be settled by arbitration under the rules of the American Arbitration Association."

▮ Some Organizations Involved in ADR Today

Many companies offer arbitration or other ADR tools to businesses and individuals. Some of the leaders are:

- *Endispute:* Founded in 1981, Endispute has offices in Boston, Chicago, New York, San Francisco, and Washington, D.C. Its dispute resolution services rely on members of a panel of attorneys and former judges. It claims to resolve matters ranging from small, two-party personal injury disputes to complex, multi-party, multi-issue commercial and public disputes.

- *Judicial Arbitration & Mediation Services Co.:* Based in Orange, California, this is one of the largest—if not *the* largest—providers of ADR in the country, handling all sorts of disputes. The investment banking firm of E. M. Warburg, Pincus & Co., Inc., is reported to have invested approximately $17 million for nearly two-thirds of the company's stock. Warburg, Pincus obviously believes in the future of ADR.

- *American Arbitration Association:* An organization that has promoted and conducted arbitration for more than 60 years, the AAA is based in New York and has offices in dozens of cities across the country. It helps businesses arbitrate at low cost by providing arbitrators, setting standard rules for arbitration, and providing form language to include in contracts and arbitration agreements. Numerous industries, such as the construction industry, now regularly rely on AAA-directed arbitrations to settle their disputes.

- *Center for Public Resources:* A nonprofit think tank based in New York City promoting ADR to corporations throughout the country, the Center for Public Resources is funded by large corporations and law firms. It has been rather successful in having corporations sign an ADR pledge by which they agree to attempt to settle disputes with other companies that have signed such a pledge through ADR rather than through litigation. The pledge is intended to avoid any concern that suggesting ADR is a sign of weakness or an inability or lack of desire to litigate.

- *Oklahoma Mediation/Arbitration Service:* Run by an attorney, it recently was designated one of the fastest growing private ADR companies in the country by the *Arbitration and Mediation Directory.* The firm apparently handles approximately 1,000 cases per year.

- *Skadden, Arps, Slate, Meagher & Flom:* The New York City-based law firm, which has an ADR practice area and an ADR coordinator, educates all of its attorneys in ADR.

▌When ADR May Be Appropriate for a Dispute

There are ten factors that a business should consider when determining whether ADR is appropriate for a particular dispute:

- The nature of the dispute, including whether the dispute is so complicated or technical that an expert decision-maker would be best

- The likely litigation costs and outcome

- The positions, relationships, and perspectives of all of the parties involved in the dispute

- The sensitivity of issues related to the dispute and whether they may require confidentiality

- The settlement options

- The importance of a jury to the parties' case

- The importance of discovery

- The importance of a speedy decision

- Whether a party believes that the dispute needs to be resolved by a court to settle a principle

- Whether there are strong emotional or ego issues involved in the dispute

▌A Final Word

Growing numbers of disputes will be resolved in the 1990s through alternative dispute resolution techniques. ADR is not just a buzzword or fleeting topic of interest. ADR is here to stay. Contract negotiators, such as marketers and sales executives, can play a crucial role in helping their employers resolve disputes through ADR. How? By negotiating for an arbitration or ADR clause in the contract.

FIVE ARBITRATION CASES

The irony of ADR is that it still often results in litigation—maybe to determine whether the parties have agreed to ADR, perhaps to have a court enforce an arbitrator's award. But even with the lawsuits that surround ADR, ADR is still a less expensive and quicker form of dispute resolution than a lawsuit. Here are five cases that show the extent to which parties involved in disputes seek to engage the courts.

1. In October 1987 the Miller Building Corporation contracted with Coastline Associates Limited Partnership to construct the Coastline Inn in Wilmington, North Carolina. The contract contained an arbitration provision and a provision that Coastline would be charged interest on all late monthly payments. After several late payments, in April 1988 Miller billed Coastline for interest due. Coastline did not pay the interest charge. Miller completed construction in July 1989. It continued to bill Coastline for interest on late payments through February 1990, but Coastline failed to respond. After receiving no response to a written formal demand for payment, Miller filed a lawsuit against Coastline on August 27, 1990.

On October 30, 1990, Coastline asked the court to compel Miller to arbitrate its dispute. The trial court refused on the ground that Coastline had unreasonably delayed in demanding arbitration and had waived any right to arbitration. An appellate court reversed. It noted that the contract stated that "[a]ny controversy or Claim arising out of or related to the Contract, or the breach thereof, shall be settled by arbitration . . . A demand for arbitration shall be made . . . within a reasonable time after the

Claim has arisen." The appellate court ruled that Coastline had demanded arbitration within a reasonable time as required by the provisions of the contract. "Coastline demanded arbitration . . . approximately two months after Miller breached the contract by filing suit," it noted. The appellate court also rejected the lower court's conclusion that Coastline had waived its right to arbitration because, during its delay, Miller incurred "substantial" attorney's fees. It noted that Miller did not have to bear the expenses of a lengthy trial, that nothing indicated that it lost evidence because of Coastline's delay, and that Coastline did not take advantage of judicial pretrial discovery procedures not available to it in arbitration. The appellate court then ruled that the dispute should be resolved by arbitration, as the parties had agreed. (Miller Building Corp. v. Coastline Associates, 411 S.E.2d 420 (Ct. App. North Carolina 1992).)

2. After a contract dispute arose between Trade & Transport, Inc. and Natural Petroleum Charterers, Inc., Trade invoked its rights under the contract to demand arbitration. It nominated Lloyd C. Nelson as its member of the proposed arbitration panel. Natural Petroleum nominated Frank L. Crocker as its member of the panel. Nelson and Crocker then chose Manfred W. Arnold to be the third member, and chair, of the panel. After the arbitrators rendered a partial final award, Crocker died. Natural Petroleum then nominated Jack Berg as its new arbitrator to replace Crocker. It then went to federal district court, seeking a court order compelling Trade to nominate a new arbitrator; it contended that the two new arbitrators should, under the arbitration provisions of the contract, appoint the third member of the new panel and proceed to rearbitrate the entire dispute from the beginning. The contract stated that the arbitration panel shall consist of "one arbitrator to be appointed by the Owner, one by the Charterer, and one by the two so chosen."

The district court denied Natural Petroleum's motion insofar as it requested the appointment of a new panel. Instead, relying on its power under the federal Arbitration Act, the court appointed Natural Petroleum's nominee as the replacement for Crocker on the original panel. The court then ordered the panel to "proceed with all convenient speed to determine all questions involved in the submission by the parties." The panel eventually awarded damages to Trade; Berg dissented in part from the damage award. Natural Petroleum went back to federal district court, objecting to the court's refusal to order the creation of an entirely new arbitration panel. The case reached the U.S. Court of Appeals for the Second Circuit, which rejected Natural Petroleum's argument. It agreed with the lower court that Natural Petroleum's naming a successor to Crocker did not give it the right to replace the existing neutral arbitrator agreed upon by Natural Petroleum's original nominee; because the contract was silent as to what should be done after a panel had been convened, had rendered a partial final award, and a vacancy occurred due to the death of the members, it was within the district court's authority to fill the vacancy as it had. (Trade & Transport, Inc. v. Natural Petroleum Charterers, Inc., 931 F.2d 191 (2d Cir. 1991).)

3. When Alphonse Fletcher, Jr. began working in the equity trading department of Kidder, Peabody & Co., Inc., he signed a standard Uniform Application for Security Industry Registration or Transfer, commonly referred to as a U-4 Form, in which he agreed to arbitrate any dispute between him and his employer that the stock exchanges with which he was registered required to be arbitrated. On March 15, 1991, he resigned from Kidder. He then filed suit against Kidder, alleging that he was constructively discharged as the result of Kidder's racial discrimination against him as a black man, in violation of the New York State human rights law. Kidder contended that Fletcher's claim should be arbitrated, but Fletcher argued that racial discrimination claims were so important that they should be resolved only by courts. The court disagreed with Fletcher. Finding a liberal public policy favoring arbitration, it ruled that Fletchers's racial discrimination claim should be arbitrated. (Fletcher v. Kidder, Peabody & Co., Inc., 584 N.Y.S.2d 838 (1st Dept. 1992).)

4. In 1975 Richards & Associates, Inc. contracted to perform the electrical work required for the construction of the Durham County Judicial Building in Durham, North Carolina. Richards completed work on May 29, 1979, and, four years later, submitted a claim to the county for more than $200,000 in damages allegedly due to delay and changes in the work caused by the county. The county denied the claim. Because the contract between the county and Richards contained an arbitration clause, Richards demanded arbitration. However, the county contended that the arbitration clause limited arbitration to timely claims, that is, claims that, if raised in court, would not be barred by the applicable statute of limitations. In North Carolina, there is a two-year limitation period for claims against counties. The county argued that its agreement to arbitrate was not effective because Richards had filed its claim four years after completing work. The case reached the U.S. Court of Appeals for the Fourth Circuit. Citing the broad public policy in favor of arbitration, the court ruled that the question of timeliness was a question for the arbitrators—and not the courts—to decide. (County of Durham v. Richards & Associates, 742 F.2d 811 (4th Cir. 1984).)

5. The Sverdrup Corporation and WHC Constructors, Inc. were parties to a subcontract agreement that provided that WHC would do certain PVC system work on a project for which Sverdrup had contracted with Sonoco Products Company in Hartsville, South Carolina. The subcontract contained the following arbitration clause: "All claims that cannot be resolved between the parties shall be decided by arbitration in accordance with the Construction Industry Arbitration Rules of the American Arbitration Association. This agreement to arbitrate shall be specifically enforceable under the prevailing arbitration law. The award rendered by the arbitrators shall be final, and judgment may be entered upon it in accordance with applicable law in any court having jurisdiction thereof."

Following WHC's work on the Sonoco project, leaks developed in the PVC system. Sverdrup contacted WHC, which had already left the job site, about the leaks. WHC agreed that Century III, another contractor on site, could perform the repair work. After Century III made the repairs, part of the PVC system exploded, causing a failure of the system. Sverdrup called upon WHC and Century III to replace the PVC system; they refused. Sverdrup then did so and filed suit against WHC and Century III for breach of contract, breach of express warranty, breach of implied warranty, indemnity, negligence, and breach of oral contract (against Century III only). WHC filed a motion to compel arbitration and to enjoin the lawsuit pending arbitration. The parties agreed to arbitrate and agreed in writing that "the award rendered by the arbitrators will be final and judgment may be entered upon it in any court having jurisdiction thereof and will not be made subject to modification or appeal except to the extent permitted by Sections 10 and 11 of the federal Arbitration Act."

On August 31, 1990, the arbitrators issued an award in favor of Sverdrup against WHC in the amount of $419,456.07. On October 8, 1991, Sverdrup filed a motion for entry and certification of the award as a final judgment. WHC maintained that Sverdrup was precluded from obtaining judgment of the award due to its failure to have the award confirmed within the applicable limitations period. The court noted that an arbitration award is not self-executing as a judgment but, instead, must be enforced by a court. Generally speaking, confirmation of an arbitrator's award can only be denied if the award has been corrected, vacated, or modified in accordance with the federal Arbitration Act. But, the court ruled, confirmation may be denied based on a party's failure to seek confirmation within one year from the date the arbitration award was made. While noting that Sverdrup may have had other remedies, the court refused to confirm Sverdrup's arbitration award. (Sverdrup Corp. v. WHC Constructors, Inc., 787 F.Supp. 542 (D. South Carolina 1992).)

ADR Checklist

✓ Courts, legislators, corporate in-house counsel, and corporate executives are recognizing more and more the value of resolving disputes through means other than litigation. Alternative Dispute Resolution (ADR) techniques are the wave of the future.

✓ All forms of ADR are subject to the agreement of the parties and therefore may be altered to reflect individual concerns in particular instances. ADR techniques include mediation, mini-trial, private trial, and arbitration.

✓ The disputes that may be resolved through ADR range from private antitrust actions, breach of contract, and dealer/distributor issues to non-competition agreements, employment, and unfair competition questions.

✓ Not all disputes are amenable to ADR. But where appropriate, ADR can lower dispute resolution costs; resolve disputes more quickly than litigation; afford the parties privacy, flexibility, and control; and help maintain ongoing business relationships by avoiding the acrimony typically associated with litigation.

✓ Marketers and sales executives play a key role in ADR—by insisting at the beginning that ADR provisions be included in sales contracts for any disputes that thereafter arise. Doing so can yield substantial value to an employer.

HOW RESTRICTIVE ARE RESTRICTIVE COVENANTS?

■ Noncompete Clauses ■ Overbroad Covenants ■ Factual Analysis
■ A Final Word

Scott Puzia was the principal sales representative for DataType International, Inc., a direct mail company, for approximately ten years until February 1992, when he resigned.

During the time Puzia worked there, DataType specialized in direct mailings for the pharmaceutical industry, comprised of pharmaceutical manufacturing companies and the advertising agencies that served them. The pharmaceutical industry sent direct mailings to physicians and nurses, intending to generate sales of pharmaceutical products, such as prescription drugs. The expertise of Gail Propp, DataType's president, was in computer programming, which played a vital part in effective direct mail operations.

In May 1988 Propp raised Puzia's base salary from $24,000 to $40,000. (Puzia also was at all times compensated by a 12 percent commission on net sales of business he obtained for the company.)

Then, on December 14, 1988, the parties executed two written agreements. One was an Agreement for Sale of Shares. It reflected a sale by Propp to Puzia of 60 shares of DataType Class B non-voting common stock for $10,000, to be paid over 12 monthly installments. The other agreement was captioned Executive Employment Agreement. It contained a restrictive covenant that provided:

> (a) While this Agreement is in effect, and for a period of Two (2) years after the termination of this Agreement, the Executive

[Puzia] shall not, either directly or indirectly, compete with the Corporation or engage in any business similar to that conducted by the Corporation, within a radius of One Hundred Twenty Five (125) miles (the 'restricted area') of the then principal office of the Corporation, whether as a shareholder, officer, director, sole proprietor, partner, employee, consultant, representative, lender, investor, independent contractor, agent or other capacity. Solicitation or acceptance of accounts outside the restricted area which entail services to be rendered to office or business locations within the restricted area shall constitute competition in violation of this Agreement.

(b) The Executive shall not, for a period of Two (2) years following termination of this Agreement, either directly or indirectly contact or solicit any 'customers' of the Corporation, wherever located. As used herein the term 'customers' shall be defined as any person or entity to whom or with which the Corporation (i) has provided services during the Eighteen (18) month period prior to the termination, or (ii) is, at that time of termination, involved in negotiations for the providing of such services.

DataType paid Puzia the money Puzia used to pay Propp for the shares covered by the stock purchase agreement. The increase in Puzia's salary, coupled with commissions generated by his effective salesmanship, resulted in his annual compensation exceeding $100,000. But Puzia remained dissatisfied with his job at DataType. He continued to work long hours. Propp had spoken of selling the company and a target sales price for the company of $5 million, but DataType's profits never brought the company anywhere close to such a consummation. Puzia became determined to leave.

In 1986, Puzia had incorporated a company called Integrated Sales Systems. That company never did any business. On November 18, 1991, Puzia filed with the New Jersey authorities an amendment to that company's certificate of incorporation changing its name to Pharmaceutical Direct, Inc. At about the same time he also reserved a telephone line in the name of Pharmaceutical Direct and arranged for office space if that company ever became active. Puzia did not tell Propp of these activities.

At a lunch meeting on November 13, 1991, Puzia told Propp that he would be leaving DataType. He submitted a letter of resignation dated February 11, 1992, effective February 21, 1992, the date on which Puzia left DataType's employ.

Puzia accepted employment with a company pursuing a different, noncompetitive business, but decided after only four days that he had made a mistake. Accordingly, Puzia activated his company Pharmaceutical Direct, Inc., and began to compete with DataType. DataType filed suit against Puzia, contending that he had breached his noncompete agreement.

▌ Noncompete Clauses

Employers frequently ask employees to sign restrictive covenants, which also are known as noncompete agreements and covenants not to compete. It seems that almost as frequently when an employer seeks to enforce them, these covenants end up in court.

Years ago, courts were unwilling to enforce restrictive covenants because they were seen as agreements to restrain trade. Furthermore, general covenants not to compete, they believed, imposed greater hardships upon employees than upon employers. Employees were prevented from practicing their trade or skill, or from using their experience in the particular kind of work with which they were familiar. Courts recognized that they might encounter difficulty in transferring their particular experience and training to another line of work and that their ability to earn a livelihood could be seriously impaired. Furthermore, courts understood that employees usually had few resources in reserve to fall back upon and might find it difficult to uproot themselves and their family to move to a location beyond the area of potential competition with their former employers.

More recently, courts in most states have held that there are situations when it is not only desirable but essential to enforce restrictive covenants. Courts that permit these kinds of noncompete agreements to be enforced place the burden on employers to show that they are enforceable.

Because enforcement of employee restrictive covenants may result in the loss of an individual's livelihood, courts rigorously examine them and enforce them only to the extent that they are reasonably limited geographically and temporally and then only to the extent necessary to protect the employer from unfair competition such as from the use or disclosure of trade secrets, confidential customer lists, or the like.

Customer lists must be confidential to be protected. A customer list is not confidential where the past or prospective customers are "readily ascertainable" from sources outside the employer's business. However, a court will prevent the solicitation by a former employee of customers who are not openly engaged in business in advertised locations or whose availability as patrons cannot readily be ascertained but whose trade and patronage have been secured by years of business effort and advertising, and the expenditure of time and money, constituting a part of the good will of a business.

▌Overbroad Covenants

Courts in different states have several different methods for treating covenants that are overbroad, which may occur if the restriction is for too long a time or covers too large a geographic area. Some courts simply refuse to enforce them or any part of them. Others take a "blue pencil" to the covenant, delete the unenforceable provisions and enforce the covenant to the extent the balance remains grammatically coherent once the unreasonable provisions have been excised. The blue pencil approach can be understood from the following example: Suppose a covenant prohibits an employee from competing in New York, New Jersey, and Connecticut. If the court thinks limiting competition in Connecticut only would be reasonable, it could take a blue pencil to the covenant, cross out New York and New Jersey and enforce the Connecticut ban. Sometimes, though, courts seem to wield blue pencils in a rather arbitrary fashion. If the same covenant had been drafted to state "the New York Metropolitan area," a court might not enforce any of it, ruling that it could not rewrite the clause or take a "blue pencil" to the phrase to delete two of the states to which it referred but could only delete the whole thing.

▌Factual Analysis

Often, whether a particular covenant will be enforced requires an analysis of the particular facts of the case. For instance, in the DataType case, DataType contended that the restrictive covenant Puzia signed barred him, within its temporal and geographic limitations, from competing with DataType. In other words, it contended that the covenant prevented him from offering direct mail services to any pharmaceutical company or advertising agency in the field within 125 miles of New York City for two years.

DataType also contended that Puzia should be barred from contacting or soliciting any pharmaceutical company or advertising agency, wherever located, with which DataType had done any business or was negotiating to do business with during the 18 months prior to Puzia's departure. Because the restrictive covenant defined "customer" as "any person or entity," DataType contended that its provision of services to or negotiation with any division of a pharmaceutical company placed the entire company beyond Puzia's reach. Similarly, it argued that any such contact with any account executive at an advertising agency placed the entire agency off limits.

The court rejected DataType's broad reading of the covenant. It noted that pharmaceutical companies were typically made up of a number of divisions, each devoted to the manufacture and marketing of a particular product. The divisions, it said, were largely autonomous. A product manager dealt directly with an account executive at an advertising agency and could play a part in the selection of vendors such as DataType. But, the court said, there was relatively little communication among product managers with respect to their day-to-day operations. The court also noted that advertising agencies were divided into account groups that dealt with their pharmaceutical company accounts on a largely autonomous basis. "There is a surprisingly small amount of cross-information and communication among account groups in the same agency," the court said.

As a result, the court found, a salesperson of services such as DataType's who had previously dealt with a particular product manager at a pharmaceutical company or an account executive at an advertising agency only had a very limited advantage in soliciting other product managers of the same company or other account executives at the same agency.

The court noted that Puzia did not make off with a particular DataType "customer list." But, it said, the law forbids employees to solicit their former employers' customers if the customers would have been unknown to the employees but for information obtained during their prior employment. Nonetheless, the court said that it would not restrict Puzia from soliciting all product divisions of a pharmaceutical company or all account groups of an advertising agency that had a prior relationship with DataType. "Given the autonomous nature of these sub entities, an entire company cannot reasonably be regarded as DataType's 'customer'; nor can an entire advertising agency be so regarded." Puzia had agreed not to solicit those specific individuals with whom he had developed a relationship while at DataType, and the court limited its order to that effect.

461

▌A Final Word

Because a restrictive covenant is a contract, an employee that signs one must be given something in return. That is an easy test to meet at the beginning of an employment relationship—the person gets a job and the employer gets the covenant. But it is a bit more complex when an existing employee is asked to sign such a document. Some courts believe that continued employment is sufficient; others have ruled that something substantial in addition to continued employment, such as a raise or promotion, is required.

The law relating to restrictive covenants is not so pro-employee as it was a dozen or two dozen years ago, but executives should realize that it is still not purely pro-employer, either. The law does not like to reward bad faith or improper use of trade secrets or confidential customer lists; indeed, an employer may be entitled to the protection of certain trade secrets or other confidential information even when an employee has signed no covenant. However, by the same token, the law seeks to promote competition—at least, fair competition. Employees that have signed restrictive covenants should not automatically assume that they are enforceable. Before jumping ship or violating the covenant, they should seek to determine whether, and to what extent, the covenant is enforceable.

FIVE RESTRICTIVE COVENANT SUITS

1. After a salesperson left to sell sanitary maintenance supplies and chemicals for a competitor, the Puritan/Churchill Chemical Company filed suit. Puritan said that its former employee had signed an employment contract at the outset of his 11-year period of employment with the company that contained restrictive covenants providing in part as follows: "Representative does expressly covenant and agree that . . . for a period of two years immediately following the termination of such employment he will not . . . 1. Solicit orders for sanitary maintenance chemicals and other chemical specialties, supplies and equipment, or for engineering and maintenance services in connection therewith, for distribution to institutional, industrial, commercial and governmental consumers. 2. Contact for the purpose of diverting any of the customers or accounts of Puritan's business as described [elsewhere in the contract]. 3. Own, manage, control, operate or participate in the ownership, management, or control, or engage as a sales representative or sales executive, of any business which engages in any phase of the business described [elsewhere in the contract.]"

The case reached the Supreme Court of Georgia, which refused to enforce the restrictive covenant. Puritan's former employee was a salesperson for Puritan but the restrictive covenants prevented him from owning, managing, controlling, operating, or even participating in owning, managing, or controlling any business that would compete with Puritan. The court ruled that "language which restricts employees from activities . . . much more . . . than is necessary for the protection of the employer will not withstand the reasonableness test so as to uphold the covenant." The court refused to blue pencil, or cross out the offending portions, of the invalid covenant and ruled against Puritan. (Puritan/Churchill Chemical Co. v. Eubank, 265 S.E.2d 16 (Sup. Ct. Georgia 1980).)

2. When John E. Ward began working for the American Mutual Life Insurance Company, he signed a form employment agreement as a condition of his employment. The agreement provided, among other things, that for a period of 18 months following termination of his employment, he would not procure, solicit, accept, or refer applications or inquires about insurance from persons insured by American Mutual within specified locations or from any person insured by American Mutual under a policy that Ward had sold or serviced. After Ward had worked there for more than a decade, American Mutual required its salespeople to sign new contracts incorporating a more restrictive noncompetition provision, or to be discharged.

Ward refused to sign, was fired, and brought suit against his former employer for damages for breach of the employment contract. A master appointed by the judge found that he had been fired in violation of his employment agreement, which provided for termination only on the anniversary date of his contract. But the master also found that, shortly after his discharge, Ward had solicited and sold insurance policies in violation of the noncompetition provision of his employment contract; that meant that Ward, too, had breached the agreement, and the master determined that that precluded him from recovery. The appellate court reversed. American Mutual's wrongful discharge of Ward constituted a breach of his employment agreement "so material as to discharge [Ward] from any further obligations" under the contract and to allow him to recover damages for total breach. (Ward v. American Mutual Liability Insurance Co., 443 N.E.2d 1342 (App. Ct. Mass. 1983).)

3. The Packaging House, Inc. designed and sold displays and packaging made to customer specifications. Although it did not do any of the actual design or packaging work, it developed special detailed working relationships with certain designers and manufacturers that enabled it to provide a full range of packaging design and display services to its customers. Most of the Packaging House's customers were located in Chicago, Minneapolis, New York, and Cincinnati. It marked its customer list confidential and kept it under lock and key; only certain of the company's officers and employees had access to the keys. The company also kept its costs and pricing information in a secured and confidential manner. All 10 of the company's salespeople signed employment agreements that contained a restrictive covenant that prohibited solicitation of the company's customers by a severed employee for 18 months.

After working for the Packaging House for eight and a half years, Marvin Hoffman resigned and began soliciting business from his former employer's accounts. The Packaging House then filed suit against Hoffman seeking to prohibit what it alleged was Hoffman's breach of the restrictive covenant. The court noted that an employer ordinarily has no proprietary interest in its customers but that it could use a restrictive covenant to protect itself from the disadvantageous use of confidential information it revealed to an employee during the course of that person's employment. The court concluded that Hoffman had acquired confidential information through his employment with the Packaging House and subsequently attempted to use the information for his own benefit. It then ruled that he should be enjoined from violating the restrictive covenant. (Packaging House, Inc. v. Hoffman, 448 N.E.2d 947 (App. Ct. Illinois 1983).)

4. Louis F. Bertoni, Delores O'Hara, and Rocco F. Catucci had known each other for some time when they discussed the possibility of establishing a business for dealing in graphic arts. They formed a corporation under the name GG Graphics, Inc. Bertoni and O'Hara each contributed $10,000 to set up the company and Catucci allegedly contributed $20,000. Each party was to own one third of the company's stock, but no stock was ever actually issued. O'Hara was to serve as president and Bertoni as vice-president, secretary, and treasurer, while Catucci was to serve as a vice president and sales supervisor of manufacturing and processing. The company was housed in a building O'Hara owned and it paid rent to O'Hara.

After a very short time, differences of opinion arose. Catucci apparently was under the impression that Bertoni and O'Hara would play the role of silent partners and that he would have full authority to run the company. After one of the disputes, Catucci formed a new corporation, Data Repro, Inc., changed the locks on the O'Hara building, and advised customers that there had been a change in the name of Graphics. Catucci took all of the assets of Graphics, pledged them as security for a bank loan, and immediately began operating Repro. Using the proceeds of the bank loan, he purchased a building near the O'Hara building and moved Repro to the new building. Bertoni and O'Hara filed suit against Catucci, alleging that he had committed a breach of trust by delivering the Graphics' assets to Repro.

The court ruled that even though Catucci had signed no restrictive covenant, he could be sued by Bertoni and O'Hara. It was well established, the court said, that the officers and directors of a corporation stand in a fiduciary relationship to the corporation, owe to the corporation their individual loyalty, and are not permitted to derive a personal profit at the expense of the corporation. While an officer or director, acting in good faith, is not precluded from participating in a business similar to that of the corporation, the officer or director "must not act so as to cripple or injure the corporation." If that happens, the officer or director may be held liable for damages. The court stated that it "would be difficult, indeed, to imagine how an officer's or director's conduct could be more disloyal or more destructive and injurious than that of Catucci." It concluded that when an officer or director has been found to have diverted corporate assets and opportunities, that person may be held accountable for the wrongdoing. (Bertoni v. Catucci, 498 N.Y.S.2d 902 (3d Dept. 1986).)

5. In 1962 Gerard H. Lavoie founded Centorr-Vacuum Industries, Inc., a manufacturer of sophisticated, high-temperature furnaces. Centorr became recognized worldwide as an expert in the specialized furnace industry and, under Lavoie's leadership, attained a 20 percent share of the world market. On January 4, 1985, Lavoie sold his entire interest in Centorr to Thermal Scientific, Inc., a multinational conglomerate, for approximately $4.9 million. Desiring to remain active in the industry, however, he simultaneously entered into an employment agreement with Centorr that provided that he would remain a highly paid consultant. The employment agreement contained a noncompetition clause that stated that he agreed not to engage "in any business activity in competition with the business then being conducted by [Centorr] at any place within the United States of America, Canada, or the United Kingdom, whether directly or indirectly, for his own account or as an employee, partner, officer, director, consultant or holder of more than 5% of the equity interest in any other person, firm, partnership or corporation for a period of three years after the termination for any reason or expiry of the Term hereof."

By early 1990, Lavoie, who had received more than $600,000 from Centorr as a consultant, regretted selling his business and sought to reenter the specialized furnace industry. He began negotiating with

Centorr for some arrangement whereby he could participate in the formation of a competition business without violating the terms of the noncompetition clause, which he admitted was enforceable. The negotiations broke down and, in March 1990, he terminated his employment relationship with Centorr.

Shortly thereafter, Lavoie met with Donald Lavoie (his younger brother), Peter Sanborn (his son-in-law), and several other individuals to discuss the formation of a corporation to produce furnaces similar to those produced by Centorr. In October 1990, Materials Research Furnaces, Inc. was incorporated in New Hampshire. Donald Lavoie acquired 30 shares of the company's stock and became its first president. The company thereafter entered the specialized furnace market in direct competition with Centorr. Lavoie provided significant financing for the Materials Research start-up. He supplied various family members with $60,000 in loans and gifts so that they could acquire Materials Research stock. He also lent Donald Lavoie and Peter Sanborn approximately $240,000. They, in turn, lent Materials Research that money. Lavoie also expressed his willingness to lend money to other Materials Research employees for the purchase of stock. Lavoie also was associated with Materials Research through his interest in the Suncook Business Park. In 1989, he gave the land on which the business spark was located to various family members. He then provided $2 million in financing for the business park and, with the assistance of Donald Lavoie, supervised its construction. Lavoie held a mortgage on the property.

Centorr filed a lawsuit against Lavoie seeking injunctive relief and damages. Citing the relationship between Lavoie and Materials Research as well as evidence that Lavoie assisted Materials Research in various other ways, Centorr contended that Lavoie had violated the terms of the noncompetition clause. The superior court found that Lavoie had not violated the noncompetition covenant because he had not engaged in "direct action" when he loaned money to family members associated with Materials Research. It also found that his relationship to Materials Research as the mortgagee of the Suncook Business Park did not violate the non-competition covenant because the park "appears to have other business purposes than to just be a home" for Materials Research and because "[n]o testimony was offered to suggest that a less than arms-length rent is being paid."

The case reached the Supreme Court of New Hampshire, which ruled that the superior court had misinterpreted the noncompetition agreement. It ordered the court to determine whether Lavoie's actions "indirectly" assisted Materials Research in competing with Centorr. The Supreme Court said that although courts normally construe noncompetition covenants narrowly, "where, as in this case, the noncompetition covenant was ancillary to the sale of a business, it may be interpreted more liberally." (Centorr-Vacuum Industries, Inc. v. Lavoie, 609 A.2d 1213 (Sup. Ct. New Hampshire 1992).)

Restrictive Covenant Checklist

✓ The days when restrictive covenants were not enforceable in any state in the country are now long gone. Although a number of states still do not enforce them, a majority do.

✓ Only those restrictive covenants that are reasonable in time and geographic limitation are enforceable, and only to the extent necessary to protect an employer. Thus, courts do not enforce restrictive covenants any more than is required.

✓ Certain forms of competition by a former employee will be restricted even when the employee had not signed a covenant. These may include unfair competition, theft of trade secrets, and improper use of confidential customer information.

✓ To be enforceable, a restrictive covenant also requires that an employee have received something in exchange for the covenant: a job, a raise, or a significant promotion would seem to fit that bill; it is not clear whether mere continued employment would be sufficient.

✓ An executive that has signed a restrictive covenant should not assume that it is enforceable. Indeed, the executive should realize that it may not be enforceable. An experienced attorney can provide the proper advice, after taking into consideration all of the relevant factors including the appropriate state's law.

FOR FURTHER READING

To a large extent, court decisions and regulatory and legislative developments are the principal sources for information about advertising, marketing, and sales law. They may be accessed through computer-aided research, such as Lexis and Nexis, provided by Mead Data Central, Inc., or Westlaw, provided by the West Publishing Company. Statutes, such as state versions of the Uniform Commercial Code (UCC), also are important.

In addition, consider the following:

Adelman, Martin J. *Patent Law Perspectives.* New York: Matthew Bender & Co., Inc., 1993. Multivolume. Patents in detail.

Arbitration Journal. New York: American Arbitration Association, 1993. Quarterly journal that brings basic alternative dispute resolution issues to rather undeserved theoretical heights while covering ADR developments rather quickly.

Bankruptcy Law Reporter. Chicago: Commerce Clearing House, Inc., 1993. Multivolume. Regularly updated, discusses and reports on bankruptcy court decisions and other developments.

Collier on Bankruptcy. New York: Matthew Bender & Co., Inc., 1986. *The* multivolume source for discussions of bankruptcy law.

Gilson, Jerome. *Trademark Protection and Practice.* New York: Matthew Bender & Co., Inc., 1992. Multivolume. Comprehensive indeed.

Hawkland, William D. *Hawkland Uniform Commercial Code.* New York: Clark Boardman Callaghan, 1993. Regularly updated, this multivolume series explains the UCC section by section with ample case citations.

Kupferman, Theodore R., ed. *Advertising and Commercial Speech.* Westport, CT: Meckler Corp., 1990. 141 pages. Nine articles on this important subject.

Lichtenberger, John. *Advertising Compliance Law.* New York: Quorum Books, 1986. 216 pages. More for those who need it or want it.

McCarthy, J. Thomas. *McCarthy's Desk Encyclopedia of Intellectual Property.* Washington, DC: The Bureau of National Affairs, Inc., 1991. 385 pages. Definitions from "abandonment" (e.g., of a trademark) to "worm" (i.e., a kind of computer virus); more than one probably needs because it has definitions that will virtually never be needed but often is valuable enough to get one started.

Marketing Management Magazine. Chicago: American Marketing Association, 1993. Quarterly magazine that regularly covers sophisticated marketing law issues.

The National Law Journal. New York: The New York Law Publishing Co., 1993. Self-described as "the weekly newspaper" for the legal profession. Often carries articles by lawyers and news of interest to marketing, advertising, and sales professionals.

Plevan, Kenneth A., and Miriam L. Sirosky. *Advertising Compliance Handbook.* Practicing Law Institute, Inc., 1988. 527 pages. Comprehensive, albeit more than five years old.

Product Safety & Liability Reporter. Washington, DC: The Bureau of National Affairs, Inc., 1993. Discusses legislative, regulatory, and court developments.

Products Liability Reporter. Chicago: Commerce Clearing House, Inc., 1993. Multivolume. Regularly updated, covers different aspects of product liability law and reports new court decisions.

Rosden, George Eric, and Peter Eric Rosden. *The Law of Advertising.* Matthew Bender & Co., Inc., 1990. Advertising law in a multivolume, updated set.

Secured Transactions Guide. Chicago: Commerce Clearing House, Inc., 1993. Multivolume. Regularly updated, covers state developments in secured transactions.

Speiser, Stuart M., Charles F. Krause, and Alfred W. Gans. *The American Law of Torts.* Rochester: The Lawyers Co-Operative Publishing Co., 1983. Updated frequently, this multivolume series discusses all one could want to know about liability for injuries to another's person or property.

UCC Cases Digest. New York: Clark Boardman Callaghan, 1992. Multivolume series digesting court decisions on the UCC.

INDEX

O

P